KV-456-606

No Fear of Flying – Women at Home and Abroad

For Grace,

wishing you every success
with you latest venture

Much love

Jenny

xx

NO FEAR OF FLYING
Women at Home and Abroad

Edited by Jocelynne A. Scutt

Artemis

Artemis Publishing Pty Ltd
PO Box 151
Market Street Post Office
Melbourne 3000 Victoria
Fax: (03) 670 1252

First published 1993
Copyright © Jocelynne A. Scutt 1993
Interviews: Gloria Lee, Ofelia Lopez
Copyright in individual written contributions
remains with the contributors.

All rights reserved. No part of this publication may
be reproduced in a retrieval system, or transmitted
in any form or by any means, electronic, mechanical,
photocopying, recording or otherwise, without prior
written permission of the publisher.

National Library of Australia
Cataloguing-in-Publication entry:

No fear of flying: women at home and abroad

  ISBN 1 875658 04 1.
  1. Women – Australia – Biography.
  2. Women immigrants – Australia – Biography.
  3. Women travellers – Australia – Biography.
  I. Scutt, Jocelynne A., 1947- .
  (Series: Women's voices, women's lives; no. 4.)

304.8092294

Typeset in Berkeley by Lorna Hendry
Printed in Australia by McPherson's Printing Group

Remembering Violet Goode

Acknowledgments

The fourth volume in the Artemis series 'Women's Voices, Women's Lives', *No Fear of Flying – Women at Home and Abroad,* is the first book resulting from my stay, in June 1992, at Eleanor Dark's cottage in Katoomba. The much appreciated award of a writer's fellowship meant that I was able to do the preliminary planning of the volume and the writing of the outline at Katoomba.

I appreciate the contribution of many to the editing, compiling and production of *No Fear of Flying,* including the contributors who wrote so cooperatively, or who willingly made themselves available to be interviewed. I thank also Trish O'Carroll for wordprocessing several drafts and a number of difficult tapes; Jocelyn Terry for wordprocessing and indexing; Anne Thacker for proofreading; Lorna Hendry for design and typesetting; Christina Neri for the cover design; Jo Steele who kindly granted the use of Barbara Hanrahan's screenprint 'Girl with Birds' for the cover; and Dairmuid Pigott for the background photograph, 'The Five Lamps of Knowledge'. Without their contribution *No Fear of Flying* would not be the book it is, and working on it would not have been so rewarding.

That I am in a position to write and edit, and particularly to have produced *No Fear of Flying,* is due in no little way to the positive support of enthusiastic friends and family. I thank them sincerely.

The photographs of Penelope E. Andrews (La Trobe University), Gloria Lee (Jenny Green), Sandra McCallum (Kathy Derham Moore) and Jocelynne A. Scutt (*Mr Neal is Entitled to be an Agitator* – Ronin Films), and the extract from Barbara Cummings, *From Kahlin Compound...* (1990, Aboriginal Studies Press) are reprinted with permission.

Jocelynne A. Scutt
Melbourne, November 1993

Contents

Introduction

Jocelynne A. Scutt *So Brave Women* **1**

Part I **Flowers Fruit Colour Smell**

Gillian Hanscombe *'Space, and Nests, and History'* **13**

Marlies Puentener *Fush 'n' Chups* **23**

Vivien M. Altman *To Feel Passionate Again* **33**

Janice Farrell *New Horizons* **43**

Gloria Lee *Sitting Out in the Hills in China* **53**

Janet Wilczynski *There and Back Again - and Again* **61**

Kathy Kituai *Point of View* **71**

Part II **This is My Country**

Mickey Zhu *China is My Mother's Home* **83**

Susan Ogier *Australian Now* **87**

Jan Mock *Australians in Alaska* **91**

Sandra K. McCallum *From Australia to Canada and Again* **100**

Kristin Henry *The Kind of Belonging* **110**

Vivienne Correa *Home – Among the Gum Trees* **118**

Part III Changes. Transitions.

Lynne Wenig *To the Unknown Island Continent* **127**

Penelope E. Andrews *The Sense of Belonging* **131**

Janet Labatut *Que Sera* **139**

Ania Wilczynski *The Cambridge Connection* **151**

Tui Taurua *No Turning Back?* **159**

Jennifer Simon *Your Flight is Now Boarding* **164**

Part IV The Politics of Country

Anne Hickling Hudson *The Other Side of the World* **175**

Sylvia R. Hennessy *Bathurst via London* **195**

Dorota Malchevski *From Poland to Australia, via Greece* **201**

Mary Ann Bin-Sallik *Harvard: A Djaru Woman's Perspective* **214**

Ofelia Lopez *Becoming A Walking Book* **224**

Gisela Gardener *As A Woman I Have No Country?* **239**

Epilogue

Jocelynne A. Scutt *No Fear of Flying* **247**

Index

So Brave Women

Jocelynne A. Scutt

'I should like to go back to Australia,' wrote Australian writer Christina Stead to a compatriot in 1950, 'but the fare there and back is so much...' Distance and the cost of travel did not, however, prevent her from going to Europe nor, later, returning home. What leads women to travel thousands of miles to make new lives for themselves, whether at home or away from home?

Australia is a nation of travellers. The traditional Aboriginal culture, centred in Australia for at least 60 000 years, bears as a prominent characteristic travelling from place to place, while at the same time Aboriginal people are strongly connected with the land of their dreaming and their country. That Aboriginal people have a tradition of moving does not mean that they have no attachment to a particular place. Far from it. As Joyce Clague says in 'Staying to the End' in *Glorious Age – Growing Older Gloriously*, of her childhood on the north coast of New South Wales, at the mission at Ulgundahi:

> Through my grandfather's descriptions, I knew of places I had never visited. He sang songs to us, telling us stories and the meaning of them. When I was old enough to travel, I often came across places I already knew because he told us about the hills, the rivers, the streams, what trees were there, the formations of rock...When I was a young child, he would be missing for a while, away doing [initiation] ceremonies. Then he'd be back and catching up on the role he had left behind...[He] was central to initiation programs right up to Tabulum near the border of Queensland, and down the coast, and particularly up in the mountains...

When colonisation or European invasion of Australia took place, Aboriginal people were often forced to become reluctant travellers. In *Take this Child...From Kahlin Compound to the Retta Dixon Children's Home* Barbara Cummings writes of the history of Aboriginal children being taken away from their parents, their families, their country, and growing up in a 'home', by reason of government policy. The children believed that 'being taken' applied only to them: it was not until later that they learned that forcible removal of children had a much longer history:

> From the official establishment of the Retta Dixon Children's Home in 1947 until its closure in 1980, no one ever tried to reunite us permanently with our families. I was more fortunate than most while I was in the Home, because my mother visited me about once a month and took me out. Parents were allowed to visit their children and take them for outings but for most of them, this was too difficult...
>
> I knew, at an early age, that the authorities took children from Aborigines; but what I, and many others, didn't realise was that our mothers before us had also been removed from their Aboriginal mothers and institutionalised at Kahlin. My mother often referred to herself as being 'in the Home', yet whenever I pursued the topic as I grew older, she didn't want to discuss it...

In 1912 Baldwin Spencer wrote a report for the federal government which provided a (spurious) foundation for the enforced removal of Aboriginal children from their homes and their country. He asserted that no 'half-caste' children should be '...allowed to remain in any native camp, but they should all be withdrawn and placed on stations'. He went on to observe that in some cases:

> ...when the child is very young, it must of necessity be accompanied by its mother, but in other cases, even though it may seem cruel to separate the mother and child, it is better to do so, when the mother is living, as is usually the case, in a native camp.

Colonisation, which brought about the breaking up of Aboriginal families and groups and which sought to destroy Aboriginal people's links with the land through government-directed emigration of Aboriginal people from their country to other parts of Australia, was founded in force. To regard the establishment of Australia as 'settlement' offends not only against the Aboriginal people who experienced the influx of the British soldiers and convicts (and, later, free settlers) as invasion or genocide. It also ignores the fact that there was no 'choice' behind the journeying of either guards or prisoners. The convicts came to Botany Bay and, later, Port Arthur, Port Phillip, Moreton Bay and the Swan River because they were sentenced to transportation. The soldiers came because it was their job, their duty, and their regiments which were ordered to come; not to come would have been desertion.

The courage it takes to travel thousands of miles from the familiar – home – to a foreign land is not lessened because force rather than desire underlies the journey.

Although under sentence or under orders, and with no choice, those travelling to Australia were brave. The courage it takes to travel thousands of miles from the familiar – home – to a foreign land is not lessened because force rather than desire underlies the journey. Nor are travellers not brave because the force which dictates the transfer from one country to another is founded in law or custom: the law of marriage, the dictates of cohabitation rules, and the customary requirement that a wife follow her husband and make her home where his is.

Women convicts were transported to Australia for lesser crimes, often, than the men. There was a perceived need to 'keep the numbers up': even before colonisation began, correspondence with the Home Office indicates that a matter of prime concern to those engineering the change from sending convicts to the North American colonies, to Australia as a destination, was that there be 'sufficient' women on hand to ensure that the men were not deprived of female company. South Sea Islander women were one noted target: kidnapping was an official British government policy to provide workers and women for British settlers and convicts. Female offenders were another: that there were far fewer women convicted of crimes than men meant that those who were convicted were at far greater risk, proportionately, of being transported.

When free settlement took place, single women were often encouraged to emigrate from Britain to Australia, the stated incentive being the greater possibility of marriage in a country where the male population exceeded the female. Children learning history in the 1950s and 1960s (and possibly still, today) learnt that women came to Australia 'to find a husband'. This information was imparted as if the women were 'ordinary', on the 'husband hunt', and unremarkable for any initiative, strength or courage. Yet

Children learning history in the 1950s and 1960s (and possibly still, today) learnt that women came to Australia 'to find a husband'.

how courageous to travel away from home and family to a country thousands of miles away. How brave to leave everything with which a woman was familiar, to chance her life and her future to the possibilities of marrying a man who would be kind. To travel with a motive of marriage does not lessen the fear of the unknown (with the veil of romanticism torn aside, it may well increase it). Nor does it discount at all the courage of the women.

And did all women travel to Australia in search of wedded bliss, anyway? Hardly. Women came to Australia for all the reasons men came, and very possibly more. Women came to find work. Women travelled to expand their knowledge, their horizons (both literally and figuratively). Women arrived at ports all around Australia seeking adventure. Some wanted to throw off the stultifying conventions that robbed them of the opportunity to operate in society as independent people. Some sought to establish their own businesses, perhaps a more difficult thing to do in Britain, a nation bound by tradition. Some thought they would have a better chance for a comfortable future for themselves and their children if they chanced their luck in the colonies, rather than remaining, starvation at the door, in Ireland or Scotland or England or Wales. Many came from modest family backgrounds, where resources did not extend to education for girls. Many were otherwise forced to work as governesses or to endure life as a burden on a brother who had succeeded to whatever fortune the family possessed: too often nepotism extended only to the male line, where money was concerned.

The courage of women as immigrants did not end with the journey to the colonies. Once landed, many women settled at the first port of call. But many women travelled further, hitching up their skirts, gathering together children and household goods, and making their way inland, to farms, or north or west or east to the goldfields. Many women went, as spinsters or widows, to establish their careers as nurses, shopkeepers, postmistresses (when women were 'allowed' by the authorities to take up such posts). Many women exercised their limited choices as women workers by working as prostitutes. Many were forced into prostitution, kidnapped in the 'white slave trade' which was real, rather than a proper subject for 'jokes'.

> ...many women travelled further, hitching up their skirts, gathering together children and household goods, and making their way inland, to farms, or north or west or east to the goldfields.

The travelling of women, spreading out all over the country, continued from one century to the next. In the 1890s Clara Saunders travelled through the Western Australian goldfields recording her impressions. As Norma King writes in *Daughters of Midas – Pioneer Women of the Eastern Goldfields*:

Clara was in Coolgardie for only a short time when Mrs Fagan called her and Florrie over to the window and pointed out a strange woman who had just come to town. The newcomer was dressed in bright colours, with some red material draped around her shoulders. She appeared to have been drinking and was parading up and down the street.

Mrs Fagan told the girls she was advertising her business. When the naive young girl wanted to know what type of business the woman was involved in, her employer explained: 'She is a woman of ill-fame...She is camped over at the back of Sylvester Street on a rise. She is the first of her kind to come here.'

Houses were spare. Camps were more often the accommodation for all living on the goldfields. Nurses found the conditions were difficult. Norma King observes that the pioneer nurses in Coolgardie were Sister Margaret O'Brien and Nurse Lena Miller, arriving in April 1894:

The Warden showed the women over the hospital, and Sister O'Brien commented later that the patients were '....the dirtiest looking objects imaginable, covered in dust and sand indescribable...tents and more tents, men everywhere, old singlets and trousers were the order of their dress. The hopeless look of everything would have discouraged the stoutest heart.

Margaret O'Brien and Lena Miller worked with what they had, at the same time forging ahead with their own plans and hiring carpenters to set up tent frames for their own twelve-bed hospital.

Women made their way around Australia by coach or waggon, and eventually by train. Catherine Bond, arriving on the Western Australian goldfields in the winter of 1896, experienced life in Boulder, Kalgoorlie and Coolgardie first hand:

> The sand is deep and loose and heavy to walk in and every step raises a cloud of fine dust. Outside of the town the small huts are made of brown hessian or canvas stretched on wooden frames and, further out, small tents. One feels how much these poor people have suffered; not a tree, not a shrub, not a blade of grass – always brown sand.

In *Goldfields and Chrysanthemums*, published in 1898 in London, Catherine Bond wrote of additional trials for women who had left more conventional lifestyles behind them. On one occasion in the Coolgardie suburb of Toorak she 'found the owner [of the house] pasting hessian over holes that mice had eaten in her walls'.

In the 1940s, 1950s and 1960s women came to Australia from Europe, particularly Italy and Greece, often after marriage by proxy. In *Forza e corraggio (With Strength and Courage)*, published by the National Italian-Australian Women's Association in 1991, women of the first generation of Italian migrants write of **...travelling to Australia, some having married men they had never seen or of whom they had photographs only.** Other women came, alone, to make new lives. Franca Arena, now a member of the New South Wales parliament, was born in Genoa, Italy, in 1937. At 21 she applied for an assisted passage to Australia and as she writes in 'No More Crumbs', published in *Different Lives – Reflections on the Women's Movement and Visions of its Future*:

> On payment of £10, I left Italy on my own, for a country where I knew no one. On leaving Genoa, some friends gave me a gold pendant with the famous lighthouse (La Lanterna) of Genoa and a scroll which said: 'As this lighthouse has guided our navigators through the centuries, may it guide you though the unknown oceans of your life.' It is to this very day one of my most precious possessions.

What motivates women to leave Australia, to make their homes and lives elsewhere? The 'colonial mentality' often dictated to Australians that it was necessary to 'go abroad' to make a life; that Australia was a lost and lonely continent on the periphery of the world – or at the end of the world, and that no one would pay attention to anything a person said or wrote, or painted, so long as she (or he) was stationed in the antipodes. Europe – and particularly England – was the place to go if an Australian were to be a part of 'the world'.

The Australian community had too readily ingested the notion that *nothing* 'made in Australia' – whether manufactured or the product of intellect or artistic strengths – could be 'worthwhile'. The 'mother country' – England (and, sometimes, other parts of Britain) held such a dominant position amongst people who saw themselves as, in a sense, in Australia temporarily only, that many Australians set off as soon as they could for 'home'. In the eighteenth and nineteenth century this manifested itself in families with the money to do so sending their children to school in Britain, or ensuring that they could study at British universities. As Franca Arena observes, in the mid-twentieth century it manifested itself in an obsession with cricket at Lords:

> Immigrants had had years of facing a policy of assimilation, being 'factory fodder' expected to leave all decisions to those 'born to rule', the very people who seemed to think Australia was not an independent nation but an appendage to Mother England. For years we saw the spectacle of an Australian prime minister making annual visits to England to watch the wretched cricket, which was alien to so many of us...

Writers like Miles Franklin and Christina Stead, and political activists like Muriel Matters and Alice Henry, left Australia for long periods. They felt alien, sometimes, in their own country, because writers and thinkers were too often overlooked when they worked and wrote in Australia. Once abroad, they were more likely to be acknowledged.

The notion that Australia is 'the end of the earth' rather than the beginning, or one of many beginnings, is falling by the wayside.

The tradition of travelling away from Australia to live and to learn continues. But today it is more in recognition that expanding horizons adds to the value of what can be learned in Australia, what life can be, to be full, rather than an elevation of 'overseas' over 'here', or overseas institutions above those existing at home. The notion that Australia is 'the end of the earth' rather than the beginning, or one of many beginnings, is falling by the wayside. Political perspectives are changing, so that Australia is being accepted more and more as a country centred in its own geographical location, and as being valuable for what it is, rather than as an adjunct to or offshoot of another country, another culture, removed only in place and time.

Women travel, bravely, from Australia – despite the distances, despite language differences – backpacking through Asia and Europe alone, or with a companion. Women make their lives in other countries, not renouncing their origins in Australia, but seeking to add to their understanding of the world and of their place in it. Women become citizens of other lands.

But still, where the traditional Australian culture is concerned, the Aboriginal culture, supremacist notions remain. Aboriginal people, goes the theory, came to Australia down the land bridge through the Malaysian Peninsula and New Guinea. Eurocentred theories of the beginnings of human life have, at last, to a certain extent at least passed into history. The generally accepted origin of human life is the African rather than the European continent. Yet even for this, shouldn't we ask why?

Australian Aborigines have lived in Australia for at least 60 000 years. Some anthropologists and geologists would venture the time span is more likely to be 120 000 years. Nonetheless, none of these scholars accept what is likely to be the reality: that Aboriginal people began life on the Australian continent, rather than originating elsewhere. *This* is where Aboriginal memories are; *this* is where Aboriginal culture is centred; *this* where every aspect of Aboriginal heritage is fixed. There are no Aboriginal memories that can be traced back to some other continent, some other culture. And even could they, why then would this mean that Aboriginal culture is derivative of that other culture, and not that the other culture derives from Australian Aboriginal time and history?

Eurocentred theories of the beginnings of human life have, at last, to a certain extent at least passed into history.

Land bridges do not operate in one direction only. Why could it not be that Aboriginal Australians are the direct descendants of the first human life, with the land bridge being used, not north to south, but south to north? Why can't it be that human life derives from the Australian land mass? That human life proceeded from the antipodean continent to the African and European continents? This makes equal sense as any theory that Aboriginal people came to Australia via the countries to the north. Yet there remains a reluctance to accept that this history is equally likely as any other – and in many respects more so. Why not?

'Flowers Fruit Colour Smell.' Gillian Hanscombe left Australia to work and study, write and make poetry, leaving scorching summers and golden wattle, like Janice Farrell and Janet Wilczynski, for snow and the delicate change of European seasons. Janice Farrell returned to the golden heat, while Janet Wilczynski emigrated twice from the picking of primroses, catkins and bluebells in the English spring, to the sun and long white beaches of Australia. Marlies Puentener left New Zealand to find flat, scorching, ochre earth in Queensland and Darwin. Gloria Lee left the red earth of Alice Springs to sit out in the hills in China, together with her sister collecting twigs to remind them of the eucalypts, the leaves, the trees of the Northern Territory – until her return. Kathy Kituai left clay soil, red dust storms, Sower Sobs and Paterson's Curse – and Kangaroo Paws and Enamel Orchids, for eternal spring in the jungle with wild orchids and passionfruit bloom in the remote Highlands of Papua New Guinea. Vivien Altman longed for the violets, blossom and daffodils, the smell and texture of eucalypts of a Melbourne spring, yet revelled in the passion, the charm and the sweaty vibrancy of Latin America.

Mickey Zhu, travelling to Australia from China, found – like Sandra McCallum who made her way from Australia to Canada – that where she is living now is home: for Mickey Zhu, it is Melbourne, Australia; for Sandra McCallum, Victoria, British Columbia. Vivienne Correa's family went from China to Hong Kong. Later she, together with her husband, set sail for Australia – and a new life, and 'home'. Sue Ogier and Jan Mock travelled to Australia as children, with their families, migrating under the £10 immigrant scheme; for them, Australia is their home. As a teenager, Kristin Henry travelled to Australia with her family, too. Like Sue Ogier and Jan Mock, the sense of familiarity stirs when she returns to 'home': for her, Tennessee in the United States of America. Yet like the others, *home* is here. 'This is My Home.'

Travelling to a different country, taking up residence away from home, signifies change. 'Changes. Transitions.' Not only did Lynne Wenig's life in the United States change when she married an Australian; her country changed, too. So it was for Janet Labatut when she married a British national who had made his life in Australia: she now lives and writes in Melbourne, Victoria. Penelope E. Andrews left South Africa for the United States of America, then found her home in Australia – a base from which she now is free to move once more to the United States, teaching, until her return. Jennifer Simon left Scotland and England for Victoria, Australia to pursue work goals. Ania Wilczynski fulfilled her own ambitions, and her mother's ambitions for her, when she backpacked over Asia, landing in Cambridge, England and completing her PhD before returning to Sydney. Tui Taurua changed countries as an escape from one relationship, and found it ironic to be teaching Australian politics, as a citizen of New Zealand. Now as a citizen of Australia, she regrets knowing more about Australian political life than about the politics of the country of her birth.

...she regrets knowing more about Australian political life than about the politics of the country of her birth.

'How can we change the entrenched negatives of stratified British-style education implanted around the world?' asks Anne Hickling Hudson, Jamaican-born and living and teaching in Brisbane, Australia. Like Sylvia Hennessy, coming to Australia from Ireland via London, she grew up in a colonised country. Mary Ann Bin-Sallik's country was colonised, too – after the British invasion. She studied at Harvard, a Djaru woman from Western Australia, adding to the ambitious program of achievements of Black Woman's Action, established to support Aboriginal Australians in expanding their education. Magnificently, on a shoe string! From Poland, escaping a repressive government, Dorota Malchevski emigrated to Australia via Greece. Ofelia Lopez escaped a repressive government to arrive in Australia, from El Salvador, as a refugee. 'Does being a woman mean one has no country?' asks Gisela Gardener, born in Germany, lived in Britain, arriving in Australia with her daughter and husband and now living in the Centre – Alice Springs – with two daughters and husband. Virginia Woolf's words ring true – but they contain a bigger story than ever she or any non-Aboriginal Australians thought. The politics of country extends to the way women see ourselves, and the way we view 'country'. Aboriginal women demand 'country'. Aboriginal women and non-Aboriginal women demand rights and freedoms in this country. Women from a multiplicity of backgrounds, from so many different countries, are working together to appreciate the meaning of country, from whichever country we come.

What leads women to travel thousands of miles to make new lives for themselves, whether at home or away from home? *No Fear of Flying – Women at Home and Abroad* recounts the lives of 25 women and their courage in leaving Australia for life abroad, or leaving home and making 'home' in Australia. *No Fear of Flying* is a tribute to the brave: to the strength, the freedom, the humour and initiative of all women who have travelled, and who plan to do so.

PART I

Flowers Fruit Colour Smell

'Space, and Nests, and History'

Gillian Hanscombe

Gillian Hanscombe was born in Melbourne in 1945 and left for London in 1969. Her Australian adolescence was filled with the usual angst and conflict, punctuated by a range of quite disparate passionate commitments: to sport, religion, poetry, and lesbian love affairs. During two decades in England, sport and religion got dropped, while poetry and lesbianism were shaped and validated by feminist theory and activism. Since 1986 Gillian Hanscombe has lived in rural Devon with her lover, Suniti Namjoshi, and her son Martin. Her published work covers a range of interests, including polemic and literary criticism, but her principal focus is poetry. Books include *Hecate's Charms*, Khasmik, Sydney, 1976; *Flesh and Paper* (with Suniti Namjoshi), 1986, Ragweed, Canada and Jezebel, United Kingdom; and *Sybil The Glide of Her Tongue* published by Spinifex Press in Melbourne in 1992.

Melbourne in the 1950s – O glamorous age! Scorching summers, with pictures in the *Sun* of how many hundreds of people slept in rows on the beaches. The young Queen's visit in 1953, thick crowds screaming with rapture all the way from Collins Street to the Shrine. The 1956 Olympics, held in an atmosphere bursting with aspiration and raw sentimentality. People wept with pride when Betty Cuthbert won the sprints, when Dawn Fraser won the 100 metres freestyle, when teams of golden girls won the athletics and swimming relays. Then there was the 1958 Billy Graham Crusade: thousands flocked to the Myer Music Bowl to pledge themselves to the God of America, and Hollywood came too – to make *On the Beach* with Ava Gardner. Melbourne might be the last remaining outpost on earth of human habitation (Tasmania didn't count) but at least it was on the map.

There was 'going to town' with mum for shopping and lunch in one of the cafeterias: Manton's, Myer's – they all had the same tin trays and the same ice cream scoops of mashed veg to go with the hot pie and sauce. Waitresses wore aprons and laced headbands, and everyone called mum 'madam' or 'dear'. The currency was pounds, shillings and pence and we learnt the aliquot parts at school. Everyone knew what a guinea was.

...my parents decided I should have my secondary education at a small independent girls' school run by Anglican nuns, so that I could become a lady.

Having mixed in for my primary education at the local state school, and my father having started to make some money (as he put it), my parents decided I should have my secondary education at a small independent girls' school run by Anglican nuns, so that I could become a lady. Manners, after all, were more important to a girl's future than brains. It's true this school didn't do much for my brains, but my lesbianism blossomed and I had a young English teacher who told me everything I wanted and needed to know about poetry. The nuns have long since departed, and the school has gone co-ed and up-market. I don't know if it still turns out ladies.

Induction into the Australian identity was quite explicit. Australia was the lucky country; no tyranny of distance, no high unemployment, no mega-buck frauds, no underclass. The word racism didn't exist in the vernacular: 'Aborigines' was a sub-category option on the matriculation Australian history syllabus, though the 'White Australia Policy' was part of the compulsory section. I never heard the word foreigner, or even the word European people; who didn't talk like we did, ran fish and chip shops, or green groceries, or milk bars, and were called New Australians. In the lucky country, everyone could do well; and if they didn't, it was their own fault.

Politics were the great white chief, Robert Menzies, who trembled with adoration when he spoke of the Queen; the hated DLP (Democratic Labor Party) which split the Labor vote and ranted about the new yellow peril of Asian communism; and trouble on the wharves. In the early 1960s, with sophistication just round the corner, Melbourne television boasted the young, black-haired Bob Hawke, preaching about wages; and the young Beatrice Faust, shocking everyone by arguing in public about abortion. There was no Australian film industry, and the television schedules offered an almost non-stop flow of American pap, with the ideology of the Home of the Brave left intact. Though I later joined anti-Viet Nam protests, along with other university students, I had no understanding of American imperialism, either military or cultural. I was an ignorant, amateur pacifist, like the other humanists of my generation. We were, after all, educated to be well-mannered and bookish: we'd been taught a lot about the theology of original sin, but nothing at all about the wickedness of the world.

At school we had Anzac Day, Empire Day and Remembrance Day, though the wars got muddled and we sang *Land of Hope and Glory* thinking it meant Australia. We sang the others, too: *Rule Britannia, O Valiant Hearts,* and *God of our Fathers.* Every year we heard the ABC (Australian Broadcasting Commission) broadcast about Simpson and his donkey, and we repeated Laurence Binyon's poem and we listened to the bugle. We hoisted the flag, vowed to thee my country and stared to see which unmarried teachers had tears in their eyes because that meant they'd lost their true love in the war.

The map of the Pacific looked different then. Papua New Guinea was under Australian mandate; Indonesia was a new and frightening neighbour, about which we were taught nothing except that President Sukarno was an uncivilised thug; Malaya had jungles and the British fighting for freedom and democracy; Singapore was where the Japanese had done unspeakable things to their prisoners; Saigon was an elegant French colonial city; Taiwan was the 'real' China. There were no jumbo jets; no tourist packages to Bangkok, Kuala Lumpur, Hong Kong; Hawaii was not an American state; there was no Tullamarine airport. Going to that mystical paradise called 'overseas' meant England and Europe. It was cheaper, when I left in 1969, to fly to London than to New Zealand.

If geo-politics didn't exist, and Australian party politics were a mere haze, then gender politics were not even apocryphal. Being a girl was a sorrow and a frustration; being a clever girl was a terrible disadvantage; being an ambitious or independent girl almost qualified as a social pathology. By the age of 15 – the old Leaving Certificate year – everyone knew that the race to the altar was the only one that really counted.

I left when I did because there was no reason to stay. Or – I fled when I did to escape my suburban destiny. The Melbourne of the 1950s had no niche for women like me; and the 1960s didn't really arrive in time. SDS (Students for a Democratic Society) and student sit-ins didn't start until I was nearly through my MA; and the Whitlam government was elected after I'd gone. The White Australia Policy remained intact; there were no gays on the streets, no feminists on the television, no socialists in office; there was no fashion for ethnic eating or community radio. The most outrageous students Melbourne University could manage were the Rationalists, whose claim to shock status was arguing against the existence of god. At a dinner hosted by Kerryn Higgs (who later wrote *All That False Instruction*) and myself, because we were editors that year of the undergraduate literary magazine, Professor Sam Goldberg declared (and I remember the exact words): 'Women can be intelligent, yes; creative, yes; but imaginative – never.' No one disagreed, and Kerryn and I dutifully paid the bill. This Melbourne was no place to be a poet. And as for being a lesbian…

But it was in London, into my third year away – post-culture shock, post-bureaucratic pigeonholing, post-travelling to Greece and back, via France and Italy, post-paying tax and buying a bit of a shared house – that I began to find out how to write what I wanted to write; because it was in London, having no history and no identity – being born adult, as it were, as all immigrants are – that I discovered the mythic power of the Australian landscape, and the passion it engenders. I mean, of course, the parts I had known. There was the 'country' of the Goulburn Valley, where my mother's father was a stock and station agent and where we visited often, though it took all day to drive the 130 miles in the

...I discovered the mythic power of the Australian landscape, and the passion it engenders.

tiny Ford Prefect that had to crawl over Pretty Sally in first gear. There was the 'bush' of the Great Divide, where my father had acquired a holiday house and where I spent many summers water-skiing on the Eildon Weir, sitting near the local waterfall, cycling and driving on the gravel roads round the district, finding the most lush patches of eucalyptus, wattles and ferns. And there was always the sea: Port Phillip Bay, the Great Ocean Road to Portland or Port Fairy, the Pacific when we went to Sydney.

I began my first sequence, *Hecate's Charms*, with the country of my childhood:

Those were the glad days,
mad, bad
(morally flawed, that is)
ring-a-ring-a-peppercorn-rosy
where the caterpillars curled
and the silly wattle shed its showers.

I want Wungnu and Numurkah,
Shepparton, Murchison and Tallarook,
and all the faded Goulburn Valley journey.

I was a quick child, glad child,
loquats-over-the-fence child,
bad child
spitting out the pips;
afraid of being chased
(puff puff)
by the square dare of the black steam trains.

Pigeons for the morning,
magpies for the noon,
kookaburras by the railway
all afternoon.

Those were the breathless, marvellous,
wheat-glazed, bonfire summers.
Everyone sat through the gum-leaf-dusted heat,
everyone's grandma pushed and pulled sweet scones
from a wood-fire stove,
everyone's children dawdled home by the creek
(and bottled tadpoles)
everyone's father noticed the stars
while mother was noticing father

The earth was mad and bad
and full of fruit, and full of people,
and full of space, and nests, and history.

Prologue 1 from *Hecate's Charms*, 1976

Being Australian might be problematic (the English were ferociously contemptuous and condescending), but being an Australian poet was unambivalent and inevitable. I sent *Hecate's Charms* to Judith Wright, in gratitude for all that her work had meant to me as a schoolgirl and student; and she wrote back, straightforwardly welcoming me to the tradition I belonged to.

Ten years later, when I was writing the sequence *Flesh and Paper* with my lover, the poet Suniti Namjoshi, it was the bush of the Great Divide that provided images of passion and connection:

...A particular place,
I tried when you smiled,
when you asked me to answer,
The women were vivid;

they were friends; they were lovers;
and the ferns in the winter
were greener than apples,
were headhigh and watering.

I was hungry; impatient.
My hands helped me daily.

My hands down the trees
were as fervent as ever
they felt down the thighs
of women, my lovers...

'Was it chance,' *Flesh and Paper*, 1986

Still later, when I wrote the sequence *Sybil the Glide of Her Tongue*, the imagery of English sheep and rose gardens, of Greek cypresses and olive groves, of Indian silk and sandalwood, became threaded through with the great Southern Ocean:

The sea breasted herself, reared, fell, and was fooled. Later, she lay flat and brooding. If I had a grain of greatness in me, I'd call her a god and be glad. I'd prepare ceremonies.

But I know better. I know she herself fawns at the come-hither of our-lady-the-moon. (My lover, who also has a secret face, beckons nightly. I beckon in my turn. We were both, long ago, imprinted by tides.)

From 'The Prophetical Songs', *Sybil The Glide of Her Tongue*, 1992

I'd become accustomed to the formulation that although I had escaped the horrors of Australian society (the small-mindedness, the bigotries, the impossibility of vision, the awfulness of the men), I had miraculously retained the gift of the mythic landscape: its ravishing, merciless, huge intensity, that still – after more than 20 years – whispered or thundered in my dreams and day-dreams. I was therefore unprepared for what happened to me in March 1992, when I spent a month, together with Suniti, touring *Sybil* in Adelaide (at the Writers' Festival), Melbourne and Sydney. Though I'd been back many times for family reasons, this was the first time I'd gone back as myself, so to speak. The experience was intoxicating. I wanted to stay. I wanted to belong.

Not that England hadn't been kind to me, despite the **England gave me** fabled arrogance of the southern English, who not only **psychological** have a genius for stoical self-satisfaction, but may even have **space to be** genes for it! England gave me psychological space to be **whoever I pleased** whoever I pleased and to do whatever took my fancy. To be **and to do whatever** young in London was an utterly benign experience, since **took my fancy.** London was indifferent in the best sense: no one cared what you wore or what you said or where you came from; and however strange you felt, there were at least a dozen other people who were just like you.

I hadn't planned to spend more than 20 years away. The summer of 1968-69 was very hot. I was sweating over my typewriter on my MA thesis, and my then lover – a violinist – was practising for a recital. We were renting a flat in South Yarra from architect friends who were spending a year 'overseas', but who would, of course, be coming back eventually. My lover suddenly said: 'Why don't we go to England?' and I replied: 'Sure, but what would I do?' It was easy after that. She'd spent two years in London already, and knew people. She arranged everything, more or less: jobs, work permits, travel details, shipping of all our worldlies ('do we really need to pack the breadknife?' I protested – but she said: 'Whatever we don't take, we'll have to buy').

I got on with finishing my thesis and enrolling for an evening degree at Birbeck College in London. We left in August 1969 and spent a month getting to London via Hong Kong (for pleasure), Vienna and Munich (for violin lessons), and Amsterdam (to see friends).

The expatriate Australian who'd secured our work permits and offered us jobs and accommodation, until we found our own, had a full house with his sons home from boarding school for the English summer. He offered us, instead, his small motor launch to live in. He showed us how it worked and said we could take it wherever we liked. It was moored on the Thames near Marlow in Buckinghamshire, the next month was spent going up and down the Thames, working the locks, emptying the chemical toilet, trudging over the fields to buy food or catch the train to London to see the tourist sights. After a couple of weeks, my lover pointed out that we'd have to find somewhere to live, in time for when our jobs began in September. I said that in all the Agatha Christie who-dun-its, it's always the barmaid who knows what's what. So we went to the village nearest where we'd be working and asked the barmaid if she knew of a place to rent. Sure enough, there was a cottage being renovated that hadn't yet been advertised...

I knew from Agatha Christie that English tea happened at four o'clock and that it meant crumpets and cake and honey, so I was properly ready when the bell rang at four...

My job lasted only a month. I didn't get on with the expatriate Australian (nor he with me) and I decided to quit before I got sacked. But what to do? Women like me weren't trained for anything and therefore had better teach. I spent a solid week with the Hertfordshire phone book looking unsuccessfully for schools: I tried E for education, S for state, G for government even C for Church of England – all categories that would have yielded a list Back Home. In the end I tried H for Hertfordshire – and there was a list: not of schools, but of Colleges of Further Education (FE Colleges). (I didn't find out for a year that schools are listed under their own names, so you need to know what they're called before you can look them up.)

I phoned up all the FE Colleges, offering myself, and getting no interest at all until I hit one near the end of the list. 'Well we DO need an English lecturer,' said an accented male voice. 'Can I come to tea to discuss it?' I knew from Agatha Christie that English tea happened at four o'clock and that it meant crumpets and cake and honey, so I was properly ready when the bell rang at four on the agreed day. 'Do call me James,' said a small, bearded, red-headed chap who turned out to be an expatriate New Zealander. He hired me for the following week.

After a year spent working, doing tourist trips and belting down the M1 motorway to Birbeck three times a week, my lover said we should move to London. She'd been offered the job of leading the Royal Ballet Touring Orchestra and was, I think, the first woman to lead a professional orchestra in Britain. I thought I'd try the independent system and got a job teaching senior English at Queen's College in Harley Street, the oldest establishment in England offering formal education to women. It was set up in 1848 by Christian socialists in order to give governesses a paper qualification, and had a distinguished rollcall of past students (including Katherine Mansfield), though by the time I taught there, it had become a girls' public day school and was full of very rich foreigners who had no motivation (it seemed to me) for knowing Chaucer or Pope or the eighteenth century novel.

I was mercilessly patronised. When I ordered a particular edition of Milton for the A level course, the Head rebuked me – in front of my class – by saying: 'But you're Australian: what do you know about this or that edition?' (She was a chemist herself and told the girls that Shakespeare was a bore, didn't they agree?) The history master, who wore a pinstripe to school and always carried a copy of the *Financial Times*,

> I was mercilessly patronised...
> 'But you're Australian: what do you know about this or that edition?'

instructed me during shared free periods about the correct titles due the minor aristocracy (second sons of marquesses are called... but on the other hand, second sons of earls... the son of a baronet...) The senior English mistress informed me that she was not Irish: she was anglo-Irish minor gentry, since her father was a Church of Ireland clergyman. 'As you're Australian,' she'd said to me when interviewing me for the job, 'how can you understand the English Lake Poets?' I'd replied (already by then tired of being treated like a barbarian from outer space): 'Well, you're Irish. How do you understand them?' But she'd given me the job.

I taught at Queen's, and also at Jews' College, for the four years needed to fulfil my British residency requirements, and then went up to Oxford. My lover had meanwhile begun a relationship with an English violinist who also worked in the Royal Opera House orchestra; after a while, the three of us set up together and bought a house in Harrow. By now I was firmly settled and thought never at all about returning to Australia. I earned money giving English cramming or coaching sessions, doing freelance teaching for Americans based in Oxford, doing typing jobs in offices, working in a restaurant kitchen, doing office cleaning and later – after Oxford – working as a journalist. Once settled in Oxford, I set about having a baby, thinking that writing a thesis was the most compatible occupation to undertake while pregnant.

The worst time of my life was the northern winter/southern summer of 1974-75. My mother died quite suddenly in Melbourne and I flew back for the funeral. I was one month pregnant and facing a threatened miscarriage. I lost the baby at 20 weeks and was given a lot of help and sympathy from my supervisor (at St Anne's) and from the principal of my own college (St Hugh's). I was amazed, therefore, when I was safely pregnant again, to have my news greeted with shock and horror by my supervisor, who immediately cancelled plans to recommend me for a fellowship and told me to keep the knowledge secret from my college at all costs. This was easy enough to do until fees had to be paid in the January of 1976 (the baby was due at the beginning of April). There was only one way out of the problem, as far as I could see: I would have to use the Oxford horror of an Australian accent to my advantage.

My Australian lover agreed to my plan. We went together to my college, me draped in a large coat and carrying a lot of books, she talking in the loudest voice she could manage, and in the broadest Sydney she could produce, all along the corridors to the bursar's office. Everyone looked the other way, as I'd known they would. Once in the office, while the paperwork proceeded, my lover kept up a constant flow of dreadful Australian, making the bursar screw up her eyes and wince with embarrassment. I had the baby and completed the thesis without my college ever knowing anything until I told them myself, after leaving Oxford, to put my son's birth in the birth announcements column of their magazine, which they duly did. Predictably enough mine was the only name sans 'nee'.

> I had the baby and completed the thesis without my college ever knowing anything until I told them myself, after leaving Oxford...

All that was more than a decade ago, a decade filled – not with expatriate identity problems, but with the power of feminism, which I found first in books (reading for my thesis) and later in activism of various kinds. Feminism rationalised why I hadn't, and couldn't, fit in; explained that not only did a woman have no country – having had no access to power or policy – but that a lesbian woman was always an exile, no matter when she started or where she ended up. Most importantly of all, feminism constructed a world-view in which a female humanbeing was taken to be the norm, and on that solid ground I could begin to flesh out my own vision and develop my own style with confidence.

Finding feminism would have changed my life and my consciousness whatever country I'd been living in – I'm sure of that. It happened to be England – so England is where I stayed. Feminism in London was, in any case, chock-a-block with expatriate English-speakers. The women's publishing houses and writers' groups were particularly extra-English: there were dozens of women from Australia, New Zealand, Canada, South Africa and the United States of America. Nearly all were white; nearly all were what the English call middle-class. Non-white input and race politics came later, during the mid-1980s, making maximum impact at the first international feminist book fair, held in London in June 1984. I met Suniti there, on a public platform: she was one of five lesbian writers invited to read, and I was chairing the event. We became friends, corresponded, became lovers. Though she'd grown up in India, she'd lived for many years in Toronto, teaching at Scarborough College, University of Toronto; and we spent a couple of years commuting. Having decided to live together, we had to choose England or Canada. Australia never occurred to either of us. The existence of my son, then aged 10, made England seem the better option; but we agreed, often enough, that if you're a lesbian, you don't have proper roots anywhere; and if you're a writer, you can live anywhere; and if you HAVE lived somewhere else, you can live anywhere else easily. In addition, we agreed, home is where each other is.

March 1992 added a new option. Perhaps it would be possible to 'go home'. Perhaps it would be possible to be a lesbian and a poet back in Melbourne; and to have – whenever one wished – the dry land, the eucalyptus forests, the technicolour birds, the mighty ocean. Perhaps one could have all this because of the women we met: women with energy, imagination, generosity, plans. They were friendly, they were hospitable, they were enthusiastic, they were capable; **they were not on their knees with anxiety and penury – as we all were in England, having become battered and fragmented after a decade of Thatcherism.** In that one long-and-short month I lived in a feminist dream, created – for the most part- by the women of Spinifex Press, whose ideas and ambitions for Australian feminist writing are secured with prodigious hard work and attention both to what books need, and to what women need. Everywhere we went there was good talk, fresh food that we could afford to buy, literary events and audiences where we could make sense, meetings and visits and parties where friendships could flourish. And wherever we went, we were given fine wine to drink! What more could a woman want?

We're cautious, Suniti and I. We know that setting up house somewhere, and filling in forms, and having to take sides in whatever fights are going on, isn't at all the same as having a working holiday. We know familiarity breeds complacency. We know people will make much more effort if we blow in once in the blue moon, than if we were part of the scenery, since we're like that ourselves when it comes to friends and visitors. Nevertheless: Melbourne in the 1990s is still quite a different proposition from the Melbourne of the 1950s. There IS now room for women like me. There are people able to want what I'm able to offer. And as for our work: there are women reading Suniti's books, or mine, who don't feel that what we write has nothing to do with them. I don't know, as I write this, where I'll end up. But I do know, for the first time in 20 years, that Australia has become a possibility.

Fush 'n' Chups

Marlies Puentener

Marlies Puentener was born in Christchurch/Otautahi, New Zealand/Aotearoa on 12 August 1966. After doing welfare work with women for five years in New Zealand, the Northern Territory and Tasmania, Marlies is studying for a bachelor of social work, at the University of Queensland. She lives in West End, Brisbane with her feline familiar and a house of madwimmin.

For Cysta Souls on the Journey,
Louise and Janine

As with any Kiwi, it was with trepidation I immigrated to Australia in November 1988. Like my sister, Janine, I moved to Australia to study what was then unavailable in New Zealand: herself, acupuncture and myself, drama. Following an unsuccessful audition for NIDA (National Institute of Dramatic Art), and being told to come back when you've lost 'that' accent, I indignantly stomped to my VW Kombi and drove north. I wasn't overly perturbed by plans going awry and so with a new plan to travel and work I set to conquer the east coast.

As a baby, I was adopted into a working-class family. I grew up in a weatherboard house in Beckenham, Christchurch: 20 minutes from the sea and one hour from the mountains. I was the middle child with an older brother, younger sister, a Swiss father and English mother. Childhood consisted of gumboots, Catholicism, the pet lamb, eeling in the Heathcote River and family outings on bicycles before we got a car. My sister and I, albeit with the most loving intent, nonetheless provoked

Chank the family cat into a state of neurosis from which he never fully recovered.

At six, I began to learn to play the piano, taught by a big hearted Baptist woman whose going rate was then 10 cents per half-hour. She was a reliable source of gossip on anyone local since the 1920s and you could accurately read the hour of the day by how far her suspendered stockings had slipped. We fed her oversized cat our seg sandwiches (New Zealand for meat sausage); and my best friend Helen Doyle and I made her year by winning the Christchurch music competition's duet section with *Marche Militaire* – me pounding away on the bass. Somehow, similar childhoods managed to produce some spirited and committed feminist women in my extended family. With two such cousins, Anna and Rachel, and a daring and incredibly determined sister, Puentener women are indeed a force to be reckoned with.

My teenage years were a time of contrast: school balls, debating teams, plays on the one hand; and punk pub bands, black op shop clothes, bikies, and copious quantities of vodka on the other. My mother, a former nurse, did paidwork at home taking knitting orders. My father, after immigrating to New Zealand in the 1950s from Switzerland, worked six-days-a-week as a house painter. Together they managed to put all three children through private Catholic high schools.

...feminist role models (albeit disguised) in the form of strong, independent, politicised nuns.

I attended Sacred Heart Girls' College in Christchurch for seven years where I first encountered feminist role models (albeit disguised) in the form of strong, independent, politicised nuns. My high school years were marked by the Springbok Rugby Tour of New Zealand, and other contentious issues. Political and moral debates were generally encouraged by the nuns and other teachers in a social justice framework, emphasising the importance of living one's beliefs. In 1981, when the Catholic Bishop allowed students time off school to participate in the huge national street protests against the Springbok Tour, the red uniforms of Sacred Heart girls featured prominently in the media. Kiwis were genuinely perplexed at the world's reaction to Prime Minister David Lange's nuclear free New Zealand stance. (We, at 18 years were all convinced it was our victory – that is, the radical youth vote.)

With this background, it was with surprise that I encountered the indifferent attitude of many Queenslanders following 20 years of Joh (New Zealand-born and now former Premier of Queensland). As part of an environmental group seeking signatures for a petition to stop the blasting of Nelly Bay on Magnetic Island, I was often met with: 'I agree with your stance – but what's the point in protesting?' Yet there are many exceptions, two of whom I have been fortunate to know through the Magnetic Island fight – courageous women, Liz Owen and the late Susie Dickson.

Generalisations are usually problematic, yet for me New Zealanders do have a sense of unity, and belief in their potential to influence political change. Australia, undoubtedly due to its geographical size and diversity as well as its state political structure, denies many of its citizens that same feeling of empowerment on a political level.

My decision when in Brisbane to head across to Darwin was made hastily. Constrained by dwindling finances, my friend and I decided to drive the 2500 kilometres to the Northern Territory capital city.

With incredible naivety as to what lay ahead, I allowed an abandoned cat to adopt the Kombi as her home. The three of us panted, sweated and cursed our way along Flinders Highway and across the Barkly Tablelands in mid-summer. 'The cat' became Shealagh, and apparently enjoyed certain parts of the journey as she produced five kittens (all sons) some months later in Darwin.

Now we do have 'hot' in New Zealand, which any South Island Kiwi would define as being anywhere between 18 and 24 degrees Celsius. Anything above – well it's just not possible – is it?

Indeed it is.

Heat in Australia is not a mere intangible concept, it is a physical entity that engulfs the whole person and dictates one's lifestyle. I had the dubious pleasure of experiencing the full force of this phenomenon in an un-airconditioned vehicle travelling 14 hours per day surrounded by flat, scorching, ochre earth.

Having survived road trains, Mt Isa police, blowflies in the ears, nose, eyes and mouth, as well as the sight of countless cattle carcasses, I began to wonder if Darwin really existed. The Kombi, deciding it did not, upped and died some 200 km outside Darwin. Having met every NRMA, RACQ, and AANT service person along the way, we were destined to meet the last who relieved us of our final pennies to enable the old VW to stagger into Darwin.

My introduction to Darwin in January 1989 was terrifying: a great expanse of flat land cowering under a jet black sky fragmented by successive white tributaries of light. Convinced Cyclone Tracy II was about to occur, I parked in a bushy street for the remainder of the night. At daybreak two burly Northern Territory police woke me up to personally deliver my $200 fine for sleeping on the street. I had parked the Kombi directly across from the home of Darwin's chief of police.

Heat in Australia... is a physical entity that engulfs the whole person and dictates one's lifestyle.

The saving feature of Darwin for a Kiwi straight out of a New Zealand winter were the sunsets and (eventually) the lightning shows. The powerful beauty of the setting sun off the Darwin coast is a magical memory, worth the munchings of marauding mosquitoes.

Australia is a land of all creatures great and small – most of them greater than smaller. Every migrant has their cockroach initiation and one cannot ask for a better (or bigger) one than is staged by Darwin's Blattodea who provide a full army or two for a welcoming parade.

I was fairly polite in my restraint when I happened upon my first tropical 'fridge complete with sugar, jams, vegemite, vegetables and flour. I came to understand these were no mere 'fridges but Fortresses-for-Food where shelf items sought refrigerated refuge from the heat, cockroaches, geckos and ants. All was revealed the first time I came home to a procession of the latter, twenty abreast marching en masse in a purposeful black line from my bedroom, down the hallway and into the kitchen – all for a honey lid I had inadvertently left on the bench. Outside the house it was commonplace to observe a frilled-necked lizard in prehistoric pose sauntering down the driveway.

...grabbed by the shoulders and turned about to cast my gaze upon my swimming partner – a two metre croc floating full length on the top of the water.

It was not until the pilots' strike of 1989 (grounding domestic flights in Australia for weeks) that I was able to afford a discounted four-wheel drive tour of Kakadu National Park. Here I became very intimate with one of Australia's 'greater' creatures. A long-standing fear of heights made me decline the tour guide's offer of a 'bump-push' up the side of a waterfall to see the view over Kakadu. After several failed attempts at persuasion he gave up and joined the others amidst mumblings of 'woosy girls'. I meanwhile decided to enjoy the now vacant series of fresh-water pools by the thunderous falls. Deafened to anything other than the descending water, I swam merrily about, waving to a large group of people on a far bank in true neighbourly fashion. After all they were waving at *me* fairly energetically, or so it appeared. It was only when I saw a friend descending the rock face with a curious urgency that I swam over to see what was ado.

In frantic sign language I got the message to remove myself from the water. I complied with slight annoyance only to then be grabbed by the shoulders and turned about to cast my gaze upon my swimming partner – a two metre croc floating full length on the top of the water. Shock was, praise the Goddess, delayed, and by this time the rest of the tour party had joined us. Still miffed at the tour guide I quietly witnessed his purple fit: 'What were you doing girlie? – You could've been a goner!' I nonchalantly replied with my Mother's favourite: 'Mate, you should know – if you don't hurt them they won't hurt you.' Rendering a male speechless is a most satisfying past time and I've since made a point of indulging as often as possible. I was awarded heroine status for the remainder of the trip.

I finished Form 7 (Grade 12) at highschool and then worked as a secretary for two years in an adventure travel agency. This involved optional weekends white water rafting the fantastic Rangitata Gorge. At 19, having saved some of my wages, I took off for the Middle East. With long, dark hair I soon cottoned on to wearing a head scarf to avoid continually being asked how many camels my Mother would like to sell me for!

The lives of women in Egypt and war-torn Israel are so vastly different from ours in Western culture. Travel opened my eyes to many more faces of oppression. Being told to stand outside mosques and synagogues with the butt of a machine gun and asked whether I was 'unclean' (menstruating) was a huge culture shock for this teenage Kiwi from down under.

Travelling as far as Lebanon, I returned to New Zealand after briefly backpacking through South-East Asia. Always one for a bargain, I had accumulated brass, olive wood, henna, you name it, from every bazaar and market I could sniff out. Arriving barefoot and bronzed with all this booty, New Zealand customs had a field day.

In 1987 I changed jobs and worked in the Department of Social Welfare in Christchurch. Equal employment opportunity (EEO) policies were being implemented in the public service. Enthusiastic and 20-years-old, I welcomed a position of women's liaison officer (WLO). With 600 staff, 79 per cent of whom were women, we had our hands full. Ours was the first office to 'win' a women's room for staff use, complete with small library.

With a handful of other WLO's, we organised speakers on issues concerning women, carried out surveys and needs questionnaires, held self-defence workshops, dealt with sexual harassment cases and were consulted on policy alongside Public Service Association union-delegates. The majority of us were young, bursting with burgeoning feminist energies. Nevertheless, the white, middle-class, chain-smoking male public servant (of the brown-suit-and-toupee variety) proved a formidable opponent.

> I stumbled into a job as a carer for six Aboriginal children and teenagers with severe intellectual and physical disabilities.

As women's liaison officers, Ruth Jones and I kept each other sane and laughing. She continues to fight for the rights of Maoris, women and the disabled. Kia Ora Ruth.

From this feminist Baptism By Fire in a bureaucracy, in Australia I have been fortunate to work within less hierarchal structures – in community-based services. In employment, I have felt very lucky in Australia. I have been accepted for most positions by interviews without the emphasis on contacting referees and so forth. My experience of seeking employment in New Zealand (whether it was full-time or casual work) was that of a great concern with qualifications, age, and specific former experience. Australians, I have found, are more prepared to 'give you a go' – allowing your work performance on the job to speak for you.

This proved so in Darwin when I stumbled into a job as a carer for six Aboriginal children and teenagers with severe intellectual and physical disabilities. After a casual inquiry visit to the home, I received a telephone call that night – the night worker was sick, could I do her shift? By 6 am the following morning, I had blundered my way through changing a stomach tube, four out of six baths, ten nappy changes, and the consequence of laxatives administered three days before. I got the thumbs up and began work forthwith.

This job was extremely insightful, giving me a new perspective on the judgemental blindness of 'normal' society's definition of what constitutes 'quality of life'. These are indeed beautiful, valuable lives.

In Darwin I also became honorary housemother in a homeless young women's independent half-way house where I lived for a year with four others aged between 17 and 19 years: a born again Christian aspiring to be a major in the Salvation Army, an atheist, a sleepwalking-bulimic and a Muslim made for crazy living!

It was here I met Ann Buxton, a dynamic youth worker who for years co-ordinated the youth services in Darwin under the auspices of the YWCA (Young Women's Christian Association). Ann provided much inspiration, linking me up with the Big Sister Program whereby young adolescent women pair up with a big sister for friendship and support. Through the 'Y', in 1989 I attended the First Northern Territory Women's Health Conference in Bachelor. This was an inevitable patchwork of diversity – in colour, philosophies and objectives. Many Aboriginal women from outback communities attended, as well as the small networks of workers from women's services in Darwin, vegan separatists from Alice, and femocrats from interstate. I helped present a workshop on young women's health with this diverse bunch – a brave endeavour!

...the First Northern Territory Women's Health Conference in Bachelor... an inevitable patchwork of diversity – in colour, philosophies and objectives.

What stood out for me at this conference were the huge differences between white and black health care in this country. I was one of 100 or so participants who walked out on a preview screening of a New South Wales contraception education video at the conference. Designed for remotely situated Aboriginal women it promoted Depo Provera with no mention of the controversy surrounding the safety of the drug. The practice of rounding up pregnant Aboriginal women within a few weeks of their 'due' date and bringing them into hospitals denies many aspects of Aboriginal culture as well as personal choice – yet my understanding is that this continues throughout the Northern Territory.

Tasmania was my next stop for almost a year-and-a-half. After the cyclone-regulation housing of Darwin, I was in seventh heaven surrounded by quaint worker's cottages nestled in the green valleys of Tasmania.

It was fairly painful to see cottages modernised: false brick veneer, metallic front doors, fireplaces filled in. However, living in my own 1830s cottage I came to appreciate all is not blissful in a house with sloped floorboards, draughty open fireplaces and no insulation in a -3 degrees Celsius Tassie frost.

Tasmania, upheld as Australia's green belt, was a disappointment. Even here, 'greenie' is a dirty word. This is a notable difference between New Zealand an Australia. To be a greenie in New Zealand usually commands a lot of respect. It is a label earned through environmental action and is not one adopted by those merely sympathetic to the cause. The logging of national parks is an horrendous concept to most Kiwis and unfortunately for most Australians it is a reality here.

Every night returning from work in Launceston I could be stopped in my car for up to 15 minutes as a train carrying hundreds of trees intersected the road outside my village. When the United States actor and activist, Whoopi Goldberg, challenged her conservative Launceston audience on Tasmanian woodchip sales to Japan it went down like a lead balloon. Fortunately, Tasmania has many active greenies, addressing environmental destruction at physical and spiritual levels... Long may the cauldrons of the Keera* wimmin bubble high in the great Western Tiers.

I loved my work in a young women's refuge in Launceston, Tasmania. The broader collective comprised radical separatists from Deloraine, the workers predominantly liberal feminists. At times this was a volatile combination but everyone involved held a sincere commitment to the well be-ing of young women.

Somewhere in the middle, and the youngest permanent worker, I found the most effective means of broadening and linking feminist perspectives was through books. I established a library at the refuge, and this became a valuable resource for both workers and residents.

While mainland Australia accepts St Kilda and Kings Cross, conservative Tasmania largely denies the existence of homelessness in a state where convict vagrancy laws remain in force. Commonwealth and state funded refuges are constrained by restrictions on length of stay for service users. The maximum first time stay is six weeks, and three weeks every subsequent stay. This, combined with survival on YHA (Young Homeless Allowance) and JSA (Job Search Allowance), inevitably resulted in high recidivism.

> Long may the cauldrons of the Keera wimmin bubble high in the great Western Tiers.

With an emphasis on 'believe in yourself and act', I choose empathy and empowerment as feminist working tools to encourage dealing with pain rather than denying it. The young women of Karinya made me laugh, scream, and stand in awe of their strength and courage. I still correspond with several of 'my' girls and use their references in my resume.

Working in Tasmania's Northern Sexual Assault Service was also a great experience; very different from crisis work. The capacity of children to heal is phenomenal, as well as their comprehension of protective behaviours at an early age.

Networking of women's services is a difficult process in Australia in comparison to New Zealand. Again, geographical distance is a major prohibitive factor. Such vastly different populations, climates, needs and access to resources does not augur well for unity. Despite all this, Australian women continue to strive for cohesion and do an excellent job. The strength of philosophy and commitment to women continue to be the most effective uniting forces.

Australia has been a source of private happiness for me in a special way. Despite three years of persistence, I had met with repeated dead ends in searching in New Zealand for my natural mother.

I came to Australia with one obscure clue left – a witness at my natural mother's wedding 17 years before. Knowing this was my final chance, I decided to leave fate in someone else's hands this time and handed it over to 'Birthlink' in Melbourne.

Within a month, I received a telephone call – they'd found her, moreover they had spoken to her! Suddenly, a name on documents became a person. She was very 'down to earth' they said and she would ring back in a fortnight. My birth mother was excited but needed some time.

The following two weeks were almost unbearable. Would she call, or might she change her mind? She called, and we met in May 1991 after a year-and-a-half of writing. To write to someone about whom you know virtually nothing yet share a unique bond, while ever mindful of adoption reunion disaster stories, is a formidable endeavour. The first letter took me three weeks to compose, very much a case of blood, sweat and tears. Yet I look back on that time of writing contact as a valuable experience: so much love and hope.

I came to Australia with one obscure clue left – a witness at my natural mother's wedding 17 years before.

My natural mother is wonderful, warm, with a big sense of humour and enormous energy. My Nana is a lovable matriarch who bakes a wicked chocolate cake. To see physical likeness was a new experience for me but perhaps what strikes everyone most are the same mannerisms, dramatic storytelling and strength of self and values.

I sit in her house now, aware of a greater sense of home in Australia with her here.

Having adopted three children as babies, Mum and Dad in New Zealand were fairly unique in their openness about our origins. Childhood fantasies about movie star natural parents were always tolerated, and when we asked, Mum provided us with the limited verbal information she had. Both were consistently sympathetic toward our natural parents seeing them as very brave and without choice at that time. Mum and Dad were brave also, when my sister had her reunion at 16 and I later at 24.

From this background I entered the debates regarding the new reproductive technologies (NRTs) with a broad range of perspective's concerning infertility, the Western Institution of Motherhood, gender roles, and non-biological mothering. This presents a major feminist challenge and will become as big an issue as abortion. In the meantime we continue to await a national pap smear program, let alone basic living standards for Aboriginal people in this country.

Now, a New Zealander cannot write on their experience of Oz without addressing accents. As a Kiwi in Australia – more over, one with a broad South Island 'accent' – one is always at the mercy of all amount of ribbing.

In my time here I have, on occasion, encountered the most pleasant Australians. Yet as soon as my mouth opens, nationality revealed, the same 'most pleasant Australians' transform into proverbial Ockers and the: 'What's the difference between a Kiwi and a...' begin. While in most circles it is not kosher to make racial jokes about many migrant groups, there are no such Australian rules for New Zealanders and inevitably all hell breaks loose with a Kiwi victim. Always outnumbered, and notoriously bad at remembering jokes, I have learned (hard as it is for this Leo) to keep my mouth shut and endure.

In pursuit of peace, every so often I attempt to be an Australian for a day (gasp!) but always get caught with any of the following: dairy (= corner shop), chillibin (= esky), togs (= bathers), duvet (= doona), wee one (= little one), blank section (= vacant block) and, of course, fush 'n' chups. However, after four years in Australia, with a gross facial contortion I can utter a fairly believable feesh 'n' cheeps.

My sister has been known to admit to entering a Sydney takeaway at a late hour and asking for 'chips'. The woman serving apologised saying: 'Sorry we don't cook chops or any meat at this time of night.' I was often asked by Tasmanians trying to place the accent if I was from Melbourne!

There are other semantic subtleties. Refuge residents thought I, as a new worker, was especially cool. When they confided: 'I went with a guy last night,' instead of a discussion on condoms, STD's and pregnancy, I would merely reply: 'Well where did you go?...in his car?...Well that's a bit boring isn't it?' It was some time before it dawned on me that 'went with' was a colloquialism for sex. The conversations changed somewhat thereafter.

But sport is the worst. Janine and I cower beside the radio forced to listen to New Zealand versus Australia rugby or cricket scores to gauge whether it's safe to venture onto public streets with our accursed 'accents'. Should Australia be victorious (although fortunately this is not often) perfect strangers overhearing a Kiwi accent have no problem approaching with: 'We licked youse good didn't we?' It's never wise to be unprepared.

It was some time before it dawned on me that 'went with' was a colloquialism for sex.

The worst occasion arose when the sewerage pipes blocked. The Brisbane City Council (in true council style) sent seven men to my home to sort out the blockage. Unfortunately this was following an abysmal New Zealand defeat to Australia in rugby. Standing in my backyard copping the full brunt of every failed All Black manoeuvre while raw sewerage spewed forth in a fountain is not one of my more favoured memories.

I briefly returned to New Zealand in 1991-92 after a three year absence. There had been many changes in the economy. Massive redundancies, cuts to welfare, benefits and pensions, increased GST (Goods and Services Tax) and heavy costs for electricity (heating) had all taken their toll. In contrast, I looked on the scenery of my home country with newly appreciative eyes. The Southern Alps in January were still capped with snow – here again were real mountains!

I had my first experience of home sickness a year before when I read Janet Frame's autobiographies, *To the Island*. The things you forget.

I miss family and old friends, unchlorinated artesian water, snow, a Nor'wester sweeping the tussock of the Canterbury Plains, Guy Fawkes night, Hudsons chocolate chip cookies, Kowhai and Kumara, hotties, Hokey Pokey ice cream, and movies with intermissions. I love Australia's white sandy beaches, tropical fruit, wombats, Louise's tuna mush, Aboriginal art, drying washing in half-an-hour, multi-cultural festivals, jacarandas in bloom, mosquito nets, new friends and a certain Border Collie.

our work and future visions should know no national boundaries

As much as I love New Zealand and will always be a Kiwi, I have no plans to return there permanently. I much prefer the Australian climate, now have a (very geographically-wide) circle of great friends, and believe I have better professional prospects here. New Zealand feminist friends and former workmates have encouraged me to return home, stressing how much there is to be done in New Zealand. There is much to do everywhere.

As feminists our work and future visions should know no national boundaries which merely serve to divide. I take strength from the view that Sisterhood is Global. This is both the journey and the goal.

Kia Kaha Tuahine
(Sisters, Be Strong)

* *Keera is women's land in central Tassie (Tasmania)*

To Feel Passionate Again

Vivien M. Altman

Vivien Altman was born in Melbourne of Jewish refugee parents from Russia and Austria. She moved to Tasmania when she was a child, and completed her primary and secondary education at the Friends' School, Hobart. She then returned to Victoria and completed an arts degree at Monash University and post-graduate courses in social work and criminology at the University of Melbourne. She has worked as a journalist and broadcaster, and in research, education, teaching English and community work.

An activist for many years around the issues of women, prisons, community legal centres, immigrants and Central America where she lived for more than five years, today Vivien Altman is far more interested in ideas, journalism and writing than activism.

At the time of writing this essay, Vivien Altman was completing an autobiographical account of her time in Central Amercia. She has recently returned to live in Central America.

I remember when they cremated my father, at the Sydney North Shore Crematorium, after we rode there in a black hearse that was strangely and coldly formal. We were surrounded by friends and family who were names to me, some more familiar than others, rather than faces I knew intimately. After all, I'd grown up in Hobart, and gone to university in Melbourne. White haired Hans Spitzer, my father's oldest Viennese friend, spoke at the funeral about friendship stretching back to their childhood in Vienna, where I had lived for six months as an 11-year-old child. There was no rabbi, or anything Jewish about my father's funeral.

When we travelled by train from Holland, to Vienna (a Holland where no one wanted to speak German), as the train was winding through the snowcapped Austrian mountains I caught my father gazing out the window. His face was deeply troubled. One day, my father fell very ill. The Viennese doctors conducted tests and confined him to bed with a serious heart attack.

My father said the Austrians behaved worse than the Germans in the second world war, and I could tell he was uncomfortable in Vienna, where they sat in their expensive leather coats in the famous coffee house Dehmels, drinking coffee with whipped cream and eating rich, mouthwatering cakes. When I sat with my parents, the anonymous faces staring at us, we looked different, and the Austrians don't like difference.

One day, a couple about my father's age turned up from New York. Elegantly dressed, they spoke with heavy Viennese accents, acting as if they knew my father as well as we did. They put their arms around me, and patted me on the head. I didn't know them, but an overwhelming sense of closeness and affection radiated between them and him. More than 10 years later, they came to pay their last tribute to my father; they were family, and coincidentally they were holidaying in Sydney when he died.

My Viennese grandmother fled to Switzerland when the Nazis came, my uncle to New York where he practiced as a psychiatrist, my step-aunt went to Italy, then Canada. I've never met any of my first cousins on either side of the family; I once spent three days in San Francisco looking for one of them.

My grandmother became a Catholic, even though she had three husbands, one after the other. My grandmother's third husband was Catholic. Having helped my grandmother escape from the clutches of the Nazis when the Russians came, he was in Baden, in Austria, at their summer residence. Both of them went back after the war, even if my aunt had to change her Jewish sounding surname so that patients would come to therapy.

The Russians marched into Baden after the Allies had defeated the Germans. A Russian soldier threw one of the maids on top of my step-grandfather and raped her; my grandfather died instantly from a heart attack.

My mother's father was a Menshevik and the Vice-Minister for Justice in the Kerensky government, falling out with the Bolsheviks over the national question. A brilliant philosopher, lawyer and writer, imprisoned by the Bolsheviks, he fled to Germany and came to Australia with his family to start a new life. He became a leading figure in the Jewish community and a strong Zionist who fought with the then Governor-General, Isaac Isaacs, over the question of the setting up of Israel.

Growing up in Hobart, I was educated at a Quaker school, the Friends School, in a family of Jewish Europeans who neither practiced religious nor cultural Jewish traditions. We celebrated Xmas and Easter with dinners and presents and, despite our family discussions about politics and philosophy, I can't recall one single conversation about Israel. My parents were not Zionists. They stood out with their accents and intellectual ways; my greatest childhood dream was for my mother to make lamingtons and butterfly cakes, and I was sorely embarrassed by my grandmother, who visited us in Hobart each summer and spoke English very badly. In the late 1960s, I was far more moved by the Viet Nam war than touched by the six day Arab Israeli war.

Who was I? Born in Melbourne, with a happy childhood growing up in Hobart in a loving supporting family, a privileged education, a student at Monash at the height of student protest and the anti-Viet Nam war movement, throwing myself far more enthusiastically into political activity and partying than my studies.

Completing an arts degree and two post graduate courses in criminology and social work, the latter at Melbourne University, I became heavily engaged in the early days of the prison movement, and the free legal services in Melbourne, hanging around Carlton, and Fitzroy, and later Glebe in Sydney. There was *Digger* magazine, the Pram Factory and The Free Store in Chapel Street, plays at La Mama and bands such as Skyhooks and Stilettos to rage to; my first feminist consciousness raising group at Melbourne University – we smoked grass and thought we were a cool, chosen generation, that would change the world.

The anarchists at The Free Store in Chapel Street and Drummond Street may have been distant from the borscht belt of my grandmother who constantly entertained her Polish and Russian friends behind the heavy blue drapes in East St Kilda in the same city, but it was much closer than the claustrophobic anglo-provincial, moralistic world of Hobart, where the most exciting event of the year was the Sydney to Hobart yacht race.

...we were Jewish, but there was nothing for me to grasp onto or to identify with. I didn't feel Jewish!

Sydney, May 1986: boarding a plane to fly to Nicaragua, via Los Angeles and Mexico for an indefinite period. At the time I thought I'd probably go for a couple of years. I'm always asked: 'Why did you want to leave Australia?' Why did I want to throw everything away, friends, family and familiarity to go to a tiny third world country in Latin America convulsed by war and underdevelopment. Undoubtedly it was something to do with the 'other'. My parents had been social democrats, and my father's privileged world had created a great intellect and an eccentric who respected Ghandi and the United Nations, but somehow we were always different. We were out of place in Hobart, out of place in the Jewish community on the mainland (as the Tasmanians called it), we were Jewish, but there was nothing for me to grasp onto or to identify with. I didn't feel Jewish!

In London, in the late 1970s, I'd been to benefits for the Chilean resistance, and the black images of Pinochet's military coup were firmly etched onto my mind from movies such as the *Battle of Chile*. In 1978, I stayed with friends in their Paris flat at the time the Sandinistas took over the National Palace. My friends were the Sandinistas Paris connection, and it was in this Paris flat with polished floors that I first learnt where Nicaragua was on the map and who the Sandinistas were.

Why did I leave Australia? In the early 1980s, I started to work with the first Salvadoran refugees who came here and as I got to know them and find out more about their tiny, stricken country, I became more interested in doing something about it. I was shocked at the brutal conditions under which most people were living, and the organised cruelty of the armed forces. It reminded me of stories that I'd heard from refugees living in Australia about the Nazis in the second world war.

I was mesmerised by the charm, impressed by the social achievements in Cuba, and in love with the mixture of ideas, vibrancy and social commitment of the people that I met in both Cuba and Mexico.

Nicaragua was a different story, too far away for most Australians to care very much, but for romantics like me, attracted to ideas and ideals, it shone out in a world that had turned out rather more sourly than we had hoped. I was becoming frustrated by being involved with something that was so far away, growing increasingly weary of listening to boring speakers who came on tours from Central America saying very little about what was really happening there.

In the mid-1980s, I decided to go to Cuba and Mexico for six weeks over the Christmas holidays. It was this first trip to Latin America that turned my head. I fell in love with my first experience of Latin America. It may sound like a cliche, but I found it alive, warm, stimulating and energetic politically, intellectually and culturally, and at some deep psychological level I warmed to the romance and warmth of human relations. On an emotional level, and as a personality, I have always felt miles apart from the dominant anglo way of doing things in Australia. On the other hand, it's part of me, and I can't disown it entirely.

I simply didn't want to become a femocrat (which is where I was heading); all my boyfriends came from other countries; most of my friends were obsessed with careers and babies; and as I was having so many problems falling pregnant, leaving the country for an open ended period of time seemed like an interesting, challenging and adventurous thing to do. There was nothing so special to stay for in Sydney, and although I was terribly nervous about leaving, at heart I'm a great adventurer eager to try new experiences.

In Latin America, people I met talked about ideas; they loved to party, facing their life realities with an energy and unbounded enthusiasm. It was all daunting but challenging. I was mesmerised by the charm, impressed by the social achievements in Cuba, and in love with the mixture of ideas, vibrancy and social commitment of the people that I met in both Cuba and Mexico. That trip was a turning point in my life, not only was I immensely attracted to the idea of living in Central America, I was sick and tired of life in Australia.

The Australia of the late 1960s and the 1970s interested and challenged me, but the 1980s in Australia were about careers, greed, and the 'me' generation, something that neither stimulated nor turned me on. I could never say that life was boring, as I was always busy with work, other commitments, lots of friends and an active personal and social life. But at some deeper level I was bored and frustrated.

When I left Australia, I was terribly nervous about the decision I'd made but deep down, I knew it was right, however lonely and difficult it was to be in those first daunting months. I have a very supportive family who respect my decisions. My friends are generally encouraging and understanding, although perhaps some of them thought I was a little crazy but probably even envied my decision to cut loose and go. As for jobs, I didn't really know what I was going to do, all that I knew was that I'd have to learn to speak Spanish fast when I got there, and that my chances of finding employment were reasonable given that I'm very well qualified, have skills and varied work experience. Certainly I knew that I'd be paid very little, but in retrospect my trip wasn't all that terribly well planned.

I tend to be an optimistic person, who believes if you want to do something badly enough you do it and sort things out as you go along. Travelling to Nicaragua, I flew via Los Angeles, and then on to Mexico City, where I was expecting an Australian friend to meet me at the airport. There was nobody waiting for me, but eventually it was all sorted out and I was moved into a tiny, rather dark and gloomy, hotel in the southern part of the city, close to a handful of people I knew or for whom I had addresses (mainly Australians or Salvadorans). Everyone turned out to be incredibly warm, friendly and hospitable. In the end I stayed with a Salvadoran family, having met the husband previously in Australia, and they welcomed me into their home and their confidence as if I was one of them, something that touched me deeply and is still part of me today. Over the years we have become close and dear friends; their house in Mexico became like a second home, and I've visited them several times since they moved back home to San Salvador.

When I arrived at the airport, a middle-aged officious woman customs officer with dyed blonde hair went through my bag and removed all my letters...

Before I went on to Nicaragua to taste my new life, I spent three weeks in Cuba. This second time round, my experience was much more sobering. Before I'd left Australia, various people had entrusted me with letters to take to Cuba, as the mail is quite unreliable, so I was carrying about a dozen personal letters. When I arrived at the airport, a middle-aged officious woman customs officer with dyed blonde hair went through my bag and removed all my letters; no amount of explaining could persuade her to give them back. I was furious, imagining her in real life in her giant 1950s rollers and headscarf, with her stretch tight lycra pants over her velvety thighs eating ice cream in Coppelia Park in Central Havana.

Then a couple of people I'd counted on seeing again were out of town, it was summer holidays, and although Havana is a gorgeous city, Cuba is a much better place to visit if someone looks after you, or if your on an organised tour. It was just one of those holidays that didn't work out, so when I returned to Mexico I was glad to get back and anxious to fly on to my destination, Managua, Nicaragua.

The possibility of spending time with my Central American revolutionary lover in Mexico had seemed remote. He was always in meetings. But even he was pissed off with me when I got back, as I'd failed to understand that he'd gone to inordinate lengths to arrange some time with me, only to find that I wasn't in town. The crux of it was that I hadn't understood the arrangements in Spanish. That hit me over the head like a sledge hammer. I was devastated by a sense of powerlessness.

As I sat at the airport, waiting for the flight to Managua (AERONICA is always late), I got talking to a Brazilian man David who'd lived and studied in the United States of America, and was also on his way to Nicaragua. We talked the whole way to Managua. I cannot explain exactly how I felt when the pilot said we were coming into Managua. Landing at the Augusto Cesar Sandino Airport, everyone seemed very friendly, and half the people on the flight seemed to know each other. Managua is a village!

When the wheels touched the ground, and we got out of the plane, the hot balmy tropical air slapped me in the face. I was excited about being there and realised I had no idea what I expected it to be like.

There were lots of young skinny boys in army uniforms. Suitcases and big wooden cartons were strewn all over the floor where hundreds of passengers seemed to be waiting for their luggage. Glancing around I noticed scruffy looking foreigners, the internationalistas and clean shaven guys with khaki pants, cream shirts and telltale laptops, but mostly Nicaraguans with endless bags and boxes. It reminded me of when you travel with Turkish or Greek gastarbeiter (foreign guest workers) going back after the holidays to work in Central Europe carrying everything with them.

My first impression of Managua as we chugged along in the little old sloping taxi was one of surprise. It was flat, unattractive, hot and ordinary; there were a few colourless billboards along the way, and the cars moved slowly along the road with the giant potholes. But where's Managua, I kept asking David, screwing up my face in a quizzical way.

Managua has no centre: it was destroyed in the 1972 earthquake and never rebuilt because it lives on a fault line. What's left looks like bombed out shells of buildings and the new Managua is a series of suburbs dotted everywhere. Managua is definitely not a place you can warm to immediately. How could I even begin to describe a city, if you can call it that, so vastly different from our Australian cities, and so indifferently ordinary.

There's a tendency to think the grass is greener on the other side, and although I was a worldly person who'd lived and travelled the world, nothing could have prepared me for life there. Nothing worked, the heat was unbearable, the buses were too crowded to get onto unless you liked the sensation of being a sardine, drenched in your own sweat, or sharing that of others, which meant I chose to walk everywhere, hitch a ride or get a taxis. There was nothing cold to drink that wasn't hideously sweet, and I detest sweet drinks that do nothing to quench your thirst. My stomach was bloated from parasites and it was hard to find out where things were, as there weren't any maps or information centres. There were no public toilets – which can be drastic in a country where newcomers are prone to runny diarrhoea, and no public phones that work unless you went to the post office and stood in a queue.

The Chileans, Rosie and Sergio, were friends of friends who turned out to be a bit of a godsend, inviting me to stay at their house until I got on my feet, although just finding a phone on which to ring them was a logistical nightmare. They proved to be an entree into the Latin, not the Nicaraguan, world in Nicaragua. In their house I was introduced to the maid or the empleada, a Central American institution that didn't go out of fashion with the revolution. No, I would never have an empleada ever, the very idea was beneath me, but that idea collapsed into a shuddering heap after a couple of months of never ending heat, parasitises, smoke filled rooms and dust.

Within a couple of days, I had a job teaching English at the Jesuit University (the Central American university) for which I was well qualified, to be paid about the equivalent of $US30 a month. The other teachers in the department, both locals and foreigners, were very welcoming and Diana, an Australian journalist, and I had caught up with each other. She'd moved in with another Australian journalist who had lived in Managua for a couple of years so that opened up another world. My Salvadoran friends had given me the number of a Salvadoran woman, and we ended up becoming close friends. Australian Simon wasn't around in Managua, he was managing a television station over on the Atlantic Coast, but vaguely through him I'd heard about a North American journalist called Maureen and within a couple of weeks we caught up at an international press event: the Sandinistas were always very good at attending to the international press. Fast talking red haired Maureen and I were to end up friends for life and later on we shared a house with a Belgian, Jan, and a Nicaraguan, Nuzzli. We lived closely and intensely. Our bonds remain firm, having lived through death, dreams, romance and war together.

Feeling hemmed in and restricted at the university, I left at the end of 1987 and began freelance reporting to Australia, Britain, Canada and the United States. I was free to travel in the region, as long as I could flog enough stories. Most of my work came out of Nicaragua and El Salvador, Mexico, and Cuba.

There was a military war going on in Nicaragua, a nine-year-war that really finished only after Violeta Chamorro won the presidential elections in 1990. That meant nearly everything went into defence and production, and the economic embargo coupled with the impoverished under-developed economy devastated the lives of ordinary people. Yet despite the war, death and mutilation that surrounded us, the tough conditions, and the chronic shortages of everything, it's amazing how people make do, become more creative, appreciating things when you have them. Life was very intensely up and down.

I would never compare my situation to that of a Nicaraguan. I was a middle-class, privileged, educated woman who had made a choice to live there, and I could leave any time. We were foreigners, and that meant we were rich, and we were rich by comparison. Given my economic situation, I was able to travel outside the country two or three times every year at least, or my friends travelled and brought back batteries, cassettes and popcorn. Earl Grey tea, Vegemite, curry and good Italian food and coffee were the things I missed the most. I would have killed for a real cappuccino, good bookshops and music collections, and the luxury of Australian beaches.

We were foreigners, and that meant we were rich, and we were rich by comparison.

Violets, blossom and daffodils, the smell and texture of eucalypts, wattle, bottlebrush, boronia, camellias, Melbourne spring, the glimmering sun hovering over the whitecapped waves, white sand as opposed to black, even burning flesh and the extraordinary ethnic and racial mix of our Australia left me feeling homesick at times. I missed my friends and family, especially when I lived through trauma or tragic circumstances, or when something exciting was happening to me, a passionate romance (of which there were many), then I would long to be in Australia although I was surrounded by love and warmth.

Perhaps it's the nature of Latin America, where human relations are valued differently, or in countries such as Nicaragua and El Salvador where conditions are really tough, that brings people together. Relations are formed quickly and intensely. To me, Latin American men are closer to their emotions, so if you can get around the machismo, it's easier to have relations with them. That was life in Managua, things happened quickly and intensely, it was the character of the place. No sooner had you met and become friends with someone or even lovers, they were moving on to somewhere else or someone else. There was an enormous international community in Managua, and within that were many different communities and layers, people from all over the world, chasing a dream, journalists, internationalistas, artists, revolutionary tourists, aid workers; those who were motivated by religion, or looking for cheap rum, fast sex, or Latin lovers; delegations, fact finding missions, brigades, groups, parliamentarians, political leaders came from all over the world, it was the Paris of Central America. It was Central America, but Managua was distinct.

It was difficult to know Nicaraguans, who grew sick of people who came and then left again, so many foreigners came to Nicaragua, or the locals were too busy trying to survive, wanting to marry you on the first night, or uninterested in foreigners unless they were important or North American. Whatever you did, however well you spoke Spanish, and however many Nicaraguan friends you had, we were foreigners, outsiders who could never really be part of what was going on.

We had Latin American friends and lovers, lived with Latin Americans, cared for their children, grieved for them when they died, cried when they were killed, went to funerals and made love with them. Sometimes we despaired at the violence and the old fashioned deeply ingrained ways of doing things. Often I hated the sexual politics as much as I hated the dust, the heat and the parasites and the tackiness of Managua.

And I hated the way that power corrupts, naked in front of my eyes, tearing away at some of my dreams placing me firmly on the ground, but never carrying me to cynicism or despair.

> ...often I hated the sexual politics as much as I hated the dust, the heat and the parasites and the tackiness of Managua.

My third trip back to Australia: this time it's different. During my other two visits, I never questioned whether I'd go back to Central America or not, it was a given, and I felt no real draw to stay in Australia. Each time, I was lured back by interesting work. Reporting from Central America had been exciting and challenging, and the call of romance was equally tantalising. With the wars over, the international media has moved on, and the Australian media has absolutely no interest in the region. So making a living has become a problem for me.

These days I'm grappling with questions of my identity and the future. In some ways Australia is less attractive in the middle of the recession and what is essentially a very conservative moment in history. These days my friends are obsessed with careers, and bringing up families. Interest in political change or the world is definitely out of fashion, most people are far too jaded, cynical or caught up with their own lives to care terribly much about anyone else's.

I'm not sure what that makes me, a silly old romantic or a worn out idealist searching for a place in her own country. Even in the six years I've been away, Australia seems even more ethnically and racially mixed, there are few jobs for young people, AIDS has devastated a generation of the male gay community, I'm surrounded by charming, good looking and talented babies and young children, most people have house renovations, answering machines, computers, no time and have given up smoking, and the bulk of my friends are successful professionals, many with a public profile.

What does that say about us? Probably nothing more than age, class and privilege, and the 1990s.

Central America is also a different place from six years ago. Not only are the military conflicts finished everywhere except Guatemala, but so has the moment, and the economic situation has sunk to an all time low. That makes working there even more difficult, accentuating the huge differences between them and us. In El Salvador, the signing of the peace accords ushered in change, but alarmingly high levels of violence predominantly from the military and the death squads continue.

On the other hand Australia is my country, for which I have a tremendous affection, there is family and there are old friends, and my long term future is here. I am not Central American.

I left Central America in February 1993 after the Salvadoran peace accords were signed after 12 years of bloody war, returning to Australia for an indefinite time. My plan is to go back to collect my clothes, and my books, investigate the possibility of researching a postgraduate degree there, to catch up with my friends, and my boyfriend, although I'm not even sure he is still my boyfriend, to live a little, to engage with the world and to feel passionate again.

New Horizons

Janice Farrell

Jan Farrell was born into a West Australian farming community in 1947. Trained as a state registered nurse (SRN) in Perth, she travelled to the United Kingdom in 1969 where she trained as a midwife. Later she married a British army officer and was 'posted' within Europe. Returning to Australia in 1984, she took up nursing once more and is now living in Melbourne.

I grew up on a farm in York, 60 miles from Perth, Western Australia, one of six children. I now see those early years as forming the basis of my desire to travel and experience a different life and culture.

My parents' background profoundly influenced this need and in essence my need to find my roots and background. At school I was very conscious of the spelling of my name (Kuhl) and its English pronunciation ('cool'). I was often mocked for expressing things the wrong way around. I was shocked when accused of being a Nazi because my father was German. Until then he was like any other father, and had served in the Australian army during the second world war. Consequently I was confused and remained silent about my home life. These feelings were not helped by my father's reluctance to talk about his life before he arrived as an illegal immigrant in Australia in the 1920s. Years later, when I had the chance to meet some of his family in Germany, they remained just as reluctant to talk about themselves until after the second world war.

My mother was born in South Australia of Polish/German descent and learnt to speak English as a second language at school. It was this, too, that gave me a hunger to discover who I was and where I came from,

43

explaining the differences between myself and my Australian friends with English backgrounds.

It was my mother who ultimately took care of the strangers my father took in. For many years it was home to a lonely first world war veteran, who helped my mother with the milking of the cows and tending the garden. A 'misplaced' Yugoslav, who had been a POW (prisoner of war) in Germany, became part of the family, besides many other people who drifted in and out of our lives during my earlier school years.

In the 1950s a nearby town became a reception centre for refugees from Europe. Sometimes we had a family to stay for a weekend or over Christmas. These people brought sad and traumatic memories, which they tried to put behind them, and so face the future with hope in their new country. My parents seemed to help bridge the gap in a small way. It gave me a longing to know more about 'ethnic' people, where they came from and the diversity of cultures. My father's policy was to bring up those of us born after the war as 'Australians only'. Whether he liked it or not, I did feel the difference. Language was only part of it.

...later I realised I could combine nursing with the experience of other cultures and travel overseas.

It was naturally accepted by my family that I would become a nurse when I grew up, and it was all I ever wanted to do. Together with the upbringing I had, I could think of nothing more worthwhile than being able to help others in need. It was later that I realised I could combine nursing with the experience of other cultures and travel overseas.

The world I knew as a child was protective, but my curiosity was certainly roused by those who passed in and out of my life. There was a greater world outside my childhood experiences and beyond Australia, and I wanted to find it. Political and economic reasons had never entered my head.

The dream became a reality in 1969. I had completed my third year nursing training and a paediatric post-graduate course. During that time I had saved the money for my fare to Europe. On my parents insistence I had sufficient for a return fare. Forgoing some of life's pleasures was a small price to pay for the experience of a dream come true.

I left Sydney on the eve of my twenty-second birthday on the SS *Southern Cross*, telephoning my parents just before the ship sailed. It was an enjoyable six week journey by ship via New Zealand, Fiji, Tahiti, Panama, Florida and Bermuda to Southampton, England.

I had enrolled to do midwifery training in Edinburgh, Scotland but just before leaving I heard that it was required for overseas students to work a year as a third year student nurse before being permitted to commence a midwifery course. I was impatient, and wanted to get on with further training, rather than being held back another year. Meanwhile I had made another application to a hospital in Swindon, Wiltshire, but had not received a reply before departure. The ship had already left New Zealand when a letter arrived that confirmed my immediate enrolment into midwifery.

I hadn't realised the extent of my parents apprehension at the uncertainty, the travelling alone and of having no definite plans for the future other than to do overseas aid work. On top of this I was rather introverted and shy by nature, and they must have wondered how I would cope. Years later I was told how saddened my father had been that I had never given him a chance to help or asked for assistance for my travels. At the time I thought he would be proud to know I'd been able to do it on my own. Like so many others, he had arrived in Australia without any means and had made 'it' with much hard work and little assistance. Now as a mother of two who themselves seek to be fully independent, I have some understanding of his feelings.

A number of young people on the ship were, like myself, off to 'see' Europe. There were also British people who had gone to Australia on the £10 passage scheme, had fulfilled their two year commitment to stay and were returning home. I remember during such conversations being unable to comprehend their return because it was apparent that they had done much better for themselves in Australia than they ever could in England. Nostalgic memories of home overrode their original reasons for seeking a better life. I was indignant when someone thought there were reciprocal arrangements between the United Kingdom and Australia, and that I had only to pay £10 for my passage to Britain to work and study there.

It wasn't until the ship berthed and I saw the docks in Southampton that an overwhelming sense of the reality of having left home, family and friends, confronted me. Life on board the ship had become secure in its routine and the people familiar. Now I had to face an altogether new environment. For several hours I was shunted between one group of officials and another, not being permitted to disembark. They wanted proof in writing of where and when I was to begin my course, only I had packed it away with my luggage which was already sitting on the wharf. I was being made to feel like a criminal, and explanations of where the relevant papers were made no difference. Finally someone took my word for it and let me go, once they had a forwarding address.

I wasn't sure whether I would be met at the wharf by someone my parents had got to know on a trip two years earlier, but she was there. It was a late December afternoon when we left by train for Newport, Wales where she lived. A bleak, dark grey landscape dotted with leafless trees occasionally shrouded in mist was all I could see. We passed through towns and villages which appeared to look the same at night – continuous strips of grey roof tops. I was in a different world.

The bright blue skies, white clouds and sunshine, even the night skies, brilliant with stars, had disappeared. That was my first culture shock. I was staying with someone very kind, but who was quite eccentric. She was an unmarried school teacher, with a passion for cats. Cats lay and sat upon the table and benchtops; cats roamed underfoot; cats licked the plates

Nostalgic memories of home overrode their original reasons for seeking a better life.

when they could chance it. It made me shudder. Next morning I awoke to the sound of something falling softly. It was very still – it was snowing! I noticed that people walked on the road instead of the pavement. The pavement was covered with black ice, which I did not know was invisible and slippery.

The midwifery course started in February. In the nurses hostel I soon learned to adapt myself to understanding the variety of accents. There were girls from Wales and Scotland, and various counties in England. We also had an American, South African and an Iranian student. Some were from India, Sri Lanka and Uganda. Nationalities seemed quickly forgotten as we endeavoured to work and study together, with a common aim of becoming 'midwives'. When money was sufficient, we travelled a little, particularly enjoying the Wiltshire Downs which was within easy reach.

...I awoke to the sound of some-thing falling softly. It was very still – it was snowing!

With commitment to complete my course and the poor pay it was difficult to travel further afield to the Continent. It took a month of savings to buy a pair of shoes! I was fortunate to be chosen to do the district part of my training in another county – Gloucestershire. I was billeted out by a wonderful couple who had boarded a few student midwives before, so they were understanding and helpful.

The area known as the Cotswolds with its rural aspect gave me an insight into the everyday lives of country English people. I was duly given a uniform – a dark navy overcoat and navy cap – to wear, and a black bag to carry my stethoscopes, watch and whatever else was necessary. My transport was an old black bicycle. I felt so conspicuous, as it seemed to belong to a bygone age.

The two district nurse/midwives with whom I worked were nurse/social worker, friend and confident all rolled into one, to people wherever they were called. The local doctors relied on their knowledge of the patients, to help give a clearer picture for understanding and diagnosis. I had great respect for them. It was a privilege to see the interaction between professional people working for the good of the 'whole' person – their physical, emotional and social needs. My curiosity to know what it was like inside some of these beautiful thatched cottages was satisfied whenever a house call was necessary to some of the more influential people; I learned that the upkeep of these places was quite high, and only those with a decent income could afford the expense of a cottage.

I involved myself with the 'general' work, too, not realising that I would be in trouble for this when I returned to the training school. Still, I would have risked that chance again for the experience it gave me over those late summer and autumn months with the young families and elderly we helped. I spent a few days with a social worker during this time and the highlight of that was a trip to a Gypsy camp. There were fewer places for Gypsies to camp and not many people wanted them around where they 'might poach' off some private land or where their camp was seen as an 'eyesore'.

Soon after commencing my training I met my future husband, Roger, who was an army lieutenant in the corps of signals, and was studying at the Military College of Science in Shrivenham. He had just spent some time in Berlin and Krefeld, Germany. I certainly didn't fall in love with the uniform: civilian clothes were worn by men and woman like those in any other academic institutions.

The officers were confident, self-assured individuals, whose training and responsibilities had given them a maturity I hadn't seen in young men of that age back home. To fit in with my new husband's life of continually being moved I had to forego my career as a nurse. At the time I didn't give this a second thought.

My parents-in-law may have been initially disappointed that their son was marrying an Australian instead of someone who was of English 'breeding'. To their minds Australia was still a colony that lacked the finer academic and cultural traditions. To an extent, time helped to break down barriers on both sides until I no longer felt an outsider but part of the family. Roger and his sister had been given an equal opportunity for an education at university and received every encouragement. My parents on the other hand had never even hinted that such opportunities could be obtained by us. It belonged to 'others' who were naturally very clever or whose parents had the money to pay for it.

Members of my husband's family came from Wales, Tyneside (north east England) and Scotland. My parents-in-law had retired to Somerset so I was once more quickly becoming acquainted with a variety of accents. I still like hearing the lilt of the Welsh accent most of all. People had difficulty in guessing my origins, as apparently I didn't have a distinctly Australian accent.

An incident some years later bore this out. At the time my husband was working in the Ministry of Defence in London and we had been invited to a luncheon party at the home of one of the colonels. I had heard him described by those who toiled under him as a pompous so and so. Trays of food were being passed around by the colonel's wife and as she was serving me she was lamenting that she picked up accents quickly, but added that at least the American accent was not as bad as the 'worst of all accents' – the Australian accent. At this, Roger announced cheerfully that she was just speaking to one. Whereupon she collapsed into a chair landing the tray with its contents in my lap. There was much silent laughter in the office for months afterwards.

I certainly didn't feel as if I fitted the pattern of an officer's wife. I wasn't English, I wasn't from the typical upper/middle-class of English society or whose parents had been part of the British forces, and as a grown woman I didn't call my parents 'Mummy' and 'Daddy'. I hadn't the finer ability for small talk. At cocktail parties and mess dinner nights a few hours of speaking trivia seemed necessary to be entertaining in mixed company. Some officers and their spouses appeared to be shallow people not wanting any depth in friendship. This may have been due to being frequently uprooted and moved on to another 'posting'. However, there were those who were prepared to let down their guard to reveal the person underneath. I suppose it helped to develop an inner strength as one couldn't rely on family or friends when continually being thrust into new situations. On the other hand there were bonuses too. People within that environment knew what it was like to arrive at a new destination, and they were helpful by giving hints on local customs, where to shop, the best markets, and by simply making a person feel welcomed. By the time we had been married 13 years we had lived in as many places as years of marriage.

Our first home was one half of an army hut. It had an asbestos roof, no ceiling and was bitterly cold since it snowed in October that year of 1971.

Housing was in short supply for married personnel in Worcester, so after spending the first month with my parents-in-law we moved to 'Wood Farm Camp' beneath the Malvern Hills. During the second world war it had been a hospital camp for the American Air Force. Our first home was one half of an army hut. It had an asbestos roof, no ceiling and was bitterly cold since it snowed in October that year of 1971. It seemed a bit of an adventure at the time, certainly not what I expected! With our belongings and some wedding gifts we made it as much like 'home' as possible. I was amused at the extent to which one couple went in making their hut more homely. They were older; he was a high ranking officer from a different regiment and came from a wealthy background. Their possessions looked so incongruous in a hut; arm chairs, antique pieces of furniture, swords and silver trophies, candlesticks, trays and tea sets, expensive rugs and animal skins were all on display.

I was soon to find out about service life with all its uncertainties, moves and separations. Roger was sent to Blandford and I stayed behind in the hut. I was lonely, so to fill the empty days I took a job in the local old people's home. It was no ordinary home, it had been magnificent in its day, belonging to the Lea and Perrins family who owned the Worcestershire sauce company, and was now a home for 'genteel folk'. The people had come from wealthy backgrounds, spending many years in places like India, Africa and China. They had worked in the civil service or as missionaries. Some of them were living in the past and we were their servants! I developed a little idea of what it must have been like in *Upstairs Downstairs*.

Was it the army's intention to put our marriage to the test? Our first year was spent mostly apart, except for some weekends. Our next move was to have been to Germany. Orders were changed only a week beforehand (not uncommon) and instead we left in a snow storm for Catterick Camp, near Richmond in Yorkshire. The area was called 'whinny hill', but it soon acquired the nickname 'windy hill'. It overlooked the edge of the Yorkshire Moors. It was bitterly cold and we awoke next morning to find five workmen ready to start putting in oil fired central heating. Ours was the first house and was basically the experimental one. Roger left for Stirling, Scotland, and I was left alone for another five months. He visited on the weekends when he could, but the camp was often snow bound.

To avoid loneliness and boredom, I filled my days baking and providing morning and afternoon teas for the workmen. No wonder they kept coming back to my house – even whilst they worked on all the other houses in the area. My reputation with the other wives, and needless to say the colonel's wife, was none too pleasing – I had started something that they didn't want to feel obligated to do. My one friend was an elderly man who was a retired inspector with the Yorkshire police, who looked after the welfare of families in the camp. He often called for tea and a chat, and when he learned I was expecting our first child he insisted on shovelling the snow from our path and driveway, suffering a minor heart attack in an effort to help me. I got to know one of the wives who had given up a promising career as a concert pianist, but she was posted on with her husband, only a few months after our friendship began. This was common.

...it was late and I heard a landrover pull up, then soldier's boots crunching on the gravel path, and I knew the impending news.

Roger and I were together again only a couple of months before our son was born. Even then most nights were taken up with some program or another, and weekends were broken up by Roger going on rescue parties or pot-holing near the Lakes District with the young recruits.

The next two years in Blandford were more normal as Roger was on another training course. It was here that I learned of my father's death. Strange that one can know something before being told – it was late and I heard a landrover pull up, then soldier's boots crunching on the gravel path, and I knew the impending news. I was taken to the guard room where a call was put through from Australia. A soldier at one time himself, it was soldiers who brought the news of his death.

In Germany we were back to the housing shortage once more and, for me, the weeks alone whilst Roger was away on military exercises or 'recce's' (looking for communication sites). By this time we had a daughter. We were living in an upstairs flat for a few months until a house became available for rent on the edge of town – it was set behind the other houses – fronting the road. The main Hannover railway line ran past the bottom of our garden. Our landlord had been a photographer who was required during the war to photograph the results of some of Hitler's medical experiments which he found extremely difficult to talk about. A year later and we had moved again, to another area of Germany close to the Dutch border.

Like most service people we made regular trips back to England to keep in touch with families. It became routine at school holiday times using the ferries from Zeebrugge or Calais to Dover or Felixstowe, with the car having to bear identification that the occupants were British military personnel. The danger of being made targets by the IRA and other militant groups was constant. On occasions the car had to be checked for bombs. My Australian passport also gave me some trouble albeit of a different nature. Many times immigration control in England stopped our entry into the country until certain details could be cleared, despite my being married to an Englishman. This was not the only time bureaucrats had caused me a great deal of unnecessary trouble and pain. Unlike my husband and children I have been unable to obtain dual nationality.

On occasions the car had to be checked for bombs. My Australian passport also gave me some trouble...

When it came time for the inevitable move, the wives were left to do the majority of the packing/unpacking, as the men always seemed to have yet another military exercise. The departure from the house had to be timed precisely to the hour so that army housing personnel could come to itemise everything that was provided and check it over for breakages or loss. Utensils and crockery had to be laid out on the tables in neat rows for quick scrutiny and the house was to be left spotless. This meant working into the small hours of the night to have everything 'just so'. I would often do the packing at night with the children in bed as our son would become most distressed to find a good many familiar things in boxes, and would try to get them out again. The goods sent by army transport, the car packed up, the children waiting, most of their belongings having gone ahead days before, with the 'marching out' complete and signed for, and the doors locked behind us, we would be off again.

We learnt to appreciate the wonderful forest walks both in Belgium and Germany, where they were called 'Volksmarches'. There were walks of different distances – eight, 12, 15 or 20 kilometres... We went summer and winter alike. One such walk in a remote wooded area in Germany bought us accidentally to a bombed out site that seemed to be the remnant of a small concentration camp. Old wooden signs, written in German, directed the elderly and children to go one way. A few intact remains of brick structures looked like ovens. The place was so still, no birds sang.

The best decision we ever made was to buy a caravan when the children were quite young. This enabled us to be a family for once, despite my husband's commitments. Often, we went to the smaller towns and villages, away from the tourist areas. For some of the holidays we travelled further afield, into the Netherlands, Bavaria, Luxemburg, through Austria and Switzerland, Northern Italy and the French Alps. There we went up to Mont Blanc by several stages of lifts, then four person cable cars suspended almost four kilometres across glaciers to the Italian side of the Alps. One Christmas caravanning holiday was spent near the Czechoslovakian border, each caravan had a Christmas tree outside, lit up with coloured lights set in the snow, and at night it looked like a fairytale. Then there was also Scotland and Wales and, before we left Europe, a trip to Athens and Crete. To our children these were normal events.

It was not common practice for families to accompany their husbands when they went away on a course. The one exception to this was a three week course in Oberammagau, Germany. It provided a holiday for me and the children without the chores of housework.

I was relieved that the children did not have to be sent away to boarding school as British schools were available for them in the places where we lived when 'abroad'. Most people saw their children only a few times a year and 'conveniently' got on with military life without any interruptions. It was in the British School of Brussels that it was compulsory to learn to speak French. The school was like an international school so they didn't develop any racial prejudices. A wonderful big African American Major called Ned wanted my son for company on a long drive back home through Germany. He was highly amused at people's response as they gaped at the sight of 'a big black American with a little blonde English boy'. There were so many people from different parts of the world either in the diplomatic services, working in the EEC (European Economic Community) or with NATO (North Atlantic Treaty Organisation), as was Roger. It was here that we had many non-English friends all living in a foreign city yet somehow there was an understanding that we are all basically the same, even though government and social problems differed from country to country. My husband was regularly away in either the United States, Canada or Portugal. The airport became like a bus stop.

> **The airport became like a bus stop.**

The only times I had any real life which was not identified with being an army officer's wife was in London and Brussels. This involved work connected with the church. In London the church ran a soup kitchen on a weekly basis and also provided accommodation for homeless people. When the regular nurse was unavailable I filled in to assist a doctor also doing voluntary work outside normal hours (he was a neuro-surgeon) to see to the medical needs of the 'street kids' and groups like the Hell's Angels – underneath often very lonely, frightened people. In Brussels, I took some voluntary work connected with an orphanage, an old people's home, and the refugee centre. It gave me more awareness of some social problems that every city faces. I also did voluntary work in the American NATO health clinic. I saw how difficult it was for 'white' Americans to get over the prejudices against 'non-whites'. A couple from Papua New Guinea attended the church and were not really welcomed.

In 1984, after much soul searching, we left Europe to settle in Perth, Western Australia. It was difficult for me to re-adjust to Australia. I missed the variety of life that people and the different countries provided. I did not know that on returning these were to be my mother's few remaining years. I am so thankful that I was there when she really needed me.

Eventually taking up studies I was able to re-register as a nurse in Perth. Through my work as a nurse I now have more understanding of human relationships than I'd have, had I never ventured beyond these shores. I didn't take the course I had planned, but even so my life would have been very ordinary if it hadn't been for the many people I met, whose lives enriched my own.

I seem to have lost the sense of 'belonging' to any particular place, but I can see the feelings of non-identity being repeated in my children. I hope I will have the same courage in being able to 'let go' as my parents did, when I wanted to discover new horizons.

Sitting Out in the Hills in China

Gloria Lee

Gloria Lee is of the Arrernte people and was born in Alice Springs in 1908. Her mother died when Gloria Lee was about four-years-old, and when she was 10-years-of-age Gloria Lee went with her father, a Chinese national, to live in China. She was educated in Alice Springs and China. When she had completed her schooling at the village school in China she travelled with her step-mother and other members of her family between the Chinese village where she lived with her step-mother and sister, and Hong Kong where the family had business interests. When she was about 21-years-of-age Gloria Lee returned to Australia. Apart from her sojourn in China, she has lived and travelled in the Northern Territory, South Australia and Queensland. In recent years Gloria Lee has been much in demand for interviews by oral historians and was interviewed by ABC Radio's 'The Coming Out Show' in mid-1993. She is currently living in Alice Springs.

When I was born there wasn't a register for coloured people. My mother was Aboriginal and my father was from China. In those days we didn't count so we weren't counted in the official records. The first Aboriginal child registered was one they called a 'half-caste'. After I married him, my husband went to check the records to see if I had been recorded; I hadn't.

My husband was an Englishman. Purdy was his name. I met him in Alice Springs. He was from Manchester and came from a middle-class family. He married me because I was expecting his child. When we were already married, we wrote to his sister and told her. Upon learning this, she said to my husband: 'You can't tell your father, because you're his eldest son.' The problem was that the eldest son gets the freedom of the city of Manchester; his family was well up in society. So he and his sister kept it quiet. My sister-in-law is still alive, living in Switzerland.

Purdy didn't tell his father, but the rest of the family knew. I didn't ever meet his family, but I told Purdy that if he ever wanted to go back to England that was alright. I didn't want to go to England. If he wanted to see his people, he should, but I didn't want to go to see them. I said I was quite happy in Australia. Purdy said that the only person he wanted to see was his brother, Bob, to whom he was fairly attached. During the second world war they met up in Egypt, so that was okay. Purdy wrote to me from Egypt saying that Bob was a real pommy, 'he's telling me all the pommy ways and speaking a bit of fancy language'. But Purdy said he didn't care; he was satisfied with Australia.

Purdy wrote to me from Egypt saying that Bob was a real pommy, 'he's telling me all the pommy ways and speaking a bit of fancy language'.

When I was married to Purdy his sister-in-law and sister wrote to me, as did my brother-in-law. I sent them food parcels during the war, putting in all kinds of things – rice, tins of fruit, anything we could send, and everything that they couldn't get. We kept sending parcels after the war and, by this time, my daughter Olive was over there, so the parcels were for her, too.

There was an uncle, Hardy. He was raised as a sibling, a part of my husband's family. He was pretty well up too. He travelled for ICI in England and he even was bombed during the war. Hardy lived in Portugal and he and his wife didn't have any children. So they wrote to me and said; 'What about sending one of the kids over?' I said alright, so I sent my Olive over to England and they sent her to school there. She went to a very good school in England, a convent.

Way before then, in 1918 (when I was about 10), I left Alice Springs with some of my family and went to live in China, in my father's village. We went in a boat, the *Mon Tora*. We shared a cabin with a Greek woman. There were only two beds in the cabin. I slept head to toe with my sister on one of them, and the Greek woman and her baby had the other. When we ate, the husband would gather up all the bread for himself and keep it. Then he and his wife put oil on it and ate it in the cabin. I had to get little pieces of bread from the table for them, too, and bring it in. I thought it was horrible, eating bread soaked in oil! We didn't go straight to China. We went to Java, Batavia, I think, and then to Singapore. We landed in Singapore and caught another boat, which came from India. From Singapore we went to Hong Kong where we stayed in a Chinese boarding house. The people who owned the boarding house sent out to the Chinese café for dinner for us. They didn't cook because there were so many guests.

We went to Macau, then travelled on to land at a jetty, and after landing we had to walk back to the village. The whole area was called Long Phu. It was the place where the first president of China, Sun Yat Sen, came from, in that area. There were brick houses with slate roofs. Chinese bricks made up the living room, the bedroom, and a little attic: that was my uncle's house. We had a block of land which created a family argument between my father and my uncle: my father had sent money back to China, but his brother didn't build a house on the land for us.

We lived on the Pearl River. At one end was Portugese Macau, and at the other was Won Poh, the military academy. That was where the writer Han Suyin's husband trained.

I went to school in China and learnt Chinese. I even came top! But after I returned to Australia I forgot how to write Chinese. Chinese is very difficult; you have to remember every word. But I know what it means when I see characters in Chinese, and I can speak it still.

I didn't speak Chinese before I went to China, but my father taught me how to count in Chinese, because I wanted to learn: 'Yut Yee Sarm Say Ng Lok Tzut Bart Gow Sup.' At the time I was going to school in Alice Springs. Mrs Ida Stanley came up to be the first teacher in the Centre. She began the Alice Springs School for coloured people. My brother and sister were the only ones who were having a formal education at the time. The rule was, generally, that we children didn't go into a school. Even many of the whites didn't go to school. In one family there were eight children. They were pretty big yet never went to school: I think their mother taught them a little at home.

It was not until my brother and sister made up the numbers at school that the coloured children had schooling. My brother and sister went to the morning school with the white kids, so they could speak English and read and write. Soon after they were ready for high school, my brother left to go to work. At that time children went to work at 14-years-old.

My language is Arrernte. I am Arrernte and belong in the Alice Springs area. I didn't go to school with the white children in the morning. I went in the afternoons because I couldn't speak English – not much, anyway. We did ordinary schooling, such as the ABC and tables. And reading. I could speak a bit of English, because I learnt some words from my brother and sister when they came back to Alice Springs, when the school began here.

Many years later, in China, I had no problem with learning to speak Chinese in the village, because I was young and running around with the kids meant I had to learn it. The Chinese children had no interest in learning English, because there was no point.

We landed in Sydney when I came home from China. On my return, I was a bit backward at the English language. I had also forgotten Arrernte. Then, after a while when I was with the other girls speaking, both English and Arrernte started to come back to me. Much later, my daughter Olive wanted to learn Arrernte. My daughter Sarah also wanted to speak it for her work. Her work takes her everywhere. She flies over the country to see what is happening with various groups of people. She picked up Arrernte

My language is Arrernte. I am Arrernte and belong in the Alice Springs area.

and has many languages. She speaks a bit of everything and understands many Aboriginal languages.

My mother died when I was about four-years-old. She'd given birth to a little girl. We lived at my father's house. My mother was at the camp. We heard a cry from the camp, which was in a gully. The workers grabbed me and rushed me down with them, and I saw my mother lying there, with some women sitting beside her crying. I didn't know that she had died.

When she was carrying the child, my mother often left me with one of our relatives – a nursemaid for me. Many years later, Marie, the nursemaid, lived at Santa Theresa before she died.

My father came to Australia to build a railway. They were **They were recruiting Chinese** recruiting Chinese labour to build the railway station at **labour to build the** Darwin, and the first railway. A lot of Chinese people came **railway station at** at that time to work on the railway. After my father **Darwin, and the** returned to China and I went with him, I lived in China for **first railway.** about 10 years. My family travelled between Hong Kong and China. The people thought it was interesting, our coming from Australia. They'd say: 'Black fellow up there now,' meaning my brother and sister and I were living in their village. My own people, my relatives, were alright to me. My aunty and uncle and other relatives accepted us. It helped that I went to school and that I was young. My sister was older than I – she was 16 – and she couldn't mix properly because she was too old, too grown up. She, my brother and I were the only ones in our family who went with my father to China. My mother had several other kids, and my father looked after all of them. My mother had three other sons besides my own brother. None of them came to China, because they were men, working out on the stations, and had their own lives. They worked for my father, too. Whenever they came in from riding out on the station, they stayed with us in my father's house, like a family.

When we were in China I missed the food we ate in Australia, although we had eaten rice in Australia; we often had curry and rice when we were living in Alice Springs before we went to China. And tea – all kinds of tea comes from China. We had it in Alice Springs and in the Chinese village. That was no different, although there may have been more kinds of tea in China.

In China we ate rice and other Chinese food. I often cried: 'I want bread.' My poor old father had to send to Portuguese Macau to get us some bread. My father gave me everything I wanted; he spoilt me rotten after my mother died. I often walked around, crying: 'Where's mum, where's mum?'

The games the children played in the Chinese village were not Australian games. I watched them play, the boys, bang bang kick things with the side of the foot. I wondered about the game and my brother said it was shuttlecock or some similar name. I thought it was ever so funny: to kick the thing with the side of the foot, at one another. It was good to look at.

The girls didn't play any games. As soon as they were old enough they left school and were trained to be mothers. They looked after the smaller children when the mother had to go to work and the father was out at work, too.

My father didn't do any work at all. He stayed in China for one year only, then returned to Australia. Before we left for China, he had stopped working on the railways, and had been running a market garden, growing every vegetable he could. Then the garden was sold, which was a very bad business because my father was not treated honestly in the dealings. He started cooking around the place, and there was no garden to come back to when he left China for Australia again. My brother returned with him, and I stayed with my step-mother. She had a child after my father went back to Alice Springs. The baby died, poor little thing.

When I left the village school, just like all the Chinese I didn't take a job. In China, we didn't work like the middle-class people unless we trained for school teaching or a position like that. But such work was mainly for the middle-class people. The ones who worked, worked in the same sorts of jobs as their parents. I didn't want to be a teacher. I travelled up and down from our village to the town, but that didn't count as work: it was not work. Although I was travelling, which was what I wanted to do, at the same time all I wanted was to return to Australia.

I really missed Australia. For us, the land belongs to a certain section of people, they love their land, and the people who belong there should have the land recognised as theirs. The land is special; a person belongs there and the land you belong to is your own bit of land, and all the Aborigines know who owns this piece of land and that piece of land, all around Alice Springs. We respect those claims.

Often, in China, I missed the sound of the voices singing in the corroboree. I recalled times in Australia when I would hear a voice singing and would say to my mother or my old people: 'What on earth are they singing about?' I would say to myself: 'I don't understand what they are singing, that's not Arremte.' And my mother or the old people would say: 'It is from a long way country.' After my mother died, there was an old grannie who talked to me. She told me of the happenings around Alice Springs, and how the people from the long way country had safe conduct through the country we lived in, because they signalled in advance that they were coming through.

> ...all the Aborigines know who owns this piece of land and that piece of land, all around Alice Springs. We respect those claims.

In China, I missed the freedom of everything – the freedom we had in Australia. After I returned to Alice Springs, I could have married one of the Chinese who was living in the town. He had money and a position, but to me it meant that once married to a Chinese, I'd be stuck. I had the idea that I wanted to travel. To go from here to there. I knew the way of life that would be expected if I married the man. When a woman is married, she doesn't move out of the home. I even explained that to a young Chinese girl who stayed with me in Alice Springs for a year or so at one time, after I came back from China and the Chinese had asked me to marry him. Yet sometimes I have regretted that I didn't accept the offer. I should have married the Chinese. I kind of belonged there. Belonged with the people: you marry, you're old and you're one of them. There are some good things about that kind of life.

If I had married the Chinese, we would have gone backwards and forwards between China and Australia. So I would have travelled, anyway.

Today, I feel half-caste Aboriginal and I sometimes feel Chinese, too. When people ask me I can say Chinese or half-caste Aboriginal Chinese. If I say Chinese, people look at me queerly as if they notice that I am darker than most of the Chinese. It is as if they are thinking about what it means, and yet I feel half-caste Aboriginal and Chinese.

But when I was in China I missed the trees and the land. My sister and I used to go out into the hills and rake twigs to bring back to burn in the fireplace. People don't chop trees in China because there are hardly any, but we got to pick up all the twigs and bring them to the village. We went out into the hills and sat out there in China. We wanted to get back the feeling of being out in the Australian land. It was to get away from the village, too, because there were so many people. We wanted the space, so we'd just go out there and sit under a tree, then bring back the twigs and branches to light our fires. It was a shock going from Australia where there was space and the great open, with so few people, to China where there were *so many* people. I was young, so I was alright. But Marge, my sister, had a bad time. She didn't come back to Australia. She went off her head a little bit afterwards, because China was so different and it affected her badly. We took her to Hong Kong. My step-mother said she could have come back to Australia with us, but this was during the war and I don't know what happened, finally. When the war broke out, there were lots and lots of troops in Hong Kong.

It was a shock going from Australia where there was space and the great open, with so few people, to China where there were *so many* people.

I thought Hong Kong was safe and that I could leave Marge there at the place where she was staying, because my step-mother was there often, too: she travelled to Hong Kong on business and saw Marge regularly. Then low and behold, the British couldn't hold Hong Kong. The Japanese overran it, so people like Marge were left with no homes, nor anywhere else to live. The people wouldn't feed them.

My family had relatives in Hong Kong. They had business there. I often went down to live with them, but I would go back home to the village. That was after I'd left school in China. In Hong Kong many people spoke English. The whites did that. I talked to all the missionaries there. They were mostly American.

When I returned to Australia I didn't miss China, at least at first. Then, after a while I began to miss the people and my mam. I wrote to them after I came back to Alice Springs. I often sent them money and other goods. At the time, in the 1930s, I didn't have much money, but I'd manage to send them £1 or anything I could. Something was better than nothing.

I noticed that Australia hadn't changed, when I came back. We often went out bush with my husband, after we were married. I liked being in Alice Springs. And then I had my children too – the four girls. I had to think about sending *them* to school. I did alright because the Catholic church helped me a lot. This was in the 1930s and we didn't have any money. The church people said: 'You can pay whenever you've got it.' This was the convent where my girls went to school.

I met my husband back in Australia. He and a friend were walking to Darwin. They were two pommies. The other one is still alive in Alice Springs; he has a family. He **We went out bush, often.** and my husband, Purdy, walked as far as Bower Creek. Then the policeman at Barrow Creek said: 'You can't walk any further because there's no water between here and there.' The two pommies were brought back to Alice Springs, so that's how I came to meet him.

Purdy and his friend had set out from Alice Springs for Darwin. They rode on the trains coming up: it was cattle trains, they were hiding in the rattlers. They hitched because there was no money. They heard that the workers got £1 a week in Darwin, for handouts. So they walked to Darwin – or tried to. They jumped on the rattlers.

I met Purdy through friends. Both he and his pommy mate married here. I was over 20 when we married. We went out bush, often. And he got a job here. He did anything. He was trained to take over his father's business. His family had a hardware distribution business, supplying smaller shops. He was the first to stay home and take over his father's business. Then he said: 'Oh, I don't want to be like you, just stuck here all my life. I want to go to see the world.' So Purdy's father sent him out to Australia with Dr Barnardo's. He paid his own fare.

After coming back from China, I didn't travel overseas again, but I did go to Adelaide, Brisbane, Tennant Creek and many other places. I went with my husband at first. I travelled up and down from Alice Springs to Adelaide often, for holidays. I didn't work in Adelaide. Then, after the war came and we left Alice Springs our marriage began to fall apart. I went to work somewhere else, and that was that. After I split up with Purdy I went to work in Brisbane, at the Mater Hospital. The children and I lived in Brisbane for a fair while. All the kids went to high school there. I had the four girls, and put them in a convent so that they could go to school. And from there, the brother-in-law who didn't have any kids said he and his wife would like to care for one of mine. So I sent him Olive. They sent her to a posh convent. It was a good convent in Manchester.

We sent letters back and forth, then eventually Olive wrote to tell me: 'Oh, uncle wants me to stop here and marry here, but if I do that I'll never see you again, mum.' So she asked my uncle if she could come back to Australia.

She got an Oxford entrance. That was about the time my uncle was married to a Portuguese friend of ours. They had a house in Portugal. Eileen, my uncle's wife, wrote over telling us: 'We've got a small house... Yes, only eight rooms.' Only eight rooms! I laughed when I heard that.

When I returned to Australia I felt out of place because the whites wouldn't accept me. The coloured people are always friendly to anybody. But we are different. I felt that the whites didn't accept me, and I could see it. They'd speak to my husband and they wouldn't speak to me. Not all of them. Some would speak to me, like one man who was something of a gentleman. He wasn't a roughie like a lot of Australians.

Then I remembered back to when the half-caste home was set up in Alice Springs. Some of the people involved in the plan had a big herd of goats. When they brought the goats in, the government began using the goats to feed the Aboriginal kids: milk and meat. The boys used to clobber the goats and bring them back every week with them, home to be eaten. At the time, the people in the Northern Territory were in favour of separating the Blacks and whites, because some of the white people recognised their kids amongst the Aboriginal children. Even some of the white women, who were married to the white graziers, saw that the children looked familiar. When the white men married the white women, they began throwing out the Black women or half-caste women they had lived with before. This happened often when the white men had made a bit of money. That was a lot of the reason the half-caste kids home was set up.

I buy Chinese food in the shops in Darwin.

I met up in a convent with some of the white mothers. They would say: 'Oh, we're here to visit our cousins.' They were visiting their half-caste relatives.

I often talked with the Chinese who lived in Alice Springs when I returned from China. But they're all gone now. For years I've had nothing to do with Chinese people, except that when I go to Darwin there are Chinese people there, and I talk with them. I buy Chinese food in the shops in Darwin. My daughter Peggy lives there, and one evening when I was visiting she said: 'Oh, you can get anything in Darwin now,' and I said: 'No, you can't, I've been looking for some salt fish and I can't get any.' She said she would get me some. I picked up a taste for salt fish in China: they salt it first, chop it up, then preserve it in oil.

I have never been back to China. I did want to. I can do it now, but all the old people of my generation are dead, everyone there is young now. I would find out from their fathers and mothers who they are, so I would know them. When I came back to Alice Springs, for a long time I wrote to the ones I knew in China.

There and Back Again – and Again

Janet Wilczynski

Born in Surrey, England in May 1939, Janet Wilczynski spent seven years in Victoria as a child, so was educated in both Australia and the United Kingdom. She trained as a secondary drama teacher at Trent Park Training College, Hertfordshire from 1959 to 1961, and graduated with a BA from the University of New England in 1988, majoring in English. She has worked as a cook, pharmacy assistant, bookshop salesperson, librarian and teacher.

Janet Wilczynski returned to Australia in 1962, marrying and living in Canberra for 13 years before moving to the Central Coast of New South Wales. She works there as a primary teacher/librarian and provides a home for two spoilt cats and also for her two daughters' possessions (and occasionally her daughters) as they move between cities or countries. Her interests include animal welfare, gender equality and legal reform – especially in the fields of family law and judicial bias, discretion and accountability.

I have migrated to Australia twice – once as a child in the 1950s and once as an adult in the 1960s. I was born in Surrey, England, where I lived until I was almost 12, for the last four years in the village of Ashtead, between Leatherhead and Epsom, where the famous Derby is run.

In childhood, I was surrounded by the Downs, the River Mole and Ashtead Woods – which provided a cycle of entertainment: picking primroses, catkins and bluebells in the spring; tadpoling, river-swimming and tree-climbing in the summer; and finding conkers (horse chestnuts), and hazelnuts in the autumn – not to mention being chased by every farmer in the district. Because my mother had her hands very full with my much younger brother and sister, I was free to range the surrounding countryside with my friends, only reappearing – scratched and filthy – for meals.

I attended the village school, from which every lunchtime a few friends and I escaped to play on the common, where our Detective Secret Society skulked behind the oak trees and tracked unsuspecting and innocent pedestrians in the firm belief that they were spies. As the headmistress said when I had half my front tooth knocked out in an accident on one of these excursions: 'It's her own fault.' And of course she was right.

Usually holidays were spent by the sea. One holiday we stayed in a caravan at Littlehampton, where German prisoners of war were cleaning out the nearby river. They were pathetically anxious to talk to children, showing us photos of their own families, and the memory of these men has counteracted, to some extent, my dawning awareness of what had been happening in Europe during the second world war.

In 1951 we migrated to Australia. In retrospect it amazes me to remember the equanimity with which I faced leaving my country. Possibly because I had rarely been outside my own very sheltered, beautiful and peaceful part of southern England (apart from trips to the London museums and art galleries and the annual summer fortnight by the sea) I had no real experience of the outside world, and it all seemed like a huge adventure.

We went to Australia House in London ('Come to sunny Australia!' screamed the brightly coloured posters in the windows) and sat on the Thames Embankment looking at a book of Victorian flowers, brilliantly coloured and strangely shaped. Some years later, in Victoria, my mother quoted to me Adam Lindsay Gordon's lines: 'Where bright blossoms are scentless and songless bright birds,' although it's not really true that the flowers are scentless.

The most upsetting thing for me was giving away a huge dolls' house, a toy theatre and our large porcelain dolls, whilst my mother left behind her oak furniture and still talks about her Welsh dresser. It never occurred to me that I was leaving a place which I would almost certainly never see again. As the boat train left London I buried my face in my last copy of the weekly comic *Eagle*, immersed in the adventures of 'Dan Dare, Pilot of the Future', and oblivious of the fact that this was probably my last sight of England.

We embarked on the *SS Ranchi*, a liner converted to a troop-ship during the war and now being used for migrants – I suspect without being re-converted. After five weeks of blue sea, flying fish and dolphins, we arrived at Port Melbourne. I wondered why so many men were propping up walls or sitting on the wharf, and was told: 'The wharfies are on strike.' (Welcome to Australia!)

We spent a week in a migrant hostel: tin huts surrounding a vast dining-hall from which music blasted perpetually. I always associate the song *Mocking-bird Hill* with this period, and when 35 years later, I saw the film *Silver City* (about Polish migrants), I recognised the setting: the huts, the grassless baked earth, and the sounds. One day, not realising that it was St Patrick's Day, we went to have a look at Melbourne. For hours we stood, unable to cross the road whilst the banners and bands of an enormous procession of Irish or those of Irish descent wended its way down Swanston Street. Looking back, I suppose that these two early experiences typified Victorian life at that time: the power of the unions, the church and the Irish.

My father had been the manager of a Boots the chemists branch, and my parents bought a pharmacy in the seaside township of Portarlington on the Bellarine Peninsula, about 110 kilometres from Melbourne. We travelled through a landscape as alien as the moon; the fields stretched to the horizon, very brown and very flat, with only the volcanic triangles of the You Yangs breaking the monotony.

And I never could adopt 'arvo' or 'beaut' or 'haitch', and why oh why is the colour maroon pronounced 'maroan'?

Our house was constructed in the prevailing architectural style: inadequately lined cream weatherboard, surrounded by a verandah and surmounted by a liver-coloured tin roof. It was alive with rats, mice, fleas and other small game, and parrots and blue wrens had a field day in the overgrown jungle of a garden.

Everyone in the township seemed to be related to everyone else. Their first names were curious – flowery or abbreviated: Marleen, Jasmine, Sharleen, Orpheus, Barry, Norm, Craig, Kev and Merv. Not a Susan or a John to be found.

Even the language was foreign. When my father was asked: 'Ow-yer-goin' mite?' he politely replied: 'Actually I'm going to Geelong by train and then by bus.' And I never could adopt 'arvo' or 'beaut' or 'haitch', and why oh why is the colour maroon pronounced 'maroan'? One of the great mysteries of life. And like all new arrivals we had the embarrassment of interpreting 'bring a plate' literally, only to realise that everyone else had scones, lamingtons or a sponge cake – the staple fare for all occasions – on *their* plates.

There was a misapprehension in Australia that those who came from the United Kingdom were simply transferring to another part of their own country, whereas Australia is in many ways just as foreign to the British as to the non-British migrant. In the 1950s, if there was a similarity it was to a Britain of 40 or 50 years earlier which had been preserved in amber.

Barry Humphries, speaking of the Australia of his childhood, said: 'It was excruciatingly boring,' and in many ways it was. My mother found it to be an 'intellectual concentration camp', and we later started having the *Manchester Guardian* and the *Observer* sent out to keep us in touch with the rest of the world. My brother, sister and I eagerly awaited our copies of *Eagle* and *Girl* comics, which arrived erratically by sea mail.

There was a love-hate relationship between the 'old' Australians and the 'new' from Britain, particularly England. This was the era of Robert Menzies, wool was a £1 a pound, Australia was riding on the sheep's back and busy exporting primary products to war-devastated Europe. Australia was proud of its British traditions – British to the bootstraps – looking upon Britain as 'home' and hoping to 'go home' at least once in a lifetime.

In spite of or because of this, and their isolation and insularity, Victorians were at the time very defensive, especially with people from 'home'. New arrivals were greeted, often on stepping ashore, with: 'Well, how do you like Australia, then?' The slightest hesitation in breaking into rapturous praise of the sunshine, the freedom, the food, in fact everything, resulted in a truculent: 'If you don't like it you can go back where you came from.' We were constantly informed that Australia had the largest cabbages (!), the best beaches and the best education system 'in the southern hemisphere'. Why not the northern hemisphere too? I wondered.

...there was a joke current that on any day, at any time, the Director-General of Education could say from which page in the *Victorian School Reader* all children in the state should be reading. It was true.

There was an odd combination of admiration and pity. No one could understand why we all looked so fit. Everyone was convinced that because they had been sending food parcels to Britain during the war we must all be starving. And there we stood: bursting with health and obviously not starving. Nor were we enraptured by the prospect of large unadorned slabs of steak, having always been very well fed on the fish and vegetables freely available even when meat and sugar were rationed.

One result of Australia's attitude to England (not necessarily to the Celtic countries) was that, although I had started secondary school six months before migrating, and had passed the iniquitous 11-plus exam (which directed children to the more academic grammar schools – or to the secondary modern schools), my parents were informed that Australia's education system was far in advance of poor backward old England's, and I was sent back to primary school from March to December.

The curriculum was totally different. In England I had been part of the 'learning by doing' revolution, where grammar and tables would be acquired (or not, as the case might be) by osmosis as one constructed models and did projects on coalmining. These methods were adopted by Australia later, when the United Kingdom had long abandoned them. Because we never heard incorrect English, and because I was raised at home on a diet of Milton, Shakespeare and Blake, the system more or less worked for me, although I am still a bit shaky on my tables. In the Victoria of the 1950s, however, education was authoritarian and inflexible and there was a joke current that on any day, at any time, the Director-General of Education could say from which page in the *Victorian School Reader* all children in the state should be reading. It was true.

I learnt a lot, including analysing sentences into columns with such unintelligible headings as 'Adjectival Clause' or 'Object'. I never knew why; like the other children I just did it. I learnt new (to me) and unfamiliar poems by heart, beginning with Banjo Paterson's *Clancy of the Overflow* and Dorothea McKellar's *My Country*. I knew all about the 'green and shaded lanes', but now had to become acclimatised to the 'sunburnt country'.

I began to learn the language: streams were creeks, and fields were paddocks. I discovered wonderful words for which there were no English equivalents: wowser and whinge, for example. Phrases such as 'Clancy's gone a-droving', 'gone walkabout' and 'Buckley's chance' crept into my conversation (but *never* 'maroan'). I tried to become accustomed to the outlandish names of the towns, such as Wagga Wagga and Bandiana – or even Hay and Hell and Booligal. So unlike the sensible names I was used to, such as Nether Wallop or Lower Slaughter. I learnt to play softball, not rounders, and became used to eating sandwiches in the school yard instead of a cooked lunch in a canteen. I took part in the ritual which started every day in every Victorian state school: standing rigidly to attention around the flagpole whilst intoning, as if it were all one word: 'I-love-God-and-my-country-I-honour-the-flag-I-serve-the-King-and-will-cheerfully-obey-my-parents-teachers-and-the-laws.' Not that most did – or at least not cheerfully.

At the weekends I worked with my father in the family pharmacy (Kwik-Tan: 3s 10d and California Poppy Hair Oil: 2s 10d) or swam at the beach and occasionally worked on local farms harvesting onions, peas or potatoes. On Saturday evenings I joined the other children in a tin hut for 'the pictures': cowboys and Indians, a newsreel of the Korean war and a glorious technicolour adventure. In 1953 we saw the film of Queen Elizabeth's coronation and watched Edmund Hillary and Tenzing Norgay on Everest, which was hailed as a great triumph for the British Commonwealth. The audience always joined in enthusiastically, making more noise than the soundtrack, and joyously rolling Jaffas down the aisle.

For the women there were various 'ladies'' meetings where garden-party hats and white gloves were worn, as they were for shopping in the two local general stores – a formality which seemed strange in the stifling heat of a Victorian summer. So did our secondary school uniforms, which were Victorian in both senses of the word. In summer we wore thick neck-to-below-knee navy dresses, and in winter pleated gym slips (which did nothing for the burgeoning female forms below), shirts and ties, with heavy lace-up shoes, navy gloves and felt berets all year round – a far cry from the check dresses and Clark's sandals which I had worn in England.

Weekend entertainment for adults revolved around the hotel and the church. It seemed to me that most of the men became very drunk on

> The audience always joined in enthusiastically, making more noise than the soundtrack, and joyously rolling Jaffas down the aisle.

Saturday evenings and then confessed on Sunday mornings. A very convenient arrangement. Coming from the home counties, where I doubt if most people cared about their neighbours' religion and certainly never discussed it, I found the obsessive church-attendance a shock to the system. I had chosen at the age of four to attend the local chapel, coming home clutching luridly illustrated cards depicting gory crucifixion scenes or tortured saints in long nightgowns, and proclaiming myself to be 'Washed in the Blood of the Lamb'. 'I don't suppose it'll do her any harm,' my mother would mutter dubiously. I had also chosen to attend Sunday school and had been taken to the parish church by my school, so I was far from being the unenlightened heathen I was made to feel on arrival in my new country.

If you stay in your own country it is less necessary to constantly examine your beliefs.

Later at high school, along with other migrants, I was regularly subjected to an inquisition about why I did not attend church and why I sewed or ironed and worked in the pharmacy on Sundays: 'You'll go to Hell.' When I was about 14 my class Scripture teacher who, incidentally, regularly hit the children violently on their heads, told us that only those who went to church would do well in the end-of-year exam. For night after night I learnt passages from the *Bible,* inspired not by Christian zeal but by a most unchristian desire to prove him wrong, to be the Devil quoting Scripture. I had the great pleasure of then witnessing his embarrassment when he realised that the only child with full marks was a non-church-attender.

I am not sure that my years at two Victorian schools were good for my character; they certainly influenced it; perhaps toughened it might be a better phrase. If you stay in your own country it is less necessary to constantly examine your beliefs. Migrants have to think and then either consciously retain or reject certain aspects of their former lives.

Education is one of the major problems for migrants. At the end of primary school, having mastered adverbial clauses and Henry Lawson, I came second in the class by half a mark, only to find on starting high school in the large provincial city of Geelong (to which we moved a few years later) that I had been relegated to the C stream, whilst the girl who came top was in the A stream. Fury drove me to work so that by the second year I was top of the A stream. Although I am by now at least half Australian I cannot forgive the injustice of being treated differently because I was a migrant. It is like being a woman: you have to work twice as hard to be recognised. However, Australia's 50 years of post-war migration have improved attitudes. I have seen the xenophobia and hostility exhibited to the successive waves of English, Dutch, Eastern European, Greek and Italian migrants subside, and hope that eventually this will spread to newer arrivals from Asia. Prejudice is still there, even if under the surface, and sadly it is often exhibited by the previous wave to the new arrivals, but a better travelled younger generation, exposed since birth to television, at least has some knowledge of the rest of the world.

Guests of Their Majesties' Governments used to be sent to Australia for seven years, fourteen years or life. We stayed for seven years, returning to England on the Norwegian ship, the *Skaubryn*. As we entered the port of Naples, a voice over the loudspeaker requested: 'All foreigners to report to the forward lounge.' An elderly woman with whom we often sat remained glued to her seat. 'All foreigners must come,' I said. 'Oh no,' she replied indignantly, 'I'm not a foreigner, I'm English!' One could almost hear the strains of *Rule Britannia* echoing around the lounge.

In the spring of 1958 we landed at Southampton and stayed for some time in the New Forest, where primroses bloomed in the remains of recent snowfalls. We then moved to a village in Epping Forest and after working for a year in the Charing Cross Road at Foyles ('The Biggest Bookshop in the World') I attended a music, art and drama college set in a glorious eighteenth century mansion and park in Middlesex, where I qualified as a secondary drama teacher. (My Melbourne matriculation would not gain me entry to a British university, as it had not been possible for me to study a classical language.) This was followed by a year's teaching.

In September 1962 I returned in the *MV Fairsky* to Australia to marry my former high school economics teacher, now a lecturer in Canberra, who had come to the school – very foreign, wearing a long black coat and a black felt hat, and with a charming European accent – in my final two years. I had been good at economics, although my reprehensible habit of seeing figures as people, instead of the more generally accepted custom of turning people into statistics, occasionally caused problems. After my return to the United Kingdom, he proposed by letter, and having read too many Victorian romantic novels, particularly those of Charlotte Brontë – ('Reader, I married him'), I once again sailed for Australia.

> My Melbourne matriculation would not gain me entry to a British university, as it had not been possible for me to study a classical language.

I must be one of the few people who have come twice as an 'assisted migrant' – the Immigration Department having discounted my first trip because I had been a child. This time I knew that I had previously not liked Australia very much, but Canberra in the 1960s was very different from the Victoria of the early 1950s.

The best way to approach Australia is through Sydney Heads on a fine, sparkling day, as I did, and that evening I arrived in the Australian Capital Territory (ACT). From the moment I saw Canberra I loved it. At first I could not understand why I felt so at home there, until I realised that it was like the cities of the future which had been illustrated in my Dan Dare stories in *Eagle*. Lake Burley Griffin, filled shortly after I arrived, was surrounded by white public buildings and spanned by the King's Avenue and Commonwealth Avenue bridges; more and more Canberra resembled the dream cities of my childhood, and I also grew to see the bush surrounding the capital through new eyes. I still remember the day I finally accepted it: riding in a bus through the outskirts of Canberra I suddenly realised that I was seeing the gum trees as if they were my trees. They too, like oaks and silver birches, had become familiar and friendly.

Canberra combines Europe and Australia. Many people dislike the city intensely, saying that it is too planned, clean, organised, even 'soulless'. Its trees are planted in rows of contrasting colours: evergreens and deciduous; wine-coloured, olive and lime green; all different and from different countries. The city's people are like the trees – from everywhere. I was told that at the time about 65 per cent of the population had been born overseas. I like 'the drunkenness of things being various'. I like knowing people who have come from all corners of the world; having friends from the United Kingdom, China, Russia, Poland – and also Australia.

I suppose I have always believed in multiculturalism. I am proud of belonging to a mongrel nation and have never understood the Nazi dogma of racial 'purity'. In looks, my brother, sister and I are probably throwbacks to Britain's succession of traders and conquerors: Phoenician (tight curls, olive skin, brown eyes); Roman (brown hair and eyes, olive skin); Viking (blonde hair, blue eyes), although we are 'pure English' – except for an Irish great-grandmother. My daughters do not believe me when I say that one of my reasons for marrying a Slav was that I thought we would have interesting children – which we did.

...one of my reasons for marrying a Slav was that I thought we would have interesting children – which we did.

In 1962 I did not simply return to Australia; I came into the Polish migrant community. Whilst in London I had been very influenced by the films of the Polish director Andrzej Wajda, and his images in Lotna of the Polish cavalry charging – gallantly and hopelessly – against the invading German tanks in September 1939 were also part of my history, although I had never been to Poland.

Until my marriage some months later, I worked in the public library whilst living with a Polish family, and after our marriage my husband and I stayed with Polish friends in Geelong. It was Christmas, and for a couple of months I was very conscious of being a foreigner. The weather was hot, I met no one who spoke English fluently, and felt guilty when those around me made the effort to converse in English. It certainly made me realise the problems faced by non-English-speaking migrants as I sat hour after hour eating *Polski ogorki* and downing vodka, whilst saying nothing more profound (in Polish) than; 'Excuse me, I am English, I do not speak Polish very well.' Deep and meaningful communication it certainly was not.

On Christmas Day I attended a Roman Catholic service in Polish and Latin and sat, tears oozing from my eyes, remembering the cold of an English Christmas and longing for English words. Words, words, words. In one of my favourite plays, *Roots,* the heroine tries to explain to her mother the importance of language: 'Language is words... it's bridges, so that you can get safely from one place to another. And the more bridges you know about the more places you can see!' All my bridges were down.

What must it be like for those who come here as adults unable to speak English?

One of the advantages of being a migrant is that one can love two countries. However, it is true that one never really fits in anywhere, always being to some extent an outsider everywhere. I suppose I finally came to terms with this when, in 1984, after years of inner debate, and whilst both retaining my British citizenship and having obtained it for my daughters, I was at last naturalised in a ceremony followed by a supper reminiscent of the Australia of my childhood: tea, scones, lamingtons and sponge-cake. I was having my sponge-cake and eating it too.

In Australia, once new acquaintances have recovered from the shock of finding that my accent does not match my surname, they usually pick it as being English. But in England I am Australian. 'Ah, from the Antipodes, I presume,' as a sweet old gentleman in the London Underground observed as we chatted whilst waiting for a fault in the line to be fixed.

On the other hand, being an outsider is not necessarily bad; it means that one remains to some extent a perpetual tourist. I still regard Australia's parrots, marsupials and wild flowers with a childlike wonder undimmed by long familiarity. A kookaburra's laugh or a currawong's call will never be merely part of the background. And on a trip to stay with my daughter in England four years ago I went out into the freezing March dawn to listen to the chorus of blackbirds and thrushes and to gaze at the daffodils, primroses and anemones thrusting through the incredibly lush green grass along the River Cam, which I would probably not have done, had I never left. Although I felt at home, I was behaving like a visitor.

One is always conscious of other places, seeing everything as different and exciting or even different, annoying and wrong, but never taken for granted. I have tried to instil in my daughters a love of their own country, particularly since both were champing at the bit to travel, and have gone overseas, the younger backpacking in Nepal and now working in London. Both have now visited the countries of their roots – Poland and England – but they knew the country of their birth first.

My own parents brought us up to appreciate the plants and wildlife of whichever country we were living in, taking us caravanning to the bush and mountains whilst in Victoria and to every Norman castle or Roman remain in southern England. I took my daughters to see as much of Australia as possible – mostly camping. I do not know if my older daughter, living in Cambridge, remembers, but before she left we travelled through the Northern Territory, and one night at Mataranka thermal springs I told her to stand and smell, look and listen: camp fires, frying onions, eucalyptus leaves, dry grass, southern stars in a dark-blue sky with the gum trees silhouetted against them, a few sleepy kookaburras. I said that she should remember.

> I still regard Australia's parrots, marsupials and wild flowers with a childlike wonder undimmed by long familiarity.

In some ways I know that I shall always be, not necessarily English but certainly European. My mythology, literature and history are European. I have learnt as much as I can about Australia's history, and I am very conscious of the dispossession, injustice and cruelty inflicted on Australia's indigenous people by 200 years of European settlement. I find Australia's colonial past increasingly fascinating, as is the Aboriginal mythology explaining the origins of places and wildlife, but deep down I do not yet feel about them as I felt when I stood at Thermopylae and imagined Leonidas and his 300 Spartans defending the Pass 2500 years ago or when I stood on the West Country downs and felt the Druids stirring in the chalk beneath my feet. Being on the site of the Eureka Stockade is an interesting experience; seeing Bosworth Field, where the last Plantagenet king died in 1485, is an emotional one.

What I hope I am is not a citizen of England or Australia but of the world.

And yet this is not entirely true. In one of those Victorian readers so long ago was the story of the great bushman, Bernard O'Reilly, who in 1937 used his common sense and bush knowledge to rescue the survivors of the wreck of the *Stinson,* a light aircraft lost on the Lamington Plateau. Seeing the scene of the wreck myself many years later, standing surrounded by thick rainforest, I found that story as moving and inspiring as I had at 12-years-of-age.

What I hope I am is not a citizen of England or Australia but of the world. The virtue of not belonging solely to one small part of the globe is that perhaps one belongs to all of it? Well, a fair amount of it, anyway. However (and for me there is always a however), unlike Dorothea McKellar, my homing thoughts will probably fly to a green and not a brown country and I want my ashes scattered on the Wiltshire Downs. Or perhaps the plains around Canberra? There are always two points of view: the endless dilemma of the migrant.

Point of View

Kathy Kituai

Kathy Kituai was born in Western Australia, has lived in Adelaide, Papua New Guinea and now calls the ACT home. She was assistant editor for the Institute of PNG Studies 1981-84, co-editor of *Our Time But Not Our Place*, 1993, Melbourne University Press, and writer in residence for Belconnen Community Centre 1990-91.
Kathy Kituai has facilitated Creative Writing Courses BCC for the O'Connor Family Centre since 1991, reviewed for *Muse* magazine since 1989 and was vice president for the Fellowship of Australian Writing 1987-90. To keep sane she writes poetry, short stories, articles and is published in Papua New Guinea, Japan, the United States of America and Australia.

I am standing at the bottom of the bed. My hands grip the wrought-iron frame. Part of me, that other part of me called 'John', is on the bed. He is ill; very ill. I am scared. Each time I look at his grey, sickly face, I float off somewhere. I don't know what is happening. I am four-years-old; grounded in fear; powerless.

Suddenly I hear IT. Enchantment. Sonorously it surges through my body. I fly from note to note. My skin ripples in response. Ecstatic, no longer scared, I become this frequency that soars above all pain and fear. I turn to my twin brother and say: 'Did you hear it?' 'What?' comes his jaded reply. He does not open his eyes. 'That!...'

Now he looks at me. Curiously. He tilts his head in the direction of the wireless. A radio announcer is talking. He opens his eyes and listens intently. Why now does he open his eyes?

'Not that!' I insist impatiently. 'That other!... did you hear it?' 'What was it called?' 'I don't know... it was on before... it was like this,' and I'm making the sound for him; humming it, recreating it, but he stares at me blankly. If I could become it again, surely he will know what I mean.

'Did you hear it?' I say again in desperation. Part of me has taken wing and flown far away. I am on one side of understanding, my brother on the other. There is a chasm between us. I listen to his voice reverberate as if he is speaking in a foreign language. 'Do you mean that song?' he says, almost nonchalantly. 'Sure! I've heard it lots of times.'

...the first time in my life in which I remember a conscious feeling of belonging; a feeling of being-at-home with what-I-am-in-essence.

Is he lying? No one could experience that kind of magic and remain aloof. I am confused. This is the only person with whom I am connected. If I became IT, why didn't he? 'What is it called?' I challenge. 'Music.' he replies. The Source-Of-All-Meaning can be encapsulated in words? Now I know that he is lying.

Knowledge does not come without a price. My discovery of music is tainted with a state of sadness. This is to be the first time in my life in which I remember a conscious feeling of belonging; a feeling of being-at-home with what-I-am-in-essence. Elevated in a wordless paradise, too young to articulate my homecoming, I am also alienated. My twin brother does not understand that I have not just heard music but encountered it. I no longer belonged to this other part of myself called John quite so much after that.

The second world war, that nameless tension-in-the-air during early childhood and I am aware of rations, the *Warsaw Concerto* and Catalinas on the Swan River. Dressed in my best starched bonnet, John in equally splendid attire, and after being sworn to secrecy (even now it is hard to write about this), we are taken off to visit a man in an airforce uniform. He is handsome. I am drawn to him in an inexplicable way but again I have no words to explain this rush of recognition. Imagine my elation in finding my mother's photograph on the sideboard. 'Mother,' I whisper. 'This man loves you.' Embarrassed she laughs. He seems pleased. 'Does she know?' he asks in a whisper. The ambiguity of the question does not affect me. Mother shakes her head and asks me why I say this. Isn't it obvious? I point to her photograph on the sideboard.

I am told all my life that the man my mother is married to is my father. Her husband is foreign to me. He sleeps in the sleepout around the back. I ask embarrassing questions that are never answered. In the final year of the war, my mother presents John and me with war medals and we are told to take great care of them. No explanation is given. My mother is distressed. My sister says we are too young to receive these. She is right. Once again I am confused. John smirks knowingly. There is no use asking him. He lied about the Source-of-all-Meaning. No one can be trusted. I never see the man in the airforce uniform again. Suddenly very alone, I am a nomad in search of me.

I find parts of this new identity whilst under another spell. Reading. Dick, Dora and Fluff provide the props; *Alice in Wonderland* – the magic wand. Visiting Enid Blyton's Faraway Tree with the Saucepan man, Silky and Moonface conjures up a sublime awareness I have about myself and life. Against all the odds, anything is possible. Adults do not know this. Again I experience a sense of homecoming. Blyton created lands on top of The Magic Faraway Tree and it is here that I migrate in my imagination. But as a member of a family of six (four boys and two girls) in an unliberated era, reading is forbidden fruit.

I learn of the Caucus Race in Lewis Carroll's Wonderland where everyone not only participates – all win the race. We play a different game at our house. There are beds to be made, dishes to be washed, floors to be cleaned and boys don't participate in those tasks; only girls. Boys are educated.

Still I read. Most times it is in the loo or under the bedclothes. If caught in the act, I am accused of laziness.

Considering my choice of literature, it's ironic that a cat, minus a Cheshire smile, brought me down to earth. Come with me to Grade 2 Forest Street School, South Perth. Listen... I am in disgrace. Why? Absenteeism and for being behind in my work. Miss C. explains that I am to draw in my sketch book. See how eagerly I comply? Drawing is now third on the list of The Source-of-All-Meaning, after music and reading. Chalk takes me on any journey I wish to go. Can you see Miss C. creeping up behind me? She is looking at what I have drawn, clears her throat and claps her hands to gain the attention of her charges. 'Class, what was it I asked you to draw in your sketch book?' 'A cat Miss C.,' they all chant. Well I'd got that right. I've drawn a cat. 'And what colour is a cat class?' Some say white, brown or black. Miss C. is showing my drawing to the class. They are laughing. I slink further down the hard, wooden seat. 'And what colour is your cat Miss Clarke?' 'Red,' I manage to reply.

> I like my red cat. I draw over it in white. My hands shake in defiance.

She throws my book onto the floor and tells me to draw it again. Once again I comply. I like my red cat. I draw over it in white. My hands shake in defiance. Miss C. is coming over to me again. I wish I were eating pop-biscuits with Moonface. She claps her hands again. The class is paying attention.

'Class...what colour did we say is a cat?' There is weary irritation in her voice. It is the same tone I have heard in my mother's voice when I'm reading and there are dishes to be washed. I know that they are going to answer something like: 'White Miss C.' So why does she look so disapproving?

My cat is pink. Red and white make pink. She throws my book onto the floor again. Many years pass before I lose the fear of drawing.

My education consists of staring out classroom windows. At home I daydream about piano lessons. I beg permission to play. Always the answer is: 'When you are serious about it, you can learn.' I spend six years sitting at the base of the piano miming my seriousness whenever my mother plays and the answer never varies. Identity rests on learning. It is time to become airborne.

Lift-off comes one afternoon when I arrive home from school and announce that I have found a music teacher. I am ten-years-old. Frustrated. Many adults have directed my journey this far in life and only I know which countries I need to visit.

Eighteen months of bliss follow. I have reached an oasis. After completing my chores each afternoon, I practise for hours. Beethoven, Bach, Beethoven, Mozart, Beethoven. My teacher sees me as her protege and urges me forward, sometimes faster than I can travel. She understands my thirst. It is almost as if she knows that I need to drink-in as much knowledge as possible. The desert is not far away. My mother has a thirst of a different kind. Alcohol. She sells the piano.

Remembering these years is like thinking in a shade of charcoal. I leave school at 13, wander the wilderness of waitressing and factory jobs. Five siblings have flown the nest. My mother is drinking heavily under the disguise of having a few drinks to relax. She is a good Catholic, and I can only surmise in retrospect that, along with other taboos, she does not cope with divorce.

At 18, I fulfil that for which I am trained. Motherhood. The night the man who is to become my husband proposes, I answer with an overwhelming: 'Yes... and we can have a family.' Startled, he steps back. Family is another word for belonging. I cannot articulate it any further than this. I only know I have not experienced it as yet. He is my childhood sweetheart. Why marriage? Perhaps it is his airforce uniform.

I have four children in five years. I am 24-years-old, grounded again, powerless. There are beds to be made, nappies to be washed, children to be fed and still boys do not participate. My husband leaves the airforce and runs a business.

The location has changed. South Australia. I am in exile in the Eastern States; that extra-terrestrial place that I have heard so much about in Western Australia. Clay soil, red dust storms, Sower Sobs and Paterson's Curse. Where were all the Kangaroo Paws and Enamel Orchids that transform scrub into spring? Gilgies are called Yabbies, rivers man-made, surf bubble-and-foam. I am slow to appreciate vineyards that produce international wines, an arts centre on the Torrens and European culture nestling in the Adelaide Hills.

The view out the window is ten acres of bushland overlooking Mylor Valley. A piano graces the lounge room. I keep a twelve year promise to myself. Locating Middle C, I reteach myself how to play. The church welcomes my organ recitals during services, but not so my understanding of Christianity. I query dogma, the insular nature of the church in suburbia and place New-age interpretation on J.C. Super Star is not yet a Rock Opera. It was the red cat all over again, only I don't slink down the hard, wooden seat this time. I run kindergarten, married groups and preach at Retreats from the pulpit. The elders of the church ask me to recolour my thinking or leave. I leave.

Likewise, after eighteen years of marriage my husband does not understand either the sense of parenthood that I expressed when he proposed or my growing assessment of fair play and so I ask him to leave. During that time I read Zen, philosophy, astrology and wonder why I have wasted so many years making beds. Exasperation turns into poetry and after being published in a Zionist magazine in the United States of America, I deviate to other pursuits. I become one-of-the-boys and go into partnership in a counselling business, based on astrological philosophy; join the AMTRA Club and climb mountains in a 175 Suzuki motor bike.

I find myself another music teacher and, after two years of theory, composition and jazz arrangement, he hires me to teach his students. No formal training behind me, teaching comes easily. My method is: find out how the student assimilates knowledge, match that with what they need to know, and guide them into the teacher within. I teach Grade 6 theory, as well as practical, and all students pass their AMEB exams with A's and B's.

But what had I really learnt after all these years? Applying my own method of teaching, I realise that I assimilate knowledge intuitively and, in retrospect, search for words to describe the experience.

Nouns do not explain things to me, make them real or enlarge understanding. I trust innate knowledge only and am out of balance. Life comes into focus more if encountered – not named. Zen makes more sense to me than Christianity. Discovering Taoism is like falling down the well with Alice all over again.

More than anything I feel different; an outsider to my family in Western Australia, the church and, in a wider sense, in the working community. I belong only when engaged in activities from The Source-of-All-Meaning and Motherhood. This was to change. About this time in my life I met a man who would further my sense of alienation. We were to climb out on a limb together; far, far away.

He talks to me about eternal spring in the jungle where wild orchids and passionfruit bloom and of a culture steeped in equality and kinship. Paradise is Emegeri, a village in the remote Highlands of Papua New Guinea: a place where everyone belongs. His people respect the aged, adore children and he proves this by almost absconding with every child we meet in the streets of Adelaide, whilst I smile reassuringly at parents and wonder if it is too late to become pregnant again. I have micro surgery to ensure this. He expresses respect for his elderly parents and sends them money even though he has little himself and his closest friends are Africans, Asians,

Papuans. While he completes his masters degree, I attend secretarial college with my daughter, packing my head with Pitman shorthand, touch typing and bookkeeping. I have either met the Red King or a Shining Knight. We marry.

I am filled with fear as I wave goodbye to my four teenage children, not of flying, but of leaving and the changes that will occur in us all during my absence. Motherhood has given me a glimpse of myself but still: 'I'm late, I'm late for a very important date,' and my offspring know this and wish me well. I cry uncontrollably all the way to Sydney, Brisbane, Port Moresby and often during the many years that follow.

It is the colours that I notice first in my new country. Vibrant purples, pinks and peach Bougainvillea growing down Moresby streets, iridescent blue butterflies, green frogs silently appearing like enamel brooches pinned to fences, red hibiscus, white frangipani.

...the humidity that sticks my laplap to my thighs, grows mildew in cupboards and cockroaches that fly

Slowly I encounter Port Moresby and my new land comes into focus. My parents-in-law are anxious to meet me. We receive word that Papa is ill. A trip to Goroka is imminent. Nimbly, Papa bounces over to meet us at the Settlement; old eyes sparkling with joy and pride for his son. We embrace, cry, embrace. He has tricked us into visiting him. My people conquered his land but not his spirit; underrate his culture yet he welcomes me – a white women as a *Tambo*; forcibly the church took his son away from the village and educated him and still he retains his sense of trust.

Never do I exchange one word that can be understood by Papa. This man whose relationships are based on the law of kinship, and to whom nationalism is a foreign concept, lives the lore that love and respect supersedes any culture or language.

Mamma worked within the limits of gender roles. Every weekend she trudged the half day's walk over mountains to the primary school, a string bag heavily laden with produce from her garden to ensure that her son ate well while he was engaged in this unfathomable whiteman's learning that interfered with her son's culture. Remorsefully I remember Miss C. and how basic education is taken for granted in Australia.

I go back to secretarial college to satisfy my hunger for formal education. I see the irony of the multi-cultured situation at the college; learn American shorthand from a Filipino teacher in Papua New Guinea. I do not stare out any windows, and top the class.

I become used to the humidity that sticks my laplap to my thighs, grows mildew in cupboards and cockroaches that fly, especially when we are entertaining, but not to the monotony of the weather – in the high 30 degrees most days. I miss cold rain, sitting beside an open fire, blossoms and autumn leaves. So too it seems do other expatriates on campus.

Australia Day, and we celebrate with Vegemite sandwiches, Ozzie beer, barbequed snags and tell yarns. I fantasise about eating fish and chips out of newspaper, Choo Choo Bars, and peaches, ripe and inexpensive, and try to recall what it feels like to be cold. I cannot get used to wearing shoes while at the beach. A tropical ulcer eats deep into my ankle.

Gradually I began to realise that the Melanesian way of life was not like the Caucus Race my homesick-husband had described to me when we first met in Australia. Not every one participates. Semi-educated Papua New Guineans can neither fit back into village life nor gain employment in the cities. They turn to rascalism. Once this amounted to stealing tinned fish, rice and clothes from their Colonial Masters, a pay-back that was tolerated, understandable in the hot-bed climate of 'Haves and Have-nots'. Papua New Guineans name them, almost fondly, Rascals. 'There is no "one, two, three, away!"' but quite a few headstrong Papua New Guineans no longer listen to the elders and have began running when they like and leave off when they like, so that it's not easy to know if this race with Law and Order will ever be over.

Some do make beds, wash dishes, clean floors. Not all who do these chores are women. They are called house boys but they lose dignity in the process by carrying out domestic chores that directly clash with proud traditional roles as men and win the grand prize of twenty-six Kina (approx. $32) a fortnight in return.

I find myself staring at Australians employed in blue-colour labour like sweeping streets, collecting rubbish, gardening.

I can obtain office work easily and earn an expatriate wage almost three times that which my highly educated husband can earn as a national academic. This was a colonial country over-seen by Australians: 1980, and although Independence has been gained in 1975, and I am married to a national, my status has not changed. I am a 'white missus'.

Homesick I return to South Australia and notice the smell of eucalyptus, the sudden shock of commercial television and of being able to catch a bus that runs to a timetable. I find myself staring at Australians employed in blue-colour labour like sweeping streets, collecting rubbish, gardening. I am uncomfortable wearing make-up and stockings again and Oh! how I long for my laplap and thongs. I despair at the close-knit circle of Aboriginals in Victoria Square, backs turned to Whites as they wait for the welfare cheques. Likewise the dependence of youth on the dole horrifies me and I sermonise about the low national wages in PNG, the Wantok system (extended family support). My eldest son replies: 'Well at least you still speak English Mum.' Whenever I cannot be understood, I do what everyone does in PNG. Lapse into Pidgin. All four children now shake their head at this person whom they once called mother.

Supermarkets completely overwhelm me. There are more than two brands of anything on the shelves. Where is the tinned fish, large bags of rice, hard plain biscuits? Often I walk out not being able to make a decision on what to buy. However it is nice to have my jokes appreciated by check-out girls when I finally quell the indigestion of Australian wealth.

I walk into rooms and automatically reach to switch on overhead fans. The switch is not there. Lacking also are brown faces in the streets, the smell of lime and beetle nut, lush mangoes, coconuts and green bananas. I know it's time to return to Moresby when I keep repeating the story about how we showed Papa the sea for the first time and he remarked: 'That's the biggest river I've ever seen,' or the time we explained the moving star in the sky. 'It's a Sputnik,' my husband simply stated. Papa gave an uncommitted 'H-m-m-h!' the way Papa did. Watching him receive this sort of information was history in the making but I couldn't help wondering if my father-in-law was thinking: 'Whiteman's rubbish! It's even in the sky!'

Why not return with me to Moresby and experience for yourself all the things I am missing? Can you see how green everything has become in our absence? The Wet has set in. Don't worry if the car swerves from side to side on our return to Waigani campus. I'm only dodging frogs. Why did the storekeeper serve us first when I stopped at the Trade Store for supplies, even though I protest because we were at the end of the queue? Perhaps our white skin makes it easier for him to see us. Would you like to join us at the drive-in tonight? I hope you like coconut cream in your rice. We will sit beside the car on a grass mat and enjoy our meal while we watch the movies. Only Kung Fu or John Wayne to choose from? I agree that Asian and American movies are a cultural overlay – the same way as they are in Australia. Similar questions occur to me each time I recognise American Blues Riffs rhythmically played with a rubber thong on ancient PNG bamboo pipes or see cartons of beer becoming part of the traditional bride price instead of pigs. Here, have a chicken leg to eat and cheer for the best fighter in the film. No it doesn't matter if he's not the hero; he's winning! Who's that waving over there? Wave back. I didn't see but no doubt a relative of ours. You heard them say that my house boy was very handsome? Oh!…that will be a colleague from secretarial college. This happens with people who don't know that I'm married to a national. Yes we leave our shoes by the door of the house when we return. What's that you say?…you can't stay?…It's too hot! I'll catch you further down in the story when I return to Australia.

John Kolia's advertisement for an assistant editor at the Institute of Papua New Guinea Studies coincides with my return to PNG. Perfect. I have a work permit and want a position offering a national wage. Utopian perhaps but not an economically wise preference considering our extended family obligations.

As assistant to the editor, I prepare the quarterly magazine, *Bikmaus*, collate entries for the literature competition, check galley proofs, edit contributions to the literature competition and prepare them for radio. The latter interests me most of all.

I convert my husband's MA thesis on the Banabans in Fiji into a four-part dramatised documentary. I can understand his work; I typed his notes for him. In 1982 it goes to air at NBC and has been played many times since. However my husband is accredited for the many hours this has taken of my time. Why? Is it because he is a national, is educated, or the gender factor?

Close, he and I have played whichever game either culture demanded. I refrain from cooking for my father-in-law if I am menstruating. My husband shares the household chores in private and plays the perfect host for visiting academics. There is one game neither of us can play much longer. I have not become pregnant.

A Big Man, my husband is expected to reproduce. In the eyes of villagers, I am falling on one side of his culture – he on the other. A chasm grows between us. Their constant reminder that traditionally he can have ten wives if he chooses reaches me like a foreign language. I listen as his voice reverberates their persistence. 'Ten wives!' I quip. 'Fine but I won't stay around to count them.'

Both cultures come up with traditional solutions. Our sister-in-law announces that the child with whom she is pregnant is for us if it is another boy. Robbie is born. We adopt. The ANU offers my husband a PhD scholarship. In 1984 we move to Canberra. Nonetheless his culture wins the race. He returns to PNG in 1988 with a new partner and a baby daughter.

Robbie and I make Canberra our home. He is the one who now stands out in the queue even though he wears jeans and Reeboks. At least one of my sons is more than interested in stories about Papa.

Sometimes we arrive at the place where we begin. Belonging is also of the heart. For some time I float off somewhere. I don't know what has happened. I work in childcare; coordinate an after-schoolcare centre in O'Connor.

In Moresby I am an expatriate because I come from another country. In Canberra I feel like an expatriate because of my experiences of marriage in another culture. Life in PNG replaced The Source-Of-All-meaning. I have not played the piano in ten years. I buy a piano.

Slowly I discover that I can write. It takes me several years to create a first draft of a novel on the culture clash in PNG. Internalised, Miss C. constantly draws my attention to red cats within the text. All too aware of expatriates capitalising on their experience, I am conscious also that my point of view is valid. Whiskers and all, soon I will redraft and hold the manuscript up for the class to read. I refuse to draw over any multi-cultured experience in white.

PART II

This Is My Country

China is My Mother's Home

Mickey Zhu

Mickey Zhu was born in Shanghai, China, on 30 March 1966. She went to school in Shanghai and studied engineering at the Shanghai University Engineering Science Textile Institute, graduating in 1988. After working as an assistant engineer at the Shanghai No.4 Textile Machinery Plant for nine months, she emigrated to Australia. She now lives in Brunswick, an inner suburb of Melbourne, Victoria, where she is studying for her masters of mechanical engineering.

On a sunny winter's day on 16 December 1989 I wait to leave Shanghai airport. Surrounded by my relatives, only I, in my heart, am not afraid at all. I tell my relatives I will be alright even though I go to a country I don't know at all. That day, at the airport, father held my hand and, with tears in his eyes, knew it was good for me to go overseas. He says so, but he doesn't want me to go away from him.

However, everything is arranged. The tuition fee for the half year English course has been paid and it cost the family a fortune. I have a visa from the Australian Embassy, although 50 per cent of visa applications are refused, and I buy only a one-way ticket to Australia. For me there is no way to go back. None of my relatives has been this lucky. I have to go.

At that time I am 23-years-old. Australia thinks I should be an independent adult, when it grants me the visa. But I was just a girl with no knowledge of overseas travel and a lot of misconceptions. I have lived all my life in Shanghai, travelling for short holidays to nearby provinces where I have relatives. Travelling to another country for the first time is risky, but exciting.

When I was 18-years-old, my mother, an associate professor in a university, realised that the best future for me is overseas. She found the information about getting overseas. She was so confident and independent. She raises the issue of my going away from home, to live in another country. My father spoils me and feels sorry that I am talking about leaving the country, but on my mother's insistence my father finally lets me go on my own way; he lets me become independent. Now I realise it is so important to be encouraged to become independent, it is a major change in my life. It is the beginning of becoming a real adult.

She raises the issue of my going away from home, to live in another country.

I want to come to Australia because it is fashionable. If your family can send you overseas, you will become known in your group of young people. You will be famous. The young people will admire you. Also, China is an isolated country; if you go through all the hassle of getting a visa and passport it means you are extremely lucky.

In every young Chinese mind America and England alone represent western society, and there are already thousands and thousands of students on overseas scholarships in those countries. So when the people in Shanghai suddenly began talking about Australia and about travelling there privately, it was a chance and an exciting idea. So all the young people open the geography books and go to the library to learn about Australia.

These young people then applied for a visa. They meet outside the Australia Embassy every morning, exchanging information about Australia. Even those who have received a visa will go there to tell us the good news, raising our hopes of being successful, too.

It doesn't matter where you go or why you go, so long as you get out of China. Even if you become a beggar somewhere far away, people still think you will become rich and famous. In China I have a good job as an engineer. My family was good to me and I had plenty of friends. My job was easy, no pressure, with the standard amount of money earned by university graduates. Father regularly gave me extra money to spend and our flat was comfortable by Chinese standards. I was busy socially, often out late – watching movies, dancing, drinking tea, talking and eating. It was a carefree life.

There was an incident in Beijing, but we heard little about it and I didn't care about it. It was only after I arrived in Australia that I heard more. Because the news we had had in China was only in passing, with no more than cursory reference to it, at first I was surprised how worried the Chinese students were about what happened in Tian An Mien Square.

In China, after an eight month wait, I finally obtained a visa. Although my visa said six months, I didn't believe I would be back in China in that time. I was confident I would be in Australia much longer. I don't know where the confidence came from, but I am a friendly person who gets on well with people and have a habit of meeting people who are willing to help me.

In the beginning, I thought Melbourne and Sydney were suburbs of a bigger city like Shanghai. I didn't realise they were miles apart, as different as Shanghai and Guangzhou. I knew Melbourne as 'the Garden City' and was looking forward to going there to look, and to make the most of it in the six months study time, earning as much money as I could, becoming a millionaire and returning to China. Become a millionaire?! At that time it was my fantasy.

When I arrived in Melbourne airport, some people who had come to meet another traveller asked me: 'Where do you want to go, can we give you a lift?' I answered: 'I am looking for a place to live, can you find somewhere for me?' They replied: 'It's difficult for a girl in this city,' so they took me to their house. After a half day telephoning around the Chinese student community, I was lucky to find a room to share straight away. The people who helped me were so friendly and nice, that they set me off on a path that somehow meant I met friendly people from then on.

Suddenly I feel safe that I have a room to be my Australian home. I am starting my new life from here.

When people see me with my yellow skin, brown eyes, black hair, I think people expect me to have an accent. I've always had a Chinese accent. I don't think that will ever change. So long as I make myself clear, even if there are mistakes in my English, I think people can understand. If I say: 'G'day mate, ow ya goin?' people will laugh or feel surprised. So I think I'd better be natural and not try to alter myself, including the way I speak.

The language is totally new. I had studied English for 10 years but never ever used it in conversation while in China. The Australian English course was little help, because my mind was concentrating on how to earn money to survive. I knew a lot of English words but didn't really appreciate what they meant. I knew what a car is but I sat in the back seat of one only once. I didn't know what a freeway is, what a highway is, and why they aren't all called roads. I didn't know the difference between a flat, a unit or a house. In Shanghai, everyone lives in a flat; no one lives in a house with a front yard, back yard and driveway. All the houses in Melbourne are different colours, the red brick, green trees and blue sky combined together looks so beautiful. In Shanghai everything is grey, including the sky. All flats are uniform; a foreigner would not be able to tell the difference. For me, the housing commission flats in Kensington are a luxurious place to live.

In one month, my mind is totally changed. I have spent all the cash I brought with me, and I still haven't got a job. I learn that the jobs Chinese students are doing are processwork in factories, office cleaning in the city, and washing dishes in the restaurants. I realise I must work very hard if I am to survive. At first, I believed I would have to stop eating until I got *any* job.

I realise at the time how unprepared I am, how little knowledge I have about Australia and western society. Most Chinese students managed to find a job, but it was well below what they were qualified to do in China. Many of them work illegally, eventually returning to China.

Fortunately for me, things changed after three months. I found a boyfriend who is born in Australia, lived in Australia and studied in Australia, and is totally and utterly Australian. It is he who helped open my eyes to western society, encouraged me to survive, helped me to stand up. Now I consider Australia is my second homeland. If one day I have a chance to travel around the world, I think I will still come back to Australia.

I feel I fit into Australia. The living standard here is better than in China. The food is better, with more variety than I ever saw in China. People here throw away fruit and food that is better than the quality we eat in China. If I'm desperate I could pick it up and eat it. I am confident I can find a job that will pay my expenses, but I hope that with my qualifications as an engineer I can get a good, well-paid job. I don't mind working as a kitchen hand so long as I work, and pay for my own food. I feel proud of this and am pleased that I do not have to live on the dole. I can even make a joke when people ask why I married an Australian when there are millions of Chinese males – 'a change is as good as a holiday'.

I've been back to China once. For me it is always my homeland and I feel familiar with it. The economy in Shanghai has improved, which was expected: compared to Australia the living standard for the Chinese should improve. I keep in contact with my parents. I know what is happening in China, and I feel I am part of it although it is far away.

When I returned to Australia after my trip to China, the only feeling I had was depression at the thought of going back to hard work and study. But I don't want to become a person who is always a trouble to others and to the country. China is my mother's home. I have made my home in Australia.

Australian Now

Susan Ogier

Born in Birmingham, England, in 1951, Sue Ogier is the sixth child of nine. In 1965, with parents and three younger siblings, she emigrated from England to Australia where she started work in an envelope making factory in Sydney at the age of fourteen. By 16-years-of-age Sue Ogier was married and a mother of a lovely little boy. In the same year her parents returned to the United Kingdom, leaving behind a young women who was too innocent to realise the finality and isolation of such an event. Now in her forties, Sue Ogier is a mother of three boys, a grandmother, and lives in Bega, a small town on the far south coast of New South Wales.

Arrival: Sydney Harbour, Australia, New Year's Day 1965. There was my mother, father, a younger sister, two younger brothers and me. We were here as a separated family: five remained in England while the younger four of us took the trip, migrating to Australia. This separation was a strong event in our lives. It was one with which my parents never actually came to terms. We were of the £10 immigrants and had arrived in the land of sunshine where the immigration board in England had said that the Australian lifestyle meant everybody had a swimming pool and two cars and lived on a large block of land, and there were horses to ride – everything was wonderful in the land of sunshine. As a 14-year-old, the politics of the country were of no or very little interest to me. I was part of the 1960s – the flower power era. Everybody was very much into 'doing their own thing'. The Viet Nam war was taking place and the turmoil and excitement of those times remains embedded in my memory. They contributed greatly to the person I am today.

Australia: the shock of how far behind the country was. To a 14-year-old-girl, fashion was *so* far behind. And the music! It took time for new ideas to take hold and for cultural values to move from one country to another. There wasn't the instantaneous communication there is today.

Sydney Harbour: there were my Mother and Father and the small family that we had become, together with all the baggage around our legs. It was daunting. A strange country where we knew nobody. We were put onto a bus and sent to an immigration camp outside Liverpool, in Sydney's west. The camp was a condemned army barracks, the 'huts' or 'houses' being made out of half of a galvanised circle. Imagine a 44-gallon-drum sliced vertically down the middle and laid on its side. This, on a larger scale, was what we were expected to live in.

New Years Day: summertime in Australia, and we had come from an English winter. My first night in Australia was spent in these condemned barracks. There were two sections, a bedroom section and a living quarter. I woke up in the course of the night, wanting to go the toilet. I was in fear of being in a strange place in a strange country and not knowing where the toilets were, being totally alienated. I crawled out of bed and just stood there, the wet trickling down my legs and onto the floor. To this day I am left with a strong impression of the fear that overwhelmed me, preventing me from going out of that little hut to fulfill such a basic need – going to the toilet.

> I was in fear of being in a strange place in a strange country and not knowing where the toilets were, being totally alienated.

There were communal toilets, communal kitchens, communal everything in the migrant camp. There were hundreds of us immigrants, all pushed in together. We all came with the same dreams, dreams that Australia was a wonderful country. We all had the same disillusionment. I met no one who was optimistic or enthusiastic about the country. Not only had we been put into an isolated, condemned place, but the mosquitoes! No one can explain the intensity of the aggravation of mosquitoes to a new pommie – a new pommie immigrant to Australia. The mosquitoes seemed to pick us up and carry us away. Then there was the intense loss of familiar places.

Lack of transport: the only way to get into Liverpool was to get on a train, travelling on the East Hills line, which passed through Liverpool on its way to the city. Once there, the trip had to be repeated in order to get 'home'. This was a major event. The bus system was non-existent as far as an English person was concerned: we were used to having a bus going every half hour, so that if an intending passenger missed the bus she had only to wait and catch another not long after. There was I in a strange country in a strange environment with a sense around me of total and utter lack of confidence, lack of belief that we had done the right thing. The fear was enforced by everyone living around us, at that time, in that migration camp.

We escaped from the immigration camp as soon as we could. We were the fortunate ones. My father had been transferred with his job. He was in the motor industry and had to travel to Zetland every day. This required a bus and train journey. I went looking for work. At 14-years-of-age my mother thrust money into my hand at the train station, saying to me: 'Go into the city and get a job.' Fourteen-years-of-age. I did that. I still marvel. I got onto the train and went into the city. I applied for a job, which was very easy to obtain in those days. Times have changed so dramatically, for in those days a person could go out and get employment without any drama. That day I returned home, with a job.

We moved to Ingleburn, which was even further out in the western suburbs. I arose every morning, walked a 2 km walk down to the train station, caught a train to Liverpool, changed trains at Liverpool station, travelled into the city centre, changed trains again, then travelled to the northern side. It was a great amount of travelling each day for anyone, particularly someone as young as I was. I earned £10-a-week, paying my parents £5-a-week for board. My travelling costs were 30-shillings-a-week. I had very little money left over.

I enrolled in nightschool typing courses. Home life was terrible. By now, we lived in a house with no indoor plumbing. I slept on the couch because we couldn't afford a bed. The lifestyle was so different from what I had grown up with. In England we had a four bedroom house, with an upstairs toilet, and downstairs toilet. Life was comfortable. I walked into the city centre of Birmingham, a very very big city. Life was familiar, I had friends and everything was easy for me. I had traded this in to live in Australia, in a place without indoor plumbing, mosquitoes that would carry you away, a wretched lifestyle, miserable parents, a brother who was victimised terribly at school because he was an intellectual type: he was constantly being pommie bashed. Now a teacher in London, to this day he has never returned, and if Australia is ever discussed he advises people never to go to Australia – it is a place (he says) where you would not dare to tread. His memories are so vivid that he is a terrible ambassador for the country. I cannot blame him for his personal experiences.

1967: a big year for me. My first son was born. I married two months after his birth. It was my sixteenth birthday. My mother and father, younger sister and two brothers returned to England that same year, leaving me behind. I was a 16-year-old mother in a country 12 000 miles away. Bringing up two small children and living in a foreign country alone, without any family support, was a daunting experience. But it had positive effects on me. It made me a decisive, strong person who knows what is right for herself.

In 1988 my father passed away. I returned home to England after having been away for 21 years. England was as alien to me as Australia had been when I originally arrived. I realised I had become a true Australian. I was more comfortable with my familiar surroundings which were now Australia. Australia was my home. But to see my family was wonderful. I realised how much I had missed, especially in the growing years of 14 to 24, without the interaction of my sisters. Now, there was instant bonding. We had the same roots, we understood where we had come from, there was no need for words. Yet they had a more passive nature than I. They had more of a tendency to accept the way of the world without questioning. I suppose they came to some apposite conclusions about me: I had become very much a colonial girl. They said: 'Sue is so strong,' 'Sue is so capable.' I became strong and capable out of necessity.

Australia was my home. But to see my family was wonderful.

I stayed in England for four weeks. It was hard to leave – not the country, but the family. The country no longer has any attraction for me. It has no deep roots into my soul or my psyche. I am now Australian. After returning from the trip I applied for Australian citizenship, so now I have dual citizenship. But I am 100 per cent Australian.

My life experiences have provided me with a great foundation for my work as a support worker for women's housing. I have an understanding and an openness and empathy for working with women. Even if I haven't directly experienced what they have, I find I am able to extend the empathy from within, not just on a superficial level. I am a good Australian, with three Australian sons and a lifestyle I am proud of. I am proud of who I am and what I am. Being in Australia has contributed to that.

Australians in Alaska

Jan Mock

The Laker family emmigrated to
Australia in 1958. Jan Mock
(nee Laker) was born 6 April 1951
in Benenden, Kent, England.
She completed her secondary
education in north-east Victoria and
Melbourne and graduated from
Monash University in 1973 having
completed an honours degree in
science and a diploma in education.
Since 1974, for the greater majority
of this time, Jan Mock has taught
in secondary colleges in Victoria.
Her interests include travelling,
bushwalking, cross country skiing, tennis and meeting people.

My family background has had an enormous impact on my life. There always have to be influences on one's life, and with most people the family is often the most influential. My parents are English, as are my brother and myself. I was born in 1951 and my brother, Richard, was born two years later in 1953.

After serving with the British Army in Sudan, my paternal grandfather transferred to the Indian Army. When my mother was only a few months old, in 1930, she went to India to live, where she spent the next 18 years. When she was three or four her parents separated, ultimately divorcing. My grandfather had custody of my mother, whilst my mother's sister and brother remained with their mother and returned to England. Due to the nature of army life, my mother could not live a 'normal' family life with her father. She spent all her school years in catholic boarding schools in northern India, seeing her father infrequently. During the second world war, my grandfather was killed and my mother, at 18-years-of-age, was sent 'home' to England to her mother, who apart from being almost a total stranger, had remarried. After matriculating and attending college, which she had to finance herself, my mother worked in a school and an office before meeting and marrying my father, who was 21 years her senior. They married in 1950. My father died in 1989 at the age of 80 and throughout their married life my parents love of each other remained very strong.

In contrast, my father's family had lived in Kent, England, for generations, rarely travelling beyond their nearest village. My father was one of five children. His brothers and sisters were married with teenage children before he met my mother. Dad, like all unmarried people of his era, lived with his parents. The situation suited the family, as the ageing parents were being taken care of and Dad often generously helped his brothers and sisters financially. For my father to be thinking of marriage at 40-years-of-age, after apparently showing little interest or desire to do so, came as a bit of a shock for some members of the family. Initially, my mother was not made terribly welcome; indeed one of Dad's sisters never did accept the idea.

My parents disregarded Canada due to its climate. Rhodesia, as it then was, New Zealand and Australia were all possibilities.

Living in England during the second world war and the years up to our departure from England in 1958 was not particularly easy, especially when rationing was in. My parents could see only hard times ahead, with few opportunities for their children. With the death of both my grandmothers within six weeks of each other in 1957, there seemed little to keep my parents in England. Active immigration programs to various Commonwealth countries were operating at the time, and my parents began to plan for a different life.

My father had always been employed with the forestry in England and so the enquiries with regard to immigrating were made in this area. My parents disregarded Canada due to its climate. Rhodesia, as it then was, New Zealand and Australia were all possibilities. Due to racial problems in Kenya, my parents ruled out Rhodesia (now Zimbabwe). New Zealand could promise a job in a very isolated area only, where hunting, shooting and fishing were the only pastimes. Going to New Zealand would also have meant that my brother and I would have had to go to boarding school. That was not what my parents wished for us. This left Australia, which had the added advantage of my mother's sister and husband (who were already living in Melbourne) being prepared to sponsor my family coming to Australia. The culmination was that my family arrived in Melbourne aboard the P & O ship, the *Strathnaver*, on 19 February, 1958. Our fares cost a total of £20: £10 pounds each for my mother and father.

My father and mother really loved the six week trip in the ship, leaving a wintry England to arrive in sunny Australia. The voyage was one long holiday for us all, even though we were third class passengers with our cabin situated close to the engine room.

My parents thought that Australia would give them everything that England couldn't; after all they had been told that in all the advertising propaganda. This illusion was quickly shattered. After a few days in Melbourne with my aunt and uncle, we set off to commence our new life. My father had a job waiting for him with APM (Australian Paper Manufacturers) in the La Trobe Valley. He was to work in the pine forests and a house was supplied. Sounded good, but no one told us where this house was. Somehow we found our way to our new address four miles south of Driffield, which in those days boasted a primary school and a school house. Our nearest town was Morwell, 20 miles away on a dirt road! After living in built up south-east England, we arrived on the doorstep and could not see another house in any direction. The house had no electricity or telephone and its water supply was a very small water tank, which constantly needed filling up. To top it all off, the house, being so neglected, was infested with rats and mice. Laying traps every night appeared to do little to cull our pests and so on good advice my parents laid Ratsak, after which (they had been assured) the rats and mice would seek water when they were about to die. Some may have, but lots never found the water; instead they fell down the wall cavities within the house. The stench was so dreadful that Dad ended up ripping out the wall-linings in order to clean away the dead and decaying bodies...and this was supposed to be utopia. If my parents could have caught another ship then for England right then, we would have been on it.

During our first whole summer in 1958-59, we experienced a significant heatwave. Apples were burnt on the branch. Our relatives in England thought the heat had got to my parents, as they had never heard of anything as absurd as apples cooking on the trees.

Probably the worst aspect of living in south of Driffield was our total isolation. Although my parents left England with little money they didn't contemplate that they would need to buy a car; they had never needed one in England! My father was picked up for work and dropped off afterwards. My brother, aged five and I at seven years, had to walk four miles each way to school. Sometimes we would be lucky enough to be given a lift in one of the quarry trucks that used the road daily. I still remember 'Ray' with great affection – I am sure he timed his early run to the quarry, so that he could pick us up and take us to school. I can't recall being so lucky for the walk back home! After a while my mother bought a push bike to ride into Morwell to get our supplies; as soon as we were able my parents bought a Vesper scooter, which made life a bit easier.

One event which highlighted our isolation and particularly our lack of transportation occurred soon after we arrived. One afternoon our entire school population, which was very small, went for a walk towards the nearby creek. I stumbled and fell onto my right side. I was aware that I had hurt my arm, but nothing could be done about it at school and so at the end of the day I walked home with my brother, as usual. Meanwhile, my arm continued to hurt and swell. My parents sensed that all was not well, but what were they to do? Fortunately a fellow student recounted the story of me hurting my arm to his family that evening, whereupon his father came to our house to see if I was alright. He ended up taking us into a medical clinic that evening. I had broken my right wrist.

Living under these conditions was distressing for us all, particularly for my mother, who was so very isolated.

Our passages back to England were booked several times only to be cancelled because something positive happened...

My memories of this period of my life include constant talk about returning to England. Our passages back to England were booked several times only to be cancelled because something positive happened, such as our being given a different house, which had electricity and a 'chip' hot water system, or my father taking a different job in north-east Victoria. These changes encouraged us to 'give it one more chance'. We were obliged to stay in Australia for two years; this was a stipulation of the immigration program.

My brother and I were soon 'Australianised'. At our first school in Driffield, we spent many play times and lunch times sitting under the Cyprus trees with a large group of other children teaching us to speak 'Australian'. They obviously did an excellent job as I have not been recognised as an English person since those days. Only this year, some 35 years later, someone asked me why I didn't sound English like my mother. Her accent is as strong today as it was the day she arrived in Australia.

Amongst all the agony of such a relocation there are always some amusing anecdotes. For our first Christmas my mother wanted to buy some 'mince meat' for 'mince pies'. She asked for it at the grocers to be told rather abruptly that butchers sell mince meat. The butcher certainly did sell mince meat; it turned out that she was wanting fruit mince, which she finally found at the grocers.

As teenagers, my brother and I regularly became patriotic when test cricket was being played between Australia and England. Although the two of us never felt terribly British, we were unable to barrack for the Australian team and it seemed we were unable to barrack for the English team quietly! We have had many sparring moments over the outcomes of a cricket match, which have generally always been in good fun. Even to this day, I find it impossible to barrack with any real heart for the Aussies, and never when they are playing the English team. This patriotism does not extend to other sports, funnily enough.

When we first arrived in Australia, a British subject had the same status as an 'Australian'; there was no difference. After Gough Whitlam became Prime Minister in 1972, British subjects could become naturalised Australians. This notion was totally out of the question for my mother. Dad felt very Australian anyway and probably was ambivalent towards his citizenship. As a teenager and young woman, I did not consider changing my nationality. I still haven't, although I have now contemplated it and even sent for the papers to do it, in 1988. The idea of attending a very public ceremony is not appealing to me (although I believe one can become naturalised in private), as that would expose the 'lie' I have been living all these years: many people do not know I am English. Sometimes I have deliberately concealed it to avoid being teased, whilst generally I can't be bothered explaining for yet another time, that yes I am really English and yes I would rather live in Australia than England and yes I have been back for a visit and so on and on. Today, being married to an Australian and having two Australian children, I see more reasons to be a naturalised Australian than I did in the past. The main reason holding me back, apart from not getting around to it, is that I want to ensure that my children can use my birthright to travel on a British passport and more importantly to be able to work in any EEC (European Economic Community, now EC) country, if they so desire one of these days. Ultimately, however, it is simply another task I have to get around to doing.

Being English in Australia meant that a lot of our family conversations revolved around a recent letter from a relative, some memory of what had happened back 'home', and if we were in England now what would we be doing. Having left England at such a young age and coming to live in such a different country, I had nonetheless built up quite a knowledge of where we lived, who my aunts and uncles were, and the various customs that made up our lives in Britain. **As I grew older I felt confused as to what I really remembered, as opposed to what I had learnt through our conversations and photographs.** I then resolved that at the end of my first year of teaching I would return to England to see it all for myself. I did. I found that I had remembered very little. I enjoyed my trip, but it was sufficient to quench my desire to learn more about where I had come from. When my husband, Kevin, and I were contemplating going overseas for our long service leave in 1988, together with our children, Peta and Andrew, (twins then aged seven years), we did not consider going to England. I realised, then, that I had severed my ties with England. It was then that I wrote for the papers to become naturalised.

Although I grew up feeling basically Australian, for as long as I can remember I have had a desire to travel overseas. Fortunately I married a man who shared that desire. In 1989, we spent our three months long service leave in Europe. As with any holiday in a different place, those on holiday are outsiders looking on, wondering what life is *really* like in a particular spot with a particular culture and environment. On our return from Europe, and on the very first day back at work, we were told I had the opportunity to take up an International Teaching Fellowship for 12 months in Anchorage, Alaska. This came as a surprise, but as we had just returned from overseas it seemed all we had to do was just catch another plane. Our children began to think this was a normal way of living and, after consulting an atlas, told us where else in the world they would like to go!

After the initial excitement wore off we began to consider seriously the implications of going. Our major concerns revolved around how we would survive in the climate, especially as we would be leaving Australia in January 1990, to arrive in a cold and dark Alaska. We decided to take the opportunity without too much deliberation, as it sounded too good to be true. As with many different and perhaps frightening situations that have confronted me, I reason that if other people can cope or achieve certain goals then I certainly can do it too. We read as much about Anchorage as we could find, which was not much, and tried to accept that Anchorage experienced a 'temperate' climate. It is amazing what tourist publications will print, isn't it? That year we experienced the coldest Anchorage February and November on record.

As it turned out, Kevin, my husband, accepted the fellowship instead of me: I was ineligible, because I was working four-days-a-week with the Ministry of Education then, instead of five-days-a-week.

The other major factor we had to consider was money. The fellowship did not provide any financial assistance, so we had to find the air fares ourselves. The fellowship was limited to organising an exchange of teachers. This meant Kevin and his exchange teacher exchanged jobs and houses. Kevin was to be paid at the same rate as he was in Victoria and I had to take leave without pay. This meant that the year would not be cheap. Kevin ended up working that year for less than half the salary of his colleagues; Alaskan teachers are relatively well paid.

Life in Alaska was different from what we had ever experienced. On arrival we were fortunate to have caring neighbours, who showed us locations of essential facilities such as the supermarket and post office. When I went to the supermarket on my own I found it with little difficulty, as it was well lit up, but to find the post office in the same complex was not so easy; even at midday on a cloudy day it is pretty dark in Anchorage at that time of the year. Hearing the children talk about the various constellations they saw in the sky while they were waiting for the school bus in the mornings was weird. The animal life is different, too, with its inherent dangers.

Moose appear to be harmless, however when they stand up to 2m at their shoulder they are an awesome sight.

Moose are common in and around Anchorage. They feed on young birch trees but when the snow is very deep they cannot forage easily for their food. This sends them into town to raid gardens and whatever else is poking up through the snow. Moose appear to be harmless, however when they stand up to 2m at their shoulder they are an awesome sight. Couple this with the fact that they will charge people and dogs and trample them; they are to be treated with respect. If a moose was in the neighbourhood the first sign was dogs barking. (I am convinced that there are nearly as many dogs in Alaska as people!) Then when someone had spotted the moose a series of phone calls were made to alert everyone as to where the moose was, and its movements were noted. One morning I even had to drive the children to school as a moose was between us and the bus stop.

Driving was another ball game; we had to come to terms with it rapidly. Not only did we have to contend with driving on the 'wrong' side of the road, but we had to cope with very icy and snowy conditions. Kevin had driven in Europe the previous year and he also drives in Australian alpine areas a lot in the winter, so he was partially prepared. I had neither driven in Europe nor in Australian mountains in the winter. I was apprehensive about driving, but realised that if I did not want to be isolated all year, I had no choice. In Alaska, public transport was non-existent where we were living. Car tyres are fitted with metal studs for winter driving and due to the very cold but dry winter climate I found it was not too bad. At the beginning and end of winter, when the snow thaws and freezes into ice, driving conditions are more hazardous, especially as most locals drive as Australians would on a dry day on the freeways. Apparently front and back bumper bars are very difficult to buy; second hand ones are impossible as there are so many bingles at intersections. The worst accident during our year in Anchorage was a 50 car pile up on a particularly icy day; as soon as someone starts to skid the rest follow suit!

I applied to do substitute teaching, relieving teachers when absent, and before I could do this, I had to be fingerprinted and pay to have my record checked out by the FBI.

Living in America is quite different from life in Australia. One of the first issues we noted was the bureaucracy we had to face. For me to gain employment, I had to acquire a work permit, but before I could do this I had to have a social security number. To organise these I had to find the Federal Building downtown and then the correct department and wait for the processing to be done. I did get a work permit after two months of hassles and then it lasted for six months only, after which I had to re-apply. I applied to do substitute teaching, relieving teachers when absent, and before I could do this, I had to be fingerprinted and pay to have my record checked out by the FBI.

I spent approximately one third of the school year working as a substitute teacher. This was not my preferred option as I thought being in Alaska was a great opportunity to try something different. I could have had numerous jobs like waitressing, but I felt that working for $4-an-hour was not very profitable and it may even cost me money to work after I took into account the cost of travelling and childcare before school, as Kevin had to leave for school at 6.30 am; he had to be at school at 7.00 am as classes started at 7.30 am. As I have an honours degree in science I explored the possibilities of working in a laboratory. I made it difficult for myself as I wanted some time off during the summer, however I was frustrated in that no one really viewed my qualifications seriously; degrees are a 'dime a dozen' in the USA. (If ever I were to attempt such a venture again, I would endeavour to obtain a letter to explain the quality of my qualification.) Nonetheless, one person was interested in hiring me for a laboratory job with the Defence Department, however the contract was delayed, putting me out of contention. This prospective employer was not American and seemed to have some understanding of my capabilities and training.

The year taught me that being employed was very important to me. It gives me a certain identity, that makes me feel myself. Like a lot of women, I don't like having to rely on being someone's wife or mother. I went to Alaska thinking it would be very nice to have a year off and do some of the 'things that I had always wanted to do'. Two factors made this difficult: one was that I really needed to earn some money so we could do some vacationing in Alaska during the holidays; the other was working out what I really wanted to do, then trying to determine how I could achieve my goal in a totally foreign city and country. I also suffered from a typical female syndrome: feeling guilty for indulging myself when I knew Kevin was not enjoying his situation. He thought I was mad for feeling guilty and tried to encourage me to look after myself and take advantage of this opportunity; as he said, if he had the opportunity he certainly would. I believed him and it made sense, yet I still found it very difficult.

Alaskans were generally excited to meet Australians. Almost every single Alaskan had seen *Crocodile Dundee* and *Crocodile Dundee II*, at least once. They were fascinated with our expression of 'G'day' and could not believe that it was used extensively. One day walking down one of the hallways in a senior high school, I recognised a student and said 'G'day' as I normally would at home. The student's reaction was of complete surprise: you really do say 'G'day'. I am indebted to Crocodile Dundee and to my wonderful 'Australian' accent; I spent many a session in all sorts of schools in Anchorage talking about Australia. I am sure life for me as a substitute teacher was more pleasant because I was Australian rather than American, and I am certain that the students were being educated at the same time!

All of us experienced some difficulty in making ourselves understood, in that words we were using had no meaning to Americans. Three examples were 'fortnight', 'backyard' and 'cotton reels'. Our children had difficulty with 'rest room'; they thought that the school was providing a room for them to have a sleep in if they needed it. Andrew also asked his male teacher for a 'rubber'; fortunately the teacher thought there must be some difficulty with the language and waited for Andrew to describe it as the 'soft pink thing usually found on the end of a pencil'!

North Americans generally have little knowledge of things that are not American and so found it hard to believe that we lead similar lives to them. The senior students whom Kevin taught were amazed that he could drive a car. Andrew was asked if he knew what a helicopter was as one flew overhead. This attitude was frustrating initially but, ultimately, the people we mixed with, grew used to us and we to them.

Living in a different climate, environment and culture was exciting. However we were all anxious to get home again. Now we would love to go back for an extended holiday or even to live for some years, if we did not have to rely on teaching. Before we left Australia for Alaska we reasoned that a year is not very long and that we could put up with almost anything for that period. I am sure that is true, however if a person is feeling homesick, lonely or just 'out of sorts', a year can be a long time. Nonetheless, given the same opportunity we would all take it. Life is too short to let opportunities of this sort pass you by.

From Australia to Canada, and Again

Sandra K. McCallum

Sandra Kathleen McCallum was born in Melbourne, Australia and now holds Canadian citizenship and is permanently resident in Victoria, British Columbia, Canada. After graduating from Monash University with a bachelor of jurisprudence and bachelor of laws in 1967 and 1968, she was admitted as a barrister and solicitor of the Supreme Court of Victoria and High Court of Australia. In 1974 she graduated with a master of laws from the University of British Columbia.

In 1979 Sandra McCallum became associate professor in the Faculty of Law, University of Victoria, British Columbia. She has been a member of the Law Society of British Columbia since 1981, and has published articles on conservation and on administrative law in legal journals. Amongst many other activities, from 1986 to 1988 she was director and chair of the Legal Committee of West Coast Legal Education and Action Fund (LEAF), an equality rights group which mounts court challenges, and has been instructor and course director for various administrative law training programs for Canadian provincial and federal departments, boards and commissions. She holds many current positions, including director of the Canadian Council of Administrative Tribunals, director of the Victoria Civic Heritage trust, and is a member of the British Columbia Liquor Appeal Board and of the Commercial Appeals Commission.

My roots in Australia are deep. My father's family came with the first free settlers to Tasmania in the 1830s. My maternal grandmother was born in Hamilton, Victoria, in 1880 and in the 1880s my maternal grandfather emigrated to Victoria from Ireland.

I grew up in Melbourne – St Kilda to be exact – in comfortable circumstances. I was the younger of two children, my brother being two years older. He, like the other members of my immediate family, has never stepped foot outside Australia.

We walked to the local school, we played tennis at the nearby courts, and we swam at the beach across the road from our house. After primary school, I was selected, along with five others from my school, to go to MacRobertson Girls High where, in 1962, I matriculated and was head prefect.

Those familiar with MacRob will know it as a competitive and selective institution, demanding excellence from its students. Some say the school creates, or at least encourages, over achievers. Be that as it may, I am grateful for its influence. It was a good background. The seeds of inquiry and curiosity which eventually led me to an academic career were planted there.

In 1963 I commenced first year arts at the then new Monash University in Melbourne. The university was so small that every member of the student population of approximately 800 knew everyone else. We ate in the only cafeteria, the basement of the first stage of the Menzies Building; now that building is a monstrous edifice.

In 1964 the Faculty of Law began and I transferred to it, graduating with the first class honours in 1969. I articled with a Melbourne firm and during my articling year had an offer from a law publishing firm to join their editorial staff at its Sydney office. For a fairly sheltered 23-year-old, the practice of law was something of a rough awakening, and it was not surprising that an offer to do something less demanding and perhaps less practical seemed attractive.

The university was so small that every member of the student population of approximately 800 knew everyone else.

I was still living at home. As a student, one could not afford to do otherwise. I imagined that the move to Sydney would be a great opportunity. It was also a way to branch out on my own. Flattered by the offer, I accepted it. I became a resident tutor at Women's College at Sydney University which gave me accommodation, a base and 'a family'.

Not surprisingly, the editorial job was a disaster. One member of staff worked at a high Dickensian style desk. The compulsory morningtea breaks were dominated by the chief who held court. She insisted that one be at one's desk as the clock struck nine. I recall dozing off in the middle of a proof-reading session, a grave misdemeanour. For someone with a new law degree and keen to do something innovative, this was high tedium, and I knew that I was in the wrong place. Perhaps the active and cooperative atmosphere of learning and partnership at both my school and university had ill-suited me to the rigid hierarchy of this old company. Personnel knew it and so did I. After three weeks I admitted I had made a mistake. The rigidity of the company is best illustrated by their response. Monthly pay, therefore monthly notice was required. So instead of lasting there three weeks, I ended up having to stay seven!

During this time I reluctantly contemplated moving back to Melbourne. It was necessary for me to speak to the principal at Women's College for, after all, I had committed myself to stay there for at least the academic year. Fate intervened. Within the same week the vice-principal of Women's College announced her plans to leave, and I was offered her job. At the age of 24 I became the youngest vice-principal of Women's College. What an interesting four years lay ahead of me! I truly loved the job, and I look back on my time there with wonder and affection. Women's College was home and its members my family. Many of the senior common room are still close friends who have visited me in Canada.

At that time Australians revered 'overseas experience' and if I were to return with stature that was what I had to obtain. I settled on Canada.

While at Women's College I did some teaching in law but my role was mainly administrative and ran the gamut from assisting students with academic and personal issues, supervising and hiring domestic staff, arranging vacation conference bookings and even fixing the furnace and dealing with burst pipes, leaking roofs and all sorts of major maintenance. It was also a time of learning, debate, ideas and challenges. The constant stimulation of visiting scholars and the excitement people conveyed about their research was infectious. I am sure this experience eventually caused me to turn to an academic career.

An academic career meant graduate school so, with the principal's encouragement, I sorted out various options. At that time Australians revered 'overseas experience' and if I were to return with stature that was what I had to obtain. I settled on Canada. It is difficult to remember all the reasons why. No doubt it was partly because of the opportunity of doing comparative research in a contemporary parliamentary federal system, partly because I was going out with a man who was planning to work in Canada. By the time I left, we had parted ways, so when I chose Canada it was in spite of him rather than because of him.

Eventually I accepted a graduate fellowship at the Faculty of Law, University of British Columbia, to do a master of laws in environmental law, which in 1973 was a relatively new field. I left Sydney with mixed feelings and misgivings; the Women's College had been a comfortable home for four years. I remember the day though not the date. It was the week of the official opening of the Sydney Opera House somewhere in mid-1973. I was probably the only person who had an official invitation to the opening yet who was leaving instead of coming to town. I flew Canadian Pacific Airlines from Sydney to Honolulu where I stopped for a few days, then went on to Vancouver. In Honolulu I had a feeling of absolute freedom. I was in limbo. The past was past and the future had not begun. There was nothing left undone and no work waiting for my return. It was an almost unique time, unusual in what has usually been a chaotic life.

I entered Canada on a student visa, which allowed me to remain for two years: all visas were for two years but I had needed only one. I had no doubt I would be going home. A number of students asked if I wanted to come to Seattle, destroy the visa, and then re-enter Canada illegally. Ironically, the amnesty provisions in effect in early 1974 made this the preferred way of obtaining landed immigrant status. I could not see the point. I did not even contemplate it as I planned to return home.

My graduate year was enjoyable. I joined a group of hopeless adults, all Australian, New Zealand or English, all keen to learn to ski but completely untalented. Eventually I succeeded, but not before a series of instructors were reduced to nervous wrecks. I also discovered muffins and Mexican food, and I even began to understand that although on paper the Australian and Canadian federal systems were much the same, the reality was quite different. A Canadian in one seminar was amazed when I explained that appointments to the High Court of Australia over the years were dominated by the heavier populated states of New South Wales and Victoria. Canadians were outraged and could not believe that residents of other states would not demand more equal representation on the court from among their residents. In Canada, regional representation together with a balance between French and English, Protestant and Catholic dominates all federal appointments, particularly the cabinet, the courts, boards and tribunals. Those of Irish origin, who were Catholic but English speaking, are excellent compromise candidates. Jewish candidates, who are almost all English speaking but not Protestant, are similarly sought after.

He advised that I get some boots and an umbrella and come to the law school regardless of the rain. I did and I used them often.

On a sunny day Vancouver is majestic. I was awed by the mountains. In winter, however, sunny days are rare. At first I thought I would work at home on rainy days but when I suggested that to my supervisor, he laughed and told me that he would never see me if I did that. He advised that I get some boots and an umbrella and come to the law school regardless of the rain. I did and I used them often.

In the spring of 1974, the dean of law at the University of British Columbia offered me a position on the faculty. I declined. I did not know what I would do after I finished my graduate work, but I did know that I was going home. Some time that spring I resiled slightly, as I accepted a job as a consultant to the federal Law Reform Commission in Ottawa in its new administrative law project. Some of the research was related to my master's thesis and I had the opportunity to work with Gerald La Forest, now a Justice of the Supreme Court of Canada. The federal Law Reform Commission had been formed in 1973 and it was an exciting place, full of new and interesting people. My year was a very positive one. All of us, no matter how junior or senior, had been hired because we had something to contribute. There was mutual respect, and an acceptance of an equality amongst unequals. I have never worked so hard and never in such a stimulating atmosphere.

If living in Ottawa was a new experience, so was the weather. When I moved to Vancouver I thought it had a cold climate. After arriving in Ottawa, I never thought so again. My apartment was only six blocks from where I was working, yet in mid-winter with temperatures sometimes down to 30 degrees (Fahrenheit) below freezing, I often had to stop in an office complex at the mid point in order to thaw out. Any exposed part of me tingled with cold, despite my boots, hat, gloves and huge coat.

Cross country skiing was popular among my colleagues, and my bumbling talent was up to it in a minor way. There was a cosmopolitan market, an active national art centre and an active anglo-Catholic Parish where I felt very much at home. One magical memory of Ottawa is walking home after midnight mass on Christmas eve with a light snow falling and a very jolly Santa winding his way down one of the main streets ho hoing all the way. Life in Ottawa was good.

...the Law Reform Commission was required to post the job across the country to see if there were any out of work Canadian lawyers who might want the position

In May of 1975 the Law Reform Commission asked me to stay on for another year. To do this I had to extend my visa. I was happy to do so, but it turned out to be not so easy. I had to seek permission from the Immigration Department. To my surprise, the Law Reform Commission was required to post the job across the country to see if there were any out of work Canadian lawyers who might want the position (even though the Law Reform Commission had said unemployed lawyers were not appropriate to fill this specialised research position). In the end I received a six month's extension. If I had begun to waver about returning to Australia, my mind had now been made up for me.

In the same month an advertisement from the Commonwealth Public Service appeared in the Canadian national papers as part of the campaign by the Labor government to bring home Australians and stop the brain drain. I was a target of that campaign.

I was interviewed for a job at the Department of Urban and Regional Development and to my delight was accepted. The department was to pay for my return expenses but for some odd reason not from Canada but from England. In the end the Law Reform Commission paid for my airfare between Canada and England and the Australian government paid the rest. It seemed to me ironic that a Labor government paid for a first-class ticket! I left Canada late in September of 1975 with few regrets. In truth there was a personal one. A promise to write never materialised. I loaded myself with things Canadian to take home as souvenirs, for I knew I would not be back.

After a leisurely trip home via London, Athens, Rome and Penang, I arrived at Melbourne airport on 11 November 1975. My brother met me and I remember him saying if it is the federal Labor government you think you are working for, you should know they have just been sacked. A few days later I called Canberra and ascertained that there was still a job waiting for me.

I waited in Melbourne to have Christmas with my family and then flew to Canberra where the government had promised temporary accommodation. I had been looking forward to this as in Ottawa, temporary accommodation provided by the Law Reform Commission gave me a suite in an hotel with a generous meal allowance for restaurant service. By contrast in Canberra, there was a government hostel with hostel-like food. It certainly encouraged one to find a place of one's own quite quickly, which was not easy. The difference between temporary accommodation offered by the federal government in Ottawa and the federal government in Canberra was in many ways symbolic of the difference in government style. I was rediscovering the hierarchal structure which I had found so stultifying before I left Australia.

On the whole, I liked Canberra but had forgotten about the hierarchal nature of both social and work environments in Australia. In the workplace there was a great distinction between those with a small cubbyhole called an office and those without. It was so different from the Canadian Law Reform Commission where we each had a small office and any idea, if it were good, would reach the top and be attributed to its author. Not so in Canberra. The credit for any idea had to be with someone senior. Often I found my ideas or those of other junior people recycled without credit by someone who had too often confused or muddled them on the way up the hierarchal line.

In the workplace there was a great distinction between those with a small cubbyhole called an office and those without.

I had been enticed to return to Australia with the challenge of a federal program in conservation and heritage. The Liberal government now in power planned to dismantle federal involvement in such programs. My job now changed from creating the programs to dismembering them. I did not like it nor did I like the internal interdepartmental meetings which appeared to be designed for each department to protect its turf and ensure that any innovation was eventually lost through inertia or exhaustion.

By early 1976 I had seen an advertisement for a senior law reform officer at the Law Reform Commission of Australia situated in Sydney. There seemed two good reasons to move. First, my wonderful memories of my experience at the Law Reform Commission of Canada and secondly, my past happy days of living in Sydney. As it turned out, this attempt to return to a happy double past was an error.

I left Canberra and moved to Sydney where I still owned a flat. I had not realised that many of the friends whom I had met during my time at Women's College were, like myself, transients; they were no longer in Sydney. I still had a base at my favourite Anglican Church, Christ Church St Laurence, so spiritually was very much at home. Church life was the only remnant (albeit an important one) of my previous connections in Sydney.

The Law Reform Commission of Australia and the Law Reform Commission of Canada was similar in name only. The hierarchy that had frustrated me in Canberra was no different at the offices of Commission in

Sydney. In contrast to the free exchange of ideas in Canada, here the only attributed ideas were those of the Commissioners. The role of the staff was to make those Commissioners look good without sharing the spotlight.

For some reason, I cannot recall now what it was, the Commission approved my travel to Canada to research freedom of information and privacy developments. I jumped at the opportunity and once back in Canada, knew that I would be returning more permanently. In Fredericton, New Brunswick I was talking to people at the Attorney General's Department about their new freedom of information legislation when a former colleague at the Law Reform Commission who was now back teaching at the law school in Fredericton told me that they were looking for a colleague in administrative and environmental law, both fields of mine. I interviewed and was offered the job and the process of obtaining landed immigrant status began.

I was elated. I returned to Sydney, sold my property and possessions and waited for the Canadian immigration process to run its course. In June I left Sydney, visited the United Kingdom, landed in Halifax and then on to Fredericton. This time I was a landed immigrant and I knew I was in Canada to stay.

Landing in Fredericton: it was mid-summer 1977 and the province was embroiled in a liquor strike, something completely unknown on this scale in Australia. There was not a drink to be had or a bottle to be bought in the province. In Canada liquor distribution and sale is a government monopoly. My duty free offerings made me popular for a day or two.

When I tried to tell my Mother where I was now living in Canada, she could not find it on the map. It was not until I told her that Fredericton was where Anne of Green Gables, from nearby Prince Edward Island, came to shop that she had some idea of where in this vast continent I was living.

Fredericton was settled by Empire Loyalists, those Americans who had fought for the Crown during the Revolutionary war, and been exiled for their loyalty. It is attractive and friendly, a small but pleasant place, particularly to raise a family. Yet I was single and at times it did seem small.

Fredericton had great seafood. In the Saturday market you could get three lobsters for $10.00. The market also introduced me to headcheese and to very expensive hand-fed lamb. As a new North American, I assumed that every city had the same service driven approach as one read of in stories of New York and San Francisco. With this in my mind, I went to Sears to stock up on furniture and supplies for my apartment. Here it was different. There was a three week delay on most things that had to come by special order. When I expressed some surprise, the salesperson reminded me that Fredericton was not New York.

In the Saturday market you could get three lobsters for $10.00. The market also introduced me to headcheese and to very expensive hand-fed lamb.

After two years at the University of New Brunswick I was invited to take up an appointment at the relatively new law faculty at the University of Victoria in British Columbia. At first I was ambivalent about the invitation but the Dean insisted I come out and look at the university. It was February 1979. I left deep snow in Fredericton and flew out to Victoria where the daffodils were up, the skies were clear and it was at least thirty degrees warmer. I was now on the west coast and although the Pacific Ocean is much colder in Canada than in Australia, it was still the Pacific. I felt very much closer to my roots.

I accepted the job and flew to Victoria on 9 June 1979, complete with all my luggage and a box of twelve live New Brunswick lobsters (an east coast symbol and popular gift).

If one is looking to a place similar to an Australian setting in Canada, it probably would be found in British Columbia. Although the geography resembles New Zealand's South Island, the coastal lifestyle and the milder climate are the closest I can come to experiencing something akin to Australia.

I took up my appointment as an associate professor at the University of Victoria in July 1979 and began teaching that fall. One of my teaching assignments involved liaising with a visiting professor at the School of Public Administration, David Anderson, on a course involving the legal foundations of public administration, which we taught jointly. Our liaison exceeded all expectations. David came to Australia in October 1982 and we married at St Peter's Eastern Hill in Melbourne in November 1982. We now have two children – James born in 1984 and Zoe born in 1988.

David is now a member of the federal parliament and I am still with the Faculty of Law at the University of Victoria. I never told my parents that I had given up my Australian citizenship in order to become Canadian. (Citizenship was required before one could be called to the British Columbia Bar.) With two children and a spouse born in Victoria (British Columbia, not Australia!) and I a Canadian citizen since 1981, Canada is very much now my home. However, while my parents were still alive I returned to Australia annually to see them. In 1982 I spent a six month's sabbatical leave there teaching at Monash University. To work in Australia as a Canadian citizen I needed a work permit. This rather pointedly reminded me that I was no longer considered Australian.

After our son was born in 1984 we planned to fly back to Melbourne to show my parents their grandson. Although I had now been a Canadian citizen for three years, it never occurred to me that I could not visit Australia as a tourist without obtaining a visa for myself let alone my six-week-old son. It was necessary, and I was refused boarding at the departure lounge. We had to delay our trip for 48 hours while a visa was processed. Getting the visa required a long and tiring day of bureaucratic coolness as minor officials seemed intent on punishing me for taking out Canadian citizenship. Obviously proud to be Canadian, but also proud to be Australian born, I do regret that there is not an opportunity for dual citizenship. New Zealand's practice seems more civilised and practical in this regard.

Because I am no longer a citizen of Australia, returning for extended periods is unlikely. The complications and lack of job prospects for a 'foreigner' are serious obstacles. I sometimes, rather impractically, imagine returning to live. I know I see Australia through rose coloured glasses. We have spent most of our holidays in Australia in the past ten years. Each time we return, we are overwhelmed by the hospitality of friends who concertina into a few weeks more activity and excitement than we probably spend in a normal year. A return to Australia always includes some Vegemite, lamingtons, roast lamb dinners and numerous visits to byo bistros. Memories that draw me to Australia include drinking Champagne with David in 1982 on the outer terrace of the Sydney Opera House at intermission while watching the boats go by; sitting in VIP seats at the Myer Music Bowl for Carols by Candlelight and listening to John Diedrich sing the *Battle Hymn of the Republic* to tens of thousands of people on the lawns on a warm summer's night.

> A return to Australia always includes some vegemite, lamingtons, roast lamb dinners and numerous visits to byo bistros.

More recently in 1991 we spent six weeks in Australia with our children who happily galloped on the beach at Noosa Heads, squealed with delight as they fed kangaroos at Lone Pine Sanctuary, and were wide-eyed as they rode the rails on Puffing Billy outside Melbourne. They love the Melbourne trams and the double-decker buses of Sydney and the rolling surf at Bondi and the experience of a meat pie eaten out of a paper bag. The latter seems odd to them. In Canada, you can have pies of almost any fruit imaginable but the classic Australian meat pie is not to be found.

I have been in Canada since 1973 and when I return to Australia, I see many differences between where I now live and where I was born. The hierarchy and the need to know where you fit in the so-called classless Australian society are still evident even on casual visits. The affluence and lifestyle of the early 1980s has been trimmed in accordance with tougher economic times. My Australian university colleagues still have offices which show rank by the number of windows with the corner location reserved for the most senior of the professoriate. The small professoriate still make the key decisions to the exclusion of others. It is apparent that the civil service is still based heavily on seniority. The workplace which I left still does not have the more easy going collegial atmosphere of its Canadian counterpart. Although it is a generalisation, with many exceptions, Canadians appear to respect merit more than seniority.

Yet there have been many positive changes in Australia, too. The mulga-wood and fake Aboriginal art has given way to sophisticated merchandise expressing a unique diverse and confident Australian society. It is not just

Ken Done but other fashion leaders who provide the stockman's coat, the distinctive wines and the famous byo bistros.

Although I rarely say petrol when I mean gas, or a fortnight instead of two weeks, or America rather than the States, I find that a strange nostalgia creeps over me when I read, as I try to do often, Australian novels and see such phrases as a sticky wicket, out for a duck, 'chook', footpath, chemist, and uni. There is a language I do not use any more but still can comprehend.

I have been lucky in Canada; I have been welcomed by an affectionate extended family whose roots go back a long way. But my roots in Canada are not yet 20 year's old and in order to commune with the friends of my youth and the people with whom I grew up, I need, from time to time, to return to Australia. There are no substitutes for the friends of the 1950s and 1960s. You cannot recreate them, you cannot replace them, nor would I want to.

The Kind of Belonging

Kristin Henry

A writer and poet, Kristin Henry has been active in the community writing movement for many years. She teaches and organises community writing programs in a variety of contexts, including schools, prisons and community centres. She is particularly interested in helping women to find their voices so that they can tell their stories. In 1989 a Community Writing Fellowship from the Literature Board of the Australia Council enabled her to set up writing workshops with country women throughout north-west Victoria.

Kristin Henry has published two collections of poetry, *Slices of Wry*, 1985, Pariah Press; and *One Day She Catches Fire*, 1992, Penguin. Her latest book, *Talking Up a Storm*, published in 1993 by Hale Iremonger, recounts the experiences and views of the 1970s consciousness groups of which she, together with co-author Marlene Derlet, was a member. Her loves include talking, feeding people, her women friends and her great family.

I came to Australia from the United States of America with my parents and younger brother in June 1965. I was 17-years-old. My father had met an American man back in the United States who operated a business here and he invited Dad to join him. Dad came six months before the rest of the family to get established, but by the time we arrived he had already parted company with the other American, so I don't think we really came because of any job. I think we came because my father was always looking for a greener pasture, and it was the looking, rather than the finding, that was important to him.

My family was descended from a long line of comfortable smugly conservative Southerners. Ironically, we left the United States just as the country was about to experience its biggest social and political upheavals since the civil war. Up to that point I'd cared more about who was taking me out on Saturday night than who was in the White House. Suddenly I was confronted by hostile teachers and politically aware classmates about the Viet Nam war, racism and social justice. I was completely unprepared, and was forced to begin thinking about these and other issues in some depth for the first time. This was an important time in my growing up because I stopped automatically believing what my parents told me about the world outside our family.

We never went in for long range plans, or for settling down in one place. My whole life had been punctuated by packing, moving, re-establishing and packing again. We had never left the United States before but I had still managed to attend more than twenty primary schools, two junior highs and three high schools in America.

Always being the new guys in town had made us a very close nuclear family. I don't remember us talking about 'migration'. We looked on the move to Australia as just another of these short term adjustments. Change was normal for us. Where one went we all went, and wherever we all were was home. Relatives were important but we saw them only when we travelled back to Tennessee on vacations anyway, so the idea of leaving them for just a little longer, to go just a little farther away, wasn't so heart-wrenching for me.

> **My whole life had been punctuated by packing, moving, re-establishing and packing again.**

But now I'm not sure what it really cost my mother to leave her family and go to the other side of the world. My brother and I saw it as an adventure. So did my father. I never asked Mother how she felt about it, because I was a typically shallow and self-absorbed 17-year-old. She turned 40 the month we arrived here, and the enormity of what we had done hit her very forcefully.

Mother, my brother and I sailed from New Orleans directly to Sydney, the only passengers on a cargo ship owned by my father's business partner. For a month we had nobody to talk to but each other, and the Norwegian officers. The three of us each paired up with one of the ship's officers, and that's the person we spent most of our time with. It was as though each of us was on a separate journey with our own personal guide and tutor. It was our first exposure ever to other accents, other food, other ways of thinking. In many ways it was shocking to us but it was also a very good preparation for living in a foreign culture.

We knew little about Australia. I had seen a short film on the Flying Doctor Service at school and my father sent letters after he arrived, in which he tried to describe what it was like. But nothing apart from the journey really prepared us.

I wasn't interested in streets paved with gold, though I was disappointed to find they weren't filled with kangaroos. My family wasn't looking to strike it rich. What we wanted was an exotic experience, but we were ambivalent.

We were relieved not to have to learn another language but enjoyed the thought of buying things in pounds, shillings and pence, and we were charmed by the idea of a monarchy. We wanted a spectacle of difference, like tourists, but we didn't want to have to change ourselves. I think we wanted to be merely tickled instead of turned completely upside down.

Although money wasn't a factor in our coming to Australia, the comparative lack of it once we got here certainly had an impact on us. For one thing, my mother was unable to get a job that was anything like what she was used to. It was still unusual for women to be in paidwork in 1965 Australia, and unheard of for them to hold executive positions. Time and again my mother was told that she was 'over-qualified'.

...we had brought woefully inadequate clothes, believing we were coming to the sunburnt country. My mother got pneumonia almost immediately

Apart from the income it provided, working was important to Mother because she saw herself as a career woman rather than a housewife. She was lonely and isolated and dependent on my father in a way she hadn't been before. Mother found it hard to identify with the other women in the neighbourhood who seemed content to stay at home. Although she eventually made friends, she never got over that sense of being different from Australian women. She was terribly depressed for the first year we were here and it was a hard time for our family. I didn't try to understand what she was going through and resented her for not being more excited about our new home. Now I realise what it must have been like for her and regret terribly not trying harder to help her through that period.

In some ways our standard of living took a big plunge. My father hadn't prepared us for a Melbourne winter and we had brought woefully inadequate clothes, believing we were coming to the sunburnt country. My mother got pneumonia almost immediately, and spent weeks on the couch in front of a little briquette fire. We had been thermostatically controlled for years, and I honestly don't think any of us was used to enduring cold for longer than a few minutes.

Mother didn't have her own car. We came from a place where everybody over the age of 15 had a car, even me. But whereas I would have felt conspicuous with one here since none of my friends could drive, Mother just felt even more trapped.

There may have been Melburnians in 1965 who had central heating and dishwashers and clothes dryers and maids, but we never met them. Nobody we knew seemed to mind not having things Mother was accustomed to taking for granted. This made her feel very alone, and as though she'd been transported back in time to some frontier town where she was expected to behave like a pioneer woman. But I don't think any of this would have mattered so much if it hadn't suddenly dawned on her just how far away from home we were, and how hard it would be to get back if things didn't work out.

I found it all sort of exciting. People made a fuss of us, and my brother and I made lots of friends. It was some time before I experienced any sense of loss or homesickness. I never felt disillusioned because I hadn't really had any expectations, and at that age I was young enough to adapt to whatever came my way. Nonetheless, there was never any question of me striking out on my own, just as there was no thought of any of us returning to the United States alone. We didn't have that kind of family. It was sink or swim together.

For the most part our welcome here was a warm one. Some teachers at school had very anti-American sympathies because of the Viet Nam war and Coca-cola imperialism. They tended to give my brother and me a rough time. But this was outweighed by the kindness and patience we found in other teachers and fellow students. We were conservative people and Australia was a conservative country so there wasn't much to fight about.

People knew much more about where we had come from than we did about where we had come to. In those days Americans were fairly rare in the flesh and there was a certain amount of good natured curiosity about us, particularly because we came from the South and had very thick accents. The lady across the street, who thought of England as her spiritual home, took me on as a project. Finding my drawl painfully slow and unattractive, she was determined to teach me how to speak the Queen's English. Others were more generous. I discovered that English wasn't a rigid code that you could carry around with you anywhere it was spoken and be instantly, easily understood. For a start, we had to speed up our tongues and our ears to keep pace with Australians. At the same time, we enjoyed the Australian colloquialisms, many of which I don't hear any more. 'She's apples' and 'come a gutzer' made us laugh, and 'see ya after' just sounded like an unfinished sentence. The tendency to abbreviate everything (telly, lippy, Woolies, Salvos, fridge) fascinated us. We were shocked by how often people referred to each other as 'bastards' without meaning or apparently giving offence, and how upset those same people could get about 'bloody' which had no meaning at all to us.

A month or so after arriving in Melbourne, I went into Myers department store. A young sales assistant came up to me and said 'Yerroit?' It was clear that she expected some response from me, but I didn't have a clue what the question was so I just had to stand there grinning stupidly. After repeating herself a few times the young woman was running out of patience. A shopper standing next to me obviously assessed the situation, and said: 'Excuse me, she wants to know if she can help you.' Relieved, I asked the assistant where the shoe department was and she said: 'Just follow the lino.' I didn't know what a lino was so I went home.

Like many Americans before us, we asked where the bathroom was when we meant the toilet. Then, embarrassed, we'd have to come back and say that word if we wanted to avoid an even greater unpleasantness. But I suppose we drew most attention to ourselves when we used that perfectly wonderful collective pronoun 'y'all', which we did constantly until self-consciousness eventually eased it out of our lexicon. And I remember that it took some time to break the habit of saying 'yes Ma'am' and 'no Ma'am' to older women. It drove teachers especially crazy.

Above all, it seems to me that I talked more – more often to more people about more things – than my Australian peer group did. Some of that had to do with my own personality, but much of it was a cultural difference. I was more accustomed to talking with older people and in front of strangers than were Australians my age. I was more accustomed to expressing my opinions and feelings than were my mates. I remember being surprised but enlightened to discover that the word 'precocious' had negative connotations in Australia whereas it was considered a compliment in America. This was a good example of the value Australians put on knowing their place, not getting above themselves. I don't think those concepts were much at home in the American psyche. At least they weren't in ours. Some people must have found me unbearable.

We were emotionally very close to our grandparents, aunts and uncles and cousins. But it was normal for us not to be around except for Christmas and summer holidays. They had accepted my dad's restlessness years earlier, and my mother's willingness to go along with it, so this move wasn't as difficult for them as it might have been. Also, I'm certain nobody ever believed it would be forever. We never did anything forever.

Once the novelty and excitement of being here wore off I became terribly homesick. Nobody who hasn't experienced it can believe how much it hurts and how long it can last. I was homesick for my extended family, and generally for my culture. Friends weren't as much a loss because we'd been such transients that we didn't have any long term friendships. The only fixed point in my life had been my relatives in Tennessee and South Carolina.

I missed, and still do, the sharp changes in the seasons, the autumn leaves, snow. There were many foods I missed and the whole family became adept at finding creative substitutes for ingredients we couldn't get here. (My most notable failure was pumpkin pie attempted with Queensland Blue.) For some reason we never got into the habit of having relatives in America send us things. We just did without Babe Ruth candy bars, okra, cornbread, blackeyed peas, pecans, crisp bacon, hot sausage, sweet rolls, cherries without pips, blueberries, sweet potatoes, good mayonnaise, Mexican food – and bemoaned the fact. On the other hand, we discovered the delights of Vegemite, Chinese food (remember when father went with kids in pyjamas to takeaway shops where they got a discount if they brought in their own saucepans instead of using the shops containers?) roast lamb, wine trifle, fish and chips, and the ubiquitous beetroot.

I missed more than anything, and still do, voices that sounded like my own, although now I no longer sound like anybody else either there or here. I remember after I'd been here a couple of years stopping an American sailor in Swanston Street and asking him if he'd talk to me. I suppose he thought I was mad but he obliged. Unfortunately he was a Yankee, but it was better than nothing.

Sometimes, even after all these years, I can get maudlin hearing a real Southern accent, the music of it. And of course it isn't just the accent, it's the expressions. Figures of speech that, for all I know, have died out in the South anyway, but they crop up in those nostalgia movies sometimes, and transport me to an equally fictional time in my life when everything was simple and good. Nobody says 'bless your heart' to me any more.

How long we intended to stay was something I was always vague about. I remember a period of two years being mentioned, but I suspect not for any particular reason other than that was our limit anywhere. I've said that I don't believe anyone thought the move was forever. We didn't consider ourselves migrants. What I think happened was that once we got here my parents realised how far away it was and how expensive it would be to go home. It was seven years before we even had a holiday back.

And of course in seven years people put down roots. I was married by the time I'd been here three years. I had friendships that had lasted longer than any I'd made in America. I was part of a community here – I worked, I had neighbours, I belonged to organisations, my husband had given me an extended family. The hold Australia had on me, in terms of my day to day identity, was by this time stronger than America's.

Nevertheless, I thought of myself as an American. I remember Dad talking about how long we had to be here before we qualified for naturalisation, but that time came and went without any of us doing anything about it. The United States doesn't recognise dual status which meant that we would have had to renounce our American citizenship in order to be naturalised here. It's hard to explain to someone who hasn't been raised in an atmosphere of fierce patriotism, as most Americans have. In those years I sometimes thought about taking out citizenship and I was almost superstitious about it. I imagined it would feel like telling your parents you didn't love them any more. I imagined it would be like severing some life line.

I finally became naturalised when I'd been here about 20 years, ostensibly in protest over something President Reagan did. But probably more to the point, I'd recently returned from a trip to the United States during which I'd felt quite an alien. I was starting to feel silly about not acknowledging Australia as my real home, my heart's and mind's home.

My parents died without becoming naturalised, and my brother still lives here but has no intention of becoming an Australian citizen. I probably will never tell my family back in the States what I've done. I know they would consider it treason. And I confess that handing over my American passport had more emotional impact on me than receiving my naturalisation certificate.

I feel that I belong to a community first, and a country second. Nationalism will never matter so much to me, but for years now I have spoken about 'we' meaning Australians. 'We' only ever means Americans when I'm remembering.

People do notice my accent when they first meet me, and it usually takes me by surprise because I tend to forget about it after all this time. When I have to speak in public I do sometimes hope people won't think I'm new here – one of those imported 'American experts'. I am always conscious in those circumstances that some people resent what they see as American dominance.

Where I grew up, in the Bible Belt, we said a prayer and pledged allegiance to the flag every school morning for years.

I have always thought that one of Australia's strengths was – watch out for sweeping generalisation – you can go a long way here without bumping into a fanatic. People don't seem to have those entrenched historical cultural hatreds and passions, unless they've brought them from somewhere else. Where I grew up, in the Bible Belt, we said a prayer and pledged allegiance to the flag every school morning for years. My family spoke about the civil war as though they could remember it. I think Australia is a very tolerant place, relatively speaking, and it's horribly disturbing to hear that thugs like the Ku Klux Klan are establishing pockets here.

I've been back to America twice. The first time was in 1972 when my son was one-year-old. My mother had to go back on business and she shouted me a trip so she could show the first great-grandchild to his family. The second time was in 1984, a couple of years after both my parents had died. I took both my children this time. I noticed a materialism that took my breath away. I don't remember growing up with that drive to buy, or that contempt for the poor. My grandparents were still frugal people who believed you should use up what you had before you got more, but I was quite shocked that shopping had become a major leisure activity for people of my generation. I really didn't want to ruin my sentimental journey by getting into arguments about socialism with my right wing relatives, but even biting my tongue caused a certain strain at times. I was less reticent about my feminism, and the result was the odd awkward silence.

I made a point of eating everything I had loved when I was growing up (fried chicken that didn't have anything to do with the Colonel, corn bread, okra, fabulous ice cream, hickory smoked barbeque, biscuits – not 'scones') and in most cases found I still loved it.

The countryside was beautiful. I had missed giant oak trees and little squirrels. It was Christmas and cold. We even had snow just after New Year. I think for as long as I live that will seem more 'right' somehow.

I didn't see one single cigarette being lit in eight weeks or a single alcoholic drink being consumed. I was amazed at how cheap the books and films were, which was just as well because the television and radio were abysmal; unless you were a cable subscriber you got the lowest common denominator rubbish and far too many commercials. I wanted to send thank you presents to the ABC (Australian Broadcasting Corporation) and SBS (Special Broadcasting Service) when I arrived back in Australia.

I watched my children's surprise at the omnipresence of religion in daily life in Tennessee. Prayers before meals, prayers before bed, prayers when you couldn't find the scissors, family *Bible* reading. It seemed very natural to me, even though religion hasn't played a part in my life for many years. We were expected to attend church every week. I saw my old Sunday School teacher, I sang with the choir, I talked to people who remembered my mother as a little girl. I found the almost tribal sense of belonging that the church gives people in the southern states very appealing, and I suspect impossible to find in a secular community, however close. Nevertheless, I had no desire to be born again.

I wanted to send thank you presents to the ABC and SBS when I arrived back in Australia.

Returning to Australia I remember looking out the window of the plane at a stretch of brown land (it was January) and getting tears in my eyes. That moment told me Australia was 'home'. And I noticed the light here. I'd heard artists talk about the light being different in Australia, but this was the first time I saw it for myself. Most of all I noticed that I relaxed. This made me compare the kind of belonging that comes from family and cultural heritage with the kind that comes from shared values and experience.

I don't want to live anywhere else but Australia. The people I love most are here. So are the people who most love me. My partner, my children, my friends. I would never willingly leave them. I've been uprooted enough in my life. Familiarity means more to me than adventure these days.

I will always be interested in what happens in the United States of America as are lots of people who weren't born there. I will continue to think fondly of the culture in which I grew up, though I see little evidence that it exists anywhere any more.

Home – Among the Gum Trees

Vivienne Correa

Vivienne Correa is Victorian State Manager of AustCare. In the late 1960s she migrated to Australia together with her husband Frank Correa. She was educated in Hong Kong, where her family resided, having established themselves for generations as traders. After spending some years in Sydney, Vivienne Correa moved, with her husband and children, to live in Melbourne. Particularly through her work with AustCare, Vivienne Correa is well aware of the struggles of women who migrate as refugees or in highly distressing circumstances. She believes that having lived in a British colony and being able speak English makes integration very easy. In working with AustCare, Vivienne Correa intends to return to the Australian community, and to those abroad who are assisted by AustCare, some of the support which she has received since coming to Australia.

I remember vividly our boat berthing in Brisbane and our first encounter with the Australian immigration official who greeted us in shorts and long socks, a new mode of dress for us colonials used to government officials in more formal attire. The official looked at our passports, my husband born in Shanghai and myself in Darjeeling, India, then drawled in broad 'strine': 'G'day, do you speak English?' His casual manner put us at ease immediately, and after attempting to understand his broad accent and series of questions that left us saying 'Pardon?' several times, we felt like saying we spoke English better than he did.

When we became engaged, my husband Frank and I had decided that we should leave Hong Kong to seek a more secure future, as times were uncertain in South East Asia with the escalation of the Viet Nam war and

China being in the throes of the Cultural Revolution. Our families were greatly affected by the second world war, particularly during the Japanese occupation of Hong Kong and many regions of China. When the war ended, our parents left Chungking (unoccupied China) to begin life again in Hong Kong, where both our mothers were well-established before the turn of the century. They left together with tens of thousands of refugees who fled to the British Crown Colony when China was engulfed in civil war culminating in the communist takeover in 1949.

In Hong Kong a little more than ten years later, in the 1960s, immigration was the topic of conversation amongst many of our friends. Where should one immigrate to? Was it wise to leave when property and the stock market were so low? Hong Kong surely will remain stable: needing foreign currency and expertise and with 1997 still 30 years away, China will surely not threaten the status quo? The Cultural Revolution is a temporary phase; reason will prevail in China; the dollar will prevail over dogma. The discussions were endless and reasons for choosing one country over another were dissected, analysed and reiterated time and again. Helen Chin, my close Chinese school friend, said she was going to the United States of America because it was easy to integrate. Being a multicultural country, she said, if there was any trouble in America the Chinese would not be picked on first, the Black Americans were there as a buffer! The United States of America, Canada and Australia were the main immigrant countries, with Australia being least popular partly as a consequence of the previously existing White Australia Policy which actively discriminated against applicants from Asian countries.

...Australia being least popular partly as a consequence of the previously existing White Australia Policy which actively discriminated against applicants from Asian countries.

My husband and I began looking closely at each of the countries, finally deciding on Australia for a wide variety of reasons. The United States was not deemed a good choice as already there were signs of drug abuse and lack of gun control laws. As well, there were potential (and actual) race problems which would not be ameliorated until the civil rights of the emerging Black community were recognised. I was not in favour of Canada as the severe winters would be difficult to withstand, and I am a lover of sun and surf. So our thoughts turned to Australia.

Australia was definitely not the favourite, but we knew several families who had emigrated during and just after the second world war and they all seemed to have settled down well. Our impression of the people was favourable: during the Viet Nam war, many Australian troops visited Hong Kong on R. and R. (rest and recreation) and, unlike the Americans who were disposed to the seedier side of drugs and prostitution, the Aussies headed for our beaches – which were poor by Australian standards.

'Bending an elbow' over a couple of beers seemed to be a favourite pastime and the Aussies seemed an easy going lot with few hang-ups and a love of the outdoors. Cricket (taken very seriously in the British Crown Colony of Hong Kong) was played like a baseball game by the Aussie team and their obvious enjoyment and informality was refreshing in the confines of the British clubs. Besides, as a young girl I fell in love with a tall suntanned Aussie, the son of one of my father's clients. He came to our home for dinner, spoke of cattle and sheep, and showed us photographs of his hobby farm. Years later I discovered he was from New Zealand!

The impression of the countries from the southern antipodes was of space and friendliness, reinforced by the people we met. The ugly Australian image of T-shirt and thongs had not yet emerged.

Why did we not choose to live in the United Kingdom? The reasons are obvious to anyone brought up in a British colony and having been exposed to the class and expatriate system whereby the local born were often discriminated against. Until the late 1960s, my husband's British company still had three toilets – one for the Chinese, one for the locals – that is, Portuguese or Eurasians, and one for expatriates. When we left, the Hong Kong Club still had not admitted any Chinese members and many large companies stopped the promotion of expatriate staff if they married a Chinese. Fortunately, these practices have been discontinued but they were entrenched when we decided there must be a better future for those wanting to redefine their own existence in a better society. In the Far East, doubts remain about any complete turn-around in racial attitudes.

> Until the late 1960s, my husband's British company still had three toilets – one for the Chinese, one for the locals – that is, Portuguese or Eurasians, and one for expatriates.

Despite discrimination, to their credit the minority community survived and prospered in Hong Kong, gaining entrance to the professions and establishing themselves in businesses. The lifestyle was comfortable. Yet, due to lack of opportunity, the older generaiton languished in the clerical positions in the banks or old trading houses. They established their own clubs, excelling in sports and the arts. The Portuguese were devout Catholics while the Eurasians were mainly Anglican. Diocesan schools were established by the Anglican Church to educate the many children who were the result of the liaisons of British personnel posted to Hong Kong. These schools are recognised as providing an excellent education.

My husband had experienced the trauma of Japanese occupation. A bone of contention, particularly for him, was the lack of recognition given to the local Portuguese and Eurasians who fought gallantly for the allied cause in the defence of Hong Kong. Many casualties were suffered and the survivors had to endure incarceration in prisoner of war (POW) camps in both Hong Kong and Japan. Following hostilities, these 'volunteers' were not offered any rehabilitation by the British government and were expected to resume their former lives without a fuss. It was only in the mid-1970s, after intense lobbying and media attention, that these former servicemen were accorded medical benefits, rights that were automatically provided to their British counterparts. A modest pension was eventually granted to this ageing group: cynically the authorities knew it was not a large financial burden to service a diminishing number of elderly and frail men. Strangely, in the many stories that have emanated as a consequence of both world wars, not much has been written about the efforts of nationals other than the allies.

We migrated to Australia for all the reasons that can be identified simply, and for many too complicated to explain in a few words. In August 1967 we finally decided to take the step and apply for immigration. We did this in secrecy as, in the past, applications from the Asian region were not often approved and we were not confident of success. We were not aware that there was a shift in Australian immigration policies and were surprised to learn within a fortnight that we were accepted as prospective migrants.

In February 1968, with great anticipation and excitement, we boarded the passenger ship *SS Tjuluwah*. A delayed honeymoon voyage to Sydney, and a fortnight of unwinding and relaxation before our new life in Australia, stretched before us. My Grandmother, a gentle and much loved individual who was a devout vegetarian and Buddhist, came to farewell us on board ship. Por Por, as we called her, draw me aside at the last minute to advise me very seriously that on no account must I eat lamb because it was believed that pregnant women should avoid this meat as it caused epileptic fits in babies! I was by then in the early months of pregnancy and not at all confident or informed about all the old wives tales relating to maternity. I obediently obeyed Por Por's instructions until, when carrying our second son Michael, I mentioned the non-lamb eating taboo to my doctor who laughed uproariously, assuring me that there wasn't a skerrick of truth in this belief.

A large gathering of friends and family farewelled us, and as the boat weighed anchor I felt the first movement of the child inside me. This step was being taken to secure a better future for the next generation. The sharp movement inside was surely a seal of approval.

The trip was idyllic. We met interesting people on board ship, including many carefree young Australians who were travelling steerage class back home after the customary visit to the United Kingdom and Europe. We also met many prospective United Kingdom migrants, and were surprised and somewhat disconcerted to learn that most paid only £10 and were given assisted passage to Australia. The immigration department seemed to have two policies for migrants. In order to attract people from the United Kingdom, these migrants were given virtually free passage. Other prospective migrants had to finance their own journey 'down under'. Although we felt discriminated against, such practices were not new to us colonials. We accepted them as a fact of life. Besides, we were in such a state of anticipation and excitement at being given an opportunity to start a new life that we brushed aside any negative thoughts. We didn't want to detract from our single mindedness: we were burning our bridges to begin afresh in a new land, terra Australis.

The ship moved south towards our first port of call, Port Moresby. One passenger, an amateur astrologer, pointed out stars and constellations and for the first time we saw the Southern Cross. The Viet Nam war was raging and it was the height of the Tet offensive. The American B52s on their bombing missions flew past our boat frequently. Over the shop's intercom we learnt that Lionel Rose had won the world lightweight boxing title. Passengers on board ship intermingled freely and we played cards and games at night. We asked endless questions of our Australian shipboard companions, and for the first time we heard the phrase 'no worries, mate'. Being in the early stages of pregnancy, I often felt bilious and was advised to drink shandy to maintain my energy levels.

When we finally reached the spectacular Sydney Heads, virtually everyone was on deck to capture the sight. I felt cheated at not being well enough to join the merry throng. Sydney had turned on one of those magnificent clear sunning mornings and when I finally emerged to go up on deck, I was captivated by the sight of the harbour and sailing ships, and in the distance the coathanger bridge spanning the water from Milsom's Point to the Rocks and the city. We docked at Woolloomooloo. Being unfamiliar with Aboriginal names, we were at once curious about what seemed to be such a strange name for the boat terminal. As the ship drew close to the docks we could distinguish my husband's old friend Chief. He was waving wildly and wearing an Akubra, an Aussie hat which replaced the baseball cap he wore 365 days of the year in Hong Kong.

In the evenings we poured over the map of Sydney and Australia...so that we could follow conversations and news items.

Auntie Sylvia and Chief took us under their wing during our first few months in Sydney, securing for us a small flat in Gladsville near their rambling old home. They were already in their late fifties with four sons all being educated at Riverview. It was a financial struggle, the parents working extremely hard towards the end of their working life to give their children this opportunity. Auntie Sylvia and Chief were attuned to an easier life in the Far East with house help and large social network. In Australia, life was comparatively spartan. Their reward was to see their children integrate and become part of an emerging multicultural Australia. Both Auntie Sylvia and Chief were wonderful role models; their enthusiasm and confidence in their new country was contagious.

The late 1960s in Sydney were exciting times. Through contacts in Hong Kong, Frank had already managed to obtain a job with a firm of stockbrokers in Sydney. It was the beginning of the Poseidon boom. Share prices were soaring. Talk about buying and selling was heard everywhere on the streets and in workplaces. People who had never before bought shares or thought about 'playing the market' sat at the end of the telephone waiting for news or seeking out advice as to when to sell or to buy. In the midst of a mineral bull market Frank felt part of an emerging dynamic nation. In the evenings we poured over the map of Sydney and Australia, looking up names and areas that were unfamiliar to us, so that we could follow conversations and news items.

After living surrounded by cardboard boxes for four months, at last we bought a modest home in a new suburb. The house was on a spacious block and a huge pinetree stood in the garden, reminding me of the old banyan tree just outside my home in Kowloon, symbolic of strength and continuity. Frank was interested in the garden. He had no warning that grass grows so quickly in summer, and that mowing the lawn is such a time consuming task.

Whilst we learnt the relaxed style of inviting friends around for a 'barbie', we continued to make our traditional Eurasian/Chinese/Portuguese dishes and were pleased to be able to find all the necessary (and many) ingredients available in Sydney. We had wonderful Australian neighbours who showed us the ropes – from how to make coleslaw, roast lamb, a pavlova and how to fix a lawnmower, to explaining odd terminology like 'lay by now'. (Notices exhorting passersby to 'lay by now' confronted me from window displays in department stores and shopping centres, intriguing me greatly.) Our great advantage was fluency in English, so integration was relatively simple, although many Australians were perplexed by our complicated background. We gave up explaining.

Notices exhorting passersby to ' lay by now' confronted me from window displays in department stores and shopping centres, intriguing me greatly.

The first generation of migrants never forget their tradition and culture. It is the next generation who really put down their roots and integrate totally. One Chinese New Year's Eve I began preparing a special dinner which required rice. I discovered to my consternation that the rice bin was empty. Chinese superstition dictates that it is very bad luck to begin the New Year without an ample supply of rice and oil. When Frank returned home, I asked him to quickly go out to purchase rice from the local supermarket. Dead tired after an exhausting day, and knowing that the shops close early for the holiday break, he refused. In the next few months the Poseidon boom became a bust. It can all be blamed on that empty rice bin!

As there was a considerable age difference between Frank and myself, we decided to have children spaced closely together. Within a few years we had three sons and became totally immersed in parenthood at the same time as meeting the challenges of our new life.

Twenty-five years have passed and a lot of water has flowed under the bridge. With the political uncertainties of 1997 for Hong Kong, and the aftermath of the Tien An Mien massacre in China, most of our relations and many close friends have also immigrated to Australia. At a recent fiftieth anniversary of a cherished Uncle, it was like a gathering of the seven tribes of Israel.

We, like many new Australians, feel very emotional as the national anthem, *Advance Australia Fair*, is played. The words reflect the deep affection we feel for this nation. Our four children are Aussies. We have placed great emphasis on their education. Having survived the war years and observing the despair and triumph of POW inmates, we are convinced that, regardless of circumstances, the spirit and the intellect can survive any deprivation.

We love bellbirds, bush walks, the beach, Box Hill market on Saturdays – and all the simple things in life one often takes for granted. Our children have been fortunate enough to attend university, working their way through and being challenged by the many aspects of university life. We are confident they will contribute to their new country and become effective members of their community. They love and participate in all forms of sport from Australian rules, cricket, basketball, to soccer. It is traditional for father and sons to attend cricket at the MCG (Melbourne Cricket Ground) on Boxing Day.

Our sons are now six foot, five inches and when we attend Mass we've been told to sit near the rear as when we stand up for the Gospel it is like the Great Wall of China: no one can see past us. Their little sister, our 'bonus issue', has effectively four fathers, her three elder brothers protectively keeping an eye on her progress.

We have learnt the Australian saying of being 'one eyed' about issues. Are we over optimistic about this country and its future?

How many countries around the world can claim to have our quality of life and sense of space? Australia has political stability, comparative racial harmony, a fair system of justice, a strong democracy and freedom of the press. Australia is a compassionate nation, having accepted and integrated successfully some 500 000 refugees since the second world war – a program of which all Australians should be proud. An Australian identity is beginning to emerge as we become more confident of our role as an independent country on the South Pacific rim. In the depths of the current recession most Australians realise that the coining of the phrase 'the lucky country' was to our detriment. We can no longer ride on the sheep's back or live high on the sales of our mineral resources. The post-industrialisation of the Western World and the emerging tiger economies have posed new challenges.

The Australian character is resiliant. We need a change of direction, a sense of vision for the future, and the will of all Australians to create a dynamic society for the twenty-first century. In the meantime, I keep in mind the words of the familiar ditty in *Burke's Back Yard*: we have found a home 'among the gum trees, with lots of plum trees... and an old rocking chair'. I can never remember all the words, but the song encapsulates my love of this country. And I am grateful that my children can say the Australian 'G'day' in the easy and confident manner of truly belonging.

PART III

Changes. Transitions.

To the Unknown Island Continent!

Lynne Wenig

Lynne Wenig runs her own consultancy to management, CentreBrain Ltd, in Melbourne, Australia. She founded and edited two national publications, *Women Australia* magazine and *The Executive Woman's Report* a bi-monthly newsletter of ideas, information, strategies, techniques and trends relevant to business women. Her latest book, *The A to Z of Time Management*, was recently published in Australia and in Asia. She is a past president of Women in Management and current interests include serving on the national executive of the United Nations Development Fund for Women (UNIFEM), the marketing and planning committee of the Sudden Infant Death Research Foundation, and the board of Dandenong Hospital.

Yes, fear of flying. I was sitting on a 'plane en route to Melbourne, doubled over, sucking ice provided by a kindly 'stewardess'. Tears of fear were streaming down my face. The turbulence of a thunderstorm mid-way between the East and the West coasts of the United States served only to exacerbate my fear – fear of the unknown island continent.

I was 20-years-of-age and had just left home, family, and friends for a country described by my Mother as being 'as far around the globe as you can go without starting to come back again'. I was also on my way to continue a marriage which, although less than a year old, was showing signs of strain. This fear-filled New York to Melbourne flight took 42 hours. Conquering my fear of the unknown took somewhat longer.

My coming to Australia began in a Brooklyn hospital. I was working as a medical assistant and finishing some tertiary study. My now ex-husband was completing a residency in paediatrics. During my second week on-the-job, someone suggested that there was a 'handsome doctor from Australia' that I might like to meet.

'It will be an interesting date,' I responded, 'as I don't speak any Australian. All I know about Australia is that Sydney is the capital and they have kangaroos.'

'His English is very good,' my colleague replied. 'You'll have no trouble understanding him.'

We were engaged four months later and married ten months after we met. Following a European honeymoon we settled in London for a time and I worked to support us both while my husband did post-graduate study.

Although my arrival down under was a great culture shock, the year in London helped. I became accustomed to different accents, the fact that people would think I 'sounded funny', and that I talked, **I talked, and** and seemed to work, faster than most of the people around **seemed to work,** me. I also learned that if I wanted to keep warm, in the **faster than most** absence of the accustomed central heating, I needed to **of the people** drink plenty of tea. 'Plenty of tea' was a newly acquired **around me.** habit: tea was something you took with honey and lemon when you weren't feeling well. When the year in England was up, I headed towards the southern hemisphere, after a brief stop in the United States of America.

My most vivid memory of the first few months in Australia is associated with fear. I was concerned about how I would find my way in this new society, when some mild anxiety was suddenly replaced by a real and quite terrifying fear – the dread of being alone at night.

My husband was doing a medical locum which required living 'out' every second evening. This was all arranged prior to my arrival, as he had a rented house in East St Kilda. Ye olde Victorian abode possessed an extraordinary number of creaks, groans, and grunts. With only one dull street light, strange, odd-shaped shadows were cast against the blinds. When you've grown up with Eastern American trees, the silhouettes of eucalypts look bizarre.

After a few nights by myself, I became distraught. Here was the brave New Yorker who had ridden subways at 3 am and walked fearlessly through Central Park at night, suddenly frightened of the dark. Pleas to my husband to change jobs landed on deaf ears, and being 10 000 miles away from 'home' meant that there were no close friends or family to turn to for help and support.

The problem resolved itself unexpectedly. Friends of my husband arrived unannounced one evening and found me panic stricken, trembling and in tears. They contacted my husband the next day, told him how concerned they were, and 'suggested' that it might be a good idea if I wasn't left alone at night for a while.

Some years, a broken marriage, and a good deal of personal growth and soul searching later, I came to realise that my dread of the sounds and the shadows was merely a symbol of my qualms. Feelings of loneliness and abandonment were the real fears. I've never been afraid of the dark since.

There is another chapter to this story. The same friends who rescued me the next day by their phone call to my husband, also took immediate action. They grabbed my coat, bundled me into their car, and took me to the theatre. 'It's a comedy,' they said, 'and it will take your mind off things at home.'

We ended up at a place called the 'New Theatre'. This was 'off Broadway' entertainment and the show was titled *The Rock 'N Roll Review*. When the curtain lifted, a man dressed in a blue dressing gown, with a red hot water bottle under his arm, walked on to centre stage. He stood quite still for what seemed like five minutes, frowned at the audience, and then proceeded to launch into a monologue about his experiences during a recent visit to the local RSL (Returned Serviceman's League, now 'Returned and Services', club). Not only did I not know what the 'RSL' was, I was completely baffled by the shrieks of laughter coming from the audience. This, was the now infamous Barry Humphries playing 'Norm'. It took a long time and many years of acclimatisation before I could finally join the audience in their 'appreciation' of the Humphries humour.

Most of my other memories of coming to Australia are associated with strong cravings for 'things American', and trying not to make too many language bloopers.

Finding a United States magazine meant going into the city to McGills. They were the only newsagent that carried American publications, and they charged what seemed like an exorbitant sum for an issue that came by sea and was many months out of date.

Eating out meant Chinese or fish and chips, and nobody had even heard of a bagel. I remember once suggesting to my husband that opening a Pizza Parlour could well be a good business for Australia. 'That's nonsense,' I was told. 'Australians will *never* eat Pizza.' Familiar foods were not available unless a kind relative overseas took pity and sent a 'care' package. Early in the 1960s, Myer opened a small 'foreign food' section in its Lonsdale Street store. What a boon that was. At last I could get US all-purpose flour so the cakes I made from my American cook book recipes would rise.

American vs Australian vocabulary caused many laughs, usually at my expense. When trying to 'make friends with the students' I once asked a group of Form 3 girls which team they 'rooted for'. It was only at lunchtime in the staff room that this *faux pas* was revealed. A request for a peanut butter and jelly sandwich sent someone into mild hysterics. But then, knowing that people were prepared to travel for miles to see Melbourne's first 'skyscraper', the 13-storey ICI building, evened the score somewhat.

129

I had one visit to the United States when I was still married and my children were very young. It took another ten years of saving $5 a week before I went home again. During that time I left my husband (taking two children aged three-and-a-half and eighteen months, £3 Australian, two cots with blankets and a washing machine), found a flat, a job and learned how to subsist on $84 a fortnight.

Australia and Australians have been very good to me. I've built a new life over many years, raised a happy, healthy family, found another partner, and fashioned a successful career. I can't imagine living anywhere else 'full-time'. But it took a long time to stop calling America 'home'.

The Sense of Belonging

Penelope E. Andrews

Born in Cape Town, South Africa on 18 September 1954, Penelope E. Andrews worked as a bookkeeper for five years before going to the University of Natal where in 1982 she obtained an arts and law degree. As a student at the University of Natal she co-ordinated the university's legal aid clinic, and became actively involved in the Black Students Society.

Penelope Andrews obtained a scholarship to do a master of laws degree at Columbia University and completed her masters in 1984. For six months prior to her journey to the United States of America, she worked at the Legal Resources Centre, South Africa's largest public interest law firm. Upon graduation from Columbia, she worked at the NAACP (National Association for the Advancement of Coloured People) Legal Defence Fund, a civil rights law firm in New York, for six months. Thereafter, she was appointed the Chamberlain Fellow in Legislation at Columbia Law School for one year prior to emigrating to Australia.

I was appointed to La Trobe University in 1986 to teach in the area of race issues and the law. Since 1986 Australia has been my home. The seven years here have been like a journey of discovery – both personally and politically. I have written on women in South Africa, public interest law in South Africa, South African labour law, aborigines and the law in Australia and Australia's *Racial Discrimination Act.* I have been educated and nurtured here, and I leave knowing that even though the journey now takes me somewhere else, I leave part of myself here, and I will return for more education and nurturing.

At the end of 1992 I travelled to New York to take up a position as associate professor in the School of Law at the City University of New

York. The decision to move there was difficult, and I left Australia with a sense of trepidation, and a great deal of sadness. But the very factors that contributed to my decision to travel to Australia in 1986 were instrumental in my decision to move back to the United States. Those factors can be encapsulated in a recurrent restlessness that has prevented me from laying down roots, as it were. This restlessness, according to Salman Rushdie, is the condition of the migrant – that once detached from one's place of birth it is impossible to reconstruct 'home' somewhere else. In fact, 'home' is everywhere.

...the condition of the migrant – once detached from one's place of birth it is impossible to reconstruct 'home' somewhere else.

In the mid-1980s I had spent a wonderful summer in Spain and Portugal, but the experience was completely ruined by my subsequent encounter with the United States Immigration and Naturalisation Service. There was some confusion with my visa papers, and I had great difficulty returning to the United States, where I had been working at Columbia Law School in New York. I eventually found my way back and in August 1985 I decided that I would leave the United States, not to return to South Africa, the country of my birth, but to find a new home somewhere else.

I began searching for jobs, and as if in response to my prayers, I found an advertisement in the *Chronicle of Higher Education*, an educational magazine in the United States. The position advertised was for a lecturer in the Department of Legal Studies at La Trobe University in Melbourne, Australia. The areas of interest advertised were in race relations and human rights and the law, an area of law that I had not only obtained some experience in, but one to which I was committed personally and politically.

I eagerly applied for the position, and since I could not leave the United States at the time, I was interviewed at Niagra Falls, by the Dean of the School of Social Sciences. He drove from Toronto, and we arranged to meet on the Canadian-American border. I shall never forget the interview: the gods were smiling on me on that wonderful, warm autumn day as I responded to questions on issues ranging from my attitudes towards teaching 'law in context', to race issues and the law, and my own research agenda. All the omens were good, and a few weeks later La Trobe University made a formal offer of appointment to me.

I arrived in Australia on Australia Day 1986.

In a very real sense I came to Australia seeking refuge. I had been living in the United States for three years where I had obtained a scholarship to do a master of laws at Columbia University in New York. My every intention was to return to South Africa after completing my one year of graduate study. A combination of factors and events resulted in my staying longer. The years 1983-86 were particularly brutal and repressive in South Africa, with wide scale and effective mass action against the white government. South Africa received considerable coverage in the overseas media, and the anti-apartheid and sanctions lobby became very active and vocal in the United States. I spent a significant part of my time travelling around the country talking about human rights violations in South Africa, practising law in South Africa, the situation of women and so on, and I grew apprehensive about returning to the country. I was nervous because on a previous trip overseas, on my return to South Africa, the security police had detained me claiming that they knew my movements overseas and alleging that I had contacted the African National Congress (ANC). During those days, contact with a banned organisation (such as the ANC) could result in a jail sentence. During my three years in the United States I was vocal and active in the anti-apartheid movement, and had shared public platforms with members both of the ANC and the Pan Africanist Congress, and naturally I feared going back to South Africa with possible retaliation from the authorities.

The reality was also that I liked living in New York. I liked living in a democratic and free society; I liked being able to participate in debates and not be concerned that security policemen were assessing every word I uttered. I liked being able to associate with whom ever I wanted. I liked living where I wanted – I felt I could be anything I wanted to be.

The United States of America shares some significant similarities with South Africa. Civil rights and anti-racist struggles there carried echoes of ours. Many black South Africans of my generation were substantially influenced by the Black Power Movement in the United States, and by the writings and speeches of leaders like Martin Luther King and Malcolm X. So there was a sense in which I felt very much at home in the Untied States. I wanted to stay, but I knew I had a tough battle ahead with United States Immigration. The only way I could remain was if I applied for political asylum – a step I was reluctant to take. For me the idea of being stateless and a ward of the United Nations for an indefinite period rankled too much at my innate insecurity brought on by the loss of my mother at an early age and the experience of growing up 'coloured' in South Africa.

I decided to apply for jobs abroad, and responded to advertisements for jobs in Australia, Ethiopia and New Zealand. The Australian job turned out to be the best deal, and I decided on Australia. It was to be another adventure – I did not know a soul in the country, except an old school friend who had emigrated in the early 1970s and who lived in Sydney. I was enthusiastic about my prospective Australian adventure.

Even though I knew almost nobody, I was aware that there was a large community of South African migrants in Australia. Before accepting my teaching position my knowledge of Australian politics and Australian lifestyles was sparse. Such a lack of knowledge meant that I had no preconceptions, which ultimately made the experience of moving to Australia one of the most positive actions I've taken.

I came entirely on my own. I was 31-years-old and relished the thought of starting afresh. The roller coaster energy of New York filled me with an enthusiasm to take on the world! I need not have fretted though – the high energy of New York stands as a direct antithesis to the muffled vigour of Melbourne.

It was my first full-time academic position, a position I had somehow drifted into. I always imagined that I would practice public interest or human rights law in South Africa, but two years at Columbia University, one as a graduate student and the other as the Chamberlain Fellow in Legislation, whetted my appetite for the academic environment. The position I was offered provided a splendid entree into the academic world.

...my professional interests have coincided so comfortably with my sense of humanity and justice.

I am extremely fortunate that my professional interests have coincided so comfortably with my sense of humanity and justice. I have always taught in the areas of law that I feel significantly committed to on a personal and ideological level. In New York, I read the job advertisement thinking that somebody had taken my curriculum vitae and decided to write a job description especially for me. The lectureship encapsulated my interests perfectly – teaching in the area of race and human rights and the law. My professional interests and predilections had been shaped early on in my career, when I spent a brief period in South Africa working at a public interest law firm, then in New York at a civil rights law firm. Coordinating the Legal Aid Clinic at the University of Natal in Durban for six years, while I was a student, had predated my professional work in the field.

I had no preconceived ideas about Australia; I did however have the image of Australia as a land of sunshine, barbecues and a laid back lifestyle. And Dame Edna Everage and Barry Humphries. I came to Australia courtesy of Canadian Pacific Airlines, flying in from a northern hemisphere winter to a beautiful and hot summer. Spending a week in Fiji on the way, I gained a delicious sense of living in the Pacific.

I was educated by the nuns and matriculated in Cape Town in 1971. My father divorced my mother when I was 10-years-old, and my mother died when I was 13. I was the first in my family to go to university, and my family, my brother and two sisters (who live in Cape Town) have always responded to my career and other endeavours with ardour, support and pride. They were always enthusiastic about my travels.

My first few months in Melbourne were difficult and lonely. Except for my colleagues at the university, I knew almost no other people. Weekends were especially unhappy for me, particularly in contrast to New York where I had enjoyed the street life and activity on the streets at all hours of the day and night. The suburban mentality in Melbourne is not always the most welcoming. It is not particularly hostile, just not engaging and welcoming, particularly for single people. Nonetheless, it was comforting coming to a country where English is the official language, and that made the transition slightly easier. Although when I travelled out of the cities I found some accents slightly difficult to understand, I did not experience any language problems.

Outside of South Africa my accent has often either been a source of curiosity or a source of ridicule. It hasn't bothered me much – the ridicule normally came from close friends. I have never felt a need to change my accent because it is so intrinsically part of my make-up – physically, intellectually and emotionally. What I have done is the obvious: I have picked up and become accustomed to expressions and words from both American and Australian English.

Life in Melbourne subsequently became, in the main, fulfilling and interesting, both on a personal and professional level. However some aspects of my life are not entirely satisfying. That, no doubt, is the condition of the migrant. There were significant gaps in my life in Melbourne. Mostly I missed family and friends in South Africa. I missed living in a society where many languages are spoken (although Australia is a multilingual country, and this is becoming increasingly obvious, particularly in Melbourne). I recall telling an Australian friend the delight I always experience in public places like bus shelters, tram stops and shops – places where one is exposed to a plethora of different languages. I miss biltong and mebos, the former a dried cured meat (ostrich beef) and the latter a crushed fruit, both popular delicacies in South Africa.

I even discovered the perfect cappuccino in Lygon Street, Carlton.

But Melbourne's variety of cuisine is amongst the best in the world. My taste buds have been seduced consistently. I even discovered the perfect cappuccino in Lygon Street, Carlton.

Being in Australia meant I also missed friends from the United States. I missed the cosmopolitan lifestyle of a city like New York and the racial diversity. Australia is a culturally diverse city, but not very racially diverse. I missed the particular tone of black politics in the United States, particularly in the echoes of the civil rights struggle there. In Australia, specifically in Melbourne, black politics has a different, and less significant meaning. Absent is the community of black scholars and activists in the United States, and I particularly regretted not being together with the small community of black female law professors I'd associated with. I missed the nurturing and support I received from groups like that.

But I did *not* miss the harsh racial realities of the United States, where drugs and drug-related crime is killing far too many African-American youth. I did not miss the anger that spills over into hatred, which makes many of the major American cities polarised and alienating.

I appreciate and like the lifestyle of Australia – the sense of security and safety not found in many parts of the world. I despaired for the apathy of suburban Australia – but an Australian friend explained that the apathy prevents Australian society from becoming a cesspool of fanatic groups like America's Ku Klux Klan. That apathy might also be a reason for issues like abortion or capital punishment not becoming major political issues tearing Australia apart. Australian society is also able to contain peacefully large groups of people who come from countries where hate is the national currency – white and black South Africans, Serbs and Croations, Arabs and Jews, to mention a few.

Initially I came to Australia for a four year lecturing position – my temporary visa was for four years. After three years my contract was extended to six years. In the meantime I married an Australian citizen. My job was converted to a tenurable one, and I applied for permanent residence. After six years in Australia I became an Australian citizen, a fact of which I'm extremely proud. The 1992 state election in Victoria meant that for the first time in my life I was able to vote. When the election was imminent, I relished the thought of having an input in the process of government that determines my life.

Early in 1992 I travelled to South East Asia using my newly acquired Australian passport. For so long my South African passport had been a source of anxiety and great inconvenience, a consequence of South Africa's pariah position in the international community. My journeys were often marred by an embassy staffer in some outpost either refusing to furnish me with a visa, or producing immense obstacles in my obtaining one. It made no difference that I did not have the vote in South Africa, or that I unequivocally opposed the apartheid policies of the minority government. The reality of sanctions (which I supported) was that any official South African document was to be regarded with the greatest disdain. In contrast, travelling as an Australian citizen gave me a sense of freedom and security.

The condition of the migrant is such that one always retains ones ties to the mother country – whether officially, spiritually, or both.

I have retained my South African citizenship for a variety of reasons, the most significant being that all my close relatives continue to live there – my sisters and my brother and their families. The condition of the migrant is such that one always retains ones ties to the mother country – whether officially, spiritually, or both.

I have come to love Australia, the people and the lifestyle. This has been a gradual and difficult process, but it's been a pleasant one. It's been like taking a journey down a long road, sometimes being distracted by obstacles at the side of the road, sometimes overcoming barriers in the way. I do not see Australia as the perfect society. Too many vestiges of the White Australia Policy linger, and while the issues of the rights of Aboriginal Australians are not dealt with adequately and satisfactorily, Australia stands to be criticised. But Australia is one of the more *ideal* societies to live in – the institutions of the state are strong, and it is a country where the ideas of a liberal democracy are at least having a 'fair go'.

It became important to me to fit into Australian society, because for so long I felt that I didn't belong. I guess as an outsider one never truly belongs, not in the way people do who have been born in Australia. But its the closest to feeling that you belong – as an outsider. I see Australian society as a bit of a contradiction. On the one hand, the modern foundations of this country was built on immigration, so there is at least an acceptable niche wherein which migrants can fit. On the other hand, there remains a reservoir of hostility to migrants, particularly migrants of colour. With this contradiction, as a professional woman working in a relatively liberal and progressive environment, I have managed to create a comfortable niche for myself – and feel the sense of belonging.

The peculiarities about Australia are the obvious ones – the relaxed lifestyle, multiculturalism, Australian league football ('Aussie rules'), the red earth of the Centre, the Great Barrier Reef, and koalas and kangaroos. For me the subtle peculiarity relates to the soul of the country, and particularly its innocence; one has the sense after living in Australia for a time that because this country has not been torn about by political violence or social chaos, there is almost a sense of naivete, a refreshing one. There is not the same level of cynicism or bitterness prevalent in places like the United States. But that innocence is changing – as Australian society matures, and particularly as the economic problems of this country grow, the innocence will be lost.

Australia's treatment of Aboriginal peoples still resemble aspects of apartheid in South Africa.

But my assertion about the innocence of this country is completely false with respect to Aboriginal peoples. To use the term 'innocent' and 'naive' to describe the experience of the first Australians since European contact is to engage almost, in vulgarity. That is not my intention. It is an accepted and undisputed fact of Australian history that the treatment of Aborigines since white settlement has left a legacy of deprivation and despair.

Being away from South Africa has given me a valuable time to reflect on the condition of my homeland. My time in Australia has also given me the space and freedom to come to terms with the sense of my identity; identity being the core at the apartheid ideology. Australia in many ways stands as a refreshing contrast to South Africa. Australia is a democracy with no official policy of political persecution (in that there are no political prisoners), there is a sense of political freedom and the positive experience of living in a democracy. It is reassuring to know you can publicly criticise government policy or court decisions, or engage in vigorous political debate, and know the sinister arm of the government, the security police, won't be harassing you. At the same time, Australia is not ideal, politically. Australia's treatment of Aboriginal peoples still resemble aspects of apartheid in South Africa. Australian political activists have over the years complained about police harassment. Despite this, there is a much greater sense of freedom living in Australia than in South Africa.

After moving to Australia I spent considerable periods of time out of the country, particularly in the United States and South Africa. I always returned to Australia – it was my base. Upon coming back from South Africa, each time I heaved a sigh of relief. It is always comforting to be back in a safe environment, to be in a place that superficially at least appears sane.

My constant belief for many years was that I would return to South Africa under a different political dispensation. But 10 years away, living mostly in Australia, is a long time. The longer I have stayed away, the more difficult the thought of returning becomes. Part of the reason is that I have changed – that there are many political and social issues I have been engaged in in Australia, which for a host of reasons would not feature as part of the political and social landscape of South Africa. In particular, certain women's rights to equality, so hard fought for and won in Australia, and which I take for granted as a woman living here, would mostly be absent from my life in South Africa. The 'national' or 'race' issue has always taken precedence in South Africa so that the 'women's question' has only recently become significant. I also like the luxury of living in a developed, as opposed to a developing, country, and having access to all the resources that are at our disposal in a country like Australia.

> ...a friend described my childhood home territory in Cape Town as experiencing an 'epidemic of rape'.

Part of the reason that I find returning to South Africa difficult is the turn of events there – that the 'reforms' and political liberation have unleashed a cycle of violence in the past few years that has left a frightening trail of misery and destruction. Apart from political violence, what we call street crime is on the increase because of the deteriorating economic and social conditions. For women the situation is particularly disturbing – a friend described my childhood home territory in Cape Town as experiencing an 'epidemic of rape'.

My new job as a law professor in the United States commenced in January 1993. I went with a sense of gloom and trepidation, because I had so come to love living in Australia. I also went with a sense of excitement and exhilaration, because it is a positive career move. My plan is to return to Australia after a few years.

I always thought I would love to retire to South Africa, because I want to die in Africa. I wanted my bones to disintegrate and become part of the African soil. I now vacillate on that desire, mostly because I think South Africa in the future will be a particularly brutal place for old people. Despite the many problems that beset Australia, I believe Australia ultimately will be a kinder place for old people. But who knows what the future holds?

Que Sera

Janet Labatut

Born in New Orleans in the United States of America, Janet Labatut travelled to Australia in the 1980s, initially to live in Perth, Western Australia, with her British-born husband. One year later she (and he) moved to Victoria. She and her husband Martin now live in Melbourne, where she works as a writer. Janet Labatut has published a number of short stories, including 'Hurricane Iris', which won the St Kilda Writing Competition in 1982. Her story 'A Tea Engagement' is published in the first Artemis crime anthology *A Modern Woman and Other Crimes.*

The story I usually tell begins at a place called Que Sera. I went there intending to eat boiled crawfish, watch the sunset, and gain inspiration for a new found interest – writing. The interest was inexplicable – hardly more than a pipe dream. I was not trained in writing and I had not read much serious literature. My background was marketing. Holding a business degree, at the time I was working as a representative for a contact lens company that literally 'turned brown eyes blue'.

I was extremely restless and disillusioned with my work and career. At times I had been successful and enjoyed the perks of selling, but at this time of my life I felt very unsuccessful. The previous awards, money and 'freedom' meant nothing. No longer motivated, I was bored out of my mind.

So I went to Que Sera seeking something – inspiration is what I told my friend J.W. Kenyon. I had intended to meet her for dinner or go to my parents' house in Mississippi for the weekend. That Friday night in April of 1988, I went to dinner alone.

At Que Sera on St Charles Avenue in New Orleans, I soaked my fingers in red hot crawfish juice. It dripped down my arms and made a mess of my lips which bulged from Tabasco Sauce. I sat outside on a wide covered porch that overlooked thousands of live oak trees and 'waited for inspiration' as I attempted to act like a writer. I was not really sure what writers were supposed to do.

St Charles Avenue is a major street in Uptown New Orleans that runs the crescent of the Mississippi River. It is lined with live oaks, streetcars, and nineteenth century Victorian mansions. The street was part of the inspiration that I hoped would zap me.

I noticed a young man eating alone, and guessed he was a writer because he seemed to bend over the book in front of him. I sent him a drink. After my dinner I introduced myself. He invited me to join him, which I did. I soon discovered that he was a writer of legal articles, an academic. He was in New Orleans doing research at Tulane University for a book on maritime law.

I knew he was foreign before he opened his mouth. He did not dress like an American. His hair was cropped, his clothes were stylish and he had an unseasonal tan. He told me that he was a Welshman from Aberystwyth living in Perth and lecturing in law at the University of Western Australia. He had a round the world ticket that would take him to the United States, Canada, a few cities in Europe, Asia and back to Australia. It all sounded unreal to me, but I could tell he was real by the way he held my gaze. He was pleased I sent him the drink.

I did not have the experience of the world which he obviously did, so I told him about New Orleans – the people, their accents and their interests. I suggested that he see some of the places that the locals frequent. From Que Sera I took him in my car to some places in Uptown New Orleans, then down to the French Quarter where we ate coffee and doughnuts at Cafe du Monde. There we talked till about four in the morning and it was time for him to go back to Que Sera where he had parked his bicycle. Although there had been dozens of restaurants near where he was staying, he had cycled thirty blocks to go to Que Sera. Before getting back on his bike he asked sheepishly if he could kiss me.

I said yes and received the gentlest kiss. I knew, then, that I had never met anyone like him. I refused to give him my number for safety reasons and told him I would call him.

The next day I went to my parents' house in Mississippi and told them I met an academic from Australia. My father prophetically said: 'I hear Australia is nice for young people.'

That Sunday, Martin invited me to hear Mozart's *Great Mass* at the St Louis Cathedral in the French Quarter. It was one of the events of the French Quarter Festival. After that we spent the entire day eating, acting like tourists, and talking. I told him about my brother, A.J., who had died

I soaked my fingers in red hot crawfish juice. It dripped down my arms and made a mess of my lips which bulged from Tabasco Sauce.

six months earlier. He told me about the recent loss of his father, then about his family in Britain, his professional acting career and his time studying at Oxford and Harvard. He explained that he was involved with someone who was in Perth. All of this had been very exciting and at times devastating for him. I told him about my recent religious experiences which included seeing the miracle of the sun – how I watched as the sun turned green, gold, and pink before my eyes as I stood on the beach in Pensacola, Florida. I explained that I thought this was part of a conversion experience that began when my brother became ill and I began saying the Rosary, which had been unheard of, for me, in my life prior to his illness. My prayer life had consisted of a few Hail Mary's and a Sunday Mass if I was in the mood.

I did not tell him in detail that I had been praying for a major change in my life – that I wanted to live my life properly, because I felt very 'far from grace'. I had had a few unhealthy relationships in the past years which had not left me feeling on top of the world, and this sign for me was a means of encouragement from heaven. In spite of having little in common, Martin and I managed to talk without ceasing, hanging on each other's every foreign word.

Martin took in everything and seemed to accept me without question. I knew I enjoyed his company but I could not see anything becoming of our friendship because he was 'on holiday'.

We agreed to get together again.

The next day, the thought of going to work was more than I could bear. I remember calling my parents and telling them I could not work any more. I wanted to quit. 'I'm freaking out!' I said. I could not handle the pressure, the tedium, the lack of fulfilment. Nothing in my life was making sense. I told them I wanted to go back to university to study literature or move either to the eastcoast or westcoast where some of my friends were living.

...there were people in the world who did not make a drama out of everything, including employment, no matter how necessary it is.

I am sure I made them sick with worry over their 27-year-old daughter who had a perfectly good job, with a secure income, and very good 'opportunities for advancement', and who was ready to toss it all in because of stress and boredom. They suggested I calm down and quit if I had to.

Martin and I continued to see each other almost every day after that. I told him how I hated my work. His advice was simple: 'Quit.' I soon realised that there were people in the world who did not make a drama out of everything, including employment, no matter how necessary it is. I continued to work in spite of the advice. Seeing Martin served as a temporary distraction from my work worries.

Over the next two weeks, Martin, the perfect British gentleman, patiently allowed himself to go through the screening process of meeting my friends and family. I was growing attached to him but it did not occur to me that I should worry about involvement with him. In my mind, he was off-limits. I was practical enough not to fall in love with a foreigner on holiday who lived as far away from New Orleans as you could get.

Eventually, he told me he was in love with me. We were sitting in the parlour of the house where he was staying. The house was an old mansion owned by a literary guild of aged academics. It was then that I realised that this house was very similar to one I saw in a dream many years earlier. The dream had been so satisfying that I told everyone about it. I also said that if I never have a house like that one, I will always have the memory of the happiness I felt in that dream. In the dream, I sat beside a fair-haired man. Martin is fair.

We both knew he would be continuing in his travels, so he suggested that I meet him for a holiday. That I could manage. But by the second week of our relationship, we were falling madly in love, spending every possible minute with each other. I kept saying: 'This is impossible.' He would correct me and say: 'Improbable but not impossible.'

The following weekend he met my parents. On the way home in the car, he said: 'Will you marry me?' I said: 'Yea, when?'

'Tomorrow!' was his reply. I said yes, but we would have to go through a marriage preparation course offered through the Catholic Church. My idea of marriage was that it is a sacrament of the Church. Martin was not phased by my need to do this. He, too, had told me on one of our early dates that he wanted to do things properly.

Well that was the whirl-wind romance that ended up taking me literally around the world. Every prayer and dream had come true. It was all better than I could have ever imagined. When I said: 'I want to move,' I had no idea that I would move to another hemisphere. When I said: 'I want to write,' I had no idea that I would be given all the time, money and encouragement necessary and a husband who would lovingly believe in me enough to help me make it happen.

This new relationship was not without trials, though. His girlfriend from Perth had arrived in New Orleans, though her stay was shortened by the news that he would continue to see me. I handed in my notice and planned to complete my job within five weeks. My parents had hoped I would wait, in case the girlfriend might change his mind.

It was probably the most difficult time for Martin because I knew he cared for the girl, and did not intend to hurt her. But, I knew that our relationship had come out of nowhere. To this day I say without a doubt it was a match made in heaven. He says I make it sound as though the heavens opened up and out dropped Martin. That was virtually the way it happened, but instead he arrived by plane.

My parents were happy for me and could see the sudden and miraculous change in mood, though there were some concerns and the reactions varied. After dinner at my parents' one day, my sister Ann was alarmed and said: 'You are moving to Australia with a man and you don't even know how he takes his coffee.' My sister Elaine said: 'Why not?' My sister Fi had said to my mother: 'There is nothing not to like about him.'

My friends were more sceptical. Peggy, who had moved to San Francisco and back to New Orleans several times, asked: 'What will you do if it doesn't work out?'

'Come home,' I said. But I had not really given a minute's thought to it not working out. It was the romance of a lifetime – one I had prayed for and got. There were no 'what ifs'. It was the easiest decision I had ever made. The timing was perfect for me. I was ready for a change, though I had no idea how large a change I was making.

> ...my sister Ann was alarmed and said: 'You are moving to Australia with a man and you don't even know how he takes his coffee.'

On my fourth trip back to New Orelans, my sister Lois reminded me that I had gotten exactly what I asked in prayer – including a visa which restricted work. She, my mother, and my Aunt Marie always say: 'Be careful what you ask for, 'cause you just might get it.'

Work was something about which I worried when I finally had time to think between packing my things, buying airline tickets, and bidding goodbye to everyone. I kept saying: 'What on earth will I do when I get to Australia?' When I started worrying, Martin reminded me that he was not marrying me because I was a 'Wesley Jessen rep.' He suggested I do whatever I wanted.

I think I had so mistaken my career for my identity that I feared that without a traditional career or lifestyle I would be a nobody. That was one of the hardest lessons I learned. Also, some reactions I still get indicate the difficulty some people have in knowing what to make of what I do. On my last visit back to America, Laura, my nine-year-old niece, asked me in typical American fashion: 'Are you, like, a housewife or something?' Her mother works outside the home, as do most of my sisters. To Laura and many others, I am somewhere in limbo. That was the feeling I had to identify before even I could accept the gift of being able to work at home. My girlfriend Charleen back in America had called her changes and the time in between those changes as 'transition'. It was slightly different for me because I was instantly doing what I wanted to do. I was just learning how to cope with so many changes.

Leaving my family behind was the other great difficulty. Not only was I no longer a part of a large extended family, I left many friends behind, some I had known for most of my life. Also, the loss of my brother was something still sharp in my mind. But these losses did not really hit me until I began travelling around Europe alone.

Martin worked most of the time. In England and Singapore he spent the bulk of his time in the library, so I was completely on my own, except for dinner in the evenings. This was a major adjustment. There were no demands on me. I had always wished and prayed 'to get off the world'. I felt that my life had moved too quickly and I could no longer keep up. I think I imagined just putting my foot out and stopping the crazy cycle like kids do on a merry go round. I suppose once it actually happened, I was faced with the vertigo that accompanied that stop.

At first, I just acted like a tourist, which was enough of a distraction. I traipsed around England, which was mind-blowing, but it did not provide the peace of mind I wanted. There was the added frustration of thinking I was a writer but not yet knowing how to write. I feared that people would think I was a phoney since I had not yet written anything.

Martin encouraged me to just 'relax, hang out, and keep up your travel journal.' This advice fell on 'cloth ears', as he says. I continued to feel compelled to do something, or be somebody. Some of that pressure is healthy, most of it was not, when I was supposed to be on a three month holiday, before breaking into a new world.

I now picture that pressure as being a barrage of images that dangled before me the possibilities of life. All were feasible, because I was capable and had varied work experiences, but a part of me rejected all these potential images. It felt more like 'the world's' values were pressing upon me to 'be the best – achieve the most – make the most' – almost like a spate of television commercials telling one what to do. The only problem was there was a great desire in me to fight the mould. I felt there was a tiny voice inside of me saying: 'This isn't natural. This isn't real.'

I discovered the wolf in me.

The challenge came for me to reject those assaults on the peace of the soul and to listen to the soft voice of calm that says: 'Leave it to the wolves.' Eventually I did, but then I discovered the wolf in me. As I learned to extricate myself from the cares of hard and fast living, I met the ugly parts of my life that do not just go away when you leave the continent and are given everything you have ever dreamed.

The other pressure we both felt was getting to know one another. This was done in restaurants, trains, planes and airports. Most people learn about someone first then commit for life. In a way, we can never say to each other: 'You're not the person I knew when we first met.' Although Martin does say from time to time: 'You've changed so much.'

My answer always is: 'Change is growth,' though the growth is often painful.

The night we arrived in Perth: from the plane above the continent, I saw a vast darkness in every direction, surrounding a patch of city lights. It was becoming clear to me that I was at the edge of the world. There seemed to be only an island of light that was to be my new home.

In Perth, I continued exploring my surroundings. Martin immediately went back to work and we slowly worked ourselves into a groove of life together. In the beginning, before Martin would rush off to work, usually nearly late, I offered to press a shirt for him. He was uncomfortable with the idea and said that I had better things to do with my time. I had a lot of trouble with this. Only a year earlier, when I was rushing off to work and I was at my mother's house, she would iron my things for me. It seemed perfectly natural to me to help him.

Martin's comment stuck with me because I really did not know what to do with my time, since I did not know what being a writer involved. Also, I felt Martin grown uneasy with the prospect of a 'wife at home'. A normal life or wife was the last thing he wanted. I was not really sure what being a wife (or writer) meant anyway, but I was slightly hurt that he did not want my help. It was all very unstructured living, which is what I thought I wanted. As it turned out, I got a part-time job (because of visa restrictions) and also did what I called volunteer work, escorting wheelchair bound patients at a rehab. hospital to Mass on a Wednesday. The memories of those few mornings on the Swan River are some of the fondest I have of Perth.

It was difficult for me. I ached to see some of the bed-ridden patients, because they were unable to do much throughout the day. I also realised that for some of those patients, just seeing a different smiling face once a week was a joy. Doing this sporadic and minimal amount of help was a way for me to 'give something back to the world, or God'. I felt I had been given so much. I saw it as a means of contributing to the world which I had not felt while working as a sales representative. In some obscure way, writing is another means of making a contribution. I decided early on that the world did not need another sales representative.

Years later, during the enrollment interview at the Catholic Theological College in Melbourne, I was asked about my time in America and in Australia. I remember thinking that the time I had spent doing seemingly capricious things in Australia was so much more constructive than the ordered and financially structured living I did while in America.

Martin's otherwise insignificant comment made me realise (only after a few years) that it is my choice to be a writer at home and that choice fills my life with seemingly unnecessary tasks which to me are necessary for sane living and more importantly are little acts of love. Martin and I resolved the ironing problem. We help each other.

Martin had to come to terms with my choice which naturally affected him. After nearly 15 years on his own, or in and out of relationships, he was now with a woman who gave up everything – for love. It was doubly difficult for him, because he saw himself as liberated and found himself living with a woman who was previously independent, aggressive and outwardly successful and who suddenly gave up any semblance of contact with 'the world' and was satisfied living, reading, praying and working at home.

These changes were not clear when they took place and neither were they always pleasant. When we moved to Melbourne after one year in Perth, we both sensed a growing uneasiness of some sort that remained until I regained confidence in my choice to be a writer and a wife. Also, mixed in with this transition was the frustration of rejection letters from editors, three house moves, grief and loneliness.

The disappointment of publishing fiction was devastating and discouraging at times. Fortunately I am a member of a writers' group in Caufield. We meet every other week to work on our stories and poems and we do so with the intention of building up, not destroying, the writers' confidence.

Yet while in Perth, when we were still blissfully happy, I cried a lot. I was terribly homesick and the adjustments were so numerous that often I was not sure why I was crying. But there had been so many changes and travel in our first year together that once again, I did not really have time to think about what was happening to me. Martin tried very hard to give me the life to which he thought I was accustomed. We frequently went out to eat, we went to concerts, clubs, films and travelled around Western Australia. Also, we returned to America to be married in New Orelans in St Louis Cathedral, where we had had our first date. That became our second trip around the world within one year. I had no reason not to be happy. I think the tears were also part of the grief of losing my brother, and leaving everything that was familiar behind in America.

In Melbourne, we finally got some sort of normal existence going. I began to write nearly every day. I had the outline for a novel involving many of the experiences I had had while working, which at times were bizarre. I wanted also to write about how I coped with the experience of losing my brother A.J. Eventually I became bored with the novel because the events were no longer relevant while I was in Australia, but it was this way that I began writing short stories.

Though I wrote quite regularly and prolifically, part of my days were spent doing very ordinary things such as laundry and shopping, which were as alien to me as my new husband and country. I had to learn how to do the most basic things, which I had never done while in America. Shopping in Australia was like solving a mystery.

While I was living with my family, I would not have a bar of the kitchen or housework. It was silly really, because my mother and sisters are fabulous cooks. The eldest sister and her husband had a restaurant specialising in Creole and Cajun food. In Australia, I struggled through the most mundane activities learning everything new, including how to write.

Martin began to work late to complete another book; he had just one year to write it. It was not until then that the loneliness caught up with me. He has since said that if he had known how much was involved he would not have agreed to the deadline. This was no consolation to me

...part of my days were spent doing very ordinary things such as laundry and shopping, which were as alien to me as my new husband and country.

when my days and nights were spent alone and my time was spent doing things in which I seemed completely inept.

I was making friends, which is not the same as having life-long friends or family members. I no longer had the comfort of Martin's many friends in Perth who had become my friends. Also, we had moved into a larger house to accommodate visitors from overseas. This coincided with the manifestation of the loss of a sense of security. This partly resulted from an incident in Perth where an alleged rapist, supposedly looking for the previous tenants, had visited our apartment while I was there with a girlfriend. This occurred only a few weeks prior to our moving to Melbourne so I was able to avoid spending much time on my own in that apartment while in Perth. With all the changes and moves, I had avoided thinking about the fear that surrounded that incident. The problem resurfaced when the Perth man and his accomplice seemed to fit the identikit of two people wanted for rape in Melbourne along the bayside and eastern suburbs.

Part of the problem of living in the new, larger house was never getting to know my neighbours. Also, we had had one burglary and an attempted burglary while living in our previous flat and then we had another attempted burglary in the new house. Until I read an article in the newspaper, I had not realised that one does not have to have been assaulted to have been a victim of whatever it is that makes you lose the sense of safety in your own home.

All of this coincided with horrendous tooth pain I suffered from impacted wisdom teeth. Until then, I had successfully avoided having them taken out.

It was one of the toughest times in my life. I felt Martin was not there for me when I needed him. I resented him and his work and blamed him for everything that was not right in our lives. However irrational the thought, the feeling of being very lonely was as physically painful as the infected tooth. I felt about third on Martin's list of priorities and I did not feel that that was what marriage was about. Not having family there was difficult. If I had been at home, I might have enjoyed spending time with my sisters and their children and someone familiar might have encouraging words about having surgery – another first for me.

Eventually the tooth came out as did much of the emotional pain and the frustration of writing. Slowly, my work was beginning to be published. Martin and I attended a marriage encounter weekend, which is designed to maintain constant communication in the relationship, by setting aside time. We moved into another new apartment, where I felt safe and where the neighbours welcomed us into their lives.

In Melbourne, I had to come to terms with all of this, which had deeply affected me. In spite of the difficult times, there were blessings. I had much more time for prayer, which was what I had always wanted since I heard about the Virgin Mary's appearances in Yugoslavia. Anyone who knows me has heard me talk about the Messages that the Virgin Mary has tried to give to the world.

When I first heard on the local news in New Orelans that the Blessed Mother was appearing on earth, I had a renewed belief that all that I had been taught about Jesus as Christ was true. I felt that God was still trying desperately to be a part of our lives, using Mary as a means of getting our attention so that we might receive all that is promised through Scripture. It was a miracle that pulled me out of living inconsistencies that had weighed me down and that stretched me in every direction but the one leading to Christ. This gradually led me to do theological studies where I felt as though I had my brain cut open and all of the intellectual and spiritual pleasures poured into it.

Since I began praying the Rosary, so much of my life had been one overwhelming blessing after another. I was able to begin writing, I was able to give up the sales work, I was able to live in another country, I was able to study literature as well as Scripture and history, and marry a wonderful man. But besides having all of my prayers answered, I began taking the challenges I had desperately needed for a sense of fulfilment which had not come to me from my previous career.

For me, Confession is an encounter with grace and a means of further growth.

Through prayer I managed to deal with the emotional baggage of a lifetime. I had to face it all once I sat and began to write. Through my writing, nasty little things about myself came out on the paper. Now that I had so much time to think, I was able to examine the life I had lived and was struggling to make sense of. Writing was a gift which had not materialised before I began to pray.

One of the first actions I took after hearing that Mary was asking us to 'be reconciled with God', was to go to Confession. Thankfully, I was given the time to move slowly towards living properly, much like St Augustine: 'Take me Lord, but not yet.' I discovered the fruits of the Confessional. I no longer see it as an antiquated means of expunging guilt, which I did for so many years when it was inconvenient to see sin for what it was. For me, Confession is an encounter with grace and a means of further growth. It is a means of letting go, a discipline of humility, not humiliation and a fountain of strength, which helps me to see where I want to learn and grow next. Such growth is not without its trials, challenges or literal persecutions, but they take on meaning when a person determinedly tries to live a life following Christ.

I now have time for frequent Mass. Nowhere else can I receive just what the Blessed Virgin Mary received when God heard her say: 'Yes.'

The challenges in my life came in every possible way but most often in just daily living. Martin has also been given his share of challenges as a result of my conversion.

In spite of our differences, we manage to live an exciting and loving life. But we both know that no matter how madly in love we are, we must work at making our lives happy and at keeping a marriage peaceful.

For me to overcome the bitterness I felt towards Martin during my adjustment period in Australia when I blamed him for my loneliness, I grounded myself in prayer and surrounded myself with people who also believed in the sanctity of marriage. I could have easily found friends who might not have encouraged forgiveness, perpetuating the hurt and anger I felt towards him. He, also, was forgiving of my less than forgiving attitude which held the grudge toward him.

Even my means of overcoming the pain was occasionally a source of disagreement between us. I attended a healing Mass, with which Martin had no problems until I decided to use 'the laying on of hands' on him. I enrolled in the Catholic Theological College which Martin fully supported until he discovered it meant breakfast services with his coffee and theology lessons at bedtime.

From time to time, Martin has had to gently remind me that he is not a Charismatic Catholic. He has returned to worship in the Church of England. He supports my pursuit of faith, but does not always share my enthusiasm. At times he finds it difficult to understand my devotion to the Blessed Mother, as I refer to the Virgin Mary. But for me, without a doubt, my life having turned completely around is in direct correlation to my recitation of the Rosary and a return to the belief of Christ present in the Eucharist. Without them, never would I have discovered the song of the currawong or the aroma of lemon-scented gums. Never would I have made close friends from about seven different countries, and discovered their cultures. Neither would I have been able to feel the bliss of returning to Martin and my new home in Australia after rushing to America because my father suffered heart failure.

All the while I have lived in Australia, I knew one day I would have a phone call bringing bad news. When it finally happened, I was stressed, but I had always prayed for strength, and received it on the long way back to New Orleans, not knowing in what condition I would find my father.

My father slowly recovered after being resuscitated. Thankfully, I was there when he and my mother celebrated their forty-sixth wedding anniversary in the intensive care unit and I was there when he defied the odds and healed quickly from open heart surgery. We spent a wonderful Christmas together with my sisters and their families, rather than a disastrous one.

The joys of moving and travelling and making new friends was something I could never have imagined possible. Having the luxury of time also enabled me to form friendships in a few short years, which some people are never able to form in a lifetime.

Though we were not together, Martin was able to spend Christmas with three different sets of friends. Whenever I think of the many countries I have visited, the dozens of friends I have made, and the very exciting life I have had in the last five years, I remember the passage from the Gospel of Mark (Ch 10 v.29-31) :

Anyone who leaves home or brothers or sisters or mother or father or children or fields for me and the gospel will receive much more in this present age. He will receive a hundred times more houses, brothers, sisters, mothers, children, and fields and persecutions as well; and in the age to come he will receive eternal life.

The Cambridge Connection

Ania Wilczynski

Ania Wilczynski was born in Canberra in June 1965. At the age of ten she moved to Gosford on the Central Coast (between Sydney and Newcastle). She went to Sydney at the age of 17 to undertake an arts/law degree at the University of New South Wales. After admission as a solicitor she travelled for three months before commencing a one-year M Phil course in criminology in October 1988 at the Institute of Criminology, University of Cambridge. She subsequently extended her M Phil thesis research to a PhD on 'Parents who Kill their Children', and in 1993 became Dr Wilczynski. She is now living in Sydney and working at the New South Wales Child Protection Council. 'The Cambridge Connection' was written when she was living in Cambridge in the United Kingdom.

I am a first generation Australian born in Canberra. I was brought up in Canberra and on the Central Coast (between Sydney and Newcastle). I later moved to Sydney to do an arts/law degree. In July 1988 I left Australia to go to England, to study at the University of Cambridge. After four years, I am still in Britain.

What lay behind my decision to leave Australia and live on the other side of the world? Having an English mother and a Polish father had made me aware that there was a lot of the world out there I wanted to discover. I had a certain restlessness, wanting to live overseas and to travel in Europe. Dual Australian/ British citizenship made it easier, in a practical sense, to go to another country (particularly England) to live. I had a strong sense of the need for me, as a woman, to be independent in terms of money, career and in other ways. My mother had encouraged me to do well academically and to pursue further education overseas. My decision to go to Cambridge to study was an example of my mother's remarkable ability to achieve what she has wanted for me throughout my life. She has generally followed the tactic of being eminently reasonable, never telling me to do anything, simply giving advice as to what she thought I should do. Usually, I would strongly disagree at first, and then ultimately (much to my annoyance) end up deciding independently to do exactly what she had suggested!

Going overseas to undertake post-graduate study also reflected a decision about the direction I wished my career to take. Whilst I had studied law as an undergraduate, I had never wanted to become a 'typical' lawyer – for instance, working in a large corporate firm. There was – and still is – a struggle within me between the 'lawyer' and the 'other' (perhaps I would now call it the criminologist/ feminist). In some ways I appreciate the 'legal' way of thinking: the cool process of dissection and methodical analysis, a 'putting things in little boxes' way of thinking. At the same time I find it limiting and constraining in other ways: the conservative nature of the legal profession, the way the law always looks backwards rather than forwards (they say that the law tends to lag behind developments in social attitudes by at least 10 or 20 years), the uncritical acceptance of the law as 'objective', 'the truth' and 'just', and its blindness to issues such as gender, race and class. The subjects which interested me most at law school were the 'policy' oriented subjects rather than those relying solely on 'black letter' law, and so I decided to do a masters course in one of these subjects, criminology. Criminology, with its focus on the 'fringe' aspects of human behaviour, concepts of 'normality' and 'deviance', and 'taboo' subjects, had long interested me.

> There was – and still is – a struggle within me between the 'lawyer' and the 'other' (perhaps I would now call it the criminologist/ feminist).

After finishing law school and being admitted as a solicitor, I had completed a phase of my life, and was psychologically ready to go overseas. I knew this would be difficult in some ways as I would miss my friends and family. However I also knew that it was something I had to do.

Finally, after almost two years of planning and acres of paperwork, I left Australia to study at Cambridge. I left by air, but travelled for three months backpacking to the Philippines, Egypt and Europe, the first half with a girlfriend from Australia and the second half by myself.

I had originally planned to come to Cambridge for one year only for the M Phil course. However I developed an interest in my M Phil thesis topic (women who kill their children) and decided to extend this research to a PhD (on men and women who kill their children). Once again this fitted into my mother's plans for what I should do with my life. When she had asked hopefully on my departure from Australia 'Do you think you might stay and do a PhD?' I had replied firmly 'No – I'll have had more than enough of studying.' Naturally she was delighted when I rang her six months later to tell her I was thinking of staying on for a PhD! Much later, after four years, my plan is to return to Australia upon completing the PhD (by the middle of 1993).

Living overseas (and particularly in Cambridge) has had both positive and negative features. One of the obvious advantages is the 'broadening of the mind' which comes from living in another country, experiencing another culture, and meeting and exchanging ideas and life-stories with people from both England and the rest of the world. This is particularly true in Cambridge's very multi-cultural graduate community. Everyone has their (often obscure) pet intellectual passion, which is interesting to hear about. Amongst my friends, these include nineteenth century radical British politics, suicides in prison, street children in Brazil, and ancient Etruscan burial tombs. During my time in Cambridge I have made some good friends, with whom I will keep in touch. I have already persuaded a few to visit me upon my return to Australia.

I have also travelled quite extensively in Europe and Britain, either with other friends or by myself. There have been visits to Germany, Holland, Denmark, Spain, Portugal, Italy, Greece, France, Hungary, Poland (to meet relatives), Czechoslovakia (on an exchange program between Cambridge University and Charles University in Prague just before their 'velvet revolution'), and walking holidays to the Scottish border and Wales. It has been much more enjoyable to do a number of short trips (for example on a one-month Eurail pass) instead of the six or twelve-month epic backpacking trip which many Australians do. Australians are well-known in England as the hardiest of backpackers, coming to Europe and in a year seeing what any English person would be lucky to see in a lifetime. The English seem to take for granted being so close to Europe, and some appear to regard it as a major journey to cross the English Channel. However, to Australians, it is a luxury to have Europe so comparatively close, and we have a totally different concept of distance from the English and Europeans. We regard it as 'normal' to take 15 hours by train or car to get between two major Australian cities such as Sydney and Melbourne. In that same time one could be halfway across Europe.

...we have a totally different concept of distance from the English and Europeans.

Living and studying overseas has been a valuable experience, increasing my independence and confidence. This is particularly true in terms of my academic abilities now that I have developed an expertise in a particular area, given conference papers and published articles. Backpacking has also been good in this respect; if you can cope with the incredible bureaucracy and trauma of having your wallet stolen whilst alone in Barcelona (including having lost the address and phone number of the friend you were intending to stay with in Paris); being obviously regarded as a major criminal by bystanders as you are bundled into a police car by officious-looking Spanish policemen who then casually stop off to book someone whilst escorting you to the police station; dealing with officials when you speak about five words of Spanish; and phones which don't work, or cut you off as soon as you get through) you can probably cope with anything!

Having a PhD from Cambridge is also prestigious and should be useful in my career since I plan to stay in the policy/research field of law or criminology. The 'networking' at conferences has been valuable too, not to mention meeting some of the people who've written the books I've read.

Britain has some wonderful countryside and old cities, and Cambridge itself is a picturesque and historic place to live with its beautiful old college buildings, immaculately kept gardens and grounds and narrow cobbled streets. As with England generally one certainly gets a sense of history – which is much more pronounced than in Australia. I will miss this when I leave.

Associated with the sense of history is seeing and being part of the Cambridge 'tradition', which is an experience in itself. There is the traditional (at times one could say archaic) college system. All the students belong to a college, and much of the student social life revolves around this. At many of the colleges (although not my own, Clare Hall) there is a 'high table' for the more senior members of the college. Often, formal dinners require the wearing of a gown and are preceded by solemn mutterings in Latin. Certain social and sporting events are held every year, such as the spectacular and extravagant May Balls (held in June!), the May Bumps (the major rowing races), and garden parties (complete with Pimms and strawberries and cream). There are also opportunities for the sociological observation of strange native rituals such as the 'burning of the boat', which takes place after the May Bumps. This involves numerous very drunk male undergraduates setting an old rowing boat alight and kicking it furiously, leaping over it as the flames roar about them, running up and down the length of the boat and almost being severely burnt in the process. The participants are expected to make a lot of noise and hug each other a lot. If this same scene occurred on a deprived housing estate with working-class boys, they would be branded as dangerous hooligans who present a threat to society. However, this is Cambridge, and therefore the exercise is viewed as a legitimate part of 'tradition' and 'male bonding'...

> ...the spectacular and extravagant May Balls (held in June!), the May Bumps (the major rowing races), and garden parties (complete with Pimms and strawberries and cream).

Starting life from scratch overseas is not always easy, or positive. It is a big step to go to a foreign country where you don't know anybody at all, where it is impossible to nip home quickly if you are feeling a bit homesick, and where phone calls home cost about $3 per minute. I don't think I quite realised how big a step it was until I had actually been in England for a few months. Before I left, everything had been so hectic with all the packing and final arrangements to make (whilst still studying) that I don't think it had fully sunk in.

One of the biggest problems anyone beginning life in another country faces is feeling 'settled' and getting to know people and making friends. This was also compounded by two other factors in my case. First, doing a PhD is by its very nature a rather isolating and intense task, demanding a great deal of self-discipline and solitary, single-minded (almost obsessive) devotion to one topic for a considerable length of time. This is not particularly conducive to meeting swarms of new people. Secondly, whilst Cambridge has the advantage of being full of young people and of having an active student social life, it is also a rather transitory place. A lot of the graduate students come for one-year courses, then promptly disappear. Even with PhD students, many finish and leave, or escape to exotic locations for long periods to do field work. The result is that one becomes attached to people who then disappear to the other side of the earth. Having a number of friends around whom I have known for many years and who know me very well is something I have missed most.

I have occasionally felt homesick, although this was more acute in the earlier years of my time in England; after a while I simply became used to being away. Homesickness has tended to hit the hardest when something significant has happened at home which has made me feel I was 'missing out' and that everyone was continuing on with their lives without me – particularly so at Christmas, or when my sister had her twenty-first birthday party, friends were married or had babies, and my much-loved Siamese cat died. This feeling particularly hit me when I received a letter from a close friend from whom I hadn't heard for two years, telling me that in the intervening period she had formed a relationship, married, had a baby, bought a new house and changed jobs.

> I miss... being able to make pumpkin soup at times other than at Halloween.

I have tended to miss people mostly (family and close friends) rather than places. Being away for such a long period obviously has an impact on friendships at home since letters tend to arrive less frequently and I inevitably felt that I was not as wrapped up in those people's lives as before. Some people lose contact entirely. However, some friends and family have visited periodically whilst I have been in England. With my closest friends the time and distance apart has not made too much difference to the quality of the friendship. When I have seen them it is almost as if I saw them only yesterday.

I also sometimes miss Australia's unique vegetation and scenery: the bush with its gum trees, native Australian flowers such as wattle, banksias and bottle brushes, the tropical rainforests of Queensland, and our spectacular beaches. I miss the sunny weather when I am locked indoors in England with the drizzling rain outside, although I do not miss swelteringly humid and boiling hot days in the middle of the Australian summer. I miss some of our exotic tropical fruits, and being able to make pumpkin soup at times other than at Halloween.

Life in a foreign country also means interacting with and getting to know the 'natives'. Cambridge is rather different from a 'typical' English city in that it has quite a high proportion of foreigners amongst the graduate students (who were the people I primarily met). I also tended to make friends with non-English people and whilst one should always be wary of making generalisations and relying on stereotypes, there are certainly distinct differences in the personality and nature of the English and Australians. The aspect I tended to notice most and which many other non-English friends commented on is the English 'reserve': the social distance, the formality and the politeness, and the time it takes to be open and personal and to get to know someone. Australians tend to be quite open, direct, down to earth, friendly and to speak their minds. I think I am typically Australian in this way. Some English people like this (and for example make comments that the Australians they have met have always been very friendly and outgoing) but others find it disconcerting, impolite or intimidating. A male Australian academic I know who has lived in England for a number of years told me that someone had commented to him that whoever he was dealing with, whether fellow academic, friend or shop assistant, he always looked them directly in the eye and smiled at them – apparently a rather unusual practice. Most had found this refreshing and engaging, but sometimes it had been misinterpreted (for example as sexual interest).

> ...sometimes I have felt that I am regarded as too open, direct, intense and asking too many questions.

I too have had mixed reactions to my 'Australianness'. Some respond to it positively and warmly; on the other hand, sometimes I have felt that I am regarded as too open, direct, intense and asking too many questions. One Englishman with whom I spoke recently told me that although he had a very respectable career as a financial consultant he was actually a closet 'anarchist'. Thinking this sounded interesting, I asked a few questions in an attempt to elicit in what ways, when, and so on. He closed up completely, refusing to answer any questions. Later that evening (after he had consumed a lot of alcohol) he asked me in a rather joking manner whether anyone managed to survive a conversation with me. When I saw him a few weeks later I made some light-hearted reference to his refusal to answer any questions and asked him why. (There I go again!) His reply? If he'd answered the questions it would have revealed some personal information about himself. Shock, horror...

In other areas too one is reminded of being a 'foreigner'. I have a reasonably broad, noticeable Australian accent which according to Australian friends who have talked to me since I have been away has diminished slightly but not very much. My accent is often 'picked' as Australian (or at least 'foreign') as soon as I say a few words. There are also differences in expressions used; I have had blank expressions in shops when asking for zucchinis (courgettes), eggplant (aubergine), sticky-tape

(Sellotape) or Glad Wrap (cling film). And I still make the mistake of buying stockings (which in England refers to the ones you wear with a suspender belt) when I actually wanted to buy tights (any type of pantyhose which go up to the waist; in Australia we use this expression only for thick winter ones).

I have become very aware of the stereotypes others have of Australia and Australians. Australia is seen as a tropical paradise where it is always sunny, we are always at the beach, and there are lots of sharks. It is sometimes viewed as slightly 'primitive' and uncivilised. The eight-year-old son of a French friend asked me whether we have roads in Australia, and disdainful references to 'the colonies' are occasionally heard. Harking back to the origins of our convict history, a number of people have pointedly asked me why I came to England to study criminology, since they would have thought that Australia was a much better place to study it! Some have also said that they regard Australia as a very 'macho' sexist place, and whilst I would not disagree, England is really no better in this regard – although these people usually implied otherwise. I am also bound to say that the aspect of Australian 'culture' with which English people seem to be most familiar is *Neighbours*.

I have been home to Australia only once since leaving, and that was one-and-a-half-years after I left. Feeling homesick, I was glad to see my friends and family again, and hear all the news that had been too time-consuming/traumatic/complicated to put into a letter. But it was an exhausting trip, trying to see everyone I wanted to see. I ended up feeling as if I needed a secretary to track down various people and coordinate my appointments. I noticed some changes, such as that everyone had become a lot more conscious of skin cancer and the dangers of too much sun; several girlfriends who in the past would have regularly spent hours in the sun in the middle of the day, with little or no skin protection, were now more careful. Nevertheless, more often I was struck by how similar everything was and how everyone was doing the same things. This reinforced my view that I was glad to be doing something different and having new experiences. There was plenty of time to 'settle down' and do the 'usual' – like climbing up the career ladder and acquiring a mortgage.

> ...there is always that feeling of being slightly 'different' and 'out of place' in a country other than that where one was brought up.

I have enjoyed the experience of living overseas and it has been advantageous in many ways, yet I would not ultimately want to settle in England. Almost inevitably there is always that feeling of being slightly 'different' and 'out of place' in a country other than that where one was brought up. Although this can be good for a period, and certainly has a 'novelty value' when meeting new people, I am not sure that I would want to live permanently in a country where I felt like that. For that reason I always planned to return to Australia when I finished my PhD. In some ways I have felt more 'Australian' and nationalistic since being away from Australia.

As I write my younger sister is going through the same stages I went through; she has recently finished her undergraduate degree and is backpacking to England to work for a few years. We will overlap by several months and then I will be back in Australia. Hopefully one of these days all of my family will end up in the same country!

No Turning Back?

Tui Taurua

Tui Taurua was born in Kawa Kawa, Bay of Islands, Northland, New Zealand on the 6 November 1956, eldest of two natural sisters and one natural brother, and four half sisters and two half brothers. Raised by her father and his wife from the age of three or four, Tui Taurua's childhood years were traumatic. Even though those times will always haunt her she is learning to deal with the experiences positively. In turn this has become the motivating force that inspires her to attain her highest goals.

After migrating to Australia in 1985, in 1992 Tui Taurua applied for her Australian citizenship which was confirmed the following year. She returned to study as a mature-age student completing the bridging course 'Preparation for Tertiary Studies' in 1989 at the Western Institute, which is now the Victorian University of Technology. In November 1992 she concluded the associate diploma in social science (community development) and in November 1999 will conclude her BA. From March 1991 to September 1993 Tui Taurua worked within the Victoria University of Technology Student Union and two years later took an additional teaching role in the Department of Technical and Further Education. In September 1993 she moved from Melbourne and is now living in Sydney.

I flew in to Australia on the 11 September 1985. Several reasons influenced my leaving New Zealand. The first was the break down of my second marriage. In 1980 I was very involved in a church which had been a major influence in my life for at least ten years. I realised that my marriage was dissolving and I was failing yet another relationship. With my marriage breaking down, church members would, I knew, attempt to influence my return to the marriage and I did not have the confidence or strength to deflect the attempts. My family thought my husband was wonderful and I knew they would disown me.

With my second marriage at an end, my travelling to Australia meant that I met up with my first husband who is the father of my son. He was living in Australia. I needed to unite my son and his father; as well, he was a means to leaving New Zealand. My ex-husband became my ticket out of the mess. This combination provided me with the incentive to leave New Zealand.

The political conditions in New Zealand were significant to me, too. I did not leave New Zealand because of the Goods and Services Tax (GST) but the GST made me glad that I was going. Fortunately, I left before its introduction.

Past experience meant that Australia was not my chosen destination. I had mixed feelings about a return to Australia once again. In 1977 I was in Australia and when I left I vowed I would never return. Just as with my second trip to Australia, marriage difficulties had precipitated my initial visit to Australia. The reason I went back to New Zealand the first time was because the marriage difficulties were insurmountable. (Upon reflection it was age problems more than marriage difficulties.)

When I decided to return to Australia I could not believe that I had reneged on my vow. At the same time, I didn't have much choice. I had to leave New Zealand because my family and friends would harass me to return to a marriage that was not working. I thought when you aged you became wiser. I seemed to have continued to perpetuate a cycle of problem relationships. My life has been a series of complications which seem to have worsened since I got older.

In 1977 I was in Australia and when I left I vowed I would never return.

My leaving New Zealand was an opportunity to place a buffer between my family, my second husband's family, and the church. I had no idea what I was going to do or whether revamping my relationship with my first husband would work out. I figured I would work that out slowly. Despite the problems surrounding my leaving New Zealand, I was excited about returning to Australia, because I enjoy new and interesting experiences. Once I had made the decision, I could not or would not turn back.

My son and I flew into Brisbane and stayed with my first cousin for a couple of weeks while waiting for my ex-husband to return. He was not leaving New Zealand for a couple of weeks. It was a matter of getting out of the country before my second husband heard where I was hiding. He had been chasing me in Auckland and I managed to stay one step ahead of him. I heard the day I flew out of Auckland was the day he found where I was staying hidden.

I was very unhappy when I came to Australia for the first time. I felt alone, with no family or friends. In Australia for the second time, my circumstances changed dramatically. I re-married my first-husband in 1987 and began paidwork in Brisbane. One year later I became psychologically and physically ill and have continued to battle both issues on a number of levels. My psychological problems stem from physical, sexual and mental abuse as a child; this continues to challenge me.

My husband and sons and I lived apart for a couple of months in 1989, then reunited. The marriage broke down again in July 1992. I returned to work in 1991 as an administrative officer with the Victorian University of Technology Student Union in Melbourne. By January 1993 I had expanded my job to include a coordinating role. In February the same year I began teaching community development at Broadmeadows TAFE (college of technical and further education).

I began my academic pursuits in 1989 in an attempt to find something to live for. I was intent, for a while, on justifying why I should die; I finally overcame this early in 1992. With my associate diploma in social science (community development) finally completed, I continued six units of the bachelor of arts, looking toward finishing my BA at the end of 1993. Late in 1993 illness forced me to leave Victoria for Sydney.

In December 1990 I came close to leaving Australia and returning to New Zealand. I had booked my seat on a flight and had every intention of getting on the plane. However, I realised suddenly that my friends are in Australia; I was and continue to be under psychiatric counselling; I have a wonderful practitioner who assists in stabilising my chronic asthmatic condition; and there were my studies. Each of these combined to persuade me that Australia is my home. Also I was not ready to start all over again. I cancelled my seat and finally put to rest that yearning to return to a productive family environment. The vision of a productive family is a story book illusion anyway.

I had booked my seat on a flight and had every intention of getting on the plane.

I remain unsure of my feelings about going back to New Zealand, ever. There are the many ghosts that I need to come to terms with and lay to rest. I cannot return to New Zealand at present and am unsure of what the future holds. Will I stay or go? I came to Australia thinking I would return to New Zealand when it is time to retire. I was intent on obtaining my Australian citizenship so I could vote and become involved in the politics of the country. I felt hesitant but recognised that if I wanted to vote I had to pursue citizenship. I obtained my citizenship in July 1993.

I was well received in Australia. Most people recognise I am a Maori from New Zealand. In Brisbane I had people introducing themselves to me on the street. I was forever asked if I knew 'so and so' or 'such and such'. I had the feeling that many Australians believe New Zealand is a small country and that we all know each other by name: many were intent on telling me how wonderful and enjoyable their holiday in New Zealand was. So many people approached me in this way to talk and pass the time, it was becoming a problem. Melbournites were not quite so forward in their approach.

The major difficulties of language are the 'colloquial sayings'. Two expressions that caught me unawares are 'sanga' for 'sandwich' and 'arvo'.

Other words are 'mell' instead of 'mall' and the way many people say the letter 'h' as 'haitch' rather than 'aitch'. Australian seems to be a lazy language because words are not completed properly.

In Australia, at first I found it disconcerting to have people laugh openly at me because of my accent. I thought 'what idiots'. I still resent being asked to say 'fish and chips' and 'six'. I am told by family when talking to them on the phone that I have an Australian accent, and Australians say I have a New Zealand accent. I just speak the way I speak and am learning not to take people too seriously.

My family are used to my comings and goings, whether I am living in Australia or some township in New Zealand. The negative reaction to my going from New Zealand to Australia for the second time was associated only with the fact that I was leaving my second husband in New Zealand. In the end, however, I suspect they just shrugged their shoulders and said: 'Tui is at it again.'

Living in Australia I am not homesick, but I do miss my culture, and now that I have become more academically minded I would love to work amongst my own people and become involved in politics. I miss my father, but recognise that I am better off living apart from the tentacles of hurt, pain, sadness and anger which surround and cloud our relationship. I have become embroiled in student politics especially regarding women and enjoy identifying and debating the issues. A minor problem is my cultural perspective which is not being addressed. This is because I have no idea how to overcome the problem.

I was raised more as a white New Zealander. This means I have experienced problems whilst having little knowledge of or knowing Maoridom. I know the feelings I experience but I don't know the language. What knowledge I have of my culture has been conveyed through the Pakeha culture. I have little knowledge of New Zealand's history. I was never involved in New Zealand politics. Now, it saddens me to know that I have more knowledge of Australia's history and political problems. I wish I had begun my academic pursuit whilst living in New Zealand: as a citizen of New Zealand it was strange to teach Australian politics. Even with confirmation of Australian citizenship, I cannot forget or excise my New Zealand and Maori heritage. I hope to return to New Zealand, but am unsure if this would eventuate because of the ties that are strengthening daily here in Australia.

I cannot forget or excise my New Zealand and Maori heritage.

I feel as if I have always had problems 'fitting in'. This is a throwback to my childhood days in which I was another woman's child and was treated as a second-rate humanbeing. I am still searching for a place for me. More and more I am at home, living in Australia: nonetheless I don't totally fit in. Compared to many of my workmates and friends I have been exposed to much emotional and economic hardship and this colours my perspective, ensuring I remain separate. At the same time part of me feels that I am very much a part of where I am. I love the different nationalities that reside in Australia. Australia is amazing. I love Australia.

I have returned to New Zealand twice. The first time was to obtain a signature from the husband I left behind. I wanted a divorce. The second time I returned was when my Uncle died. I realised I had forgotten what it was like to see Maori faces everywhere, it was wonderful. But I found the price of food extremely high and white goods were approximately the same price as Australia, different from what they had been previously. Another difference was my name: every time I tell people my name in Australia, I must spell it. I found myself doing the same thing in New Zealand. I had to consciously stop myself.

At times I yearn to go home for a holiday. The problem is where can I stay? I would be obligated to visit family. I would be even more lonely if I went home for a visit or to live permanently.

Nonetheless in 1990 I came close to returning to New Zealand, and envisaged completing a law degree encompassing a cultural perspective. This meant I would be learning about my culture from an academic perspective but that was better than what I presently know, which is limiting. My personal philosophy regarding feminist views and cultural heritage is being met from an Australian perspective and this concerns me because the more I learn about Australia the deeper entrenched in Australian society I become.

> **I had forgotten what it was like to see Maori faces everywhere, it was wonderful.**

Yet if I were to return to New Zealand I should have done so before now. To return would mean I would have to start again from the beginning. It has taken me a long time and a lot of hard work and perseverance to build networks, and find friends. I am not sure I have the energy to begin again.

Where would I like to end up? When I returned to New Zealand for my Uncle's funeral I came to yearn to return to Australia. I wanted to come home. I suspect New Zealand does not have the pull it used to have. Australia is my home now.

Your Flight Is Now Boarding

Jennifer Simon

Jennifer Simon was born in 1950 in Aberdeen, Scotland. A journalist by profession, she flew on Concorde and piloted a light aircraft while based at London's Heathrow airport as a reporter for British Airways. Badly bitten by the travel bug, she managed to get to Burma, China and Macchu Picchu in Peru before McDonalds. Before emigrating to Australia in September 1990, Jennifer Simon worked in the press office of the Greater London Council and for a major financial services group. She was a public relations consultant, then manager, of the Bank of Melbourne's media office, prior to going into partnership in business in Melbourne.

I was in the departure lounge at Edinburgh airport in Scotland. My connecting flight to London/Melbourne had already been called when the tannoy system crackled into life. 'Would Jennifer Simon, travelling on the 5 pm British Airways Shuttle to London, please contact airport information.' My heart missed a beat. 'That's me,' I told the member of ground staff as I handed her my ticket. 'How can I do that?' 'I'll have the call put through here,' she said unperturbed, showing me a telephone hidden behind her.

I waited, heart pounding. Who could it be? Had the friend with whom I was to stay in Australia had a last minute change of heart? Had one of my parents taken ill? Had my job in Australia fallen through? My flat in London was sold. I'd left my job in Edinburgh less than two hours earlier... The phone rang. It was a friend who'd been away and just received my letter telling her my news.

'I couldn't let you go without trying to wish you good luck and bon voyage,' she said. 'I just hoped I'd be able to catch you in time.' I laughed with relief and delight. 'Your timing is perfect,' I assured her. 'But you nearly gave me a heart attack. I'm looking into the aircraft from here. Ten more steps and I'd have been on it.'

The call was typical of the good wishes and support I had received from my friends once I had told them of my decision to emigrate. A huge smile spread over my face as I boarded the plane. Even the cabin crew smiled, probably because they were looking at the straw hat with corks bobbing round the brim which I was clutching. It was a present from my colleagues, who had gone to a lot of trouble to give me a good send-off. They even managed to locate an Aboriginal musician in the Edinburgh Fringe Festival and persuaded him to teach me how to play the didgeridoo. My efforts were heard 500 miles away in London, but only because of an inter-office phone link. My colleagues were helpless with laughter. I was blue in the face. The instrument is every bit as difficult to play as the bagpipes.

At Heathrow, I transferred to the international terminal where I was met by a friend with the remainder of my luggage. (In the preceding months, I had been commuting between Edinburgh and London every other weekend.) A clink of champagne glasses, a fond embrace, and I was on my way. Or so I thought.

This time, I was detained by airport security who wished to examine my hand luggage for a suspicious object. It turned out to be the Caithness glass paperweight my colleagues had given me as their 'serious' present. Being solid, it showed up as a black blob on the security screen.

The flight to Australia was as long as ever. At the beginning of it, as instructed, I opened an envelope given to me by a good friend in Edinburgh. It contained a card with words of love and encouragement and another envelope not to be opened until the plane touched down in Melbourne. I didn't know whether to laugh or cry, so did both. The second envelope contained a card depicting the 'other' Melbourne, in Derbyshire, England, lest I forget.

'Welcome to Australia,' said the man at immigration. It was early on Sunday, 2 September 1990. I had arrived!

There are many reasons why I had decided to come and live in Melbourne as a permanent resident. I wanted to have some adventure in my life. Living in a new country would be an adventure. I had a close friend in Australia with whom it would be wonderful to be reunited. And I had been to the country twice before, to Perth and Sydney in 1976 and to Melbourne in 1987. On both occasions I was struck by the friendliness and openness of the people I met, and the lifestyle. I appreciated the country's space and lack of pollution. I felt a sense of freedom. I had none of these things in London, where I was living at the time. I wanted them.

The thought of moving to Australia wasn't something I acted upon immediately. But I didn't want to get too comfortable where I was. And the thought wouldn't go away. One day, I asked myself how I was going to decide what to do. And I thought, when I'm 70, will I regret not giving myself the chance to live in Australia? Quick as a flash, I had the answer. Yes. I had turned down a marvellous opportunity in London, a job which would have paid me in pounds what I get in dollars here, because I couldn't see myself living much longer in London and managing to be happy.

My London flat was in a quiet leafy street just off Clapham Common. I had lived there happily until new neighbours who had moved in downstairs held amplified practices of their rock band and never cleared up the mess their two German Shepherd dogs left in the backyard. The house next door became derelict and squatters moved in. The police arrested a glue sniffer outside on the pavement. Getting to work was a daily nightmare because of breakdowns or incessant strikes on the underground. The trains were jam packed in the rush hour and not the most pleasant smelling. How things had deteriorated in the seven years I'd been there! I led a stressful existence.

A cannon is still fired every day at 1 pm. It's tradition.

I was then offered, and accepted, promotion, which meant working in Edinburgh, the capital of Scotland and one of the most beautiful cities in the world, with its castle towering over the city centre. A cannon is still fired every day at 1 pm. It's tradition.

So there I was, with a terrific team, wonderful employer when BOOM! My application to emigrate was granted, nearly a year after I'd made it and when I had all but given up hope. I slashed the price of my London flat, which had been on the market for a similar length of time, and began replying to the job advertisements which a friend sent me from Melbourne. She also sent me these words by Goethe: 'Whatever you can do, or dream you can, begin it. Boldness has genius, power and magic in it.' Within weeks I had sold my flat and was offered a job in Melbourne.

I had mixed feelings about what I was doing. I felt sadness, reluctance or relief depending on whom or what I would be letting go. There were moments of trepidation about how things would turn out. A perceptive friend lent me an inspiring book entitled *Feel the Fear, and Do It Anyway*.

I also felt a tremendous sense of excitement, and eagerness. The support of my family, and of my friends in the United Kingdom and here in Australia was enormously encouraging. Older colleagues shook my hand and said they wished they'd done the same when they had the chance.

My parents, who are in their seventies, were amazed at this step I was taking. They were disappointed, not least because only a few months earlier I had returned to Scotland to work in Edinburgh, which is a few hundred miles closer to Aberdeen, where they live, than London. But they accepted my decision without any attempt to dissuade me, as they had 16 years earlier when I threw in a good job in Aberdeen to take on the challenge of living and working in London.

I sought change, challenge, the opportunity to develop. All those years ago, when I had sought the same things on leaving Aberdeen, I had also sought my parents approval, which I think surprised us all since I had always been in the habit of behaving very independently. They simply said they knew I'd be all right. I felt humble and encouraged they had such confidence in me.

Being a journalist had led to my meeting lots of interesting people, flying on Concorde, visiting different places. As the youngest of a family of three I definitely broke the mould. My parents and my two elder brothers still live in Aberdeen, where I was born and brought up. But I wanted to spread my wings and seek new horizons.

When I was in my twenties, a friend who was formerly a Roman Catholic nun remarked that she could not see me other than restless, searching. She counselled me: 'Keep looking, but I think you'll find – and I lean on Buddhism here – that the journey where you find what you're looking for will be a journey inwards.'

I did not come to Australia thinking it would be some kind of nirvana. I did not come expecting to find the secret of life, rather to enjoy it more. I believed I knew more or less what to expect having been here before, and having made my third and most recent visit in May 1990, within four months of emigrating. I had wanted to make sure, if my application for permanent residence was approved, that I really wanted to live here and that I had a reasonable chance of finding employment. By doing so, the risk I was taking was a calculated one, but it still had a delicious thrill about it.

There were surprises. I had known that salaries were approximately two-thirds of those in London, but hadn't realised until I got my first pay cheque how much tax is taken out. In the United Kingdom, a 25 per cent tax rate applies to salaries up to the approximate equivalent of $45 000, whereas here the tax rate is 47.5 per cent. Certainly in the United Kingdom there are other forms of taxation like VAT (Value Added Tax – equivalent of GST) which is applied at 17.5 per cent, but I suddenly appreciated having been able to have more money in my hand in the first place and then be able to spend it as I chose.

What's more, you can usually manage to park your car almost outside the restaurant.

Inner city house prices are comparable with London's. I had expected them to be cheaper but then, I suppose, what price access to the city – any city? Certain items, like petrol and cappuccino, appear cheap to me. A United Kingdom friend was astounded by the cost of dining out until I explained that there is no VAT (GST), no service charge and – if you're dining in Melbourne – no need to buy wine, because you can bring your own bottle. What's more, you can usually manage to park your car almost outside the restaurant. Not much wonder Melbourne was rated the most livable city in the world in 1991.

What I was not prepared for was the insularity of the country and its politics. Since arriving I've been embarrassed by politicians posturing Australia as a world power, whereas I have perceived politicians, the general public and media (SBS – Special Broadcasting Service – excepted) as having too strong a domestic focus for that to be so. It's noticeable that Australia hardly rates a mention in the British, American or European media. It's difficult when you are here to find out what is happening in the rest of the world, apart from major disasters and the like.

In late 1990, the economic situation had deteriorated noticeably since my visit a few months earlier. In Victoria, the Labor (ALP) government was under harsh criticism for the state of the state as it were. By Christmas, I knew five people who had been retrenched.

Nor was I prepared for the pettiness of federal politics. I arrived when Paul Keating, the then treasurer, was trying to oust Bob Hawke from the prime ministership. Most Australians of my acquaintance seemed to find this personal power struggle, and the manner in which it was conducted, a crashing bore. All of them, media included, seemed to view the battle in terms of who would win the race to The Lodge, rather than question the damage being done to the country while this protracted struggle was going on. I was led to contrast it with how swiftly Maggie Thatcher resigned from office when she was challenged as British prime minister.

Why, if you want to register a business name, should you have to register it in every state so that no-one else in the country can use the name?

Having worked for the now abolished Greater London Council, which serviced nearly 15 million people, I find it curious that Australia, with a population of just over 16 million, has so many layers of government. Local councils, state government and federal government all seem to act out of self-interest rather than a spirit of co-operation. Why else would a law exist in one state, but not in another? Why, if you want to register a business name, should you have to register it in every state so that no-one else in the country can use the name? Why isn't there a national speed limit?

When I first came to Australia in 1976 I was impressed by the spirit of enterprise abroad; this made me want to return. The sense of conviction that you could do well for yourself by working hard, and with your share of luck, was so strong it was almost tangible. Where has that gone? It was one of the country's strengths. People don't lack the will to tackle issues and problems – I'm sure the pioneering instincts are still there – but there seems to be a lack of incentive. Government, state and federal, could do a lot more to help. In Britain, a reduced rate of taxation is a great incentive and assistance to small businesses. For Australia, on 26 September 1992 *Business Review Weekly* reported that small business was to be the target of a Tax Office crackdown. Is this the best time to be doing that, I wonder. Is this really the best step to be taken for small businesses right now, in the midst of a recession?

In a country as big as Australia, it's ironic that the people in power can't see the wood for the trees. What would happen if the broader picture came into focus? Perhaps the country would start pulling together more, with a positive effect, even in respect of the racism and sexism that I've been surprised to encounter. References to wogs, and other disparaging remarks made on account of someone's race, I may have expected to hear 10 years ago in Scotland, but not today in a cosmopolitan country like Australia.

My own reception was typically Australian – friendly, welcoming and, for some people, curiosity as to why I had come here. It took me some time to get used to how friendly people are. The first time I went into a shop and the man behind the counter (whom I had never seen before) said: 'Hi, how are you?' I looked round in surprise, thinking I had been the only one to enter the shop. I was. He was talking to me. I still enjoy it every time I am greeted like this, because it is such a welcome contrast to the United Kingdom where customers are more likely to be ignored or glared at if you dare to interrupt two members of staff chatting.

> The first time I went into a shop and the man behind the counter (whom I had never seen before) said: 'Hi, how are you?' I looked round in surprise...

To widen my circle of friends, I joined Bayside Business and Professional Women's Club (BPW), the local branch of an international organisation (Australian Federation of Business Professional Women – AFBPW). I was received warmly and within months, to my surprise, elected president. It is a custom of the club to go round the table at the start of a meeting so that members can share anything that they have experienced, or wish to draw attention to. When I said at the September 1992 meeting that I was celebrating the second anniversary of my arrival in Melbourne, I found a spontaneous burst of applause quite touching.

Some Australian expressions have been quite an eye-opener. In my first job, I was disconcerted when my boss enthused: 'Cool bananas, Jen' when something was going well. But that was nothing compared with my bemusement when something hadn't gone well, and I was told: 'Oh, that's tough titties.' I would never in a million years have heard such phrases uttered in the financial service environment in which I had been working, and which now appeared ultra-conservative.

Feigning nonchalance, I casually inquired of friends whether these were commonly used expressions. It transpired they were not, except in the advertising world where I was working on the fringe.

The first time I was greeted with: 'G'day mate, how're you going?' I thought my colleague was being funny. Surely real Australians didn't speak like that, only caricatures. But they do!

I had to learn what 'rorting' meant, and a 'double whammy', the list goes on. Words and names are frequently abbreviated. My house, being near the beach, is apparently in a good possie (position). Accent has caused mirth or bewilderment, depending on the circumstances. In the early days, before I became attuned to the Australian accent, my boss, who was little, came into my office with a man who was huge. 'Hi Jen,' she said, 'I'd like you to meet Tiny.' 'Oh, Tiny,' I grinned. 'That's a good name.' They both looked blank. Then I realised she meant Tony. It was the accent.

On another occasion, my accent prompted someone to remark it was a pity I wasn't Australian, to which I replied in mock exasperation: 'I can't win. In London, I was told it was a pity I wasn't English.'

There are advantages to having a Scottish accent, because it stands out and seems to be instantly recognisable to people I call on the telephone. It's only occasionally a problem, because generally I try to speak clearly. My accent is a part of me and I see no reason to change it.

When I hear a Scottish accent, I feel an instant spark of recognition and, I must confess, a twinge of homesickness. I haven't been back to the United Kingdom in the three years I've been here, not because I don't want to but because I made a deliberate decision to give myself a chance to become established here first. Other factors have a bearing on planning my return visit. For a start, there's the cost involved, not to mention the fluctuating exchange rate, which can make the trip even more expensive. Then there's the fact that Australia is so far away from the United Kingdom that I would like to take at least four weeks to make the trip worthwhile. As four weeks is the annual average leave entitlement here (I was accustomed to six weeks in the United Kingdom) I would have had to wait for a year to accumulate this anyway.

Last, but not least, with jobs disappearing the way they have been, I feel disinclined to tempt fate by requesting four weeks leave at this time. Nevertheless, I am curious to see how the recession has affected Britain, where many homes are now worth less than the mortgages taken out on them and where the unemployment rate is similar to that in Australia. Inevitably, I remember it as it was when I left. I want to see my family, and friends, and visit my old haunts, so I think a trip is on the cards soon.

The newness of Australian buildings sometimes makes me long to see something that is really old...just for a change.

Meantime, when it rains heavily I am reminded of Scotland. A travel article about Scotland can bring back memories, particularly if it features a picture of rivers and mountains. The sight of a British newspaper, especially the *Guardian* or the *Times*, makes my heart leap as if at the sight of a long lost friend. I hanker after the joys of reading a columnist like Bernard Levin, and for quality journalism generally.

The newness of Australian buildings sometimes makes me long to see something that is really old, as in the United Kingdom, just for a change. Christmas without the cold, and turkey served without mealie pudding, makes me think of the Christmases I have spent in the United Kingdom. (Mealie pudding is a traditional Scottish dish comprising oatmeal and chopped onions heated through – very warming and filling.) However all this creates not so much a yearning to be back among the people and the places I know but rather a renewed appreciation of them.

I feel that I fit in here as much as I would in any other country. I feel different because of my accent, but I am comfortable within myself, and that's what matters. People respond to whatever is projected to them, be it friendship or awkwardness.

If things hadn't worked out, and I still hadn't managed to make them work out in a year or two, I'd probably have gone back to the United Kingdom because I have friends there, because my work experience would be comparatively recent, and because I could renew my contacts without too much difficulty. I would not have seen any ignominy or failure in doing that: if something doesn't work out, you move on to the next thing, whether it's a relationship, a job or whatever.

As it happened, my first job didn't turn out. I realised from day one it wasn't me, and my boss realised it soon after. A young and dynamic Australian, she had hired me on the strength of a telephone interview and a meeting with her sister in London. We had both taken a chance. We parted amicably five months later, when I found another job. In all other respects – the freedom of space, the easier lifestyle, the reunion with my friend – I have what I was looking for. And it has been an adventure.

As a permanent resident, I can live here indefinitely. I have no plans to live anywhere else. But having made the move once, it's possible I might want to do it again, perhaps to Europe.

I have the words of William Jennings Brown pinned up on the noticeboard in my kitchen: 'Destiny is not a matter of chance, it is a matter of choice; it is not a thing to be waited for, it is a thing to be achieved.'

That's a tremendous attitude to have to life.

PART IV

The Politics of Country

The Other Side of the World

Anne Hickling Hudson

A lecturer in cultural and policy studies in the Faculty of Education at the Queensland University of Technology (QUT), Anne Hickling Hudson was born and raised in Jamaica and can trace the African and British origins of her Jamaican family on both sides back to the 1830s, before slavery was ended in the British Caribbean. Her studies in history, education and the media have mainly been at universities in the West Indies, Hong Kong and Australia, and in 1991 she spent a four month sabbatical at Stanford University in California. A question of enduring interest in her work is: how can we change the entrenched negatives of stratified British-style education implanted around the world.

During the Grenada revolution, Anne Hickling Hudson worked in Grenada as a teacher educator and education planner, while her husband was physical planning adviser to the government. Their two boys had their primary schooling in Jamaica, their first two years in high school in Grenada, and the remainder of their secondary schooling in Jamaica and Brisbane. Both young men are now working in Australia and visit Jamaica whenever they can.

1984: a hot Jamaican summer day in July and I was driving the familiar route along the Palisadoes road to the airport to pick up Brian, my husband, who was returning from a university business trip to the Barbados Campus of the University of the West Indies (UWI). He had been a lecturer in geography at the Jamaican campus of UWI for nearly 12 years. My career in education had stretched over more than 12 years and included teaching at a comprehensive high school in London, at primary and high schools in Kingston, curriculum development and education planning in Kingston and Grenada, and lecturing at teachers' colleges in Jamaica and Grenada. Australia was the last thing on my mind. Brian changed that when he stepped off the plane. He had seen in his professional journal *The Planner* an advertisement for a senior lectureship in urban and regional planning at the Queensland Institute of Technology (QIT) in Brisbane. He had dashed off an aerogramme to the QIT expressing interest, outlining a hasty resume, and asking whether they were interested. The question was: was I interested? Should he pursue a job in Australia if the QIT encouraged his application?

Australia? We had recently been making tentative enquires about university job openings in Britain, Brian's country of origin, and the United States of America, where I had close and dear cousins with Caribbean origins and US nationality and culture. Why not Australia? I shrugged and said to Brian that he might as well pursue the application. Australia was notorious in the Caribbean for its White Australia Policy (many people don't realise that it has long been stopped), but we had felt the sting of racism in London and knew at first hand about it in the USA: we were not expecting Australia to be much different from any other majority-white country. Yet our images of it were much more vague than of anywhere else. Australia was a cricket team. It had kangaroos, wheat, sheep and a few cities scattered along its coast. It was where my first cousin Anne had lived for nearly 20 years with her Dutch husband Jan Langbroek and their two Australian offspring Jean-Paul and Kate. Anne was the daughter of my father's older sister Catherine who had migrated to New York in the 1930s. The Langbroek family had visited Jamaica in 1983, and they seemed to like Australia. We had encountered very few other Australians. There was a postgraduate student from Melbourne at the University of Hong Kong, where Brian and I had met while we were doing postgraduate degrees there in the late 1960s. In Jamaica lived two brilliant Aussies. Barry Higman, a shy, well-liked lecturer, now a professor in history at UWI in Jamaica and one of the world's experts in the study of Caribbean slavery, is married to my Jamaican friend Merle who joked that she couldn't resist marrying him when she learnt that he had been born and raised in a place with the delicious name of Wagga Wagga! Then there is Pam O'Gorman, at that time the director of the Jamaica School of Music, another pleasant Australian who had encouraged some excellent innovations in the study and practice of Caribbean folk and popular music among people training to be teachers and professional musicians.

So we knew a few Australians, but really, it didn't make much difference to us whether we went to Australia, North America or Britain. Any of them would have afforded us a better salary, better professional career prospects, and, we thought, a safer, less politically tense environment than the Caribbean had turned out to be. Push factors were

Australia was notorious in the Caribbean for its White Australia Policy...but we had already felt the sting of racism in London and knew at first hand about it in the USA

more important in our decision to leave Jamaica than pull factors.

Prominent in the push factors were frustration, anger and sadness at the political situation in the Caribbean. In October 1983 the Grenadian revolution had been defeated, collapsing when fratricidal conflict among leaders we had known, trusted and respected for their achievements, paved the way for the invasion of one of the world's smallest countries by thousands of US soldiers sent by the Reagan government which claimed to have been 'invited to intervene' by neighbouring island governments. This was similar to the reversal of the 1970s experiments in social reform in Jamaica, when the mildly left-leaning government of Michael Manley was defeated by a right-wing backlash suspected to be underpinned by clandestine US government intervention. Our position was with Caribbean radicals who worked for the kind of change that introduced minimum wage laws, the strengthening of trade union rights, subsidised health, housing and education, worker participation in decision-making at the workplace, maternity leave laws and other reforms which encountered the subordination of women, and – here was what the then United States government could not stand – a greater share of the national economy for the local government and people, and for the first time a small exchange of trade and assistance from socialist countries.

Like many Caribbean nationalists, we were angry at the bullying intervention of the United States government, its interference in Jamaica and Grenada joining a long historical record of 'Big Stick' politics in the whole Latin American region which it arrogantly regarded as its backyard. Absolutely no innovations were to be tolerated that posed even the mildest departure from the structure that ensured the dominance of North American ownership and control of the majority of the region's important resources and the subordination of our economic progress to this pattern.

In 1980 Jamaica experienced a frightful political year. The flood of guns from the United States of America contributed to the killing of 800 Jamaicans in unprecendted battles between two main political parties. A stream of US preachers, in ranting sermons in makeshift religious tents all over the country, advised Jamaicans against supporting the Manley government which they equated with evil by drawing analogies with *Old Testament* tales. We saw the manipulation of the newspapers that was so amazingly similar to what had occurred in Chile before the overthrow of Allende. And in 1983 came the invasion of Grenada, putting to an end what had seemed like the most successful effort in the history of the English-speaking Caribbean to start reversing the centuries of colonial neglect and abuse which left the majority of the region's population dispossessed and in extreme poverty. Worse than the invasion was the betrayal of Caribbean hopes by the Grenadian leaders. Their inability in a crisis to solve disagreements about strategy without resorting to a power struggle left Grenadians on both sides of the argument dead and gave the US government the excuse it had been waiting for.

Could there be any hope for the small and defenceless Caribbean whose position put it constantly in the shadow of the great jackboot to the north? If there had seemed to be a real prospect of progress in the sense of strengthening national economies to counter poverty, we would have put up gladly with the low professional salaries, the relative lack of sophisticated consumer goods, the economic constraints that forced us, with two salaries, to have to take out a house improvement loan to repair the car. But the prospect of social progress appeared to be halted by the extreme economic rationalist solutions of the eighties which seemed to fly in the face of common sense. Caribbean countries, like other Third World countries the world over, had to open up their economies even more than before to 'market forces'. 'Market forces, indeed!' says **Caribbean** Caribbean scholar Rex Nettlefold. 'It is easy to believe in **countries, like** market forces if one controls not only the market but the **other Third World** forces.' In Jamaica market forces meant privatising ownership **countries the world** to the ridiculous extent of selling off the government-owned **over, had to open** bus service to private minibus operators, and allowing into **up their economies** the country floods of consumer goods from the United **even more than** States of America, from clothing to cornflakes, toilet paper **before to 'market** to trinkets, fatally undermining the effort to make them **forces'.** ourselves. It meant slashing government spending on health, housing and education, accepting the low prices that the 'First World' deemed suitable for our raw material resources. In the meantime, poverty deepened, and so did the increasing danger of personal violence – robbery and murder – which is inevitable in societies where 20 to 40 percent of the population is unemployed without the safety net of welfare payments which are taken for granted by the ten percent of unemployed in rich countries.

Brian was offered the QIT lectureship, after an hour's long-distance interview by telephone and another in-the-flesh interview at QIT's expense, in Brisbane. He said Brisbane looked like a livable city, with arcades of interesting shops, the Queen Street Mall full of people obviously enjoying its outdoor cafes and entertainment, old pubs and historic buildings to counter the urban impersonality of glass skyscrapers, the Botanic Gardens bordered by the Brisbane River and beautiful with familiar tropical trees and flowers. We had to decide whether to make the tremendous break involved in going to the other side of the world – a 30 hour journey by air across the United States of America and the Pacific. We did not conceptualise just how much of a wrench it was going to be – how much of a culture shock, how we would yearn for family and friends and the familiar loud, gregarious warm and vibrant culture of the Caribbean, how we would miss the University of the West Indies, how expensive it would be to visit home, how difficult it would be for our two 15-year-old boys, son Dominic and nephew Alexis, to adjust to school and make new friends in Brisbane. A sense of adventure joined the push factors to persuade us to 'give it a go' (one of the many neat Aussie expressions I've picked up). But this does not put us in the same category with those migrants who queue up for years in the dream of going to Australia, or with those like the South East Asian refugee we saw on Brisbane television recently who said that coming to Australia was like moving from hell into heaven. The pull factors were minimal. The push factors made up our minds, together with thousands of other professionals who had migrated from the Caribbean in a crippling brain drain, transferring a significant amount of wealth in the shape of expensively educated human resources and scarce skills from the poor to the rich world.

1992: we have been in Brisbane since February 1985, a long time to have spent on the other side of the world. We have an understanding of and attachment to Australia, its people and problems and environment, that we never dreamed of in those early years which were focused on the struggle to survive and adjust, to overcome the weight of depression at leaving home, to persuade ourselves that new friends and better career opportunities and conditions were some sort of recompense for the loss of ready access to our nearest and dearest.

Have we fitted in? To an extent, but people who migrate as adults with teenagers will never feel completely at ease with their adopted society. I'll counterpoint what we like with what we miss to try to illustrate the bitter-sweet process of resettlement.

The vastness of the continent takes on a human scale by the excellent transport and telecommunication facilities that enable people to keep in touch with their networks of relatives and friends all over the country. **The distances flabbergasted us.** The distances flabbergasted us. Sydney is a 16 hour unbroken drive from Brisbane, and Melbourne is a further 18 hours by road from Sydney. Perth is a four day rail journey across the continent, and Darwin is a five day drive, or a four hour flight, from Brisbane – as far as Jamaica to Trinidad. But even we as relatively rare Jamaican migrants soon established a relative-and-friend network from one end of the continent to the other.

There's my first cousin Anne and her family, who helped us immensely to settle in during our first three years in Brisbane. Anne, Jan and daughter Kate have now moved to Melbourne after having lived in Brisbane for 20 years. Jean-Paul has a dental practice in Surfer's Paradise. Other Jamaicans in the continent-wide network include Beverley Evans-Ormerod in Perth, Ian and Pat Isaacs and their family in Darwin. We are linked not only by close ties of culture and friendship, and by the close association that we have all had with the University of the West Indies, but also by our work in Australian universities. We stay with each other when we can make the long trek, and make good use of Telecom's long distance phone facilities (we can't think why there would be any need for the new private telephone service, Optus, when Telecom seems so excellent).

Caribbean contacts in Brisbane have led to our being able to enjoy regular supplies of Jamaican 'Scotch Bonnet' peppers, the hottest in the world, gungoo peas, guava jelly and guava stew. Then there has been the occasional visitor from home, friends and colleagues who have travelled here for conferences and other academic work, including Pauline Samuda, who was a fellow teacher with me, Gladstone Mills, Ina Barrett and Hyacinth Evans of UWI, Peter Figueroa (snr) and his wife Carol of Southampton University in England, and Phyllis McPherson-Russell, formerly an education minister in Jamaica, Joan Tucker, Audrey Cooper, and Pam O'Gorman, all music educators. A cloud of homesickness descends on us when such visitors leave, but that's one of the penalties of exile.

Australians are mostly very friendly and hospitable people, and many hands of welcome have been extended towards our family. People are intrigued. 'Why in the world would you decide to leave the Caribbean?' they ask, full of brochure visions of beautiful beaches, waving palms, luscious tropical fruits and a holiday atmosphere, and oblivious that this comes accompanied by a range of exceedingly difficult, real life problems and pressures. Cricket, initially, figures prominently in the conversation, until it becomes amazingly clear how little we know about it. Aussie cricket fans will tease us: 'Call yourself West Indians and not know about cricket??' This led to our two lads, who were mainly soccer fans when we first came, quickly becoming very familiar with cricket. By the time the West Indian team came to play Australia in 1988, they were following the matches with an intensity that riveted them to television and radio. It intrigues me that during a test match, many Australians are as glued to the cricket as many West Indians, and that the Woolloongabba cricket grounds in Brisbane will be as packed as Sabina Park in Kingston with equally fervent fans. The complexities of a British colonial heritage!

Counterpoised against the making of a new network of friends in Australia is a feeling of desperation at being so far from friends in the Caribbean and, even more, family. Long letters and all-too-brief phone calls don't compare to the cosy cohesion of being next door. Now that our lads are 23, they have flown the nest to set up their own apartments. They are within 10 minutes drive of us in Brisbane, but I hate being without children in my house. Their departure makes me realise that in Jamaica we would not have been so bereft, for our house would have been frequently visited by my nieces and nephews aged four to 21. I miss them acutely – my brother's two daughters and son, my sister's two little sons, and my adopted sister's daughter and son. I am lucky enough to have both parents still alive – now both in their eighties. But I have missed most of their evening years. I've travelled home to Jamaica four times to stay with them, and I have been putting on the word processor my father's memoirs, a

> Long letters and all-too-brief phone calls don't compare to the cosy cohesion of being next door.

fascinating overview of his youth in rural Jamaica, his long career with the government civil service in the ministries of agriculture and housing, his post-retirement work with statutory bodies including the Jamaican Folk Museum, the Scientific Research Council and the Bureau of Standards, and in general of the changes in Jamaican life that he had witnessed in his 81 years.

In 1990 I went home to join the family in celebrating their fiftieth wedding anniversary, when my brother organised a big party for them. But I was not there in 1989 when he put on a special music concert to celebrate the fiftieth anniversary of my mother's music teaching studio, which she established in 1939 after doing her professional training in the piano and violin in Britain. My mother is as close to me as second skin. She taught me to read fluently by the age of four, and it feels as if since then she formed every important skill that I since developed. She taught me the piano, saw to it that I learnt the violin, and inspired me through all eight examinations of the British Royal School of Music in both instruments as well as coaching me for the exams in 'O' and 'A' Level music in the British GCE (General Certificate of Education). Caribbean people are still taking many of these British external exams today. Through her own love of books and people, and her success in writing plays and historical pageants and having them performed, she developed in all of us a love of the wide world of literature and the arts, she taught me how to study and achieve, she taught me how to be warm and gregarious. To have missed the fiftieth anniversary of her music studio, and then later to miss the ceremony at which she was one of the outstanding Jamaicans awarded a silver medal for her contribution to the arts, sent me into real depression for some time. All four of us still have our passion for the fine arts. My brother Frederick, one of the Caribbean's leading psychiatrists, integrates drama and music therapy into his practice and regularly writes and produces musical plays. My sister Gillian, who trained as a plant pathologist and is now a high school teacher, also studied the piano and violin and spent years involved in lighting and stage management work for various dance and theatre groups. My sister Kathryn, who like me was successful in all eight piano exams, trained as a special education teacher with expertise in the education of the mentally disabled, but is now the only one of us who has made music her full-time career. She has taken over the administration of my mother's piano studio and teaches the piano there, and is director and producer of the very successful folk singing group, the Carifolk singers. A lot of their folk music is researched and arranged musically by her, and Carifolk concerts are a wonderful experience. As for me, I still gain my deepest relaxation from practising the piano and violin, and am an ardent listener to classical music on Australia's excellent radio stations.

> Through her own love of books and people, and her success in writing plays and historical pageants and having them performed, she developed in all of us a love of the wide world of literature and the arts...

In Brisbane, people who look like me (dark brown with an 'Afro' hairstyle) are often assumed to come from 'the islands', by which Australians mean the Pacific Islands such as Fiji, the Solomons, Samoa, Papua New Guinea. From 1986, our second year in Australia, I continued my career in teacher education at the Brisbane College of Advanced Education, now amalgamated with QIT to become the Queensland University of Technology. In my first few years there when a new class of student teachers would ask where I was from, I would sometimes ask them to guess from my accent. Usually the first guesses were 'The Pacific?' and occasionally even 'Thursday Island?' but if there were students from Britain, they would generally identify the Caribbean. In one of these classes, one woman replied immediately 'The West Indies, of course! I don't listen to cricket for nothing!' And when I visited a school and was talking to a group of Year 12 students, I was surprised when a boy asked me: 'Are you from Jamaica?' I asked him how he knew. He had never been there, he said, but he was a great reggae fan and listened constantly to Jamaican reggae performers. It was a matter to ponder over that my accent was immediately comparable to reggae songs. Often people assume, when I tell them I work at Kelvin Grove, that I am working with the Aboriginal Support Unit. Or they assume I'm an Aboriginal student. 'How well you have done!' say some when they hear that I am an ordinary, everyday lecturer teaching in the degree programme. Their surprise reflects my unusual position of being one of the very few black lecturers in Brisbane, apart from those in Aboriginal Support Units who are obviously Aborigines. Most of my students have never had a black teacher in their lives. Sometimes my foreignness is useful in teaching cross-cultural studies. Sometimes it feels terribly isolating, and it's irritating that people are so puzzled at encountering a black professional. How patronising they can be!

It was a matter to ponder over that my accent was immediately comparable to reggae songs.

Australians like our West Indian accents. But when I'm speaking in a large meeting of colleagues, it sounds to me so different from everyone else that it adds to my feeling of being like a goldfish in a bowl. The differences in Aussie pronunciation took us a little while to get used to. During our first few weeks here, I went into the Cole's supermarket on the Queen Street Mall to buy a bottle of wine to take to a friend's party, and searched high and low for the alcohol section. At last I saw an assistant and asked her where the wine was kept. 'The what?' she said. The wine. 'The what?' she kept repeating. 'Wine! Wine! The kind that you drink at dinner,' I said with increasing desperation, miming pouring out wine and drinking it. 'Oh – you mean the woine!' said she. 'We don't keep woine here. You have to go to the bottle shop for that.' I am told that my 'wine' sounds more like 'Wayne', and apparently my 'Hudson' sounds so much like 'Hodson' that I have had to get used to spelling it before it is written down. I am a bit put out, however, when I'm on the phone to my son Dominic, ask how he is, and he replies that he's 'foine'!

Anne Hickling Hudson

My first job in Brisbane was as a research assistant in a 1985 teacher education project at the University of Queensland. The questionnaires that were sent out to first year teachers asked what they thought could usefully be added to the diploma of education course. Analysing the responses, I had to put aside one which said that the course should have 'more wine and cheese arvos', and ask later what this meant (picturing an arvo to be another item of food to add to the wine and cheese). I still haven't got over the amusement of being told that it was short for 'afternoon'! Dominic and Alexis were of great use to us in translating the long list of new expressions which they seemed to learn at school within a month or two. These included: galah, sticky beak, hard yakka, cossie (for swimming costume!), pressie, wanking, Claytons, Buckley's chance, gung ho, crook (meaning ill), wog (meaning both flu bug and dark-skinned foreigner), and chook. I learnt at a union meeting what it was to 'do a Dorothy Dix' and what it meant to be 'behind the eight ball'. But the list continues. Recently my husband asked me to get a six pack of beer from the bottle shop. The assistant said to me: 'Do you want stubbies?' 'Stubbies?' I replied, puzzled because I knew that I'd clearly said the brand name I wanted. Patiently she said: 'Do you want bottles or tins?' This Christmas we received a card from a friend in Jamaica that bore the message: 'Hope you are rooting for the West Indies at cricket!' I hadn't known, until Brian told me, that 'rooting' here means something totally different from 'supporting' or 'cheering on'.

The language experience has brought home to me the extent to which there are different 'Englishes' all over the world. Being unable to speak Jamaican English except to my family is a severe cultural blow to me. On the few occasions that I have slipped into it, I've become involved in such long explanations that it seems hardly worth it. One winter in Brisbane I was picking mulberries off a bush in the Kelvin Grove car park (it was intriguing to see mulberries come to life after all those years as a child singing 'here we go round the mulberry bush' without the faintest clue of what a mulberry was). Well, how was I to know that they stained? I reached up high to get the sweet clusters at the top of the bush, and a whole clump of juicy berries fell onto my new red blouse leaving a deep purple-black mark. When my colleagues saw it, they immediately recognised that I'd been at the mulberry bush and told me how hard it was to get mulberry stains out. 'Greedy choke puppy,' I lamented to them. What? I had to explain, first, about our everyday use of proverbs for expressing emotions and morals, and second that 'greedy choke puppy' meant that if I hadn't been so greedy as to reach up for yet more mulberries at the top of the bush, my shirt wouldn't have been stained. But what did that have to do with poppies? they asked. Not poppy, I said, puppy! If a puppy is so greedy as to try eating a bone that's too big for its throat, it will choke. Oh yes. Hmm. Next time it will be much easier to say: 'If only I hadn't been so greedy as to pick the mulberries at the top of the bush!' However, I can't help slipping occasionally into such observations as

'Cockroach don't business inna fowl party' or 'Rockstone a river bottom don't know sun hot', or 'they're giving us a basket to carry water'.

My understanding of the complexities of attitudes about race has immensely increased since living in Australia. The Caribbean still suffers from a colonial legacy of racial attitudes and structures, but these are more overt and extreme in Australia. Australian views about race fall along a continuum. At one end there are the extreme right wingers, like the notorious retired army-serviceman who on radio called Japanese 'slope headed, slanty eyed little bastards' and who would like immigration laws revised so that Black Africans and Asians would have to show 'bloody good reasons' as to why they should be permitted in Australia. In the middle are those who are vaguely uncomfortable about sharing 'their' country with non-white racial groups on grounds that this would dilute the 'Australian' ethos – by which they usually mean the British derived ethos. People with this view don't usually know anyone from ethnic minorities, and tend to be limited by insularity and a narrow education, but some seem to be quite open to change. A lot of the students I encounter seem to be in this category. At the other end of the range are warm-hearted, culturally adventurous Australians who see immigration of a variety of races and cultures as a positive cultural benefit to the country, and go out of their way to make newcomers feel welcome. We, as a Caribbean migrant family, have been lucky enough to meet mostly the latter type. Is it to do with levels of education and cultural sophistication? In other words, does the fact that we move in university circles insulate us from the racism that is so clearly directed at Aborigines and Asians?

We have met our share of people who, though friendly, are nevertheless so completely ignorant of black cultural developments that they freely talk about 'Negroes' and 'niggers in the woodpile' (this apparently means something like 'fly in the ointment'). I've been told by some Australians that I am the first 'Negress' they have ever met! Unselfconsciously, people like these used the word 'black' to mean everything that is negative, undesirable and illegal, including the black (illegal) economy, 'Black Tuesday' of the 1987 sharemarket crash, the 'black' deeds of Tian An Mien Square, black feelings of depression or anger, black (or sick) humour, black film (confusing, this!) black days where everything goes wrong, and many more. I started to keep a list of them but got too fed up to continue. Quite an education for us. Not since my childhood of reading European fairy tales and English text books have I seen 'black' so negatively used in such an immense variety of contexts: I thought that since the 1960s the whole world had deliberately brought to an end this usage. But there seem to be numbers of Aussies, including just about every newspaper editor in the land, who have never heard of this development, judging from their frequent, unselfconscious and interchangeable use of 'black' in headlines and articles, both as a negative and as a skin colour description.

Australia's ethnic diversity makes it a far more interesting place to live than if it were monoculturally anglo-celtic, as it was before the second world war. It surprises our friends abroad when we tell them that with about 25 per cent of the population being of non-British stock, more than 100 different languages are spoken in Australia, with some 120 newspapers printed in more than 30 languages other than English. SBS (Special Broadcasting Service) television has one of the most advanced multicultural programming approaches in the world. Its world news is informed and excellent when compared to the selective distortions on other stations and, being a real film buff, I've enjoyed its fascinating variety of some of the world's best films from countries including France, Spain, Italy, Germany, the Soviet Union, the Middle East, Egypt, China, India, South America and Cuba, all with English subtitles. It gets top marks, too, for its Aboriginal programs and the opportunities it gives to migrants to voice their views and show their cultural creativity. We are regular ABC (Australian Broadcasting Corporation) watchers and radio listeners as well. We love, too, the variety of restaurants in all the big cities, which makes eating out an adventure – there is even a Jamaican restaurant in Melbourne which, I understand, serves ackee and saltfish as well as other delights and is a great success. There's no authentic Caribbean restaurant in Brisbane though, and plenty of room for one, judging from the enthusiastic reactions of some of our friends when they sample my adaptations of jerk chicken, escoveitched fish, stew peas, run-down (mackerel with coconut sauce), baked sweet potato, rice and peas and other Jamaican delicacies.

With Aboriginal Australians, I've learnt how complex is the issue of cultural identity. There is no doubt that they are culturally Aboriginal rather than anglo-Australian, yet apart from the handful still living in traditional tribal communities, they share a lot of white culture, and I admire the success of many of them in combining the traditional and the new. We are always very aware of the tragic devastation of Aboriginal Australia and see the scenery with a mental image of its ancient settlement. We have to point this out to many of our students who commonly refer to places in Australia being 'first' settled by the English. In response, some have argued that Aborigines never really 'settled' anywhere in Australia since settlements refer to civilised towns. Another student used this line of thought when arguing that Aborigines were primitive because 'they didn't even have any music worthy of the name – even Africans have good music'! What does one do in the face of this kind of ignorant arrogance? Aborigines give Australian culture a unique standing, that of being special and different from anywhere on earth. Their vital contribution to anglo-Australia has never been meaningfully recognised or acknowledged, not even in today's more enlightened climate. Their complex, sophisticated and uniquely beautiful art has been to some extent recognised, but even this is sullied by the extent to which it has been exploited and sometimes stolen for commercial gain.

Today's racists by and large have been restrained from killing Aborigines, but are still violently hostile to them. 'Blaming the victim', they criticise blacks for the poverty into which the white economy has forced them, and resent them for refusing to be assimilated into the white culture that tried its utmost to destroy and degrade them. One of the most challenging tasks of my career has been to work with colleagues to sensitise student teachers to this situation, and to explore ways of countering it in teaching. Most of my colleagues are among the liberal and radical white Australians who have supported Aborigines in their struggle to reclaim their rights as human beings and their cultural inheritance, and to establish political equality. The struggle has to make headway against a deeply entrenched redneck strand in the Australian ethos which is horrifying to us. It is a strand which taunts Aborigines not only as 'rockapes', 'boongs' and 'niggers', but also as 'no-hopers' and 'bludgers' (another new term for us). Are racists a minority or a majority? I'm not sure. Outside of the student body I rarely meet a racist, but their nasty views and actions are as regularly visible as are the racist manifestations of white North American and English culture. All laws and social institutions are supposed to be anti-racist, but there is still a degree of institutional racism that makes it harder for Aboriginal people than for any other people to enjoy the benefits of Australian society. We were horrified to watch Jana Wendt's television program that showed how Aborigines were denied rental, jobs and services in shops when whites were offered these same services immediately afterwards.

Are racists a minority or a majority? I'm not sure.

Our boys have settled well here, but they have been more exposed to racist attitudes than I have. At school, they were subjected to an extremely eurocentric curriculum with all its racist connotations. Dominic was asked whether he was a 'half-caste'. Never having heard the term before, he felt insulted, thinking his schoolmate meant something like 'half-wit'. In the Caribbean he would be regarded as relatively light-skinned. Here, he's told that he is 'blackish', 'darkish' or 'half-caste'. Alexis, who is a bit darker, was regularly called 'Blackie' at school. Very popular, he ran for the school and made a wide circle of friends. But when he was leaving school some of these same friends wrote in his autograph book things like: 'You're the best blackie we've ever known,' and 'It's been great to know you, blackie – as long as too many of you don't come'. Most astounding was the 'friend' who illustrated his farewell message in the autograph book with drawings of Ku Klux Klan hoods and burning crosses. I said to Alexis: 'How could you have friends like these?' He said: 'They just don't know any better – they are totally ignorant.' Sometimes I tell this story to tutorial groups of my students, and ask them to comment on it. The students argue about it. Some see it as shocking and 'scary' to think that schools are full of youths like this, and others see it as part of a quite acceptable tradition of humour that playfully knocks the other person. 'Blackie,' say some student teachers, is just a joke, no worse than 'Fatty' or 'Shorty'. It toughens up young men, I'm told, when they have to take insults from each other. What about 'nigger' and 'boong' I ask. Is that no worse than 'Fatty'? Well, it's part of life, I'm told. It prepares kids for what they meet in society.

Once, when Alexis was walking on a street in Brisbane, a police car pulled up beside him. The policeman in it told him to get in and roughly asked him where he was going. As soon as he answered in his polite Caribbean voice: 'Officers, I'm on my way to a kung-fu class,' they became instantly friendly – he was obviously not Aboriginal! 'And how are you enjoying your stay in this country?' one asked. It made us realise what Aborigines must go through every day. Apparently they don't have the right to be walking on the street particularly in a predominantly white area. It's good that politicians are talking now about the need for 'reconciliation' with Aborigines. But I think Mr Keating has his communication approach wrong when in his prime ministerial speeches he includes all today's whites in his blanket admission of white guilt for the racist wrongs of the past. What he should focus on is how white Australians today continue to benefit from those wrongs. He should remind people what it is like to live as the target of racism and what they as well as the government can do to bring it to an end.

Talk about 'no fear of flying' – I have certainly developed that in Australia. Each year here except our first one has seen me get on a plane for at least one journey overseas, sometimes two, and to this is sometimes added interstate journeys. In 1986, 1988, 1990 and 1992 I went home to Jamaica to visit my family. In 1987 I went to a conference in the Philippines, followed by university business in Brunei, followed by a stopover in Darwin to visit our Jamaican friends Pat and Ian Isaacs who are teaching and lecturing there. In 1989 Brian and I spent a short holiday in Bali. In 1991 I spent three months study leave at Stanford University in the US. I have presented papers, usually on education policy and planning in developing countries, but sometimes also on multicultural education, at conferences in Los Angeles, San Franciso, New York, London, Manila, Kingston (Jamaica), and Prague, as well as in Hobart, Sydney, Melbourne, Canberra, Darwin, Adelaide and Brisbane. I feel lucky to have developed international contacts and horizons that I would never have had the chance to develop in the Caribbean.

My interstate visits have given me a fascinating glimpse of the rest of Australia. In the days when Joh Bjelke Petersen was premier of Queensland, when I travelled by air interstate, southern Australians would strike up a friendly conversation with me, expressing their horror at my misfortune in having migrated to Queensland rather than one of the southern states! This attitude is noticeably less nowadays – is it to do with the new Goss government or with Queensland's relative economic boom in a sea of recession? We are amused that Australians in the southern states mockingly refer to Queensland as the 'Deep North', with the connotation that it's as backward as the United States' Deep South, and call Queenslanders 'banana benders'. I had to ask what that meant – apparently it has implications of not very bright farmers who spend their time bending bananas into a nice curving shape.

We are constantly aware of this sense of difference, bordering on hostility, between the Australian states. The popular perception in Queensland about the Northern Territory is that its inhabitants are outback country bumpkins who know little but cattle ranching, and that Darwin is the least desirable town in which any Australian could possibly want to live. Yet when I visited Darwin (which has not been done by most of the Australians who sneer at it), I fell in love with it: so tropical, so verdant and vibrant, it reminded me of the Caribbean. It has a relaxed, slowed-down atmosphere and a very multicultural population. Though there are only about 73 000 people in the city, these comprise some 60 different ethnic groups, and this variety was visible everywhere you went. This was so unlike the predominantly white ethos of Brisbane! Street food was a lovely feature of Darwin. There were people from all sorts of Asian countries wearing their national costume and selling a variety of most delicious cooked food, from fried noodles to satay sticks with peanut sauce, in open stalls in the city mall and every Thursday evening on the beach. The food markets are heaped with all the tropical fruits and vegetables you find in the Caribbean, besides other exotic produce from Asia that I've never seen before. I saw more Aboriginal people in Darwin than I have seen in any other Australian city, and they were walking around the town as if they belonged there, a refreshing change from the embattled, almost ghetto conditions that they seem to experience in other cities. In Brisbane it is noticeable how absent they are from most streets and most cultural events. They are ghettoized. Darwin's cultural centre has what must be one of the best and most representative collections of Aboriginal art in the country, besides excellent exhibitions of art, sculpture and craft from Malaysia and Indonesia.

I visited Hobart, Tasmania's capital, for a week in July 1985. It was winter, very cold with flurries of snow, and Hobart with its nineteenth century buildings and cobbled streets looked in part like a scene from an English Christmas card. I was presenting a paper on in-service teacher education at a conference of the South Pacific Association of Teacher Educators, and met many warm and wonderful people including some from the University of the South Pacific in Fiji, from Goroka Teachers' College in Papua New Guinea (PNG), and Aboriginal teacher educators from various Australian states. Before my visit to Tasmania, I was told that there were no Aborigines there as they had been virtually exterminated by the British invasion. This turned out to be one of the prevailing myths that some white Australians seem to hold. I was taken by the Aboriginal friends I made at the conference to visit several families of Tasmanian Aborigines and some of the very interesting historic places and sites sacred to the Aborigines. Why are they perceived as invisible by many in white Australia? Apparently because most of them are not 'pure-blooded' Aborigines but mixed with British ancestry, and the deep subconscious desire of many whites is for Aborigines of mixed race to disappear into the white majority and become thoroughly assimilated into anglo-Australian culture, rather than to be a unique group cleaving to their own historical and cultural traditions.

The tragic story of the Tasmanian Aborigines during the British invasion has been immortalised in a brilliant historical novel entitled *Dr Wooreddy's Prescription for Enduring the Ending of the World*. Written by West Australian Aborigine, Mudrooroo Narogin (formerly writing as Colin Johnson, and now Nyoongah) 'Dr Wooreddy' traces the life of an Aboriginal man from his traditional boyhood and manhood when he was initiated as an elder or doctor, to his old age and death, by which time the English were firmly established in Tasmania. Dr Wooreddy has to find ways of surviving with remnants of his family and tribal group through the cultural conflict, the massacres, the disease and the forced resettlement which marked the British invasion. With satirical irony the author portrays the missionizing impulses of English do-gooders in their attempt to 'civilise' a native people whose culture was in many respects arguably more sophisticated. As a powerful study of the clash of cultures, it is a novel which is not only compelling for anyone interested in the history of 'the West and the rest of us' (as the African writer Chinweizu has put it), but also should be required reading for every Australian. I certainly will never again be able to visit Tasmania without a pervasive awareness of its historic background through the vivid scenes from the novel.

The cities I like best in Australia are Melbourne and Darwin, though Sydney, at least parts of it, is the most beautiful of the capitals. But the visit that more than any other reconciled me to being in Australia was to North Queensland. There I experienced the awesome beauty of the Daintree and the Great Barrier Reef. Cairns and its hinterland reminded me of the Caribbean in that real mountains, that is, those covered with tropical forest, swept down to plains of silver-green sugar cane which met the town sitting on the sea coast. It was comforting to think of that whole beautiful region being in the same state as Brisbane, though several hours flying time distant. The environment surrounding Brisbane is attractive enough to be getting on with. We like the long river winding through its heart and suburbs, and sometimes go for weekends and short holidays to nearby Stradbroke Island with its beautiful white beaches and clear green sea. When we want a weekend with a bit more glitz than Stradbroke, there's Noosa on the north coast and Surfer's Paradise on the south coast.

One of the things we like about these seaside resorts is that you can stay at elegant hotels, modest motels or just adequate campsites. That's the great thing about Australian seaside towns – they provide all sorts of facilities which are not just for the rich. People overseas are amazed when we tell them about all this variety and beauty in Australia – it's clear that Oz hasn't done very much to promote its real image abroad. I mean, *Crocodile Dundee* is hardly an adequate update for the geography book images that most people have of sheep, wheat, sport, kangaroos and the Sydney Opera House.

That's the great thing about Australian seaside towns – they provide all sorts of facilities which are not just for the rich.

Brian says that I won't have a clear picture of Australia until I experience the outback. But liking my creature comforts, I'm reluctant to go on the kind of adventure he had with Dominic and Alexis while I was spending a month in Jamaica at Christmas 1986. They packed a tent, sleeping bags and a box of tinned food and drink into the back of our beat up old car (which we brought here on a container ship from the Caribbean) and drove 3000 miles to Darwin to spend Christmas with our Jamaican friends Ian and Pat Isaacs. Three thousand miles is three times the distance from Jamaica to Trinidad! and they drove the same distance back after a week in Darwin – an intrepid 6000 mile journey in four weeks. Much of the journey was through the outback: semi desert with endless miles of flat red land, the road punctuated with dead cows, dead cars and dead tyres, and the desert scape punctuated with strange, ten-foot high termite skyscraper nests (what kind of sophisticated community life must the termites live in there?) and enormous boulders. It is amazing that some of this dry land supports vast cattle and sheep ranches. Think of small cowboy type towns and hamlets in American Westerns, and that apparently is what some of the Australian mid-west desert towns look like. In one of these tiny hamlets in the middle of nowhere, they stopped at a petrol pump tended by a white Barbadian migrant and his wife! In another place, called Richmond, it was so lonely that a passing train driver waved to them as they drove past each other.

The most enjoyable part of the car journey came when they drove through, and camped in the Northern Territory, with its spectacular river gorges, plunging waterfalls, hot springs, crocodiles, a profusion of wild flowers, and ancient Aboriginal cave paintings. At camp sites, they rubbed shoulders with tame and friendly kangaroos, wallabies and six foot tall emus. On the return journey they visited Cairns. Some Jamaicans who have migrated to Australia have gone to settle up there, where some have thriving professional practices in medicine and law and others are into commercial enterprises. Because of the warm climate, these fortunate people can even grow a fruit-vegetable, ackee, in Cairns, and they would be the only ones who know how to prepare it, for it is eaten only in Jamaica.

When I left Jamaica, I was getting to the stage of feeling that I knew the education system inside out, having been a student in the elite section of it and a teacher who deliberately set out to experience how the other half lived by working in the poorer schools, preparing teachers for the poorer schools, getting involved in adult literacy and the Womens' Movement, and doing consultative work with the Ministry of Education. I'm not yet at that stage of familiarity with the Australian education system, but I've learnt a lot about it. Brian left a Jamaican career as a successful and popular university lecturer of 12 years experience. Not only had he contributed to the education of many Caribbean geographers, he had initiated the training of a generation of physical planners, who are now working in many Caribbean islands and welcome him warmly when he visits. He also became an actively conservationist member of the Jamaican Geographical Society, giving many lectures which illustrated his deep understanding and appreciation of the historical landscape and architectural heritage of Jamaica and the wider anglophone, Spanish, French and Dutch Caribbean.

In February 1985 when we arrived in Brisbane as a family, we soon learnt about the state school or private school options that existed, and got our teenage boys into one of the city's leading state high schools (if we could do it again, we would send them to a good private school despite our ideological misgivings). I kept in close touch with the school through the Parents and Citizens Association, in one of whose meetings I was for the first time called a 'stirrer'. While Brian got to grips with his new senior lectureship at the QIT, I applied for registration as a secondary school teacher in case I decided to go back into the classroom. This brought me into contact with the Board of Teacher registration which carefully scrutinises and monitors the qualifications of every teacher in the system. The board not only interviewed me but also checked out the equivalence of my overseas qualifications. It invites me to pay $15 every year to renew my registration.

In February 1985 when we arrived in Brisbane as a family, we soon learnt about the state school or private school options that existed...

I joined the Association of History Teachers, became involved in several of their interesting projects, was elected to their executive committee, and co-edited an edition of their journal. I also joined the Association of Teacher Educators and attended national conferences on teacher education, the sociology of education and technology in education. In August 1985 I was offered a post at the University of Queensland as senior research assistant in a project that was studying the experiences of beginning teachers in Queensland secondary schools. This research gave me a useful overview of the school system, and led to my meeting a variety of colleagues in education careers. Though I was wondering whether I should give teaching a rest for a few years, one of these colleagues persuaded me to consider further steps into the education maze. In 1986 I secured a part-time lectureship, then in 1987 I won in open competition with 40 others a full-time, tenured lectureship in the sociology of education at the Brisbane College of Advanced Education, now amalgamated into the Queensland University of Technology (QUT).

I also decided to experience tertiary education as a student, by enrolling part-time in a graduate diploma in media with the Sydney-based Australian Film, Television and Radio School (AFTRS). This was an innovative and exciting programme, which allowed me to combine groups of media subjects from several universities in Brisbane with courses from the AFTRS. So I studied film and television analysis at Griffith University, video, slide-tape and radio production at the Queensland University of Technology and with the AFTRS, and computers in education at the University of Queensland, and got my graduate diploma in media in 1988. It was a wonderful way of making new friends, of being introduced to Australian academic and film culture, and of learning a whole new set of media and computer skills that would enrich my existing academic and teaching experience. When I finished, I certainly had an insight into the tertiary education system in Brisbane, and was happy when Dominic later did a BSc at Griffith University, where I had particularly enjoyed the innovative and challenging programs of study.

As a lecturer at the QUT I have taught several hundred students by now, in large-scale lectures, in small tutorial groups, in undergraduate and in masters classes. I've taught white Aussies and Aboriginal and Torres Strait Islander Aussies, as well as students from Brunei, Thailand and the Peoples' Republic of China. I love the colleagues in my department: I don't think I've ever been in a job with so many like-minded or at least empathetic people. We have been through thick and thin together: fighting for the kind of amalgamation we wanted, protesting new parking regulations and getting them changed, organising retreats to plan for our collegial and departmental improvement, collaborating in creative and exciting team teaching, research and community outreach, supporting each other in exchanging seminars and colloquia, celebrating each other's academic publications, conference papers and PhDs. For two years I was one of the staff representatives on the academic union, and I've learnt how to coordinate subjects involving hundreds of students. Because of my interstate and overseas airline travels to conferences, I have met new colleagues and made new friends at several universities. I'm on the executive committee of ANZCIES (the Australia and New Zealand Comparative and International Education Society), and have learnt the skills involved in co-organising a conference in Brisbane and organising a specialist theme section at another conference in Canberra. Because of my interest in media and information technology, I have also joined societies which focus on media and computer education and on futures studies. My articles have been published in academic journals, and by the end of 1994 I should have three chapters in edited books. One day I hope to follow the example of my more literary-minded colleagues, writing a book or two of my own.

The point of articulating all of these facets of my career is to express how rich an experience Australia has been for me. But to those who think that Australia does migrants a favour, and I've heard enough of those attitudes, Australia is lucky, too, in enriching the society with so many other cultures, and in getting so many people who have been expensively and highly qualified in other countries and who have valuable career experience to draw on, to share with Aussies, and to develop. Australia is one of the wealthy beneficiaries of the brain drain that contributes to the impoverishment of countries least able to afford it; I never quite get over a feeling of guilt about our part in this.

Would I do the same thing all over again if I could do just what I wanted? Perhaps I would reconsider the destination of our migration. I might go to North America or Britain where there are large clusters of Caribbean people, I'd develop a career that interacted with them as well as that broadened my horizons, and I'd prepare for going back. Yet having experienced Australia, not for the world would I want to have missed this unique and fascinating place. We've developed a real affection for it, the physical place as well as the people. Dominic is quality control manager at a brick factory, and Alexis an assistant manager in a large supermarket chain, and both have Aussie girlfriends. We **I want my ashes** have had interesting and rewarding careers, we have **sent back to** recently decided to take on formal citizenship, and a whole **Jamaica...** new world in the Pacific and South East Asia has become real to us. But losing deep interaction with the Caribbean has been like losing a limb. My navel-string (umbilical cord) is buried there, so I have to go back some day. Maybe it will be through the sort of job that allows my skills to be utilised in an Australian/Pacific/Caribbean education consultancy, or maybe I'll just work in Jamaica. Brian says that he doesn't care what's done with his body after he dies, but I care. If I should die here, I want my ashes sent back to Jamaica to be buried in my native land alongside my extended family. There is no way that I want my last resting place to be on the other side of the world.

Postscript:
It's 1993 and there's been a lot more flying. I travelled to the Caribbean on study leave, spending from January to May researching adult and higher eduation policy, while Brian travelled the opposite way, visiting Hong Kong, Japan and Britain to do research for a book on urban planning. We met in Jamaica in March to celebrate our twenty-fifth wedding anniversary with a party put on for us by our Jamaican family. Guests included lots of people who had attended our wedding in Jamaica in 1968, and nieces, nephews and cousins born since then. Dominic, Alexis, their girlfriends and other friends were there from Australia, and many friends from the various phases of our lives and careers in the Caribbean, Britain and the USA joined us too. We travelled back to Australia through the US in May, visiting colleagues at universities in Indiana, Berkeley and Stanford.

Five days after arriving back in Brisbane the dreaded phone call came: my beloved father died in Jamaica on 5 June 1993, at the age of 82. It was as if he had been waiting to see the whole family gather once more, before slipping away from us. I turned right back and retraced my plane tracks across the Pacific and the USA, making the exhausting 36 hour journey to Jamaica to help my mother with the funeral arrangements and to join in the beautiful service of thanksgiving for this life held at the Uniting Church where my father had been an elder for over two decades. After 53 years of marriage my mother was shell-shocked. I scooped her up and brought her back to Brisbane with me. She has travelled frequently to Europe and the United States ever since she was 19, but hadn't thought that at the age of 80 she would have been trekking to Australia and back. Her first experience of Brisbane was a six-week bout of pneumonia, but when she got better we had a wonderful remaining three months together, going to concerts, the theatre, movies, parties, visiting Sydney and Surfers Paradise, and seeing some of Brisbane's attractions. Though her sadness at her bereavement is deep, her glimpse of Australia helped her through the initial shock of it. At the end of October she returned to Jamaica – where her music students, friends and family were eagerly awaiting her return. I hope that when I'm 80 I will be following in her footsteps – still working creatively, surrounded by a loving network, and traversing the globe!

Bathurst via London

Sylvia R. Hennessy

Born in January 1956 in Dublin, Ireland, Sylvia R. Hennessy emigrated to London after leaving school and completed general nurse training and midwifery training at the Whittington Hospital, North London.
Sylvia Hennessy remains a long time member of the 'Troops Out Movement', believing that the presence of British Troops in Ireland is the most serious obstacle to any progress towards peace. During the Gulf war she, along with the Bathurst Coordinating Committee for Peace, organised two peace rallies, with Patricia Brennan and Tom Uren as speakers. Active in Left Connection (formally the New Left Party), a new networking organisation for progressive left and green individuals and organisations, currently Sylvia Hennessy is working as a research assistant. She has recently completed a bachelor of social science at Charles Sturt University in New South Wales.

How could I ever forget the morning in March 1987 landing at Sydney's Kingsford Smith airport? My partner, Larry, and I were exhausted. Our two young children Niall, then 17-months-old, and Sean, two months, were wide awake. We felt as though we had spent the entire flight feeding them, changing nappies and generally trying to keep our toddler away from other passengers' food trays and out from under their feet. After we bundled the children into strollers and collected our luggage, we were met by Larry's overjoyed mother, who only a few months previously had been informed by us that we would be settling in London.

Many thoughts raced through my mind, not least of all whether I had made the right decision. Larry, my partner, as an Australian was coming home; somehow I felt less in control of this occasion than I had 11 years earlier, when as a teenager I left rural Ireland to emigrate to England. I was excited at the prospect of living in London. Life appeared so simple then. I would do my nurse training and then – well, I would travel the world. Now with an Australian partner and two young children life was much more complicated. In London, I had an identical twin sister and twin brothers. Home was less than an hour away by air. Australia now seemed so far away from everybody.

As I sat in the car, my thoughts went back to the evening we broke to my family the news of our decision to emigrate. It was a very cold January. I was pregnant with Sean, and due at anytime. My parents were in London visiting us all. Reactions at the dinner table varied. My parents and brothers were obviously happy. They perceived our decision as a natural next step in our lives, although they were saddened at the prospect of losing us. My parents nearing retirement, would have more time for grandchildren and we could have looked forward to summer holidays together on the west coast of Ireland. Alas this again would not be so. My twin sister Ann, her face said it all. I knew exactly what was going through her mind. We are very close, always have been; I would miss her terribly as she would me. We had experienced similar feelings some four years earlier, when Larry and I had gone to the highlands of New Guinea to work, I as a midwife and Larry as a surgeon. We were away for just two years, yet I managed to come back to visit Ann and she managed to visit us in New Guinea. *Then* we knew our parting was to be temporary. Ann and I had until now done almost everything together. In London, we did our nurse training at the same hospital, took our first flat together and, after I met Larry, continued to live in the same street. We were always there for each other. For me to emigrate to Australia would change our relationship and we knew it.

At this time I was also reviewing my relationship with my mother. As a mother myself now, I felt I could understand her better, appreciate her more, I wanted to spend more time with her and I felt somewhat closer. Again Australia would disrupt this process. My six brothers, whom I love dearly, I would miss, and my children would miss out on relationships with their uncles and also with their first cousins. I would miss my friends, and north London, the area where I had lived for over a decade. We would both miss the English countryside and also the proximity to the continent which we liked to visit from time to time.

Why would I want to emigrate at all? My decision was not an easy one. Our collective decision came after some consideration of our current situation and future prospects in London.

The political and economic situation had had an impact on our lives. Margaret Thatcher was at the helm, again, having been re-elected as prime minister. Economic rationalism was her game as she pursued her policies at an even considerable pace. Health, education, housing, transport, all these services were traumatised by her policies, thus creating favourable environments for private sector growth. Unemployment was soaring, now nearing three million. All appeared gloom and doom. We could see a future Britain we did not want to be part of. Larry worked for the National Health Service (NHS): Margaret Thatcher seemed to single out this institution for special treatment. Larry's long term career prospects appeared bleak, and not least of all because he was a foreign national. The Thatcher policies were making it more difficult for foreigners in the labour market.

Our housing situation also needed attention. Our one bedroom flat, now with the arrival of Sean, was obviously inadequate. While we liked the area, we could not at this stage buy.

Another issue was how Britain's war in Ireland would affect my children's lives. I had been shocked at the anti-Irish racism in the British media when I first arrived. I did not expect it nor was I prepared for it. I was sick of anti-Irish jokes stereotyping the Irish as drunks, dole-bludgers, and stupid, but now with the war there were sinister changes. We were now all possible terrorists. While some may attempt to ignore or deny the effect racism has on our lives, I was very much aware of the injustices of the British judicial system. Aware of how the lives of innocent Irish people were being wasted in British gaols. Aware of the injustices being suffered by the Guilford four, the Birmingham six, the Maguire seven, the Winchester three, the list goes on. I had become politicised by my experiences. I did not want this for my children, I wanted to spare them the trauma. I didn't want them to internalise a sense of inferiority, which could so easily develop in such a political climate.

Back in the car with Phillippa (my mother-in-law) on our way to Sydney's north shore, I couldn't help being impressed by the ultra modern high buildings, the wide roads, everything new and big, the harbour was magnificent, as was the Harbour Bridge, and the Opera House. I was amazed how new everything was. Of course, Australia had been colonised by the British only 200 years previously. I was also surprised I hadn't seen any Aborigines. Where were they? In time I was to learn many Aboriginal people lived in rural areas and later on I was to see for myself the ghettos of Redfern. I was learning. I had somehow assumed Aboriginal people had a special position in Australian society. I was right, the special position was one of marginalisation, discrimination and cultural genocide! This shocked me, and I could only empathise. Our nations peoples had similar pasts. We had also been colonised by the British and dispossessed of our land, and suffered the consequent physical and psychological repercussions of an ideology developed to justify dispossession, marginalisation and cultural genocide. Ireland now is not quite independent, the war for the six counties continues. The original Australians, the Kooris (as I learned many prefer to be called), are fighting, together with the Islander people, for full sovereignty, self-determination and Land Rights, and should be compensated for nearly two centuries of dispossession.

Back to the Harbour Bridge then on to the leafy north shore where we stayed for six weeks with Philippa. Meanwhile Larry, a competent, accomplished and resourceful surgeon, and a caring and responsive partner, was out there searching for a suitable position. The job situation was better than we had anticipated and we looked at several places where positions were offered. Canberra, Gosford, Windsor and Bathurst. As Australia's oldest inland city, Bathurst was aesthetically pleasing, had an airport, a university, most amenities we thought necessary, and was only three hours drive from Sydney, not too far for relatives. Larry and I found the people of the central west warm and friendly. This was our choice.

> I had associated Australia with warm to very hot weather not -7° centigrade...

On arriving in Bathurst, I was not prepared for the cold. We had left London after a very cold winter, and we were now experiencing another. I had associated Australia with warm to very hot weather not -7° centigrade, as it was one night when I got up to feed Sean.

My first six months in Bathurst were not a happy time for me. I cannot remember a period in my life when I felt more unhappy. Life with two young children in a new country was tiring and lonely. I know to have two young children anywhere can be tiring, but I missed home, my sister, my friends, my interests. I now had no time for anything other than the children.

Larry worked all hours trying to set up a practice. I knew it could only get better, but when? My self-confidence and self-esteem had taken a battering. Eventually I found the courage to contact the local childcare centre, although places were scarce. I secured a morning on one day, and an afternoon on another, for Niall. Things were looking up, the break felt like heaven. I immediately applied to Charles Sturt University to do a part-time degree in social science, and was accepted. I began the course in February 1988, less than a year after arriving. By now the two boys had childcare places, which allowed me time to attend lectures and do some study. At last a break from housework and childcare. It was a relief to be able to be me again. As a feminist I was none too keen on the role allocated to women by men, a role which meant women had to take full responsibility for childcare at the expense of their careers (which after all should be the responsibility of *both* parents), and consequently lose their financial independence. This can cause an imbalance in the power relationship that exists between partners. Financial independence is not everything but it goes a long way in making it possible for women to assert themselves in relationships in the private and public spheres.

Once at university, I began to meet more people, young students and mature-age students like myself. I found them friendly, outspoken, 'no beating around the bush', not at all reserved like the British. Of course, I am generalising, I like their openness. It meant I knew where I stood, I felt comfortable.

On occasion I had to repeat myself, but I felt more relaxed about this than I had in Britain, where on some occasions I was very conscious of my accent, especially when not among friends. Some Australians even remarked on how they liked the Irish accent. I can't say I ever remember this being said to me in Britain! While I never felt the need to change the way I spoke, to modify it yes. Again while in England I would consciously make attempts to speak more slowly and so avoid having to repeat myself. In Australia this was not necessary. My accent hasn't changed much as a consequence of living in Australia and living in Britain.

Some Australians even remarked on how they liked the Irish accent. I can't say I ever remember this being said to me in Britain!

On many occasions Australians on hearing me speak would inquire whether I was from the 'North' or 'South', was I a catholic or protestant, and generally show an interest in the war in Ireland. Others expressed pride of their Irish ancestry and related their forefathers' and foremothers' journey to Australia whether on the first fleet, on a later convict ship, or otherwise. Many expressed a wish to visit Ireland one day and those that had sang its praises. Only rarely did I meet persons who reacted to my accent by either trying to imitate it, usually badly, or who would immediately launch into an 'Irish joke' which I didn't appreciate; unfortunately they rarely comprehended why not. While I didn't have a problem with the Australian accent, I did find I was learning new words and phrases all the time, like galah, dag, whingeing, pom, battler, not referring to me, ha! barbie, footie, 'a suck', squattocracy, words and phrases I had never heard before. In Britain and Ireland, people now receive their daily and weekly dose of *Flying Doctors, Neighbours, E Street* and so on, so perhaps are more informed, today, of Australian terms than I was when I arrived.

One summer I recall being brought out to a farm/property for a picnic near a dam. I was unprepared for what I saw. I must have been expecting something like the Aswan Dam, because I was very disappointed. Now looking back, it was rather naive of me to expect anything other than what was there, a rather small but deep reservoir of water specifically for stock, in a paddock (rather than a field, a word we used at home). I live and learn!

One peculiarity about Australia which I observed on my first arrival was roofs, or should I say the abundant use of corrugated iron as roofing on homes. In Ireland and indeed in England, iron roofing is usually reserved for farm buildings. At first I didn't like these iron roofs, I thought them ugly. As time passed I acculturated, and my home has a typical Australian iron roof which I like very much. Now I can appreciate the delight felt by farmers on hearing the pattering of rain on the tin roof, especially out west, and particularly today, as we are living in a drought stricken area.

In 1992 when I visited home – Ireland – I encouraged my mother to begin to write her autobiography for me, for my children. She has time on her hands to write, though she tires very easily. I also went to Dublin to see her mother again, hoping to pick up some family history. Gran lived through the 1916 Easter Rising, the executions and the Black and Tans, all significant events in the fight for independence. I wanted to know it all. Alas, she was partially deaf and almost totally blind, and communication proved difficult. I had left it too late. My only hope was to have my aunt (who spent a lot of time with Granny Brennan) to write down all she could remember and all she was told. My children may one day become interested in our family history, so I want to gather as much as I can.

While in London I couldn't help but notice the changes. There was a visible increase in the number of private cars; at rush hour the traffic hardly moved down Kentish Town Road; the air was heavy with exhaust fumes; the streets were filthy; rubbish lined the pavements; and everywhere at bus stops, on benches, outside tube stations and sitting on the pavement were winos or drunks, of all ages, the majority of them male.

One evening while out to dine with my brother and his partner we were stopped by young men, begging on both occasions, asking for money, for bus fares, for food. This was a new experience for me in London: it had not happened to me in the decade I lived there. Within days, while in Oxford Street with Ann, I noticed two young adults sitting on either side of the pavement each with a cardboard placard asking for money for food. I wondered whether what I was witnessing was the result of Margaret Thatcher's economic rationalism which John Major, too, was pursuing. I thought maybe we made the right decision after all, would we want our children to live in London now? I am fortunate to be able to afford to go home from time to time; maybe I would not be so contented were this not the case. Either way, I only hope that Australia learns from Britain, and does not in the future reproduce the conditions in Australia which we did not want to be part of there.

From Poland to Australia, via Greece

Dorota Malchevski

Dorota Malchevski was born in Poland on 7 July 1954, in the town of Pela. She studied at Poznan University, majoring in philosophy and graduating with a masters degree in the early 1980s.
In 1984 Dorota Malchevski left Poland, together with her daughter Magdalena and her (then) husband. First living in Greece for a year or so, she arrived, together with her daughter and husband, in Australia – their intended destination – in July 1985. After living in Sydney for two-and-a-half-years, she now lives with her daughter Magdalena in Melbourne. Dorota Malchevski is a University of Melbourne graduate in social work.

The day I left my country, in July 1984, it was with all the outward signs of going on a summer holiday in Greece, where I would lie down on one of those fantastic beaches to enjoy nothing. Our 'dream holiday' was supposed to change our lives forever, but none of us realised how much this 'month trip' to Greece would affect our lives.

My husband, our four-year-old daughter Magdalena, and I, felt excited and scared. It was like setting out on an adventure, it didn't feel real, there were too many conflicting emotions, we were in a haze of fear, joy, sadness and hope. I could not believe that it was actually happening. Finally, we had managed to sell most of our possessions, buy the tickets, obtain passports and travel visas for the whole of our family. A story was unfolding in our lives, but it was as though we were watching another family's story, not living our own.

The last few weeks were emotionally painful for us, for our families and very close friends. I was leaving my parents. It was horrific. I did not know when I would see them again and they didn't have anybody but Magdalena and me. They loved Magdalena very much, she was for them a little copy of me. They had someone to live for. Magdalena was five-years-old. I felt that I was making a decision for my daughter that would affect her life tremendously. I was taking her away from her family, from her grandparents whom she loved, and from all her extended family. She was going to miss them very much. I was losing my close friends, the people with whom I grew up. Those friendships could never be replaced by friendships in the new world. I was afraid that even if I could see my friends in the future it would not be the same, that we may not have much in common any more.

> I was losing my close friends, the people with whom I grew up. Those friendships could never be replaced by friendships in the new world.

I grew up as an only child in Pila, a town of 55 000 people in Poland. Both my parents came from strong Catholic backgrounds, although from the age of 18 I was allowed to make my choice about religious beliefs. My mother was a dentist and my father a doctor. They worked in a government hospital. They did not want to run a private practice, and they preferred to work for the government and were not comfortable with the idea of charging patients. I practically grew up in the hospital.

When I finished high school, I moved from my parents town to Pozan. In 1977 I was accepted at the faculty of social science of Pozan University to major in philosophy. Our class was small, and the majority of students were male. Even the philosophy lecturers discouraged the female students with their comments, and questioned why we were studying such a 'male orientated' course. However, our group of students strongly supported each other.

About this time I met my future husband. A year later he finished his technical high school and had to move to Koszalin, two hundred kilometres away, to study engineering at the Polytechnic. Most weekends he visited me.

At that time more and more Polish people began to support the role of Solidarity. Like many Poles my boyfriend and I were hoping that historic political and economic changes would take place in the Eastern Block. People saw that Solidarity represented the first opportunity for change. We were not allowed to talk openly about it, but it blossomed out in Polish music, theatre and cinema.

The university administration was under the control of the communist government. University staff members who did not follow the rules and supported Solidarity were forced to leave the university. Some of the most influential university lecturers were imprisoned or forced to flee Poland, including a few of the internationally recognised philosophy lecturers who had been teaching me. Students of philosophy were told to sign a declaration that we would become members of the communist party when we finished our studies. Most students strongly believed in Solidarity and refused to sign the declaration. The future of those who did not want to join the party was uncertain for a long time. I was one of these students. I was not actively involved in political changes at the university but Solidarity provided my boyfriend and me with a sense of hope for our country. I started to believe that Poland would be part of the world again.

Two years later, in 1979, during my third year of study, our lives changed dramatically. We married. A few months later our daughter, Magdalena, was born. Even though our circumstances were difficult, especially financially, I was a very happy mother. Magdalena was the most important person in my life, she changed my world. My husband was happy and surprised when Magdalena was born, and this look of surprise has remained in his eyes ever since.

We lived on the fourth floor in a dark little attic. We had no kitchen or bathroom, no access to water except in the common laundry, and no washing machine. In winter it was unbearable to put your hands into the cold water. The room was very cold and snow would blanket in through clefts in the roof during the winter. The narrow corridor to our attic was used as a shelter by men, usually drunk, who slept on the floor. The university administration decided to give me the minimum financial support available for a full-time student (similar to Austudy) because our parents were considered to have high incomes. As we were not working full-time, we did not have access to childcare for our daughter.

The room was very cold and snow would blanket in through clefts in the roof during the winter.

One year later, in 1980, my husband was unexpectedly dismissed from his engineering course at the Polytechnic for his political beliefs. While I took care of Magdalena and continued studying full-time, he had to find work to support us. This period was difficult. He did any casual work he could find, and for a long time he worked at the railway station unloading wagons. Then he found a job as a technician at the office. He did not stay there for long as he hated the idea of having a supervisor. He wanted to be his own boss, and do something that would give us independence, money and a comfortable life. He and his mother visited his aunt in Iran a few times and it set his hopes on becoming wealthy like her Iranian husband.

Although our situation was bad, we were happy to have our own place. I felt that our marriage would survive if we were able to take control of our relationship. In 1981 my paternal grandmother died. We moved into her single room in a flat that we rented from my aunt, who also lived there with her children. At that time my husband and I decided to start our clothing business. Our little workshop became a well-organised business within a few months. Quickly, we had to learn how to manage our business. My husband and I both learnt from our mistakes. We employed two full-time and a few casual workers. We paid them much more than they could earn in the government factories. Our clothes were well-made and our style of fashion began to be popular. Many of our clothes were sold in well known boutiques all over Poland. My husband started to travel regularly to West Germany to buy good quality fabrics. We enrolled in a housing co-operative to buy a house in two years. This was part of the government housing programme for financially stable young families. In a short time our financial situation improved, but we realised that this situation was very unreliable and insecure.

When we started our business I was in my fourth year of university. I had another two-and-a-half-years to complete my masters degree. During this time, students and politically involved staff members openly expressed their radical opinions about the communist government, fully aware of the consequences of their actions. They organised student strikes. Philosophy students from my university organised a hunger-strike. Many of us signed a petition to the chancellor of the university demanding that the university protect the student's rights to freedom of speech and political expression. Nobody was thrown out of the university as a result of these demands. This meant a lot to everybody.

In November 1981 the communist government introduced the State of Emergency. This meant greater restrictions on personal freedom. It increased the fear that people operating small businesses would be reported to the government for breaking regulations and controlling imports and so on, and that people would be gaoled indiscriminately. An 8 pm to 6 am curfew was introduced.

Our marriage was going through more and more difficulties. We had become people with different interests, opinions, priorities and values. Also our parents, especially my husband's mother, were destructive to our relationship. She was psychiatrically ill and would not seek help from a doctor. She thought everyone was plotting against her, attempting to steal her money and trying to drive her mad. She was obsessed with her son and could not stand him giving me his attention. She abused Magdalena and me. My husband did not know how to deal with this situation. Neither did I. Separation from my husband became inevitable. For six months Magdalena and I lived on our own whilst my husband lived with his mother.

The rights of a single mother were unknown to me...

Living in the room next to mine at my aunty's flat was my drug addicted cousin. He terrorised his family and threatened to kill one of us or himself. At one stage he threatened to rape me and throw my daughter out of the fourth floor window. Whenever the opportunity arose he stole from the flat or demanded money from me. Several times I had to call the police to protect Magdalena and myself. In these situations my aunt and her 18-year-old daughter would close their door, and pretend that they were not there, until the police came.

The rights of a single mother were unknown to me and it was easy for my husband and his mother to threaten to take Magdalena. Applying for maintenance at the court was unpleasant. I was frightened and could not speak. My husband, in his speech to the court, made me feel a bad mother, guilty of destroying my daughter's family. That very day I decided to reconcile our marriage.

During these years the economic situation in Poland deteriorated badly. To buy bread, milk and butter people had to wait for hours in long queues with their ration cards. To buy meat and fresh vegetables for dinner was a luxury and to buy clothes from the government shop was impossible. People were desperate for any products at all. They would join a queue even though they had no idea what was at the end of the queue. The control of the media by the government resulted in confusing and false information about the country. Despite this everybody knew that workers were calling for more and more strikes. Information was spread quickly by the underground media. My husband distributed news bulletins for Solidarity as he travelled around Poland selling our clothes.

Polish industries were practically at a stand still. The church and the Pope strongly supported Solidarity. The government was losing control of the country. People were imprisoned, tortured and murdered. Many people took to the streets to demonstrate. My husband and I joined in. Small businesses provided goods, but for much higher prices. They sold goods mainly imported from capitalist countries. Many Poles took great financial risks in business. People started from nothing: no money and no skills. It was like a lottery. Many young people felt a great need to improve their standard of living in a short time. They did not want to repeat their parents' struggle.

Our business had been slowly losing all connections with the Polish textile industries. Nobody wanted to sell textiles to small private producers. We had been accused by the government of cheating the Polish people and the government, of making more money than the average Pole. The government organised special commissions, consisting of police and communist party officials who often had no knowledge of business, to enforce regulations that suffocated business and were impossible to comply with. We were allowed to import only very small quantities of textiles from other countries. We could not buy foreign currency to import textiles. The situation was bad. The Polish zloty did not mean anything outside Poland. We decided to go to France for a few months to work, pick grapes, and save money. I also wanted to look at life in the 'forbidden world'.

The Polish zloty did not mean anything outside Poland.

In France, we met my husband's aunt and her husband who, because of the political changes in Iran, had moved to France. They invited us for a few days holiday. I could observe how wealthy people in France lived, it was my first experience with a capitalist country. We had very little money but life was easy in France. People were friendly, the shops full of food and anything anyone could buy. In Poland, we had Polish money and we could not buy anything. In France, we did not have money but were surrounded by everything a person could wish for. What would we prefer?

We thought about the possibility of living in France, but only if our daughter would be with us. I missed Magdalena badly and after three months we returned to Poland. We had to go back to think. That year I completed my masters degree.

A year later we sold what we could, giving our friends everything else. We left our lives behind to begin a new life without so much struggle. In Poland, we could not see a future for our business and I had no prospect of a job in my profession. To save our family from falling apart and to be free from parental influences, I clung to the hope that it wasn't too late for us.

We had about three weeks in which to organise ourselves and prepare to flee our country.

In June 1984 our passports had finally been issued. We had about three weeks in which to organise ourselves and prepare to flee our country. A number of our friends knew what we planned and this increased our fear that the government would find out. We were the first of our family and friends to go and these people wanted to know how we were doing it because they wanted to follow us. Many have since fled and now live in many different countries, some in Australia.

Convincing ourselves to be positive and optimistic about our future we put everything on one card. The world, we wanted to believe, was kind and we could choose any place on the map to build a happy life for ourselves. For two years immediately preceding our flight, we absorbed any available information about Australia and New Zealand, mainly from libraries and friends of friends who knew somebody who knew somebody from Australia. This information, with the exception of interesting material on Australian geography, was not reliable. Australia was promising, it was a new country. We concluded that this country would have many opportunities for new migrants. My major concern was the enormous distance from Europe, from my country. We also chose Australia for this very reason – to be far away from all the problems in Europe, particularly those of Eastern Europe.

We left our country with three suitcases of clothes, little money and our passports. After a few days travelling on the bus, we arrived in Athens. With great fear we started to look around. In two days we found the organisation for refugees in Athens. That day, people from the organisation gave us a letter and the address to a hotel in the middle of the city. They told us that we were not allowed to meet with people from our holiday excursion. Each member of our family was eligible for a monetary allowance that we would collect every morning at the hotel. We could apply to see a doctor at a public hospital. We could attend part-time English classes. We did not have work permits, we were not allowed to leave Athens. At that time Greece was not a popular destination for refugees.

The situation for refugees in Greece changed dramatically soon after we left. A few months later refugees couldn't get any money or accommodation.

People had to survive without any support. The number of refugees in Greece was out of control.

We were considered lucky. In three months we were granted political asylum and refugee status in Greece. With the money from the refugee organisation I could shop every day at the market. We could survive.

During the next 11 months in Athens, we had three interviews at the Australian Embassy. We were granted permanent residence status for Australia under the special humanitarian program and we were given visas and tickets to fly to Australia.

In Greece, we lived in the hotel, in a suburb well known for the rough life, especially at night. I did not understand what it actually meant, so at first it did not matter to me. The weather was beautiful and the streets full of life. We were given a room on the second floor, with a bathroom that was exclusive. We did not have a kitchen, and nobody was allowed to cook in the hotel rooms. We had to eat so we turned our bathroom into a kitchen. My husband is a very friendly person and we met many people in a very short time. The first four floors of this hotel were occupied by refugee families from Eastern Block countries.

All new refugees went through a familiar pattern. At first they were fascinated by their new circumstances, freedom, by the beauty of Greece. They were very enthusiastic. They organised themselves visiting the coast, buying new clothes, going to the beach. It was also a time to make friends with other refugees. Some chose to isolate themselves from the rest of the community. We found that most of the refugees were applying for visas to the United States of America and Canada. They usually waited about six months for acceptance by their chosen country. Very few of the refugees wanted to go to Australia, because it was too far from Europe. There was also a much longer wait and only a few refugees were accepted by Australia. We tried to find out more about Australia from other refugees. What we found sounded promising – the adventure of our lives.

AUSTRALIA – a great, distant, exotic and tropical continent. The multicultural country with many opportunities for migrants, respect for the freedom of people, no discrimination of any kind. We suspected that because of its geographic location the cultural and economical situation in Australia would be closely linked with Asia. A new country, free from European influences. A small population for such a big continent seemed to provide opportunities for migrants. Australians were reputed to be very friendly and easy going. I heard that Australia looks like a big village where everybody could own a house. I heard that fashion was, unfortunately, two years behind Europe.

I knew very little about Australian Aborigines. In one of the geography books about Australia, I found a few photos of Aboriginal people living in the bush, a photo of an Aboriginal painting and some information about Aboriginal history. I could find no information about the current situation

> We had to eat so we turned our bathroom into a kitchen.

of Aboriginal people in Australia. The painting was fascinating and I expected to see many of these paintings in Australian galleries. I promised myself that an Aboriginal painting would be the first painting I would buy for my new home in Australia. I also wondered about Aboriginal music, which I had never heard anything about. I imagined it was exotic and wild.

Those months of waiting were difficult for me. I cannot explain exactly what I felt at the time. You have to be there to understand the fear and uncertainty for the future of your child and your family. A refugee's experience does not have to be a criminal horror story to be threatening. Our family was another unit in this strange, artificial, isolated community. We did not know how long we would have to wait, and we were struck by a feeling of powerlessness. We were people who were frozen in time.

What would happen to us if we were not accepted by Australia? Would we have to go back to Poland and to prison? The Polish government considered our flight to be a betrayal of our country. I questioned – Why?! I love my country but I could not live there any more. Why couldn't I be free to make my choice to live somewhere else in this beautiful world? I wanted my child to have a happy future, not to live in fear as I had in Poland.

In Greece, we were just another number for some participating government to support and at the same time we were considered to be trouble. Refugees are often brave people fleeing the worst of nightmares in order to build a future for their families. This is a basic human right.

After some time I felt that I wanted to leave this little community at the hotel, and Greece, as soon as possible. The important values in people's lives can become very unstable. It was easy to be trapped into thinking that the 'real life' would begin again when we left this place of refuge.

It was easy to be trapped into thinking that the 'real life' would begin again when we left this place of refuge.

My husband quickly found a job selling sheep skin coats to tourists visiting Athens. He became absorbed with his work and the people he met. He had to earn extra money that he tried to save but mostly spent on entertainment. We were able to buy new clothes and extra food. He bought an old car. This was an achievement in our circumstances. At that time our friends from Poland visited us. We had spent a week together. It was a very emotional time for all of us: they had to go back to Poland where the situation was even more difficult than when we left, and – we had to stay in the 'nowhere country'. We promised to see each other again.

Gradually my husband and I lived two separate lives: my husband – around his working life, and Magdalena and I – lived family life. In Athens social life begins after 9 pm. My husband liked to go out. I wanted to be with him, but I was afraid to leave Magdalena in the hotel at night even if I managed to organise neighbours to look after her. I was afraid that someone could steal her and I may lose her forever. I had learnt what it meant to live in a rough suburb of Athens. I was afraid that I was losing my husband, that his life was not with us any more. He adapted to these circumstances much better than I and he enjoyed it. It was an emotionally confusing time for our family.

I did not have much in common with my husband's work friends. I was his wife and that was all. However I made a few good friends at the hotel. I was especially close to Jerry. She was from Rumania and was with her son. Her daughter and husband were still in Rumania and she told me that Magdalena reminded her of her daughter. We had something in common – we both knew many people in the hotel but we both felt lonely. She was a supportive friend. She could speak English and this gave me my first opportunity to practice English. I was trying to break this strange fear of speaking in a different language and not feeling stupid when I made mistakes. I carried my English dictionary everywhere and slowly I started to talk a little English. Through Jerry, I met other Rumanian people. Many of them had to leave families in Rumania. Some stories they told me about Rumania were upsetting and horrible. They did not like to talk about Rumania very much.

I did not want to see my daughter and other little children playing on the hotel floor. She was five-years-old and I did not want her to waste her childhood. I decided to organise a class for Polish children in the hotel. I taught them to write and read in Polish. The group had children Magdalena's age. We met for one hour a day and it gave me satisfaction to see the children coming every day and progressing. I began to have problems with the hotel manager who insisted that our classes could not be held at the hotel. He would give no reason for his decision. None of the parents wanted to have anything to do with this man, especially when he threatened to throw my family out of the hotel if we did not stop the classes. The group shrank to four children, but we somehow managed to meet almost every day until those families left for America.

After ten months living in Athens my husband decided to stay in Greece and open a business. I knew that I did not want to stay in Greece. We did not have any rights there nor did we have the right to stay. I wanted to go to Australia. I could apply to America as it was taking single women, but I was not even divorced. I was nothing, I was just somebody's wife. I could not go back to Poland. We had heard many frightening stories about refugees who went back voluntarily, and those who had been deported to Poland because they were not accepted by any country. If you were not accepted by the country of your choice it was difficult to be accepted by the next one.

We were called for an interview at the Australian Embassy. I went only once. My husband had three interviews. I felt that women did not mean much for the Australian Embassy either. Fortunately, my husband satisfied their conditions. He had good skills as a technician, specialising in building roads and bridges, and he could speak English. I could not speak English and my degree was not needed in Australia. I understood that labourers and practical professions were what was wanted.

Every interview gave new hope that we would be accepted by Australia. I desperately wanted to get a visa to Australia and get away from this mess. I had had enough of watching families fighting about every little thing, swapping partners, leaving them, drinking too much. People spent time with each other not because they wanted to but because they had nothing else to do. Children were left on the stairs because their parents were busy with their own problems and were not coping with the stress. The hotel staff abused the children, yelling at them, hitting and kicking them without reason. Nobody would stand up for the children. I could not see the beauty of this country any more, I wanted to 'Go Home'.

More and more people were leaving the hotel for America or Canada. Suddenly, all my friends had left – gone to America. I felt very lonely. I missed Jerry.

One day my husband called me a lesbian, which had an enormous impact on me. I had never met a woman who consciously expressed her sexuality as a lesbian. In Poland, where the majority of the population is Catholic, to be a lesbian was unacceptable. There was no place for lesbians in Polish society. Being called a lesbian in Poland could do a lot of damage, because of the discrimination. A woman, at that time, would be ostracised. I had not realised this previously.

I was upset that my husband could question my sexuality. I had never questioned it. I had been a mother and a wife all those years and it had not occurred to me that I could have a choice. In Greece transvestites and homosexuals were very obvious. Even if it was something new for my husband and me, it was part of life in capitalist countries. I spoke to one of my Polish friends about my husband's 'accusation'. I was horrified when I noticed that some Polish people in the hotel started to avoid me. I was stunned. I began to question whether my husband could be right. How should I feel in the company of women if I was a lesbian? To question myself and find an honest answer to this previously forbidden subject was an interesting experience for me. I spent time with Magdalena on the hotel terrace teaching myself English, teaching the children in my Polish class a few basic words of English, going to the beach, parks, shopping. I did not have any Polish books to read.

I did not have any Polish books to read.

After eleven months in Greece, we finally obtained permanent visas to Australia. My husband decided to go to Australia with Magdalena and me. Unbelievable relief, excitement and joy! I hoped that we could rebuild our relationship, save my family for my child.

Our destination was supposed to be Melbourne, but the night we went to the airport in Athens, they gave us tickets to Sydney. It didn't matter!

We were farewelled by many people. Two days before we left, our closest friends from Poland arrived following in our steps. Grazyna, Jarek and their daughter Halshka waited in Greece for almost two years before gaining entry to Australia.

The end of July 1985 in Athens – mid-hot summer. Early morning in Sydney – COLD. After four hours waiting at Athens airport, approximately 30 hours flying, and several hours to clear customs in Sydney, we ended up at the 'Endeavour' hostel for refugees.

The first time I looked at the streets of Sydney through the taxi window I was not impressed. I saw dirty streets, small houses, poverty. In the middle of the Australian winter people dressed in thongs and third hand T-shirts with beer guts exposed. I felt cheated. For the first month at the hotel I did not unpack our clothes. I wondered what I was going to do now. Then we got to know Sydney from a different side, to see the beauty of Sydney and its beaches.

> In the middle of the Australian winter people dressed in thongs and third hand T-shirts with beer guts exposed. I felt cheated.

The first thing that surprised me was that the Australian sky was much higher and more peaceful than in Europe. We bought our first car, an old Holden Kingswood station wagon. It was huge. That car took us to wonderful places around Sydney, and gave us a sense of freedom.

At first the Australian sunburned red landscape seemed very plain to me, empty and still compared to the forests I remembered from Poland. With time I discovered how wrong I was, how beautiful and full of life the Australian bush is, how fascinating and exotic are Australian rain forests. It was completely different from the flora and fauna that I grew up with in Europe. I missed the richness of colours with the changing of seasons, the characteristic scent of autumn leaves and the cold winter air. White Christmas and the spruce tree, the variety of tree leaves, the beauty of European deer forests and the swarms of Polish sparrows in the towns. I remember the characteristic landscape of lakes, rivers and the cold Baltic sea, the beauty of the old Polish towns.

The Australian life style is different from what I grew up with. Australians are usually less spontaneous and not very affectionate. Even with their closest family members or friends they are rather reserved compared to Polish people, but they are friendly. They do not express themselves much through body language. In Australia people are supposed to be under control, self-confident, cool, successful. Life is very practical here. We listen to the radio and watch television, we talk a lot about our careers, politics, the economy, sport, trendy music, murders. For me there is not enough discussion about the development of the sciences, history, the fascinating variety of Australian culture, literature, classical music, theatre, Australian flora and fauna. We do not teach our children enough about the meaning of friendship. The word 'my friend' has a different value here. We like to have a lot of 'friends' and to be popular. It can be confusing especially for very sensitive children, who long for a real friend. The typical: 'How are you?' confused me at first. I had to learn that people are not really interested in how I am.

It surprised me how different the Australian sense of humour is, and very few of the television comedies are funny to me. I do not like the male approach towards women: 'If you want to be a bloody feminist, open the door for yourself.' Men who take this attitude do not understand the importance of basic human rights, especially for women. Australian women have a different status from Polish women. More and more of them openly about touchy subjects and they stand for their rights. The treatment of Aboriginal people has been the most disturbing aspect of Australian society that I have observed. I hope for Australia that being born an Aboriginal will not be considered, as it has been in the past, unlucky, but that it will mean being somebody special.

> The typical: 'How are you?' confused me at first. I had to learn that people are not really interested in how I am.

With time I realised that it was easier to be critical of what I saw of Australia, than to be positive, but it was also difficult to live in a new country with such a negative attitude. I wanted to have an open mind, to learn about this country and then do something about those issues I was not happy with. Being proud of my Polish identity, I wanted to feel part of this country where I will spend the rest of my life. Putting the positive and negative aspects of life in this country aside it was up to me to achieve the best I could. This more realistic approach helped me a lot in the process of adapting to our new circumstances.

We lived in Sydney for the first two-and-a-half-years. We met many wonderful Polish people and started to build new friendships and make our new home. My husband worked hard as a painter, he learnt the trade and established his own business. I worked at the library, then as an ethnic welfare worker, and as an agedcare worker under the Community Employment Program (CEP). I went to school to learn English, did a basic computer course, and studied ethnic welfare. Magdalena attended school and, although the first few years were difficult for her, she learnt English quickly. The cultural differences confused her for a long time.

Even if we had been trying, our marriage relationship was not working. We had different interests, very different opinions about our future, we had not been happy together. At the end of 1987 my husband invited his mother to visit us for a year. A few months later, we sponsored my husband's brother and his family to Australia as refugees via Spain. At the end of 1988 I decided to move to Melbourne with my daughter. At that same time our close friends Grazyna, Jarek and their daughter Halshka arrived in Sydney from Greece. Their marriage did not survive the migration. Grazyna decided to take her daughter to Melbourne with Magdalena and me.

The four of us arrived in Melbourne in our Kingswood just before Christmas. It felt like a second migration for me, but this time I was in total control of my life. Something new began for all of us, and although we did not know anybody in Melbourne it did not scare me. Our flat was empty and we did not have much money, but it did not matter because I knew in my heart we could make it work.

Grazyna quickly established a new relationship and moved out. I could not find any employment. My qualification from Poland was not fully recognised. Although I had a masters degree it was considered to be the equivalent only of an honours degree in Australia. It was impossible for me to get work, my main weakness being my lack of experience. In Victoria the Community Employment Program did not exist anymore.

Magdalena went to school. She was adapting to her new family circumstances for a long time. She wanted her father and mother to be together. I felt great responsibility for taking her away from her family in Poland and then from her father. At this time I could only hope that I made the right decision for both of us. The school she was attending in Melbourne had a conservative approach to single parent families. This made her feel even more lonely and isolated. For a year I had a few casual cleaning jobs. I then undertook the two years full-time social work course at the University of Melbourne. Working and studying in my second language was difficult and for quite some time I felt lost at university. I did not know the basic regulations and students rights. Fortunately, I met several supportive people who stuck with me through my studies. The best reward for completing this course was in 1991 on my graduation day, when my daughter told me that one day she would take me to celebrate her own graduation day.

> Working and studying in my second language was difficult and for quite some time I felt lost at university. I did not know the basic regulations and students rights.

We moved to a different suburb. Magdalena changed her school. She met new good friends and supportive teachers. Magdalena is a wonderful, strong, friendly, enthusiastic person. I love her and I am proud of her. I would like to compensate her for all that she lost and the pain that she went through as a result of our struggle. If I had to go back in time and take her through the migration once more, I am not sure I would want her to go through this again, but I am glad we are here. I believe, it is worth it. I hope my daughter believes so, too. One day I will find courage to ask her.

At the moment we go through a difficult time in Australia because of the recession, and we have a long way to go to improve the situation. Even though Australia has a good democratic system, we are often forced to challenge our government's failure to protect the human rights of Australians: the intellectually disadvantaged, the homeless, Aboriginal people, women, children, the elderly, migrants and many other groups of people living in this country.

Australians have a great sense of security, which is real compared to many other countries, particularly countries similar to the Poland we fled, living under outside domination and tyrannical governments. We really don't have any excuses in Australia for not tackling these problems.

Harvard: A Djaru Woman's Perspective

Mary Ann Bin-Sallik

Mary Ann Bin-Sallik is an associate professor at the University of South Australia and holds both a masters degree in education administration and a doctorate from Harvard University in the United States of America. She has served on the Commonwealth's Committee of Review of Aboriginal Employment and Training which produced the Miller Report in 1985. This report was the forerunner for the federal government's major policy initiatives in Aboriginal employment, training and education. She has served on the National Aboriginal Employment Development Committee, the first Council of the National Museum of Australia, and the National Committee Against Discrimination in Employment and Occupation. She was also a member of the National Population Council and the Council of the Australian Institute of Aboriginal Studies and is currently on the Board of Tandanya: The National Aboriginal Cultural Institute, and the Executive of Black Women's Action in Education Foundation (BWAEF).

I was born in Broome, Western Australia, and am a descendant of the Djaru people of the East Kimberley region. My family moved to Darwin when I was nine-years-old. This resulted in my having a strong affinity with that area and its people. In 1985 I was accepted into Harvard University in Boston, Massachusetts, and obtained both a masters degree and a doctorate from its Graduate School of Education. I was motivated by Harvard's international reputation for academic excellence; its culturally appropriate courses; the need to take Aboriginal education into the international arena; and the barriers confronting me in Australia.

As the first Aborigine to graduate as a nursing sister from the Darwin Hospital in February 1958, my 17 year nursing experience during the periods of governmental policies of assimilation and self-determination has shaped my present career path. I realised that the nursing profession at that time was too rigid for changes and, if I wanted to undo some of the wrongs that had been inflicted on Aborigines since the inception of British colonisation, I needed to get into academia to facilitate Aboriginal access to higher education and to participate in changing the attitudes of academics and students who would be the future policy makers.

In February 1975 I was appointed to the position of student counsellor/lecturer to Aboriginal students studying at the Aboriginal Task Force (ATF) program (now the School of Aboriginal and Islander Administration) at the South Australian Institute of Technology, now incorporated into the University of South Australia, in Adelaide. The ATF was the first Aboriginal higher education program in the country and I was the first Aborigine to be full-time employed within this sector. My contract: to complete an associate diploma in social work, majoring in community counselling part-time over four years. This I did whilst working full-time and raising my two daughters, Rokiah and Lisa, on my own.

> I needed to get into academia to facilitate Aboriginal access to higher education...

On completing the associate diploma I realised that this was just the beginning. I needed higher qualifications if I was to remain in this sector. So I applied to the University of Adelaide for enrollment in one anthropology unit for each semester of the 1980 academic year. I was confident that I would gain entry on the basis that I was employed in a tertiary institution, I had an associate diploma and a background in nursing. However, I received a letter, dated 15 February 1980, from the academic registrar of the University of Adelaide. I still have that letter. In part it states: 'To be eligible to be selected for admission to a course in the University, an applicant must be educationally qualified for matriculation. I have, with regret, to say that you do not satisfy this requirement.' I was outraged, but determined not to give up my pursuit for higher qualifications.

In 1982 I had become the coordinator of the ATF program, and by 1984 was active on a number of national communities including the National Committee Against Discrimination in Employment and Occupation, the National Aboriginal Employment Development Committee, and the Council of the National Museum of Australia. Furthermore, I had contributed to major developments in the ATF, for instance the implementation of the Associate Diploma in Community Development in 1982 and the accreditation of the Bachelor of Arts in Aboriginal Affairs Administration. This was the first bachelors degree in the country to address Aboriginal cultures and issues. I was a member of the curriculum development committee and the advisory committee for both of these awards, as well as the advisory committees for the Bachelor of Arts in Aboriginal Studies and the Diploma of Teaching Anangu for the South Australian College of Advanced Education (now also part of the University of South Australia).

In 1984 Aboriginal higher education was gaining momentum. There were some 14 Aboriginal higher education programs across the country all based on the Aboriginal Task Force model. I contributed to the developments of six of those programs. However, there were mounting pressures on people such as myself, not only to contribute to this sector but also other areas of Aboriginal affairs. This left little time for personal life, let alone studies. My daughters were now working and living independently so I began seriously to consider giving up work to engage in full-time studies. Because of my ever growing heavy work load, I had already withdrawn from a bachelor's degree at the South Australian Institute of Technology which I was pursuing part-time in June 1984.

Dr Roberta Sykes, our first Harvard graduate, suggested that I apply to Harvard for entry into its masters degree program. It was October 1984. I asked her if she was joking and stressed that I did not have the necessary prerequisites. Her response was to the effect: 'I don't joke about matters as serious as this. Further, I have followed your career and I know you can do it and I know that Harvard will accept you.' She then went on to explain that Harvard had a policy of accepting people whom they consider have made exceptional contributions to their fields. Having convinced me that I had a chance I confessed that I would prefer to get a doctorate. She diplomatically explained that I needed to get my masters degree first, and suggested that I apply for an Aboriginal overseas study award (AOSA). Failing that she assured me that Black Women's Action in Education Foundation (BWAEF), of which she was the executive officer, would sponsor me.

In April 1985 I received an offer from the Harvard Graduate School of Education (HGSE) for entry into the masters program for the September 1985 intake. I was jubilant. My family, friends and colleagues were all happy for me. But some people tried to dissuade me and, for their own reasons, wanted me to believe that Harvard degrees were not recognised in Australia! That is another story.

During the hours spent winging across the Pacific Ocean I kept asking myself what the hell was I doing on the aircraft, and whether I could adequately cope being away from my family and country for so long. I had travelled overseas several times before but as a tourist, the longest trip being only three months. This time it was to be for one academic year; I was hopeful it would be four. Possessed by the fear of the unknown, within no time I found myself at Harvard University, the oldest institution of higher learning in the United States of America. In 1986, the year I obtained my masters degree, Harvard celebrated its three-hundred-and-fiftieth anniversary. It owns and occupies 180 hectares and over 400 buildings, including 30 libraries and eight museums, in Cambridge and spreading into Boston. Off-campus facilities are located in Massachusetts, New York, Washington DC, and in Italy. An undergraduate college and ten professional graduate schools make up Harvard: arts and sciences, business administration, design, divinity, education, government, law, medicine, dental medicine, and public health. The latter three facilities are on the Boston side of the campus. I had seen nothing like it before, not even in my wildest dreams. And I had had many of those prior to my arrival.

Harvard Graduate School of Education has orientation programs for each of its minorities groups – Afro-Americans, native Americans, Hispanics, gays, and international students. Each group has its own office and provides services for its students throughout the year. At the end of their orientation programs the minority groups come together with the other students to commence a general orientation program, which I attended. All of us experienced separation from our families, cultural ties, and countries. We knew we were ambassadors for countries, and we were all determined to excel. This was our common bond, and proved to be our strength during our 'highs' and 'lows'.

How nervous we were. Students were saying: 'You know, I think the computer made a mistake and I really shouldn't be here.' It was comforting to hear this as I was secretly thinking the same. Then, at the end of our first session, in a huge auditorium packed with anxious faces along with all the other students, we attended the dean's welcoming speech. After welcoming us, she said: 'You are probably wondering what you are doing here, and thinking that the computer made a mistake, and that you should not be here. Let me tell you, our computer does not make mistakes. You were all carefully selected. You all belong here, and you will all graduate and leave here in the shortest possible time.' My South African friend leaned over to say: 'Hey, sister! It looks as if we've got the brains after all. We belong here.' The dean's words were very comforting.

During the next two weeks at the numerous student and staff functions, we were continually told that we were good, and that every one of us would succeed. No one talked about failure. The atmosphere was so positive, I thought it was all a dream. At one of those functions a male student from the United States asked me what was the subject of my undergraduate degree. I did not have any degree, I replied. His response? 'Holy hell! What sort of a genius are you?' He then proceeded to tell everyone about the 'Aboriginal genius from Australia'. I was taken aback. Then moments later one of the professors told me it was the students and the experiences they brought that made Harvard great, and that it needed us more than we needed it.

The Graduate School of Education was established in 1920 and was the first professional school to admit women to degree candidacy. It now boasts the most demographically and ethnically varied body of students representing 42 countries besides the United States. Students' backgrounds included teaching or school/university administration, experience in educational media, government, community social service agencies, health organisations, and the corporate sector.

Consequently classes comprised a mixture of people who brought with them a diversity of experiences and goals from various professional ethnic and religious backgrounds. In one of my classes there was a colonel from the United States army, a chairperson from the training and development division of a major corporation, the manager of personnel services of a bank on Wall Street, and a womens' rights activist. As one of my colleagues succinctly put it: 'We were Black, White, Christian, Jewish, and Muslim, all joined in a common and cooperative effort.'

The richness of the Harvard experience is so hard to put into words. Can you imagine studying in an environment that nurtures cultural diversity? Can you imagine going to classes each day with **Can you imagine studying in an environment that nurtures cultural diversity?** people from 41 other countries all contributing from their cultural backgrounds, and all respecting each other's differences?

Doctoral and masters students attended the same classes but, while pursuit of excellence was foremost, the atmosphere meant that students worked together as a body complementing each other with their expertise. I regard this as the hallmark of a great learning institution. The experience is one of my most treasured memories of Harvard. We had to maintain a B- average for the masters program and a B+ average for the doctoral program. Expectations from the professors were extremely high. I remember thinking that I would get an A- for one of my accountancy exams only to find that the 89 per cent was graded as a B+.

The master of education is a one year course-work program designed to meet the diverse professional needs of students who have had a number of years experience in their professional areas, and are returning to study with clear goals and academic expectations to enhance their professional competencies. Students had the responsibility of selecting the eight units required to complete the program from some 60 courses offered at the Harvard Graduate School of Education (HGSE) with the option of cross registering in any of the other graduate schools and the Massachusetts Institute of Technology (MIT). There were so many courses from which to choose, making the selection of courses one of our most difficult tasks. The doctoral program was even more difficult because it required students to undergo two years of course work before embarking on writing their 50 page qualifying paper. All this was a forerunner to writing the thesis proposal and, finally, the thesis.

Having successfully completed my masters degree, I applied and was accepted into the doctoral program, during which I cross-registered in two leadership courses at the Kennedy School of Government. Some of the people with whom I studied were politicians, bankers and diplomats from around the world, as well as federal government bureaucrats from Australia and personnel from the Central Intelligence Agency (CIA). Yes, that's right.

My first class at Harvard was community psychology. The professor began with an overview of his book and our major text, *Boiling Energy: community healing among the Kalahari Kung!* and how it related to synergy, the major paradigm. As he gave his definition of synergy: '...being a pattern of relationships in which renewable sources expand exponentially...' I thought to myself: 'This sounds familiar. It's like the Aboriginal extended family network.' At that moment he said: 'We can learn so much from the Kung! and the Australian Aborigines, because these people have so much to offer us.' I couldn't believe my ears.

One of my most exciting courses was ethnographic research in educational settings. The professor invited me to give a guest lecture to the class. The subject? The ethics of doing fieldwork, with emphasis on the negative research that has been done on indigenous peoples. I enjoyed the course so much that I took the advanced course in the second semester. The reading was heavy but interesting and created lively debates in class. The course also required students to carry out field research. Since I was undecided on a topic, my colleagues suggested I could undertake research on a number of groups like Native Americans, Afro-Americans, Hispanics, or some other minority group.

After class I went to see the professor, who later became my doctoral supervisor, and told him that I had no intention of studying any of these groups. I wanted to study 'White people'. He said: 'Fine. Why don't you do a role reversal and study anthropologists for a change?' Once more, I could not believe my ears. Within a week I was off to the Anthropology Department equipped with notebook, pencils and a tape recorder, eager to embark on a new and challenging adventure. On my way over I thought of the possible reactions to me by this 'tribe of White anthropologists' some of whom were internationally acclaimed experts in their fields. I also thought of the Australian anthropological experts, some of whom I had met, wondering what their reactions would be to having an Aborigine study them.

> I wanted to study 'White people'. He said: 'Fine. Why don't you do a role reversal and study anthropologists for a change?'

The seminar participants were social scientists and doctors with backgrounds in the social sciences. They were being trained to undertake clinically relevant cross-cultural research in the area of depression, anxiety, schizophrenia and somatisation. All were very supportive of me and within no time treated me as a fellow researcher. In a sense I was. They even invited me to become a participant in the seminar. I declined as I was having too much fun studying them.

In my second semester I enrolled in managing negotiations. Had I realised how challenging and threatening it was to be, I never would have entertained the idea. Half the class came from the Kennedy School of Government, so there was a large number of lawyers as well as American and foreign politicians in the course. We had two classes a week and at each class we had to discuss a case study – some were 60 pages. Prior to class each student would read and analyse the case. Study group discussion followed where ideas were exchanged and copious notes taken in preparation for the class discussion. Students had the responsibility of setting up their own study groups. To my surprise I was invited into a group where all other participants were from the Kennedy School of Government.

In each session the professor randomly called on one of the students to describe the case and give a brief analysis; we all feared this. Then he would open class discussion. It was a competitive class comprising 120 students, so I managed only two chances to contribute. This worried me as 25 per cent of our marks came from class participation. All case studies were based on real issues. One revolved around the kidnapping of the American hostages by the Iranians. Another related to false advertising charges brought against the Nestle company. The professor had a practice of singling out students who came from areas to which the case studies referred to describe the town, city, country, lifestyle, culture. In some instances students had been involved in the actual cases.

...the professor said to me in class: 'Mary Ann, do you know much about PNG and the culture? It's not far from Australia

In the previous year, two of the American hostages were in the class. In my year, one of the women was a member of a pressure group opposing Nestles. I felt quite safe; there were no case studies from Australia. The last case study, however, was the re-negotiation of the contract between Papua New Guinea (PNG) and the Bougainville Mining Company.

With a week to prepare for the Bougainville exercise, the professor said to me in class: 'Mary Ann, do you know much about PNG and the culture? It's not far from Australia; perhaps you can address the class next week.' My first thoughts were: 'What the hell do I know about PNG? Besides, it's so close to the end of semester exams and I don't have the time to go to the library.' I was overcome with anxiety. But since one never ever says no to a professor, dares indicate discontent, or tries to postpone a presentation, I replied: 'Not much. I will by next week though!' After class I asked him: 'What are you expecting from me?' He replied: 'Oh, you know, a bit about the culture, missionaries, language barrier, exploitation, the impact of mining on an indigenous culture. No one in this class understands any of it, but they have to get a feel for it so they can act out their roles properly.' I was greatly relieved. The only thing I had to do was read a little on the PNG environment. I had an understanding of the cargo cult, pidgin English, and who Michael Somare and Julius Chan were. For the rest I could draw from the Aboriginal experiences with mining companies.

When the time came for me to make my presentation to the class, the professor, for some reason of his own, asked me to address the class from the podium. I extended the 10 minute time limit and talked for a half-an-hour. It ended in a huge round of applause from the class and high praise from the professor. What a relief. I knew I had gained my 25 per cent participation marks!

On receiving A's and B's for my first semester's work I knew that there was no stopping me. I had the Harvard Crimson (doctoral robes) in my sights. With encouragement and references from three of my professors I successfully applied for entry into the 1986 doctoral program. The Commonwealth Department of Education refused to extend my Aboriginal Overseas Study Award to the doctoral program. I guess it did not believe in the importance of a doctorate. Consequently, I received a scholarship from Harvard and one from Northern Building Consultant in Darwin, owned and governed by eight Aboriginal communities in the top end of the Northern Territory; but it was the Black Women's Action Education Fund (BWAEF) which picked up the shortfall amounting to almost half the costs and was prepared to raise all the funds.

The BWAEF is a non-government funded organisation – which is both small, and *incredible*. It is probably the only women's organisation that encourages male membership and has men on its executive, and probably the only Aboriginal organisation that encourages non-Aboriginal membership. Hence its membership comprises Aboriginal and non-Aboriginal women and men including Jewish and Asian members, and European migrants, gays, prisoners, ex-prisoners, reformed alcoholics, pensioners and a range of religious groups as well as universities, government departments and voluntary organisations. It raises the funds for what it considers worthy projects within the Aboriginal community. It has sent four Aboriginal women to Harvard and between us we have amassed two doctorates and four masters degrees. It financed an Aboriginal man at Harvard, and supported another, a BWAEF member, with his application, and provided a reference. Both men graduated in June 1993 with masters degrees. In 1994 a young woman, Larissa Behrendt, will graduate with a masters degree from Harvard Law School, our first law graduate and the organisation's seventh Harvard graduate. Given its accomplishments it is surprising that Black Woman's Action has only 300 members. Unfortunately it does not have the money for advertising to promote itself and its achievements. It has no office or paid staff. All its work is done on a volunteer basis by members, and from a private residence. Members constantly send letters and cards of encouragement to its students and on return BWAEF honours them with a graduation dinner in Sydney.

During my four years at Harvard I lived on campus at the Cronkhite Graduate Centre. It was a mixed hostel providing accommodation for 141 graduate students representing half the Harvard graduate schools, with the majority of students from the Harvard Graduate School of Education and the Kennedy School of Government. As all graduate programs are demanding and leave little free time, most of our socialising was carried out in the dining room, learning about other people's countries, cultures, politics and lifestyles. This in itself was a wonderful learning experience. I learned about countries I had never heard of before, like Senegal in Africa and the Arab state of Yemen. I went down to meals asking myself things like: 'Where shall I sit today? Do I want to learn about mainland China or Iceland?' What we learned outside the classrooms was equally stimulating and important to our intellectual growth.

> I went down to meals asking myself things like: 'Where shall I sit today? Do I want to learn about mainland China or Iceland?'

There were some organised social activities, the annual Christmas dinner dance, Halloween party, and our end of year spring dance. There was also the odd celebration like the 15-minute-party in 1988. Two Cronkhite residents, a Japanese American who had just received news of a job commencing after graduation, and a Greek diplomat who was having a birthday, decided to give what they called a 15-minute-party in the two-bedroom suite they shared. The invitation stated that although they were aware that we were all swatting for our final exams they believed that we could spare 15 minutes to celebrate with them. The party was from 5 pm to 7 pm. Their suite was filled with the comings and goings of people staying mostly for 15 minutes only. The party was a roaring success. It gave many of us the excuse to have a break from our books and computers.

I worked part-time in my last year at the Harvard Institute of International Development (HID) as a research assistant for a joint research project with Harvard Graduate School of Education. The project was a collaborative agreement among the participating host governments of Burundi, Egypt, Indonesia, Pakistan, Sri Lanka, Thailand and North Yemen. I was responsible for summarising research reports for, and helping to edit, the program's newsletter. This provided my pocket money and financed two trips, one to Mexico for three weeks over Christmas and New Year 1988 and one, two weeks later, to Venezuela. I had to get away from the United States as the media was full of, and everyone was talking about, Australia's bicentenary celebrations which represented to me the theft of my country and the dispossession of Aboriginal people.

Not once when I was at Harvard did I have to justify my Aboriginality. This was just accepted on my say so. People were anxious to learn about us, so I spent hours discussing with them our cultures and current status. I was invited to give guest lectures in classes, seminars and conferences. The students from the United States were the least informed in relation to Aborigines. Some Afro-Americans asked me when did Aborigines leave Africa. My response was that we hadn't reached there yet. This either surprised or offended them.

My four years in the United States was the first time in my life that I felt free of racism and discrimination. I was always treated and respected for who I was and what I represented. However, I did observe the racism towards Native Americans and Afro-Americans, especially the latter because they were more visible. It is sad that a Black person is given more respect and credibility outside their country. For instance, I was treated better than the Afro-Americans in their country, and they are treated better in ours. On my way home from the United States I observed a significant number of Blacks both in London and Paris, and in Hong Kong I mixed with predominantly Asians. Not until after a few days back in Adelaide and I went into the city did I become aware that I was the only Black person in sight. This was a most profound and terrifying experience. For the first time in my life I felt so alone and vulnerable.

On 8 June 1982 my dream was realised. I proudly donned my Harvard Crimson, a gift from my widowed mother, Mary Brigid Bin-Sallik, and escorted by my daughter and son-in-law, Rokiah and Rodney Lacey, I set off to the graduation ceremony. It was one of the most wonderful days of my life. Unfortunately, my daughter Lisa Fereday and her husband, Robert, were unable to be present as they were preparing for parenthood.

After the pomp and circumstance of a Harvard graduation ceremony, I could think of no better way to celebrate than a weekend at New York's Waldorf Astoria and shopping at Tiffany's. Despite only affording a bookmark, it felt great. A Tiffany diamond could not have made me feel any happier. I needed to spoil myself because I knew that on my homecoming I would have to re-condition myself to coping with Australia's racism.

Becoming a Walking Book

Ofelia Lopez

Ofelia Lopez was born in El Salvador on 14 December 1961. She became politically active through the church, and spent almost two years as a political prisoner in an El Salvadorean gaol. She participated in the formation of a women's organisation named after Lil Milagro Ramirez, an activist who died in the clandestine gaols. On 18 May 1987 Ofelia Lopez travelled to Australia (together with her daughters) as a political refugee. In Australia Ofelia Lopez worked to establish the Women's International Network for Democracy and Development in El Salvador (WINDS). With the signing of the peace accords, and since being interviewed, in 1992 she returned to El Salvador to continue working for the improvement of living, working and political conditions for all El Salvadorans. Her reflections here are of the El Salvador from which she emigrated as a refugee. Ofelia Lopez is now director of a women's health project, which is supported by the International Women's Development Agency (IWDA).

My political activist ideas were learnt from the Jesuit priests who were breaking the silence and organising new ways of resolving the peasants' needs. The priests implemented the liberation theology, which provided a different perspective on the church. I attended seminars to learn about liberation theology and what it meant for us: why we were so poor, learning about our system, our government, our policies. The teaching was to put yourself in life, not just live in the theory, or the church, or in a religious way unrelated to what real living was about. I learned that religions shouldn't place women in a position of disadvantage and give the man all the rights. I helped with the Sunday religious services. We used

Nicaragua and the Brazilian liberation theology. We had a lot of books and songs such as:

You are the voice of the poor,
you are the christ of the poor.
The poor who you defend,
the ones you speak about,
the ones that you would die for.

The songs gave us such a strong message. It was enough. When I sang them, I was labelled a communist.

In El Salvador I lived in the countryside, in a town called Cuscatelan, 25 kilometres from San Salvador, the capital city. I had to travel long distances so that I could stay on at school, to finish each year. The El Salvadoran dream is to have a place to live and a little piece of land to maintain the family. This is what my father didn't have. We were always on the move.

My father tried continually to rent land from a landlord. When he was working their land, the owners gave my father a house to live in. He had to pay the rent from the crops he grew. Many times he didn't have fertilisers or the resources necessary to avoid diseases of the grains, so many times my father couldn't afford to feed us or to pay the rent. He then had to move from that place to look for another easier way of living. This happened every six months or, at the longest, every year. It meant I had to re-establish myself in a new school.

In my family there were ten children. 'A woman should have as many children as god will give her.' Once you are married you should have as many children as your husband will allow you to have: this is the rule in El Salvador. A mother will always be taking care of the children at home. Women had no other opportunities. This happened with my mother. I was like the second mother of my brothers and sisters. In El Salvador, a daughter is seen as the person who will take care of the youngest children and help her mother.

In El Salvador, a daughter is seen as the person who will take care of the youngest children

My brothers and sisters did not become activists when I did. I was always trying to discover the reasons 'why'. I was anxious to study, and this made me curious. I wanted to be a doctor, with a medical career. I dreamt about it, and searched to find ways of getting it. My father supported the idea emotionally. He couldn't afford it, so he also dreamed: 'I want you to be the one who will study and have a career.' But he couldn't offer me financial support. So at the time I was helping my mother, I became an activist in the church. I learned why there were so many poor people and why there were so few people who were rich, enjoying everything in life. I identified myself as being the poorest class and in El Salvador that was a mistake. My father and I were together the black sheep of the family, and so the whole family was identified as communist. The government authorities began to persecute my father and me.

I didn't and still do not understand the exact meaning of communism and the ideology for which we were accused of struggling. I only know that I didn't have the chance to study or have reasonable health care for me or for my children, my brothers and sisters. That is what put me in my political position.

I had to start working at the age of 12 and that gave me a new way of understanding the lie. I had to help my parents with providing the most basic food, sugar, grains, with what I earned from my work. I went out cleaning houses, taking care of somebody else's children, and stayed away for a month at a time. Each month I came home with money. Nothing was left for me. I wanted to study but I couldn't. I did my studies when I had the opportunity.

The traditional church didn't permit us to sit down to discuss what the *Bible* was telling us, that it didn't just happen thousands of years ago, but also was relevant at the current moment we were living. The traditional priests preached in Latin, keeping the people's eyes closed, never letting them read by themselves or study. Liberation theology, implemented through the christian based communities, was the reverse of that. We studied the *Bible,* with everybody's opinion in the open. It was so lovely to hear, to have freedom of expression, and take that message from the gospel, not hear it and then forget about it, but to listen to it carefully, read it, think about it, and comment on it. It was like eating a piece of bread, sharing, everybody taking from one piece of bread, getting a little bit.

> It was like eating a piece of bread, sharing, everybody taking from one piece of bread, getting a little bit.

I became one of the government's opposition. That put my whole family in danger. It wasn't easy because at the same time I didn't have a deep understanding of the whole social and political structure. I did understand a little about how to break the silence and speak out, not just by myself but standing up together, sharing the same kind of suffering. I had thought that I was the only one, but through the christian based communities I found there were many of us. What we needed was to become united and express our feelings and our needs strongly.

The level of literacy was not high, so there were no newsletters. Our singing conveyed the message. Simple words. The person who knew how to write and read taught the others, and so on. We tried to resolve our problems in a community way. Everybody shared whatever skills they had. It made us feel that we were not alone any more; people learn by doing that. A person develops a kind of socialising, integrating herself on a social level. Before, it wasn't like that. Everyone had to live their own lives, support themselves and find solutions to their own problems. This new approach was threatening to the government, because we got together and consolidated our visions, our thoughts and decisions. For the government that was very dangerous.

I had never thought to leave El Salvador, and I was frightened of the outside world. I was 24-years-old when I left. I was scared of the unknown. Very, very scared. I didn't intend to live permanently in Australia. I had one reason, security, and the other, medical. I said to myself: 'Yes, I will go, but only for six months,' because I thought that would be sufficient time to receive my medical treatment. Then I would return to El Salvador and go wherever was safe for me. The mountains.

But six months was not enough. I arrived in Australia as a refugee, which meant I had to stay two years in order to be allowed to return to El Salvador. When two years had gone by, I did not have any option. I had not realised how far away El Salvador was, and how difficult economics made any return. Then three years, then four years and it became each time more and more difficult to go home. I told myself: 'Well, yes, I decided to stay two years, against my own wishes, but I had to.' But after four years I became so desperate to return to El Salvador I thought: 'Oh, my God, how am I going to manage to get back?' Where would I get the money for tickets for myself and the two children? Then, what would I do there? I hadn't anticipated that in six months many changes could occur in El Salvador, and in two years many more. This made me feel so scared, again, of the unknown. This time it was in relation to my own country.

> I was scared of the unknown. Very, very scared.

When I was in the mountains, I wasn't recognised as a citizen, so I spent seven or eight years out of the real society, first in the mountains and then in prison. In Australia I had the time to think over and over again, slowly and carefully. I would need to reintegrate myself into El Salvadorian society. It made everything more complicated.

In Australia, my whole perspective became wider, bolder. I learnt things I didn't know before. This helped me to overcome other difficulties easily. I understand and look at the world differently, look at myself differently, in this multicultural country. So many people are going through so many difficulties. It is not only me. That gives a person courage to carry on with her own life.

As well, there was the learning of another language. Not knowing my own language very well, I never thought of learning any other. I had no English at all before I came to Australia, and learning was difficult. I identified American English as the language of imperialism; I saw Americans as the enemies of my people, as responsible for so many dead people in El Salvador.

How can a person learn a language which is that of the enemy? Yet in Australia I realised I had to learn English if I wanted to be part of society. Otherwise I would be isolated perpetually. Paradoxically, there were political reasons for learning English. I had to get the message about El Salvador through to the Australian people.

A large group of about 15 or 20 families came to Australia with me under the special humanitarian program. In El Salvador contact with the foreign immigration authorities is so secret, very quiet, because it is against the law. It is essential not to talk to anyone, not to tell anyone else how to go about it, not to share information. Some of the families in my group needed to get out for political reasons. In El Salvador, their lives were in danger. But a large number did not need to come to Australia for such imperatives. Most knew English; they had worked in a section of foreign relations in El Salvador and were our translators. They had good jobs and their lives were not at risk. Coming to Australia wasn't even a way of improving their work place. Perhaps they just wanted to know what it was like to live in another country.

My mother knew in advance that I was leaving for Australia. She was relieved, because she was worried about me. I was unable to communicate with her for a whole year because my letters kept getting 'lost'. Hers arrived, but she was not able to write to me often because she had economic and security problems, too. She was captured twice and released. I was prepared for that because of my own experience.

The Australian embassy is in Mexico. The consul in El Salvador looked after us. We were interviewed. The consulate did everything for me, including preparing my passport, helping me with transport and whatever else was necessary. For many people, there is no assistance. They do everything by themselves, which puts them at great risk. Most are running from persecution, and some don't manage to get out, being captured before they leave, sometimes on the way to the airport.

Rumours went around: 'You will live in camps, like refugee camps.' Rumours about Australia went around: 'You will live in camps, like refugee camps.' I thought: 'Never mind, as long as I receive what I need, which is good.' They said: 'You will receive interpreters, you will receive food and some unemployment benefits.' I didn't know anything about that because we don't have such assistance in El Salvador. How was I to understand what they were talking about? Everything was new. I had no idea what they meant. Whatever it is, I thought, I will receive it, anyway.

I came directly to Melbourne. In El Salvador I had met someone from Melbourne, when I was in prison in the most terrible circumstances. He had helped me and meant a lot to me. That was the only hope I had within all my fear. In Melbourne I had someone to meet me at the airport. I knew him only a little, but at least he spoke Spanish.

My Australian friend had visited Nicaragua and El Salvador several times, organising delegations of highly influential people, including Australian parliamentarians. The authorities couldn't treat these people badly; it wasn't politically appropriate. Security passes and permits for the prisons were given out. The government wanted to show how well the political prisoners were treated; the reality was the opposite.

Once these people got in they could hear for themselves the political prisoners' testimonies. Tape recorders and cameras were banned. The visitors weren't allowed to take paper, or write anything, but it didn't matter. People will hear. That couldn't be avoided, and it was a strong weapon.

My friend had gone with delegations through both the men's and the women's political prison. It was an educational process, learning from one side and the other. The government presented the best image, but there was also the people's side. The government was democratic, at least in ensuring that the gaols became crowded, because the number of disobedient people increased.

I was never sentenced. In El Salvador people were captured anywhere. We knew the authorities were looking for me. A special police security force worked as plain clothes detectives. Wherever you go, they go. Unfortunately that kind of infiltration existed in the mountains as well. By this means many, many people ended in prison or disappeared.

The torture in prison meant a prisoner had to say something. It was a case of making up some story that would be accepted. It is impossible under torture to keep quiet without speaking. Even then, it doesn't matter what anyone says. No one will be stupid by saying the truth, but they don't use what you say, anyway. The security police make up their own file, with an extra-judicial declaration which they force prisoners to sign, whilst blindfolded. With that declaration they can put you in prison for as long as they want, without trial. There is no way of knowing how long you will be kept.

I was in a cell with a lot of other people. The men had to share beds and toilets, and sleep on the ground. Their conditions were worse than ours. But we had male prison guards. The only females were the social workers and the prison director or governor. Often the prison guards raped the prisoners, stole money and took personal belongings. They came at about 2 am or 3 am, with the story that they were looking for drugs, dangerous weapons (like knives or scissors), or fermented fruit. They said we were making alcoholic drinks, which was not allowed. If our visitors brought such fruit it was confiscated, so why did the guards look for it?

Prisoners received no medical assistance after coming from a torture place. A lot of women were mad, crazy after the torture they received. Some people are physically and emotionally strong, but others are not. We had to deal with our own problems and those of everybody else.

We could have visits from our family twice a week. Most people were scared to come. Not many did. In many cases, the visitors were allowed to get through, visit their relatives, then on the way out they were captured. Brothers and sisters were taken into custody after visiting. I was glad not to receive visitors. My mother came to visit me only after a year had gone by, because she was scared. I said to her: 'Don't come here too often, because it is dangerous. It is enough for me to be here. I don't want you to be here with me as well.'

We had our collective in the prison, dealing with the food. We had our own rules, also: to clean up, to cook for ourselves. That was achieved through a great struggle. We negotiated with the governor to leave us alone, not to interfere. There were a lot of fights to have the authorities give us the food raw so that we could cook it ourselves. At first, the political prisoners were together with the common prisoners: women dealing with drugs, or thieves, without any political understanding of the situation. The first achievement in the women's prison was for the women to be divided, political from non-political prisoners, not to have to live together.

I was in prison for 26 months. I was very active, and my photograph and my story appeared in even the most conservative newspapers in El Salvador. Our struggle in the prison was so strong and so solid that we kept on fighting to achieve new measures. We wanted to open negotiations between the political prisoners collective and the director of the prison and also the minister for justice. We demanded a stop to the 'search', the raping and beating up of the prisoners, to receive at least one nurse to look after us, one psychologist, one good, professional social worker and a doctor, a dentist. This was for the common prisoners too. The authorities didn't want to provide them; they hadn't allocated any budget for such resources.

When I was shot, the ministry of justice came with their mass-media, their journalists, newspapers, television, cameras.

We got what we wanted, but only after a strong fight where the guards and reinforcements attacked us and wounded some prisoners, including me. After that, there was no more search. We also gained the right to have the children with us, and to receive the newspapers. After the attack where I was shot, we received tape recorders and cameras – with permission, legally. We demanded to receive delegations; the Australian delegation came in to the political section in this way. It meant visitors came to us, rather than into the director's office, so that she could not interfere in the conversation.

We provided many testimonies to the delegations, breaking through the barriers. It was dangerous but we did it. When I was shot, the ministry of justice came with their mass-media, their journalists, newspapers, television, cameras. They talked to us, sitting with our banners in the background, emblazoned with the committee for political prisoners' slogans.

We used careful methods to get materials for the banners into the gaol. Say that you are a political prisoner. Your mother comes, bringing you fruits. Sometimes she would wrap the fruits, because we needed red and black material. That became too obvious. She needed to hide it better. Maybe she would bake it inside a loaf of bread.

So we made our own banners and we had the 'National Liberation Front' and the 'Left Front' banners. The minister of justice sat between the two banners, and appeared on television flanked with National Liberation Front, Left Front. He was the highest justice authority. The prison guards were so angry. By then we had television and we saw it on the news after it happened. It was so funny and such a victory for us.

The media took photos. The story the government gave was according to their convenience. They said that I came into prison already wounded, that they captured me in the mountains and I was shot in military action. They didn't say how long I had spent in prison. One year later, in 1986, they used the same story again and published it. They couldn't tell the truth about my being shot in prison, by the guards. There was a woman with me who appeared in the courtroom. She had no name and lost her leg in the military hospital. She was captured in the mountains with another woman, and was shot there. These two guerillas ended up in prison. The other woman was 19-years-old and pregnant. After she was captured, the woman was admitted to the military hospital. She shouldn't have lost her leg; it was a sort of torture, cutting off her leg. The pregnant one lost her baby. Then she was sent to the prison. They put the same story of being shot in action about me.

We won the right to receive apples, pineapples and pears, fruit that fermented. The guards had been searching and raping every three months. The fight that sent me to hospital was the last one. They were about to do the search again, and we said: 'No.' We said: 'No more search.' That was it. It was a big fight. The airforce came. Helicopters were flying overhead and there were soldiers on the roof. The armed forces came to the front of the prison, with big trucks of soldiers, as if we were armed people. We did not have a single weapon of any sort inside. It was ridiculous. They called up the other guards from the men's prison. The entire force was used.

'No.' We said: 'No more search.'

Journalists came and we did the demonstration, taking over the director's office and saying: 'We want to denounce what you are doing to us.' It lasted two days: 20 and 21 January 1985. All night on the twentieth, we were alert, in case they came, but next day we made a telephone call directly to air, announcing the strike on the national airwaves. The director didn't want us to do it but we said we would burn up all the office if she didn't let us. We told her we had kerosine and matches, 'so think about it'. She let us after all. By the time the troops attacked us, the mass media knew what was happening in the prison.

I came out of prison in a political exchange. The man from Melbourne who could speak Spanish was there. The left front had kidnapped a colonel, so demanded negotiations with the government for release of a number of political prisoners in exchange for him. I was under the protection of the International Red Cross. They took us, because it was a big event. They provided transport and we went in the car of the International Red Cross. I was temporarily under the protection of the Catholic church, too.

I had no knowledge of Australia. I didn't even know how far it was. Maybe I didn't want to know. We flew Continental Airlines. I was so scared of the plane. It was a monster for me. Initially I didn't think what it would be like to go on an aeroplane, because it was such a foreign idea. Once aboard, it was shocking for me. I was half dead all the way through, so deeply shocked that I can hardly explain how I felt. I was by myself with nothing familiar. It was terrible.

With my children, I went to a migrant hostel, somewhere in Footscray, when we first arrived. There were sad moments, because of the food, and the aftermath of the trip. I was half dead. I don't know how I managed, with my two girls, and my health condition. The little daughter was one-and-a-half-years-old and the older girl was four. The little one had an earache on the plane, and she was crying, and I was crying, and I thought: 'Oh my God, my child is going to die. I can't cope with this.' I felt that all my body was shrunk because of the air pressure. All my muscles were seized up, my heart felt as if it was under intense pressure, and I didn't eat, I didn't sleep, even for a second. I didn't even go to the toilet.

When I arrived at the hostel, I hadn't eaten anything, and I didn't want to eat anything. I felt dizzy, completely lost, with no English at all, such disgusting food that I have ever seen before. I didn't want to know anything. I just wanted to sleep, sleep, sleep. I was there for nearly two weeks. Then I was sent to the Daughters of Charity. I felt so relieved, that's why again I think I was lucky. Very lucky, because everything changes. I could cook my own food, and for the kids. They felt better. There were other refugees in the house, but they were all single. I was the first one with children in that house. It must have been a special case for them to have me. I felt so relieved. They helped me a lot with their medical treatment too. They looked after the kids for three months when I was in hospital.

The little one had an earache on the plane, and she was crying, and I was crying...

I took another three months to recuperate. At the end of 1985 I began school, leaving one of the kids in the house to be looked after by the nuns, the other in kindergarten. At Myer House in the city I did two courses in English as a Second Language (ESL). Being in the city, right in Elizabeth Street, made me feel a part of Melbourne. But no more than two courses can be done there by any one person, because the places are given to new people. So after two courses they said: 'Okay, you have been given what everyone is normally given, so you go somewhere else to look for other courses.' That's what I did. I so desperately wanted to learn the language.

I thought I sounded funny, speaking in a foreign language. It is as if everybody else is laughing at you. If that feeling takes over, then you have lost the entire opportunity. You have to ignore the feeling, but it is difficult to do so. When you are among so many people in the same situation it's better, then you feel that there is no reason to feel the way you feel. Everybody's in the same boat.

I met a man from Viet Nam and then I understood that people from other countries have similar problems. I was head of my family, I had two kids and myself, and no one else. So I had to learn the language, because who else would do it for me? But there is a macho and racist notion that the women shouldn't learn.

The majority of the students in the English classes were men. Women like myself had no choice. I had to go to classes and suffer discrimination from the men who come instead of their women. (They will never give the chance to 'their' women to come to learn English.) I didn't know why there were so many more men than women. Now I realise that the women had been left at home. In only one class was there another woman – one. For the men, it was shocking: they thought my man should be there, not me. When I tried to make conversation in English, they jumped over me immediately. I didn't understand why this was happening. Now I know that it was a cultural issue.

The women born in Australia will never understand, because they have never been in these shoes. They never had the chance to learn a new language. Probably they do not speak another language, so this takes another possibility for communication away from the newcomer.

I just kept going and didn't take any notice of the absence of women. I was quiet, always, just learning and taking everything in. I spoke outside, not inside, the class. I was too shy. I suppose I wasn't brave enough and my confidence to speak was not developed to a point where I could speak up in a classroom full of men.

For the men, it was shocking: they thought my man should be there, not me.

Next, I went to a four week course at Preston. Then I did another six weeks in Box Hill, then looked for courses in Collingwood TAFE, to be closer to home. I did three courses at Collingwood, finishing off my formal learning of English with a certificate awarded in 1992.

Being able to study was important, particularly to me as a woman, because in El Salvador it is not compulsory to study, nor to go to school. Parents have to pay for schooling. This means that many El Salvadoreans come into Australia with nothing, and with no education. I was not just learning a new language. I was developing the study habit. It was a huge challenge. The majority of the people in the class were educated people: at least, that is what they said. This made it even more difficult for me. But it meant that I learnt English. I learnt also to become a student, and to be a student in a foreign country. It meant that I had to develop the courage to go everywhere: I travelled in to the city for classes; I went to Box Hill, and had to be there by nine o'clock. First, I had to put one child in at the kinder, then take the other to childcare, very early. I left home every day at about seven o'clock. I had to go by train.

I lived in Carlton, in a flat. The train took 45 minutes. I had to make sure I caught the early train and was happy doing this because I wanted to keep going. It's rather like when you warm up, not wanting to go slowly because then you will cool again, and that makes it more difficult to keep going.

After studying English I did further study, most recently in social and community services. After graduating I took several short jobs on a part-time or casual basis. I also did a two-week placement with the Brotherhood of St Laurence at the elderly people's centre in Clifton Hill.

Most were retired people, many of them in their nineties, and my job was to enhance their independence. They had many problems, especially with rheumatism and arthritis, so couldn't manage to look after themselves. But it was beautiful to be with them, because they were fighting to be independent, and I was helping them. I went with them for walks, bought goods for them from the shop up the street, helped them in the kitchen. I talked with them, too, because often the permanent staff didn't have time.

These old people are books with two legs, walking books. They have so much experience of life. They have come from so many different countries and will tell you of what it was like before the second world war and the first world war.

I did a placement at the community health centre in Collingwood, organising activities in the Spanish language, especially camping and recreation, to help the people feel they are a part of one community and are not suffering isolation. I took part in research for a La Trobe University study. Beryl Langer was finishing her masters degree in sociology and her work involved the El Salvadoran community. I did interviews. I was pleased to be working on such a large project and to be receiving a wage. I gave it up after eight months because working, studying, political activism, and being a mother became too much.

In 1991 I went to El Salvador, for four weeks, after being away for four years. Changes I thought would never happen, had happened. Most of the women and men who were doing as I did four or five years ago at the hospital in the mountains were working legally, with proper documentation. They were working openly. They had medicines, bandages and instruments. They didn't have to come clandestinely to the city to buy basic medication, using a false name, and with no documents, to save women and children's lives, and afraid to be captured, shot, dead or disappeared. The country had changed because the people had been pushing so much, without caring for themselves, that the barriers had had to 'give'.

In El Salvador the Women's Movement is engaged in a civil war. It took more than one-and-a-half years to coordinate a delegation, but I did it through the financial support of the International Women's Development Agency (IWDA). I had lost so much knowledge of the current situation, and knew I couldn't explain El Salvador to others if I couldn't understand it, or know of it directly, myself. I could read about it, but this was not the same. I wanted to go to see, and I wanted to give the women from Australia who made up the delegation the opportunity of seeing for themselves. But underneath all this, the real point was for myself: for me it was so important having to be the advocate in the Australian community for the El Salvadoran Women's Movement and to gain that sense of renewal.

The women's struggle in Australia, Germany, Mexico and North America gave me an entirely different picture of the Women's Movement. The international solidarity women in the Women's Movement express and the experience of looking at the issues from another angle has helped to develop my understanding. The Women's Movement says that women should fight for our rights, and that lesbians must fight to be given the same rights and respect as all women. Feminism is seen as a way of recognising the oppression men exercise against women. I am not a feminist from that point of view, but I do respect the ideas of women who express this viewpoint.

It interested me to accept and understand that we in the El Salvadoran Women's Movement have the same basic aim. But when it comes time for a woman like me to talk, with my background and my understanding of the Women's Movement in my country, I know it is very different to be a woman in El Salvador. I do not see feminism as a separatist movement, but as part of the whole process of education. I see it as important to educate men, because the men are bound to be macho in a macho society. They must be educated too, otherwise we have lost the whole struggle, and the way will not be free in El Salvador for the necessary changes.

In El Salvador, the strongest message to be given relates to education and the question of women's position in the household and family. One of the biggest problems the women experience in El Salvador is why they should have so many children. When the delegation discussed how to approach women in El Salvadore, I said: 'The man makes his wife have as many as he says, and because she is his wife and because the church told her that she should have as many children as God gives her, she shouldn't do anything about that. However, if we put a bucket full of condoms in the middle and everyone can come for as many as they want, that would be a much more educative message than to burn a bra. Burning a bra would not give them any message. Our women are from the countryside, they are not literate women, they are the market sellers. They might not have a bra anyway. But if we present them lots of condoms that will teach them something. Why should a woman be always tied up with a little baby. Why shouldn't she be learning something about the baby question?'

The women with me in the delegation learnt something too. The message was not as complicated as they had thought was needed to raise the women's consciousness.

International feminist solidarity is important. It is one of the aims with the new focus of WINDS, which is partly to organise women's delegations to El Salvador. Women can go to look and share and live and learn from the El Salvador Women's Movement. We share many common aims, but there are different ways of overcoming the difficulties we as women have in each country. In El Salvador we have had 20 years of civil war. We are dealing with so many women who carry around the trauma from the war: who knows how many children or relatives have been disappeared so long ago, or killed. Or they may well have had their own awful experiences. It is necessary to learn how to deal with this.

Women participating in the delegations will return with new ways and alternatives to deal with the problems of women in their own movement in their own countries. Women are not traumatised in Australia or New Zealand by war or institutionalised torture, but they are traumatised by domestic violence. We can use the learning in El Salvador for all women.

Sometimes women in Australia think: 'If I am happy in my family, why should I join the Women's Movement?' They need to see the ways they can learn, which in the end is the aim of the Women's Movement. It is also important to have an international understanding of women's struggles. We need cooperation from woman to woman.

Women make up 65 per cent of the El Salvadoran population, so it is important to support the women's struggle. Before coming to Australia I was giving as much as I could, in my country, with my limited education.

Women are not traumatised in Australia or New Zealand by war or institutionalised torture, but they are traumatised by domestic violence.

In the mountains I was trying to heal, in accord with my dream of becoming a doctor one day. I had a natural dedication and enjoyed doing the work. I was trained by a Mexican sergeant and was working with an American doctor in giving health assistance to the civilian population. I was trained in midwifery. I was trained also for small surgical tasks and participated in the theatre rooms helping the surgeons. I was trained in deontology as well. I then trained other people. We had patients with all kinds of illnesses, including wounds from the bombs. I had so much dedication and did the work with so much love, that that helped me when I arrived in Australia. People had heard about the work I had done.

In Australia I worked at developing the knowledge and understanding of our position in El Salvador. The financial and moral support of the women in Australia for projects in El Salvador has been important, so I am returning to El Salvador with a special project, a health training program for women in midwifery. This is based on traditional preventative medicine, particularly preventative health for the women. Women's health in El Salvador is threatened by illnesses and infections, and children suffer high malnutrition, beginning from the time of a woman's pregnancy – pre-natal and post-natal care is poor. Later on it affects the children's health too. If the woman is not healthy, how can she take care of the child appropriately?

Today, I feel that I am a part of the Australia society, because I have come through so much and overcome so many difficulties; it is easier for me to live in Melbourne now. Yet I will not be happy if I stop being a political activist towards my country. I have developed a way of understanding, and know how to lobby and approach people in various sectors in Australia, so that the issues are not lost.

I have been on aeroplanes, now, many times. It is different from the time when my hands were cold, I was shaking, sweating, and so nervous, not believing I was travelling all the way by myself. When the plane moved down, or when it shook, I thought I was dying. The first time I flew locally, I applied to represent the Committee of Mothers for Australia, New Zealand

and Japan. I had to get onto an aeroplane to go to New Zealand to carry out the job. (I have never yet been to Japan.) Now, I enjoy so much being in a aeroplane. I don't get cold hands any more, or shake. My hands are dry and warm. I like to sit in the window seat so that I can see out.

I am so familiar with the way of working in Australia that it seems I will have to begin all over again in El Salvador. I will have to re-integrate myself. It will be difficult but now I have so much confidence in myself. When I arrived in Australia I didn't know how to resolve difficulties. Now I can find alternatives because I have developed new capabilities. I have improved my social communication.

I don't think Australia will change as much as El Salvador will. Australia is a far more settled society. When I am in El Salvador I want to keep in contact with people in Australia, for however long I remain there. If something happens in El Salvador I would be able to return to Australia and would do so, particularly from the point of view of the children. The future is not as promising in El Salvador as what I would like to offer them.

Yet El Salvador is my country. I identify it as my home. When I left El Salvador, it was my homeland. Nothing has changed in five years. I feel the same. Returning to live there will be the test: is that really my homeland or not? Now, I have learnt from another country, a new culture, another langauge and more. I need to find out which is home.

So many differences between our two countries are not realised by women living in Australia until they visit El Salvador. Transport – to get into the city by a bus or a tram was so new for me. You sit in the tram and push the button for the next stop. In El Salvador there are so few buses, in such bad condition – so that if you are not prepared to leap out at the appropriate moment when the bus stops, the risk is tremendously high. The drivers drive like mad, terribly mad. They do not respond to traffic lights or the laws. They ignore everything. You can get into a bus and rarely find a seat, because though they say 'don't overload this bus' and the capacity is 40 passengers, there will be 150 or 200 people on board. You are squashed in. You can hardly get in. There will be another 50 on top of the bus, hanging on to the roof: if you cannot get into the bus, then you have to get on top of it. Sometimes you may be hanging there by one foot, with the other flying, and with one hand you are just able to hold on, because so many hands want to hold on and are grabbing at every available surface, and the bus is simply flying. There is no cause, in Australia, to think about this possibility in public transport.

To cross the street in El Salvador is so dangerous. Apart from the way the traffic flies about, ignoring the rules of the road, for Australians it is necessary to remember that the traffic drives on a different side of the road. No one worries about red lights in El Salvador: you cross when you can, and take your life into your hands.

Theft and vandalism are high in El Salvador, because the unemployment rate is high. There is also massive under-employment. In El Salvador you are likely to end up deaf because of the noise at the market: 'Buy my tomatoes.' 'How much?' 'He bought them at the other one for much less.' 'Are you trying to rob me?' 'Thief! Thief!' You see a pair of shoes and a dress? 'This dress costs only...' 'This is a special price.' They are competing so much. Everyone is screaming, trying to sell their products. And it is so crowded. Suddenly – not just at the market, but on the bus, too – you have to be cautious about your money. You can't wear any gold earrings, rings or other gold jewellery. If you look too well dressed you are at risk of being robbed. If you are carrying a handbag and manage to

Returning to live there will be the test: is that really my homeland or not?

hold onto the bus, you may not realise that someone else is managing to hold onto the bus with one hand whilst tearing at your handbag with a knife in the other. They are away with your money and all your other accessible valuables. Then – suddenly – you notice there is nothing in your bag but a hole in the bottom.

Government authorities in El Salvador have lost their authority. No one obeys the laws. Not the traffic, not the people. People throw rubbish anywhere, dirty water anywhere, peels of banana are simply thrown. There is a people's uprising against the system – a passive resistance against the government. It seems that the people are saying: 'You (the government) do horrible things to me and I will not respond. I will not cooperate.'

It will be difficult in El Salvador to teach the people once more to respond: to take care not only about themselves but about the well-being of everyone else.

Yet I had a humiliating experience with the public transport system in Melbourne, mainly through language. I had a child in one hand and was trying to hold her so I could buy a ticket. The conductor spoke in curt tones: 'What you say, pardon?' I was scared to speak up again. I was so frustrated and frightened, but also was very angry. It wasn't my fault, it wasn't his fault, it was just lack of confidence. In New Zealand it was frightening, too, and in Sydney and Adelaide: you don't talk to people any more. There is a machine system for tickets and it gives a person a very isolating feeling. This is what development means to developed countries. It means an increase in the unemployment rate. It means that people are not communicating with each other as in the past.

I would rather live in a developing country, a third world country, and be 'behind', with greater communication. We can say hello to each other without worrying about whether people think this is strange, to communicate by language. If you go to El Salvador, the people say hello to other people, they stop and comment about issues, the situation, what is happening. This is good. If we lost that because we were to become a part of the developed world, we would lose something valuable. I value it very much, keeping in communication rather than having machines for everything.

As A Woman I Have No Country?

Gisela Gardener

Gisela Gardener was born in Neuwied am Rhein in 1949. After finishing her secondary education in Germany, she took a degree in English literature and became an English teacher in London. She was active in campaigns against racisms, patriarchy and the nuclear threat. In the early 1980s Gisela Gardener realised that Britain wasn't big enough for Maggie and herself and migrated to the antipodes. Since then she has taught in Victorian state schools and in an Aboriginal school in Alice Springs. While working for a Victorian women's refuge and a women's health service in Victoria, Gisela Gardener co-authored a book with Bill Williams *Men, Sex, Power and Survival*, 1989, Greenhouse/Penguin. She is currently living with her family in the Northern Territory where she administers the Pintubi Homelands Health Service.

An elderly woman is roasting a bird on glowing coals. A swan: a black swan. She lifts it by the wing and turns it over with casual dexterity. She is describing the devastation that will follow uranium mining in her country. As she singes the feathers of this strange and beautiful creature, she relates an ancient story which tells of the dangers hidden in the rock. Beside me in the cinema, Hazel is reeling with horror at the treatment of the swan, her compulsive vegetarianism overwhelming her desire to support the embattled indigene. As the credits roll at the end of *The Partizans*, I marvel at the number of organisations – unions, community groups, activist organisations, churches – which have contributed funds to this cinematic expose of the Australian uranium mining industry.

Australia was beginning to occupy my thoughts. It was early 1981 and I was doing a booming trade in political paraphernalia for the communist owned Collet's International Bookshop on London's Charing Cross Road. A fellow worker waxed lyrical about the beaches and the sunshine he had left behind to pursue confidence and contentment out in London.

It was a time of energetic resistance to Thatcherism. I was active in the Campaign for Nuclear Disarmament (CND), which had risen like a phoenix, drawing one quarter of a million people to protest in Hyde Park. Women in our tens of thousands embraced in protest against the United States cruise missile base at Greenham Common and fired the imaginations of sisters across the globe. There were acts of anger and resistance to Tory vandalism in every corner of the country. But the writing was on the wall. The establishment in Britain – flushed with resurgent imperialist pride – shed its Edwardian anachronisms and asserted its mystical newfound 'rationalist' truths.

Women in our tens of thousands embraced in protest against the United States cruise missile base at Greenham Common and fired the imaginations of sisters across the globe.

The energy and enthusiasm I felt in the meetings, rallies and workshops was not, however, mirrored by my domestic situation. I fell out of love with men in general and my passionless playwright husband in particular. Women were sisters and more; and resistance meant survival.

The political climate became more wintry, the grime and greyness of London intensified, marriage got duller. London was a prime nuclear target and the doomsday clock stood at five minutes to midnight. Living in Chiswick, I contemplated the lead from the vehicles on the M4 depositing in my two-year-old daughter's brain. I pondered in graphic detail the cumulative impact of 'accidental' releases of radioactive and other toxic substances all over the small island I'd made my home for the previous 12 years.

Thatcher was dismantling the services which made living in London palatable – reasonable public transport, housing and health care. This, combined with my accumulated knowledge of the ecological disaster that is Britain, weighed heavy on my soul. I began to yearn for the sandy beaches, the unpolluted seas and the clear blue skies that my Australian co-worker described. My existence had become too subterranean and enclosed. I worked in a basement, travelled on the tube, sat in rooms and smoked and talked and woke up with a headache in the morning.

Then my nights were filled with dreams about swimming in the ocean – up and down tall waves just before they broke. During those nocturnal swims, I experienced a lightness and flexibility of body I had not felt for many years. I started to fantasise about striding across plains and breathing the clear air of lush forests.

I thought of the Australian coast as a combination of Greek Islands, cafés serving fresh fish in dappled shade and the wild Dutch coast of my teenage holidays. I knew there was a flat centre with a big rock in the middle and I had also heard about a bush which was apparently riddled with poisonous snakes and spiders. *Skippy* and *The Flying Doctors* had been on the television. The films *Walkabout* and *Storm Boy* were my only references to black Australia before I encountered the woman with the swan in the anti-uranium film.

I had some expectations of Australia. It was 'out of the way' and therefore not a nuclear target, which, of course, proved to be untrue. It seems, in retrospect, that my main informant and future husband knew less about the country of his birth than what was happening in London.

My friend Hazel had asked him what kangaroos ate. He thought they came to the side of the road at dusk to eat animals killed by cars during the day. Hazel insisted they were herbivores. I thought that since this big fifth continent was inhabited by the same population as greater London, pollution would be minimal. I had no idea of how much damage so few people could cause in such a short time. I could not read it in the pictures I saw, because I had no image of what had been wiped out and created in its place in less than two centuries.

In an etching from 1840 of my home town in the Rhein Valley the surroundings have not changed so very much from what I knew as a child.

For my sense of history, 200 years is not very long. My family tree goes back to the sixteenth century, for what that patriarchal version of events is worth. In an etching from 1840 of my home town in the Rhein Valley the surroundings have not changed so very much from what I knew as a child. The Protestant church, the hotel I grew up in, the provincial palace, the shores of the Rhein and the hills covered in vineyards continued to be features in my youth.

I craved change and set out to bring it about. I had to be practical and organised. A route needed to be plotted from the maisonette above the betting shop in Chiswick W4 to that beach on the other side of the world. Why an Australian beach? Because I could make it possible with my available resources. I spoke English and was told I would not find it hard to get a teaching position and rent, or even buy, a house. My fellow worker and good friend in the Charing Cross Road basement offered me his hand in marriage in front of the English dictionaries. Life became a series of well planned and kept appointments to organise the necessary paperwork for our departure. At home I packed, trying to work out how much I could afford to ship of my personal belongings and books.

In November 1981 we were ready to leave London to have a holiday and to look for teaching jobs and accommodation in Geelong. My little daughter and I travelled on return tickets purchased on credit cards. We had to collect our residents' permits the following April in London.

I was rarely anxious and often excited about my imminent adventure; after all, this was not the first time I had left home, friends and family. At the time I had a Women's Press postcard hanging over my desk: 'As a woman, I have no country, my country is the whole world!' Virginia Woolf.

I was born on the banks of the Rhein in the eighteenth century manufacturing town of Neuwied. My mother's family had owned the Hotel 'Zum Wilden Mann' for over two centuries, and she became its proprietor after the second world war. During the war she had visited wounded officers from the Russian front in hospital. She married a particularly dashing one. He returned from his war service on the losing side, dishonoured and penniless. My grandfather offered him a job as a waiter. This ignominious position and my mother's managing role were unforgivable. When I was three my mother sued for divorce, an almost unheard of act in the 1950s Neuwied am Rhein. She had decided she would no longer tolerate his coercive affairs with hotel staff, his arrogant temper, his emotional violence and eventually a slap in the face.

> **My grandfather offered him a job as a waiter. This ignominious position and my mother's managing role were unforgivable.**

My mother ran the hotel with a staff of 30 and I spent most of my time with my devoted governess Tante Marga. She was a refugee from Silesia and had spent some years in a subsistence farming village near Coburg on the former East-West border. She reached Ahlstadt on foot a day ahead of the Russian front and was given shelter and work by one of the peasant families.

For about two months every year Tante Marga took me to visit the Höhns Family. I learnt about the seasons, the hard work of subsistence farming and traditional German village life in those years. Three generations lived in three storey farmhouses, all grouped together in the village. The bakehouse and the village pond were communal.

The village was ringed by a patchwork of fields and the forests which surrounded them were co-operatively managed by all the farmers. There was no enclosure and no 'Trespassers will be Prosecuted' signs. We picked the wild berries, mushrooms and herbs where we found them; only planted crops were the property of the farmer. In later years in England I missed the freedom to walk where I pleased, but at least there were some footpaths. In Australia the English model of land as private property is even more severe and to walk across the country is possible only in national parks and similar islands in the sea of ecocidal monocultures. My support of such Australian alternatives as permaculture are based on my visits to Ahlstadt; but I do not underrate the hard and often repetitive labour which is needed to establish and maintain such systems.

When we were 16, my best friend in the village, Gerlinde, was contemplating suicide because of her limited opportunities, whereas I saw my future as one big adventure. At home in the hotel on the Rhein I was the boss' daughter and had a happy, privileged life. I ordered my meals from the restaurant and never learnt how to do housework in a nuclear family setting.

When I was 14 and getting into trouble at school and at home, my mother decided to send me to boarding school, a boy's boarding school, which had become co-ed only two years before my arrival.

I was of the generation of German school children who, in the 1960s, were taught the history and consequences of the Third Reich. Some of our teachers believed passionately that the lessons of history must be learnt, if it were not to be repeated. We learnt about anti-Semitism, fascism, Hitler, Goebbels, Auschwitz, Dachau, Bergen-Belsen and the Kristall Nacht. We watched newsreels and cine footage, read books, saw photographs. The horrors of a decade in my recent German past were not hidden.

In the background, however, lay my own connection to that decade: my father's role in the war, and his failure, ever, to condemn National Socialism. Also his mother, one of the first women to gain a chemistry degree from a German university and a founder member of her local party branch, continued her allegiance to the 'faith'. On the other side of the family, my mother's French uncle had ended up in a concentration camp because, in his Protestant church in the Alsace, he had preached against the Nazis.

> We learnt about anti-Semitism, fascism, Hitler, Goebbels, Auschwitz, Dachau, Bergen-Belsen and the Kristall Nacht. We watched newsreels and cine footage, read books, saw photographs.

Overlying all of this was the American and British popular culture which saturated West Germany with the occupation. Movies, television dramas, documentaries, comics and story books sharply contrasted allied fortitude and decency with German stupidity, arrogance and brutality. My adolescent consciousness was raised by teachers ensuring that Nazism was poison in our heads, whilst through the media the honour, charm and wit of the anglo-American liberators were held aloft for us to admire.

It was only many years later, after teaching in the Australian education system, that I fully appreciated the importance of teaching the history of genocide, and the ease with which indiscriminate violence and orchestrated massacre had been swept under the national carpet.

After I passed my Abitur (equivalent to matriculation or higher school certificate (HSC)), I wanted to study English literature. London was the belly button of the universe in the late 1960s. The English were everything the Germans were not. I became a rabid anglophile and could see little to admire in my homeland.

While applying for university places, I worked and lived in the five star Savoy Hotel in London. I learned a lot about the habits of the rich and famous, and from my bedroom on the eighth floor I overlooked St Paul's Cathedral and the Embankment Park which lay between the hotel and the river Thames. On winter mornings uniformed men removed the hypothermic corpses of the homeless from the park benches.

I took an English degree and enjoyed life in London, going to clubs and parties and often to the theatre. I met a playwright and lived with him in a basement flat off the King's Road in Chelsea.

During my postgraduate year in Oxford I became a member of the middle common room at Magdalene College. No one had warned me that until that year the college had been men only nor that the 'proper' pronunciation was 'maudlin'. I learnt several salutary lessons relating to the English upper-class twit and found myself starting to identify with feminists, especially the two Australians – Germaine Greer and Dale Spender.

On my return to London I taught English at an East London senior girls' high school for four years. Just over half the students were from Asian and Afro-Carribean backgrounds. In the mid-1970s the fascist National Front was polling 10 per cent in some elections and I received my initiation into direct political action when that party decided to hold a public meeting in our school hall.

By then I had decided not to see my father any more. His best holiday behaviour was less and less convincing. I had learnt from a variety of sources that his maltreatment of my mother had been cruel and repeated. His political tendencies and his attitude to the past – to one who had abandoned Germany as a sort of cultural exile – were undeclared but disturbing. I knew he'd been an officer on the Russian front, but in which unit, especially towards the end of the war, I never successfully ascertained. The helpful staff at the British Imperial War Museum could tell me only that he was not on the regular army lists in their possession. So, after a series of incidents which reinforced my impression that he had no disquiet about his Nazi past and an act which I considered treacherous to me, I took the unusual step of severing my remaining bonds to him.

During my involvement with the Anti-Nazi-League (ANL) in the 1970s I learnt that the Germans were not the only racists in Europe; that the ANL was not chockers with pipe smoking tweedy charmers á la David Niven and John Mills. Petrol bombs, thrown through letter boxes, were burning Asian homes; West Indian party-goers died in a bomb attack. Black youths met abuse and violence on the street and on the 'tube'.

Petrol bombs, thrown through letter boxes, were burning Asian homes; West Indian party-goers died in a bomb attack. The press were uninterested, the police unhelpful. It was mainly members of the 'loony left' who bothered to protest about the situation. After one rally, Blair Peach, a teacher, was clubbed to death by police.

I learnt about the history of the British Empire from a black point of view. My movie faith in British officers and gentlemen was lost and I began to understand that the British establishment was no less rigid and corrupt – just more successful, charming and subtle – than the German industrialists and bureaucrats I'd fled seven years earlier. My desire to 'de-Germanate' had been so intense, I'd swapped my nationality and had become quite anglicised – carrying much of the baggage of cultural stereotypia. Germans were like 'that', and I didn't want to be like 'that'.

In 1981, my first impression of anglo-celtic Australia was gained before I got off the plane. Two men wearing shorts, knee socks, sandals, diggers' hats and moustaches boarded the plane holding a can of insect spray in each hand. Stewards opened all the hand-luggage lockers and the men sprayed the cabin and us with hazardous chemicals. The day outside was as grey as the London we had left. My partner's parents were collecting us from the airport. I was glad to be taken to the security of their modest suburban home.

On the way from Tullamarine to the other side of that endless city my new found father-in-law narrated: '...the Children's Hospital, the Royal Melbourne, the Royal Dental, Prince Henry's, the Alfred...' A hospital on every street corner it seemed; Maggie would never allow that.

The big trees lining some of the wide streets were the same kind as those which had stood by the pavements of my street in Chiswick.

I spent much of the next few months lying on the beach, feeling the strain of political campaigning and the grime and muck of London slowly leach out of me. I lay on the sands of Chelsea – with milk bars selling Chico rolls and instant coffee, brown brick veneers, blue skies and blue ocean. No King's Road, no Sloane Square, no Royal Court Theatre, no punks, no number 19 or 21 bus in this Chelsea. I was and still am very confused about the location of all these London suburbs in Melbourne – Kew, Kensington and so on.

No King's Road, no Sloane Square, no Royal Court Theatre, no punks, no number 19 or 21 bus in this Chelsea.

I made mistakes, got things wrong; when asked to bring a plate, I did, an empty one. I have not been treated as a 'migrant woman', a NESB (non-English speaking background woman), even though I am one. My accented English is fluent, I do not wear a black scarf and so do not fit that stereotype. At parties people often inquire about my origins. When I tell them I was born in Germany, they usually fall silent. Why do they want to know in the first place? What assumptions do they make about me once they have that information? That I am tidy and punctual and have no sense of humour?

The lucky country has been lucky for me. In Geelong, at a Peace Movement meeting, I met Bill, my friend and lover of the last nine years and the father of my second daughter – Lily. What I have learnt in Australia has given me a different perspective on being German and I spent two years in England and Germany in the 1980s. I re-established my bond to the place of my birth in the Rhein Valley. In the last decade I have climbed the Kerries, walked across high plains to Jagungal, surfed six foot waves at Cactus, loitered with intent at Roxby Downs, Pine Gap and Nurrangar and other notorious beauty spots. I conceived my second daughter under the full moon in the Snowy River Gorge. I've been awe struck by the arid zone, falling in love with the luxuriance of the myriad gorges, which hide in the rugged mountain ranges: Carnarvon, Bracchina, Weetootla...

Over the past decade I have followed the efforts of indigenous Australians to express their dispossession and the resistance. Some Australians seem eager to heal the 200-year-old festering wounds. Others respond with increased violence. Meanwhile the 'majority' appear paralysed by the inertia of guilt. 'I am not personally responsible! What can I do?'

Australia is a magnificent land, but what a dominant culture of denial and destruction! When I first read the anthropologist W.E.H. Stanner's description of 'the cult of disremembering', I thought of those German school teachers who tried to impart to us a sense of bad news history. The difficulty of telling the truth.

...my daughters still learn at state schools an Australian history which romanticises convicts, squatters and gold diggers, relegating Aborigines to prehistory and the Dreamtime.

Hardly a week goes by on television or in the magazines or the newspapers without a 'special feature' on Hitler, the Nazis, the second world war. Anglo-celtic Australia attends to the heroic deeds of its men abroad in inverse proportion to their deeds at home against the indigenes. That the latter infamies were committed by folk remembered as explorers, adventurers, pastoralists, miners and policemen has surely made them easier to 'disremember'.

Although things are slowly changing for the better, my daughters still learn at state schools an Australian history which romanticises convicts, squatters and gold diggers, relegating Aborigines to prehistory and the Dreamtime. I marvel that I left Germany partly in defiance of the history of racism and totalitarianism, only to live in a culture where more subtle versions reign supreme.

The British government flatly refuses to accept responsibility for its quarter-of-a-million-year nuclear attack on the people and lands of the Pitjantjatjara at Maralinga and their neighbours. Eminent members of the Royal Society still cling to collections of Aboriginal skeletons, 'specimens' culled desperately from the dwindling 'stock' of intriguing evolutionary material. Meanwhile, in the midst of an upsurge of violent racism, the united German state is committing billions in reparation to Jewish people for atrocities which occurred 50 years ago. And so they should. There seems no comparable process in place for the survivors of the Coniston massacre of 1929, which was one of innumerable atrocities against Aborigines in living memory.

Now living in Central Australia, I was teaching English as a second language, my second language, the language of invasion, to Western Arrernte children in a 'both ways' school. In my present job with the Pintubi Homelands Health Service, when Pintubi woman take me hunting, they sometimes sing in a low voice as we walk across the spinifex plains looking for goannas and other bushtucker. They are intimately linked to their country and Woolf's line about women not having a country does not pertain to them, nor to the children from the town camps whose concepts of time, place and number make a mockery of European 'universals'.

There is resistance and resilience, poverty and alienation – and there is the future.

No Fear of Flying

Jocelynne A. Scutt

Jocelynne A. Scutt was born in
Perth, Western Australia and
graduated in law from the University
of Western Australia. She did
post-graduate studies at the
University of Sydney before going
abroad, living and travelling in the
United States of America, England
and Germany. She has worked,
and been active in the Women's
Movement, in Sydney, Canberra
and Melbourne.

Alone. In company. With husband. Friend. Lover. Women travel. Goodbyes
are said all too quickly. The distances widen, the miles fly by, the plane rises
above the clouds. Look! The harbour is a mere speck on the horizon. The
sun is coming nearer. The weather changes from searing heat to lip-chilling
cold. The winds roll in from the west and the sun sets into the ocean. For
the first time, she sees the Southern Cross. Somewhere, a world away, an
unknown woman looks into the sky and notices dark, massing clouds. The
snow flurries she has never seen before turn into sleet. The streets grow
silent as they change from grey asphalt to white, like melting ice cream, then
to a grey slush coating the footpath and the verges, where once there grew
green grass. Miles away, a great inland lake begins frosting over. And further
still, she knows, there is the ocean. She has never been so far from the sea
before. What do people do, inland, she wonders. How do they live?

Living in Ann Arbor, Michigan, in the heart of the United States mid-
west, I realised for the first time in my life how closely Australians cling to
the coast. In Western Australia, I had lived in the country for six years,
together with my family. York – 60 miles from Perth – and Meckering, all
of 80 miles from the city, were s-o-o-o-o f-a-r from the ocean. Yet the
distance was as nothing compared with that I confronted when studying

for my master of laws and, a few years later, researching and writing my doctoral thesis. I missed the smell of the sea. Missed the white sandhills of North Cottesloe and Swanbourne beaches where my grandmother had taken my sister and me so often, struggling up the dunes together then running down toward the waves rolling in, waves crashing against the white beach where seagulls circled, anxious for a stray crust or a cake crumb, or a sliver of crusty pastry from a real meat pie.

Going abroad, women travel alone, in the company of a friend or husband, with a partner or lover, or in mobs or groups or delegations. I set off from Sydney in May 1973, alone, for Dallas, Texas, and Southern Methodist University. In 1977 I returned, briefly, to Houston, Texas, accompanying the Michigan delegation to the Huston Women's Conference. Ten thousand women met, argued, agreed, laughed. And I was part of it.

Alongside others, or without adult company, women travel with children and, sometimes, 'with child'. Vivienne Correa, emigrating from Hong Kong to Australia in 1967, was going to a new world. Some 20 years later, Sylvia Hennessy was off to a new life, too. The awaited birth of her second child, Sean, restrictive housing and poor job opportunities for husband Larry precipitated the move. Vivienne Correa, leaving relatives and friends behind, set sail with her husband Frank Correa and the *SS Tjuluwah*. The ship weighed anchor. 'This step,' she says, 'was being taken to secure a better future for the next generation. The sharp movement inside was surely a seal of approval.'

> ...borrow money, scrape together cash for fares, pack a few clothes, all that they can carry in three suitcases, sometimes take the bread knife

Why travel? Wanting to find a kinder present and the hope of a secure future for themselves and their families, women escape from prison, avoid the oppressive intrusions of repressive governments, borrow money, scrape together cash for fares, pack a few clothes, all that they can carry in three suitcases, sometimes take the bread knife, purchase plane tickets on credit cards. They pray, despite every rule preventing it, for the grant of a passport and visa approvals. Unless the gods frown and a bureaucrat changes his mind, a valid visa means making it at least to the first stopping point on the journey out.

Dorota Malchevski and Ofelia Lopez came, from thousands of miles away from the country and from each other, to Australia. For Ofelia Lopez, the aeroplane trip from El Salvador, organised in secret, was harrowing. Her body seized up from terror, her tears mingled with those of her daughter crying from earache and anxiety. Yet she was met, at the airport, by a Spanish speaking friend, which eased a little the shock of being, for the first time, in a strange and different country. The special humanitarian program brought Dorota Malchevski to the antipodes, too. South by coach and stealth to Athens. A wait for months. Marital breakdown. Marriage make-up. By plane to Sydney and the shock of beer-bellied, thong-footed Australians roaming George Street in their T-shirts, then a safe, secure and reliable trip in a magnificent old car, the Kingswood, to Melbourne, leaving the marriage behind to make a new life with her daughter, Magdalena.

For Sylvia Hennessy, leaving London and Ireland for Australia meant leaving behind her twin sister Ann, her parents and six brothers, as well as the familiar surrounds of home and work. Yet precipitating her into accompanying her husband Larry back to his country were the consequences of British government policies, both economic and political. Back in the mid-1970s, I was heartened, travelling up to London in the train from Dover, by the staunch expressions of the English who sat, silent with the assurance of knowing they belonged, in the comfortable carriages of BritRail. Ten years later, as Gisela Gardener worked, contemplatively, amongst the books in the basement of Collet's International Bookshop on London's Charing Cross Road, reaching her decision to leave behind the rundown national health system, poorly serviced public transport, the grime and the lead and the bleak winters' days, so Sylvia Hennessy made up her mind. Should she endure any more the 'joke' of the stupid, drunken, dole-bludging Irishman? In Australia, and in her recollection for the first time ever, some people say they like her accent.

Tui Taurua flees her own private torture, a harrowing marriage break down and sexual abuse as a child. She came to Australia once, some years before, and left for home, vowing never to return. The prospect of a new life, with an earlier partner, and escape from a man intent on tracking her down in Aotearoa/New Zealand leads her back.

Women escape for more mundane, but intensely experienced, reasons. 'I left when I did because there was no reason to stay,' writes Gillian Hanscombe, poet, writer, traveller contemplating, now, a return to Australia. 'Or – I fled to escape my suburban destiny.' She escaped with a vengeance, taking with her the memories of driving through the Goulburn Valley and the bush of the Great Divide in the family's tiny Ford Prefect. The prospect of a 'suburban destiny' did not impede her poet's tongue and voice.

I left Perth in 1969 going, like Kathy Kituai, to the Eastern States. She landed in Adelaide, I several thousand miles further on, in Sydney. Not going nearly so far as Gillian Hanscombe, then, I too sought to escape the destiny of a solicitor's office. The law, to me, was stimulating. Working up the ladder to a partnership did not fit in with my picture of what the law could be, would be – for me.

Some left home, went to study. Ania Wilczynski, a 'first generation Australian' followed her British and Polish heritage, searching for her roots. She enrolled in the master of philosophy course in the Institute of Criminology at the University of Cambridge, in England. For Janice Farrell, a 'second generation migrant' on her father's side and daughter of a second generation migrant on her mother's side, Europe and Britain called. Trained as a nurse, it was not until after she qualified that she realised how usefully the profession would fit with her desire to trace her and her family's origins. (Sylvia Hennessy deliberately 'did' nursing, from the outset determined to combine it with her plans to travel.)

Plans are bound to develop and change. Travelling often takes over. Sandra McCallum was bemused when other foreign students at the University of British Columbia in Canada advocated destroying her visa, across the border in Seattle, and becoming an illegal immigrant back over the Canadian border. With an amnesty in place, this was the quickest way to set oneself on the road to Canadian citizenship. 'I had no doubt I would be going home.' With a two year visa when she had need only for one year to complete her master of laws degree, why should she take on the role of illegal immigrant-with-status? Not so many years later, after gaining one extension on her visa, Sandra McCallum returned to Canada as a (legal) landed immigrant. To stay.

Ania Wilczynski was not enthusiastic upon hearing her mother's encouraging tones intimating that a PhD from the University of Cambridge would be a good and fitting goal. Six months after she commenced her course, she found herself at the end of a long distance telephone line announcing to Janet Wilczynski that yes, she was intending to take the option to complete both an M Phil and a doctorate of philosophy. Four years in England instead of one? So it was.

For Janice Farrell, studying midwifery in Britain would provide an opportunity to improve her qualifications and 'see Europe' at the same time. Not long into her course, she met Roger Farrell. Life as a student turned into life as the wife of an army lieutenant in the corps of signals, and years of packing and unpacking, living on this base and that, finding an identity through voluntary work in various capacities, and being able to laugh about the hierarchy of service-life.

Janice Farrell laughed, too, about the intensity of reaction to the Australian accent – although she escaped censure because her tones were muted through childhood exposure to the European-intoned English spoken by her parents. Haven't we all, who take with us an accent from 'down under', known so well the colonial tincture that is embedded so firmly in our voices?

Marlies Puentener didn't laugh when she auditioned for the National Institute of Dramatic Art (NIDA), having come all the way from Christchurch, New Zealand, to fulfil her career ambitions. 'Come back when you've lost that accent,' she was told, in response to which she stomped out to her VW Kombi and into a full life.

Anne Hickling Hudson was recognised instantly as Jamaican by a student in one of her classes. She could be none other *than* Jamaican with her accent. 'It was a matter to ponder over that my accent was immediately comparable to reggae songs,' she expostulates. Jan Mock spent hours in the school yard, as a child, together with her brother, being taught by the locals 'how to speak Australian'. 'They obviously did an excellent job.' No one recognises now, nor have they since the play times and lunch times spent learning the language, that she is originally from England.

Restlessness is the condition of the migrant, says Salman Rushdie. 'Once detached from one's place of birth it is impossible to reconstruct "home" somewhere else': Penelope Andrew's words mirror his. Travelling first to the United States of America then, fortuitously (through sighting an advertisement in the *Chronicle of Higher Education*), taking up a position lecturing in legal studies at La Trobe University in Melbourne, Australia, she finds that 'home' is everywhere. Coming from the political wasteland of South Africa, with a good dose of United States democracy (with all its positives and negatives), Penelope Andrews arrived in Australia in 1986, on Australia Day. Six years later she became an Australian citizen and voted in an election for the first time in her life: the 1982 Victorian state poll. Yet, she observes, in the midst of this extension of democratic rights to her, rights denied her in her home country, it is 'an undisputed fact of Australian history that the treatment of Aborigines since white settlement has left a legacy of deprivation and despair'.

> Six years later she became an Australian citizen and voted in an election for the first time in her life...

Mary Ann Bin-Sallik knows this legacy well. She has fought all her life to overcome it for herself, her children, and her fellow Aboriginal Australians. The Djaru people are from the East Kimberley area, in Western Australia. She was the first Aboriginal to qualify in nursing in the Northern Territory, graduating from the Darwin Hospital in February 1958. More than 20 years later and holding a position in a tertiary institution and additionally holding an associate diploma, she was rejected from entry to study anthropology at the University of Adelaide, on the basis that she was 'not qualified for matriculation'. Five years later she was accepted into Harvard University in the United States of America, graduating with a masters degree and a doctorate in education. For her enthographic research unit she completed a paper on the 'tribe of White anthropologists' located in the anthropology department of Harvard University. Her equipment? Notebook, pencils and tape recorder. She declined (although invited) to become a participant in the anthropology seminar: 'I was having too much fun studying them'!

Mary Ann Bin-Sallik's experience echoes that of so many Yamagee people, Kooris, Murris, Nungas and Nyungas, all the Aboriginal people of Australia. So it was for Marie Andrews of the Bardi people, who come from the Broome area in Western Australia. Writing 'For My People' in *As a Woman*, she recounts her treatment in the tertiary sector. With an anthropology degree and having worked for a year as a producer and presenter in radio, as well as holding an executive position in the (then) Department of Aboriginal Affairs, Marie Andrews applied to study law at the University of Western Australia. 'You are not qualified,' said the registrar, '...these are not the best grades and we have only the best students.' 'University was such a foreign experience for me,' she replied, 'but as you can see, my grades have improved in the last couple of years. I am an anthropologist, I can do research. It was a learning experience for me. As I learnt more about learning I got better.' Her rejection did not stop Marie Andrews. In 1993 she graduated in law from the University of Melbourne – which (just as for Mary Ann Bin-Sallik) is not the end of her story.

Ofelia Lopez had to teach herself to study: she learnt English, at the same time gaining a learning experience in the macho-method of learning English in several Australian institutions. The economic and political conditions in El Salvador militate against most people gaining an education: many people are illiterate. In Australia, conditions are not so different for Aboriginal people. Gloria Lee found, as a child, that distinctions were made between her compatriots and other Alice Springs dwellers. A 'half caste' school was established for those whose fathers were European and mothers Aboriginal or, more rarely, with 'white' mothers and Black fathers. Later, she learnt Chinese in China. Much later, her daughters took up tertiary studies in Australian universities and one of her daughters gained entry to Oxford University.

Ofelia Lopez holds ambitions to train and work as a medical practitioner. She gained practical experience working in the mountains alongside trained doctors, during the El Salvador civil war. She is continuing with her work in a health project supported by the International Women's Development Agency (IWDA). Not only did she need to learn English in Australia. She needed to learn to study. She saw, too, the need to overcome her resistance to learning the language of oppression: to Ofelia Lopez, one of the people of El Salvador struggling together for peace and freedom, American English is 'the language of imperialism'. Paradoxically, she writes, 'there were political reasons for learning English'. She needed to use it 'to get the message about El Salvador through to the Australian people'.

Subjected to torture and imprisonment when fighting for the right to be free, the right for her people to share equally in the wealth of El Salvador, Ofelia Lopez endured. More, she organised amongst her fellow political prisoners. In January 1985 she and her fellows confront the authorities, demanding access to the minister of justice. He eventually arrives. Flanked by the flags of prisoners demanding liberation for themselves and their country he sits, his image projected into the homes and hideaways of El Savadorans. 'Left Front' screams the banner, black on red, over his left shoulder. From the wall to his right another, with equal impact, cries 'National Liberation Front', its black harsh against the brilliance of the red material, smuggled in by brave women bearing loaves of home-baked bread.

Food is the centrepiece of many migrant experiences, and that of the intrepid traveller, too. For Ofelia Lopez, there was the intensity of the demand that the prisoners be entitled to raw food, which they could cook themselves. (They demanded, and gained, the facilities for cooking, too.) Upon her arrival at a migrant hostel in Melbourne, one of her worst memories is of the food. Horrible!

Food has a resonance for other women. Often it has many more pleasant memories and associations. Tabasco sauce and boiled crawfish is wrapped up in the sweetness of love for Janet Labatut. Sitting, alone, at the Que Sera restaurant on St Charles Avenue, New Orleans, she reflected on her desire to change direction in her life: from zingy, go-getter salespersonship to reflective writer and novelist. Across the tables she saw a lone diner, clearly a writer so intent was he on his book. She sent across a glass of wine. And, reader, like Janet Wilczynski and her romantic, darkly handsome Polish teacher of economics, she married him.

Marriage takes many women around the world. Love plucked Janet Labatut from her place at the restaurant table to home on the Swan River in Perth, Western Australia and, later, across the continent to Melbourne, Victoria. And it brought with it a realisation of her central ambition – to be, to become, a writer. She has found her forte in short story writing.

Lynne Wenig flew, crying, across the ocean to Australia from the United States of America via Europe. In London she worked, putting the husband she had met whilst working in a New York hospital, through graduate school. Sucking on ice and holding her head in her hands, like Mary Ann Bin-Sallik who flew in the opposite direction, from Australia to Massachusetts, she wondered at her fear and her courage in flying half-way around the world. For me, that feeling of being quite, quite mad in being so, so far away from *home* came upon me later, as I lay comfortable and calm in my luxurious student's room in the Law Quad in Ann Arbor. 'What am I doing here,' I wondered. 'What on earth am I doing here?' Yet – I stayed, and the feeling went, and Michigan became home for me, at least for a time. Alongside the roar of the jet engines, Lynne Wenig's mother's words rang in her ears: 'You're going as far around the globe as you can go without starting to come back again.' In Melbourne, she longed for writing from America: oh for an American magazine! At McGills on Elizabeth Street in the 1960s she found international papers – months old, coming by sea as they did, then. And oh! for a bagel or pizza. 'Nonsense,' said the erstwhile husband. 'Australians will *never* eat pizza.'

Mickey Zhu was afraid she might have to stop eating until she found work. All the Chinese nationals she knew were working in restaurants, washing dishes, or in factories, doing processwork. They might be found in city offices, cleaning. Still, the fruit and other food thrown away is often better than that available in China. Do 'use by' dates provide useful information to the consuming public, or are they incentives to the public to consume? Kathy Kituai found confusion in the local Adelaide supermarket when she returned, visiting, from New Guinea. I was overwhelmed by the profusion on the shelves of Dallas' supermarkets, and simultaneously taken with the familiarity of so many of the packages and packets. The products were those I had seen and bought in Sydney supermarkets. Yet the brand names were different, the cardboard colours varied. Still, this didn't spoil the romance of walking up and down supermarket aisles at four am, and travelling back in a car with the radio playing country and western music – perpetually. The whine of a sad guitar is wonderful in the mid-west, on a warm night, with the breeze blowing in the open windows of a gently driven car. But – in the supermarkets, why so many brands? What's the difference? No difference? Why so much paper, so much packaging, so many spurious distinctions between products and produce?

Choo Choo bars. Biltong. Cajun and Creole cooking. Fish and chips. Or fush and chups. Guava Jelly and guava stew. Hokey Pokey ice cream. Hudson's chocolate chip cookies. Bushtucker. Mealie pudding. Mebos. 'Scotch Bonnett' peppers. Janet Labatut's Tabasco sauce. Street food. Pavlova and lamingtons. Muffins. Janet Wilczynski's feasting on vodka and *polska ogorki* and declaring: 'I speak only a little Polish. I am English.' Pumpkin pie pumpkin soup mulberries meat pies borscht salt fish Chico rolls. Chinese cafes. Rice, rice and more rice. The May Ball and the May Bumps and Ania Wilczynski with Pimms and strawberries and cream. And mayhem on the Cam. Kristin Henry speaking of a peanut butter and jelly sandwich (not even eating one!), greeted by hoots of laughter: is this real? the listeners seem to be saying. We heard it on the radio/saw it on television – but do Americans *really* speak like this? Do they *really* have – eat – such a thing as a *peanut butter and jelly sandwich*?! And Gloria Lee's plaintiff cry, as a child living in China, away from her Alice Springs birth place: 'I want bread!'

As a child, in Australia, Gloria Lee learnt from her father how to count in Chinese. As a child, in China, she (like Jan Mock learning Australian English) learnt from the other children, in the school playground, to speak Chinese. She came top of the class. When, ten years or so later she returned to Alice Springs, she had forgotten Arrernte, her language, and English. Gradually, her ability in those languages returned, just as she had returned to the great open spaces and the trees, and the scent of the eucalypts. Bush walks. Bread. Yet now, she longs for the taste of salt fish, a taste learned long ago in China. Her daughter Peggy buys it for her, in Darwin.

Mickey Zhu learnt English for ten years at school in China but, once in her new English-speaking country, she realises she has never used it for speaking, never had a conversation in China with anyone in the English language. 'The language is totally new.' This realisation came home to me, too, in Freiburg im Breisgau. In Australia, studying German for matriculation meant perpetual translations, on paper, from German into

English, English into German. At the Goethe Institute, for two months I spoke nothing but German. German was the common language of us students, 'brushing up'. Their first languages were Spanish, Yugoslav, French, Japanese. We developed a fast familiarity with Pidgin German, and I found walking around the shops and soaking up the signs and sounds of hoch Deutsch and dialect a useful supplement to classes.

Ofelia Lopez and Dorota Malchevski had not learned English before making their way from their countries to Australia. Ofelia Lopez settled into classes upon arrival. Dorota Malchevski used the time she spent waiting in Athens, together with her family, for the Australian authorities to approve their travel. She established English classes for herself and the children on the balcony of the hotel and, when the hotel owner made this difficult (for no good reason) persevered with fewer in the class, and added the teaching of Polish to her repertoire. Magdalena Malchevski learnt Polish, and Dorota Malchevski and Magdalena began their learning of English together.

English speakers are greatly advantaged by the wide recognition of English as (an almost universal) language. Ofelia Lopez, Mickey Zhu and Dorota Malchevski found this disadvantaged them: surrounded by English speakers who rarely spoke any other language, concentrating on a new language for them, fast talk, strange accents, was difficult. To traverse the public transport system became a hurdle to be confronted. How does a person buy a stamp, in English? The seemingly most simple means of communication is difficult. You want to keep in contact with your home country, write home in your own language? It takes more than putting down the words on paper. The paper must be purchased, the pen bought, the envelope acquired and posted. With a stamp. In Italy I purchased stamps and pens and paper, receiving multi-coloured sweets in change: a cheekily practical solution to the one and two cent problem, I thought!

Yet even English speakers can 'come unstuck'. Ania Wilczynski found this, with her 'five words of Spanish' in Barcelona when she was relieved of her wallet. Unable to communicate through that 'easiest' of mediums, the native language, and being bundled into a police car to the interested eyes of onlookers is embarrassing – as she found. For me, the loss was bag, money, passport... in Milan, where the police at the head of a queue of complainants were matter-of-fact – in Italian, and the station assistant charming – in Sicilian dialect, and a new passport was issued by the consulate in less than 24 hours.

Vivien Altman discovered, to her chagrin, that a planned meeting at the airport in Mexico was thwarted because she didn't understand sufficient Spanish to know that her male friend was intending to be there – to meet her, and take her around the sights. To make her welcome, to be together, in Mexico City. In a comedy of errors (which she did not consider comic, in reality – at the time, or after) she and friend missed one another at the airport, and neither understood the error until much later.

Not only 'different languages' can create difficulties. 'Different Englishes' can be a problem, too. Together with Frank Correa, Vivienne Correa was greeted by the quintessential Aussie upon her arrival at the Woolloomooloo dock. 'D'you speak English?' they were asked. Between their Hong Kong and his Australian English, they were convinced at the end of the interrogation that their Crown Colony English was probably better than his!

Kathy Kituai found that a little learning of Pidgin English can be good for communication – but it depends upon the geographical location of the conversation, and the participants, just as Pidgin German has its place and time. Living in New Guinea she learned, by necessity (and by reason of her good commonsense and courtesy) that learning a basic language that can be used across cultures, across language barriers, is wise. This made for ease of living in New Guinea. But her family in Adelaide regarded her lapses into Pidgin English with amused concern. At least she could still speak English, they reckoned.

Going abroad to study is one of the best ways of living overseas and coming to appreciate other cultures, other customs. In the late 1960s and early 1970s a move began in Australian universities for students to go to North America to do post-graduate study. Sandra McCallum was part of this wave. So was I. Fifteen years or so later Mary Ann Bin-Sallik caught the wave, too. South Africans had similar (although often more intense) incentives to study abroad, and the United States of America became a chosen destination. This was so with Penelope Andrews, who studied at Columbia University, completing her master of laws degree in 1984.

...greeted by the quintessential Aussie upon her arrival at the Woolloomooloo dock. 'D'you speak English?' they were asked.

Penelope Andrews found there was a strong group of Black feminist scholars, supporting one another in intellectual debate, emotionally and socially. It is a Black activism that she missed in Australia, when teaching at La Trobe Univesrty. Like Sandra McCallum, Penelope Andrews originally went to North America intending to return to South Africa after completing her year of graduate study at Columbia University. The political situation in South Africa led her to remain in North America for several years. She was strongly influenced in her political development by the United States Black Power Movement, the writings and speeches of Martin Luther King and Malcolm X. In the early 1970s in Texas, these texts had a strong grip on me, too. It was impossible to come from elsewhere and live in the United States without being caught up in the debate, in some way. For Penelope Andrews, her South African heritage made the message even stronger, the debate more pronounced.

Mary Ann Bin-Sallik found, like Ania Wilczynski at Cambridge in the United Kingdom and Penelope Andrews at Columbia, that the students coming from such diverse backgrounds meant that there was great intellectual stimulation at graduate school. The diversity lay, as it did for Sandra McCallum in Canada, in the ethnic backgrounds of the students, their professional backgrounds, their race and their varied countries of origin. There were irreverent advantages in being together with a group of 'foreign' students, too: Sandra McCallum found this in her efforts to learn cross country skiing. Much laughter, stretched limbs (but without torn ligaments) later, she qualified as a steady though unspectacular skier. (I never did manage the feat.)

Gisela Gardener did post-graduate work at Oxford University, as did Gillian Hanscombe. Gillian Hanscombe found that pregnancy was unacceptable for the model student. She successfully completed the pregnancy nonetheless, just as she did her post-graduate degree. Gisela Gardener converted to an anglophile as the swiftest method of rejecting her German background and dealing with the fears and concerns she had about the period of the Third Reich, its ethos and consequences. She felt it was all *...rejecting her German background and dealing with the fears and concerns she had about the period of the Third Reich* too close to home, and that she must remove herself from it not only bodily, but psychologically. It was only after the anglophile conversion that she realised there was another way of looking at the British Empire, another way of experiencing it. The Black way. The colonial way.

The West Indian experience in Britain was part of Anne Hickling Hudson's life, for a time. The White Australia Policy was no surprise to her: Australia was notorious for it, in the Caribbean. But she had felt, first hand, racism's sting in the streets and institutions of the British establishment. Australia could be no worse.

The colonialism underpinning so many cultures and countries, and the oppression and damage wrought by King, Queen and Empire are evident in the experiences and understandings of so many women. For Vivienne Correa, Anne Hickling Hudson and Sylvia Hennessy, British invasion and occupation of their countries is central to race relations within their countries, and relations of their countries with other nations, other powers. Tui Taurua, too, notices this in her country's culture: there is the Pakeha way and the Maori way. Maori by birth, she has been taught the Pakeha way. Although pleased to be surrounded by friends and friendship, and a culture and politics she is learning to appreciate – at the same time teaching others – she regrets, in some ways, having developed such a strong attachment to Australia and to Australian friends. She is sad to know more about Australia's culture and politics than her own.

Sylvia Hennessy sees parallels between the British invasion and occupation of Ireland, and the invasion and occupation of Australia by the British. Cultural genocide has taken place as a consequence for Aboriginal people and for the Irish. Anne Hickling Hudson is concerned about education and the underpinnings of the British heritage – and at the same time appreciates with wry humour the cricketing legacy that all former British colonies have inherited.

Jan Mock comments on the heritage of 'the cricket', too: she and her brother Richard *still* barrack for the English team in cricket, and can't bring themselves to cheer for the Australian side. But cricket is the only sport where they harbour this 'pro the English team' spirit. Vivienne Correa's family has a regular pilgrimage to the MCG (Melbourne Cricket Ground) for the test cricket. Anne Hickling Hudson observes that the Woolloongabba cricket ground is packed for the tests in the same way as the Kingston ground swarms with West Indians at test time. I remember the days of my childhood and my father listening intently to the ABC broadcast, groaning at bad play and joining in loudly the 'Howzzats?' And Sandra McCallum, with a heritage that goes back to the first fleet of free settlers to Tasmania in the 1830s and now a Canadian citizen with Canadian born children, misses the familiar Australian language of cricket. Sticky wicket. Out for a duck.

Is sport – cricket – a method of conquest or a means of communication? Does it represent the banality of colonisation or invasion, or is it a sign of crossing cultures, learning to live together?

In New Guinea, Kathy Kituai found that Asian and American movies are a cultural overlay. 'Only Kung Fu or John Wayne to choose from?' she queries. Is the new language of cultural invasion film and television? This is an old question that many would deem well and truly answered already. Yet is there a reverse invasion going on? Is Australia, at least, fighting back? *Neighbours, Home and Away, E Street, The Flying Doctors* and the rest and, much earlier, *Skippy*. And *Crocodile Dundees* I and II have coloured the vision of continents. 'G'day,' they expect Jan Mock to say, way over in Alaska in the snow-up-to-the-knees. 'If I say: "G'day mate, ow ya goin?" people will laugh or feel surprised,' writes Mickey Zhu. But Australians are expected to talk like that. Doesn't Crocodile Dundee?

The pervasiveness of language through film and television is met by Kristin Henry, talking with that wonderful soft Southern twang. 'Y'all.' 'Yes, Ma'am.' 'No, Ma'am.' Maybe these expressions exist, now, only in nostalgia movies? 'Nobody says "bless your heart" to me any more,' she says wistfully.

Some language is pervasive. Gloria Lee and Mary Ann Bin Sallik, like Tui Taurua, have experienced directly the consequences of British colonisation. Gloria Lee's observation of the schools established for 'half caste' children in Alice Springs and Brisbane resonate with Vivienne Correa's recounting of the establishment of the diocesan schools by the Anglican Church in Hong Kong – for the children of the British posted to the Crown Colony. Mary Ann Bin-Sallik is determined to ensure that her people gain access to education and have a firm grounding in their own culture so that access to various forms of education becomes a reality. Gisela Gardener has worked with two-way education in Alice Springs, gaining insights into dispossession, colonisation, destruction of culture – and the ways that Aboriginal people are working to restore culture and reaffirm values that are antithetical to colonisation and dispossession. The Land Rights struggle continues.

Kathy Kituai found colonisation very close to home. In New Guinea, colonisation lies at the foot of Australian governments and the Australian people, responsible for the policies and practices which have arisen out of intrusion into the original culture. 'House boys' do the housework – in European or 'elite' households – alongside the maids, known by many different titles whether in Hong Kong, the Caribbean or South Africa. I can 'trace the African and British origins of [my] Jamaican family on both sides, back to 1830s, before slavery was ended in the British Caribbean', writes Anne Hickling Hudson.

'House boys' do the housework – in European or 'elite' households – alongside the maids... in Hong Kong, the Caribbean or South Africa.

Many women go abroad to find work, voluntarily. Economic and political power, unevenly distributed though it is, has given women greater independence. Jennifer Simon 'sought change, challenge, the opportunity to develop'. She found all three in a varied career in journalism and public relations and, more recently, in establishing her own business together with a partner.

First, Jennifer Simon left Aberdeen, Scotland, for London. Her visits to Burma, China and Macchu Picchu in Peru preceded McDonalds. (A universal sign of invasion rivalling Coca-cola.) Travelling to become a permanent resident of Australia meant selling her London flat, resigning from her job – and knowing that her parents knew, as they had many years before on her first leaving home, that she would 'be alright'.

Vivien Altman's family appreciated her need to meet the challenge of living and working in Nicaragua. After working in the early 1980s with the first Salvadoran refugees arriving in Australia, she became increasingly concerned to 'do something about it'. In her early childhood she (like Janice Farrell in Western Australia and Janet Wilczynski in England, and Gisela Gardener in Germany) had heard the refugee stories told from a world away – life under the Nazis in the second world war. After her first trip, to Cuba and Mexico for six weeks over December-January in the mid-1980s, she discovered she was 'in love' with her first experience of Latin America. Cliché-ic but true: it was 'alive, warm, stimulating and energetic politically, intellectually and culturally'. She 'warmed to the romance and warmth of human relations...miles apart from the dominant anglo way of doing things in Australia'. Yet, she recognises, whatever the pull of Latin American culture and character, she cannot disown her anglo heritage entirely.

A working holiday as a freelance journalist developed into years of staying, learning Spanish (so that no more disastrous 'missed sightings' at airports, anywhere in Latin America or the Spanish-speaking world could occur) and travelling back and forth between Australia and Central America. Back in Nicaragua now, Vivien Altman recognises that the international media has moved on: the wars are over. Yet as Ofelia Lopez knows, the hard slog has just begun. A different slog, this time: no more clandestine visits to the cities and towns to buy medicines to save lives and ease pain of women and children in the mountains. No more ducking to avoid the authorities, and lacking official documentation. Ofelia Lopez has gone back. Still in Australia, settled and graduated in social work from the University of Melbourne, Dorota Malchevski wonders about her family in Poland. Just as in Central America, there have been changes in the Eastern Block.

Mickey Zhu has been back to China. In Australia, she gained more knowledge of the Tian An Mien Square massacre than she had in China. 'There was an incident in Beijing,' she writes, 'but we heard little about it…the news we had had in China was only in passing, with no more than cursory reference…'

The Australian Broadcasting Corporation (ABC) and Special Broadcasting Service (SBS) gain plaudits from Kristin Henry and Anne Hickling Hudson. 'Lowest common denominator and too many commercials,' Kristin Henry mutters, returning to Australia from Tennessee and wanting to send 'thank you presents' to the ABC and SBS. Gillian Hanscombe, leaving Australia for Britain at the end of the 1960s, held a more circumscribed view of the Australian Broadcasting Commission (ABC), as it was back then. Every year in late 1940s and 1950s Australia, on Anzac Day 'we heard the ABC… broadcast about Simpson and his donkey'.

Travelling independently for jobs, adventure, challenge, Jennifer Simon, Mickey Zhu, Janice Farrell, Sandra McCallum, Penelope Andrews, Vivien Altman, Gillian Hanscombe, Mary Ann Bin-Sallik and Ania Wilczynski and others found jobs, intellectual stimulation, language difficulties, theft, fame, new citizenship…

She's not sure, now, how long it was intended the family would stay.

A child has no choice: the family goes, and they go too. Kristin Henry travelled on a Norwegian-crewed ship to Australia from Tennessee in the United States. She's not sure, now, how long it was intended the family would stay. Yet, after three years in Melbourne she had made more long-lasting friends than had earlier been the case, in the family's moving from place to place in North America. After 20 years (was it something Ronald Reagan said or did?) she became an Australian citizen.

Susan Ogier, Janet Wilczynski and Jan Mock travelled as migrants with their families, too. They and Kristin Henry recognise, now, the enormous strain the move must have placed upon their mothers. Women in their early forties or early middle-age, they were lifted out of the worlds in which they had grown up, to a world vastly different. Even the illusion that 'we all speak the same language' is just that – so much an illusion. It's not only the language, the expressions, the accent, being understood when you *know you're* speaking English – so what are *they* speaking! Australian, North American, British – all derive from the same origin, the same cultural background. But how much difference there is, as a consequence of time and space, distance and geography.

Kwik Tan and Californian Poppy are the same the world over. Are the highlands of New Guinea or the mountains of El Salvador, now, unknown to them? Ubiquitous, they strode the shelves of Janet Wilczynski's father's Boots chemist shop in England, and sat squat and cheerful on the pharmacy shelves in Geelong, Australia, too. Once, they were what Coca-cola is to the world today. Or McDonalds? But the recognition factor is matched by that of 'not being understood'. And not being understood goes far beyond the lack of a 'backyard' in North America, or Scotch tape versus Sellotape versus Gladwrap versus Clingfilm. That 'rubbers' aren't 'erasers'. Or erasers aren't rubbers. And pantyhose versus stockings versus tights. And – as Lynne Wenig and Anne Hickling Hudson and so many others have discovered: 'Dreadfully sorry but you must know that "the 'r' word" means something quite other.'

The mother of the family is often isolated, arriving in a 'new' country as a consequence of husband's change of job – as for Kristin Henry's mother. Finding that, in the 'new' country the man has a place, because he *must* have a job – like Jan Mock's mother, Susan Ogier's mother, and Kristin Henry's mother, too. Seeking to make her way in a country where so many 'givens' are no more: no central heating; f-r-e-e-z-i-n-g in winter. Wives don't have cars – much less teenagers. Grin-and-bear-it with the chip heater for warming up the bath water. And this house has electricity on!

> Grin-and-bear-it with the chip heater for warming up the bath water. And this house has electricity on!

Although conditions have changed, whichever the country of origin, whatever the country of destination, the difficulties for the woman of the family remain pronounced. Sylvia Hennessy found life most difficult in those initial months of arriving in Australia and transferring to Bathurst. Establishing an medical practice is not easy. Nor is mothering two young children when the cold gets into the soul at that four o'clock in the morning feed and the two am nightmare. Learning English 'from scratch' is difficult whether the student is male or female. Yet it's even more difficult when the student confronts macho attitudes from fellow members of the class who talk over her, asserting and implying that she has no right to be here. 'Why isn't your man here?' was the unspoken question greeting Ofelia Lopez every morning in English classes. She stayed on. Kept going back. Took further courses. Learnt. Despite it.

Finding yourself, a young mother with a child and a husband, in Sydney instead of Melbourne as did Dorota Malchevski, is not easy. Still, the husband gains the job. Then there are questions about the relevance of your qualifications, although they are from a respected university and have been gained in the approved way. Approved in *your* country, that is. And the difficulty goes not only for European or Eastern European qualifications translating back into Australia. Jan Mock found that her science degree was in question, despite its quality and recognised status in her home country, when she sought commensurate work in Alaska. And Mickey Zhu, qualified as an engineer in China, hopes that her qualification will gain recognition as the basis of her new career in her new country – Australia.

Single women travelling across the world to make new lives. Mickey Zhu leaving China alone, with the encouragement of her family. An adventure. Would the streets of Melbourne be paved with gold? She arrived, unheralded, at Tullamarine airport. Janice Farrell had the possibility of being met at the wharf as the boat docked in London. Would the hold up at customs, where she was required to produce documents that were already safely on dry land, mean there was no one to meet her? Jennifer Simon had a friend in Australia when she decided to leave Scotland and London to live in the antipodes. Whether or not there was someone to meet her, she had a grand send off: digger's hat with corks bobbing on the brim, a lesson on the didgeridoo, and a last minute call at Heathrow airport. 'I'm just telephoning to wish you good luck,' says a friendly voice from the depths of the telephone, whilst Jennifer Simon gazes into the depths of the aeroplane gangway, only yards (and minutes) away. The trip takes 42 hours – or thereabouts.

Mickey Zhu had no meeting-at-the-airport planned, she met people anyway: 'Where do you want to go, can we give you a lift?' A half-day telephoning around the Chinese community secured her a room. 'I was lucky,' she says.

Public transport. Jan Mock found it practically non-existent, living as she did in Alaska. She learnt to drive with chains securely wrapped around tyres. In Australia, living in an isolated house in isolated Driffield with her parents and brother Richard, she and he walked miles to school, often grateful for a lift with a (relatively) nearby worker who detoured to collect them. Her mother gladly acquired a bicycle. In Alaska, Jan Mock's children travelled to school by bus – when there was no moose in the way, roaring and snorting and scraping at the dirt with its hoof. Or so we envisage it: concerned locals ensured that the Mocks were on the telephone tree alerting them to any proximate moose impeding the path to the bus stop.

Susan Ogier was sent into the city at 14-years-of-age to 'get a job'. She found one – and did the regular two kilometre walk to the railway station, and the long train ride into town then across to the north shore every day, five-days-a-week. In Melbourne, Ofelia Lopez travelled 45 minutes to English classes at Box Hill, after depositing children in kindergarten and childcare, and taking a tram to the city.

Lynne Wenig missed the hustle and bustle and speed of the New York subway. I gloried in the prim and proper railway carriages that sped to the affluent suburbs of Manhattan, and rode the subway, too. Once, quite lost,

I realised my error in time to alight at Central Park subway station. Would my mistake land me with a knife in the back, there on Central Park station, my life slowly ebbing away under the uninterested eyes of hundreds of commuters. Asking directions is always the best solution, and I lived.

In Canada, Sandra McCallum remembers with affection the double decker buses of Sydney and Melbourne's trams. In Britain, public transport lost its vigour and reliability through the 1980s. This, together with the breakdown in the health system and the growing sense (and reality) of poverty on the streets that greeted Sylvia Hennessy when she returned, for a family visit. Nonetheless, in Australia Gisela Gardener, Jennifer Simon and Janet Wilczynski longed for the familiarity of the London underground. But 'Black youths met abuse and violence on the street and on the "tube"' in London Gisela Gardener found, in the 1970s, when West Indian party-goers died in a bomb attack.

Fear. Women travelling abroad, whether for relatively short-term study purposes or long-term working holidays, like Vivien Altman, Janice Farrell and Jennifer Simon and others, feel fear and experience courage. Whether migrating and leaving home behind, to make 'home' somewhere else, like Kathy Kituai, Mickey Zhu, Marlies Puentener, Vivienne Correa and Gillian Hanscombe, the terrors of 'leaving' and not knowing where she is *really* going are real. Whether flying or sailing alone or together, like Lynne Wenig, Janet Labatut, Tui Taurua and Susan Ogier or Gloria Lee, it is frightening to leave everything behind, whether permanently or just for a 'long time'. Whether traipsing around Europe on a Eurail pass as did Ania Wilczynski, or selling up her flat and flying off for a second time as did Sandra McCallum, or emigrating twice to Australia from Britain – as a child, first, then as an adult, as did Janet Wilczynski: a person inevitably is scared, for a time, at least, however momentary, however quickly passing.

...there are heartaches and heartbreaks, coming together and splitting apart, finding new life, new loves.

However they come to a new country, however they travel, whether with all their goods in three suitcases, as did Dorota Malchevski, or with the bread knife safely packed, as Gillian Hanscombe was advised, the women are brave.

And there are heartaches and heartbreaks, coming together and splitting apart, finding new life, new loves. Kathy Kituai returned to Australia from New Guinea, with a new son and now makes a new life in Canberra, writing, editing and publishing. Janet Labatut has travelled from one side of the world to the other, and from one side of the Australian continent to the other. There have been changes and the need to find herself as a writer and now, she identifies as a writer. Lynne Wenig travelled to Australia to live in a large rambling house in St Kilda (only suburbs away, today, now, from where Janet Labatut lives in a large rambling house). She learned to conquer fear, to find pleasure in eucalypt trees dancing against the windows and, although it took many years, finding a familiarity with a certain Australian sense of humour.

Gisela Gardener learned about England from the heights and backstairs of the Savoy Hotel in London. Today, she lives in Alice Springs caring and contributing to the improvement of health services for Aboriginal people. Mary Ann Bin-Sallik has achieved one of her goals – the Harvard Crimson – and continues working hard at the other: access, and education, and more education for her compatriots. Marlies Puentener would not, now, return to New Zealand to live permanently. Tui Taurua is not so sure. Australia has brought to them both valuable experiences in work and in life. Tui Taurua lives free of violence, and is finding security and psychological strength and support in Sydney. In Australia, Marlies Puentener had found her birth mother, after searching for years, and 'a name on documents has become a person'.

Janet Labatut finds support and strength in her Rosary and her writing. Jan Mock is ready to go to the opposite end of the earth again, when the opportunity arises. (It will.) Susan Ogier's family found that she had developed into a strong and resourceful woman: 'I had become very much a colonial girl,' she reflects. What strength of purpose and vision this simple statement contains. 'They said: "Sue is so strong," "Sue is so capable." ' Susan Ogier 'became strong and capable out of necessity'. At 14, she had a job. At 16, she had a child and a husband, and her family had returned to England.

The meaning of 'foreign' is peculiar to the person and the situation. Janet Wilczynski muses on the elderly woman who remained 'glued to her seat' when a voice boomed into the ship, upon entering the port of Naples: 'All foreigners to report to the forward lounge.' 'All foreigners must come,' said Janet Wilczynski. But 'I'm not a foreigner, I'm English'.

Yet who hasn't 'felt foreign' in some place, some situation. But, in the end 'out of place', the migrant condition of restlessness, of difference, of 'not belonging' becomes a condition with its own familiarity. I loved the bagels and the *accents* – they all had them – and the sharp intellectual wit of law school classes. Belonging, and not belonging, there was an extra latitude for the 'foreign students', a tolerance of difference. And sometimes, simply – indifferences.

Penelope Andrews finds strength in knowing that Australia is her 'base'. Sandra McCallum was bemused by the need for her to obtain a visa in order to return, for a holiday – and to proudly display her new child to grandparents. 'But I'm *Australian*,' she finds herself thinking. 'I was born there.' She's a Canadian, now. Why can't there be dual citizenship, runs the plaint of many women, while there is misunderstanding and confusion, contradictory rules and regulations, about who can and who cannot hold dual citizenship. Yet, as Gisela Gardener asks, what does 'country' mean? To Gloria Lee, 'country' is vital. 'There is a special connection for us, with and to the land,' she says.

Snow. Ice. Scorching sun. Heat.

Fear of flying? Not these women.

Index

A to Z of Time Management, The (Wenig)
127

Aborigines and Torres Strait Islanders
30, 53-60 *passim*, 70, 137, 184-9
passim, 192, 197-8, 207-8, 212, 213,
214-223 *passim*, 245-6 *passim*, 251
see also Black Women's Action
Education Fund (BWAEF)
and assimilation/forced removal of
children 1-2, 189, 215
and anthropologists 219, 246, 252
and colonisation/cf Irish 2, 8, 185,
197-8, 257
and Depo Provera/health 28, 246, 264
and discrimination/racism 53, 60,
137, 186-7, 212, 214, 223
and education 55, 192, 214, 215-23
passim, 251, 252, 258-9, 264
and genocide/invasion 2, 8, 185,
188-9, 197, 243, 257
relationship with the land 57
and studying anthropologists 219-20,
251
and travelling 1, 7, 53-60 *passim*,
214-23 *passim*
treatment of 'half-caste' children 2,
53, 55, 60, 258
Aboriginal
art 32, 108-9, 185, 188, 207-8
culture/history 1, 7, 14, 70, 188, 207,
215, 241, 245, 246, 251
dreaming/mythology 1, 70, 246
family 1, 219
Land Rights 198, 259
languages/names 55-6, 122 *see also*
language
names 122
abortion 14, 30
accent/accents *see* language
activism/demonstrations 24, 137, 224,
225, 234, 236, 240, 244, 256 *see also*
Viet Nam war
anti-apartheid/sanctions lobby 133, 136

anti-racism 133
Campaign for Nuclear Disarmament
(CND) 240
civil rights struggle 133, 135
hunger strike/passive resistance 204,
238
peace rallies 195, 240
prison movement/struggles 35, 228-31
protests 24, 35, 132-3, 193, 240
and Spring Bok rugby tour 24
shot/injured during 230, 231
Alice in Wonderland (Carroll) 73
All that False Instruction (Higgs) 15
Allende government 177
Altman, Vivien M. 7, 33-42, 255, 259,
260, 263
ANC (African National Congress) 133
Anderson, David 107, 108
Anderson, James (McCallum) 107
Anderson, Zoe (McCallum) 107
Andrews, Marie 251-2
Andrews, Penelope E. 8, 131-8, 251,
256, 260, 264
Anne of Green Gables 106
Aotearoa *see under* New Zealand
Arena, Franca 5, 6
Arrernte people 53, 55, 246 *see also*
Aborigines and Torres Strait Islanders,
Aboriginal, language
As a Woman (Scutt) 251
AustCare 118
Australian Broadcasting
Commission/Corporation (ABC) 15,
117, 185, 258, 260
Australian Federation of Business and
Professional Women (AFBPW) 169
Australian Labor Party (ALP) 14, 168

Bach, Johanne Sebastian 74
backpacking *see* travel
Bank of Melbourne 164
Bardi people *see* Aborigines and Torres
Strait Islanders, Aboriginal

Barratt, Ina 180
bathroom *see* toilets/lavatory
Beethoven, Ludwig von 74
belonging 18, 72, 74, 79, 137, 264
    see also home, outsider
Behrendt, Larissa 221
beverages *see* culture/traditions
Bin-Sallik, Mary Ann 8, 214-23, 251,
    252, 253, 256, 258, 260, 264
Bin-Sallik, Mary Brigid 223
Birth Link 30
Bjelke Petersen, Joh 24, 187
Black Students Society (Sth Africa) 131
Black Women's Action Education Fund
    (Black Women's Action/BWAEF)
    (Aust.) 8, 221-2
black women law professors group 135
Blake, William 64
Blyton, Enid 73
*Boiling Energy: community healing among
    the Kalahari Kung!* 219
Bond, Catherine 5
Bougainville Mining Company 220
bravery *see* courage
Bronte, Charlotte 67
Brotherhood of St Laurence 233
Brown, William Jennings 170
Buxton, Ann 28

CentreBrain Ltd 127
Chamorro, Violeta 39
Chan, Julius 221
character/identity 70 *see also* colonial
    mentality/colonialism, culture/
    traditions, discrimination
    Australian 6, 14, 18, 29, 66, 89, 90,
        108, 116, 119-20, 124, 161, 168,
        169, 198, 199, 244-5
    British 17, 18, 199, 244
    Canadian 108
    Central/Latin American 7, 36-37, 259
    Chinese 57-8
    German 243, 245
    macho/machismo/'male bonding' 40,
        154, 157, 232, 235, 252, 261
    New Zealand 25, 30-1
    North American 98-9, 114
    Polish 212
Chilean resistance 35
Chin, Helen 119
Chinweizu 189
Christie, Agatha 19

CIA (Central Intelligence Agency) 219
citizenship/nationality 6, 50, 69, 77,
    90, 94-5, 100, 107-8, 115-16, 136,
    151, 159, 161, 162, 237, 250, 251,
    258, 260, 264 *see also* passport/visa,
    permanent residence, work permit
Clague, Joyce 1
Clancy of the Overflow 65
climate/weather 7, 25, 32, 40, 83, 88,
    96, 97, 104, 107, 119, 122, 128, 155,
    170, 175, 188, 203, 207, 211, 240,
    247, 261, 264
    Cyclone Tracey 25
    driving conditions 97
    English summer 19
    rain 76, 103, 155, 170
    snow/ice 46, 48, 49, 66, 96, 97, 114,
        117, 188, 203, 247, 258
    sun/surf 119, 157, 240
colonial mentality/colonialism 5-6, 21,
    47, 119, 120-1, 157, 170, 184
colonisation 1, 2, 47, 76, 77, 214, 247,
    257, 258, 259 *see also* Aborigines and
    Torres Strait Islanders
Committee of Mothers (Central/Latin
    America) 236
Commonwealth Employment Program
    (CEP) 212, 213
communication 233, 237, 238 *see also*
    language, newspapers, television
    by correspondence 30, 37, 60, 95,
        104, 155, 157, 176, 180, 228
    by sea mail 63
    by telephone 39, 44, 149, 152-3, 154,
        164, 171, 178, 180, 230, 262
    telecommunications 179
    freelance reporting 39
condoms 31, 235
convicts/transportation 3, 29, 66, 157,
    246
Cooper, Audrey 180
Correa, Vivienne 8, 118-24, 248, 256,
    258, 263
Correa, Frank 118-24 *passim*, 248, 256
Council for the National Museum of
    Australia 215
country 137
    the meaning of 8-9
    the politics of 9, 21, 173-246
courage 2-3, 6, 9, 24, 28, 30, 128, 129,
    166, 198, 208, 213, 227, 233, 248,
    252, 253, 263

cricket 6, 31, 94, 109, 119-20, 124, 176, 180, 183, 258
criminal assault at home *see* violence against women
criminology 152, 157
culture shock 128, 178
culture/traditions *see also* activism/ demonstrations, character/identity, colonial mentality/colonialism, discrimination, education, landscape, national, provincial or state landmarks/ events, newspapers/comics, politics, television, sport
Australian, 18, 22, 47, 101, 119-20, 184, 245, 257
    adherence to British 'ways' 6, 101
    Aussie rules 124, 37
    'bring a plate' 63, 245
    (no) central heating 112, 128
    ethnic diversity 185
    Flying Doctor Service 111
    hierarchical structures of bureaucracy 104
    lifestyle 28, 41, 85, 86, 87, 89, 90, 94, 112, 116, 134, 135-6, 137, 165, 240
    McGills Newsagency 129, 253
    'the lucky country' 14, 124, 245
    racist expressions 184
    RSL (Returned Serviceman's (now Returned and Services) League/clubs 129
    trams/double-decker buses 108
    taxation rates 167, 168
    upbringing of children 44
Austrian life style 34
beverages 39, 165
    Australian wine 74, 182
    cappuccino 40, 135, 167
    Earl Grey tea 40
    Stubbies 183
    tea 56, 79, 128
    vodka 24, 68, 254
British 8, 19, 64, 166, 170-1, 200
    British Airways 164
    BritRail 249
    Caithness glass 165
    Collet's International Bookshop 240, 249
    establishment 244
    Foyles bookshops 67
    Greater London Council 164

lifestyle 89
Royal Ballet Touring Orchestra 19
British Empire 244, 257
Caribbean
    Jamaica School of Music 176
    lifestyle 178
Central/Latin America
    civil war 235
    lifestyle 38-41 *passim*, 224-6, 227-8, 229-31, 233, 234, 235, 236, 237-8
Chinese 53-60 *passim*
    upbringing of boys and girls 73
    lifestyle 57, 85
dress customs 14, 76, 77, 78, 103, 104, 109, 112, 140, 165, 178, 244, 245, 262
    Akubra hat 122
    hats and gloves 65
    jeans and Reeboks 79
    lap-lap 76, 77
    scarves 26
    school uniforms 65
    thongs and T-shirt 120, 211, 249
European fairy tales 184
food 32, 35, 54, 55, 60, 76-77, 106, 108, 114, 116, 123, 135, 163, 178, 180, 185, 229, 230, 232, 253-4, 264
    borscht 35, 254
    byo bistros/restaurants 108-9, 167
    Babe Ruth candy bars 114
    biltong (ostrich beef) 135, 254
    Cajun/Creole 146, 254
    Chico rolls 245, 254
    Chinese/Chinese cafes 54, 129, 254
    Choo Choo bars 77, 254
    crawfish 139-40, 253
    bushtucker 246, 254
    ethnic eating/'foreign food' 15, 129
    Eurasian/Chinese/Portuguese dishes 123
    fish and chips 129, 254
    guava jelly/stew 180, 254
    Hokey Pokey ice cream 32, 254
    Hudson's chocolate chip cookies 32, 254
    Jamaican delicacies/restaurant 185
    lobster 106
    McDonalds 164, 259, 261
    mealie pudding 170, 254
    meat pies 108, 248, 254
    mebos (fruit) 135, 254
    Mexican 103

muffins 103, 254
mulberries 183, 254
pavlova 123, 254
peanut butter and jelly sandwich
129, 254
Pimms with strawberries and cream
154, 254
pizza 129, 253
Polska agorki 68, 254
pumpkin pie/soup 114, 155, 254
rice 54, 56, 77, 254
'Scotch Bonnett' peppers 180, 254
'street food' 188, 254
Tabasco sauce 140, 253, 254
Vegemite 76, 108, 114
German - lifestyle 241, 242-3
Hong Kong
attitudes toward Eurasians/Chinese
120-21
lifestyle 120
Kwik Tan/Californian Poppy 65, 261
multicultural/multiculturalism 119,
137, 153, 207, 237
New Zealand/Aotearoa 23, 24, 31-2,
163
Maori 162, 257
Pakeha 162, 257
North America *see also* Ku Klux Klan
(KKK)
Canadian Pacific Airlines 102
central heating 112, 128
civil rights 119
Continental Airlines 231
drug abuse 119, 135
lack of gun control laws 119, 135
lifestyle 96, 97, 112, 116, 133, 134,
135
teaching methods 220
Papua New Guinea/New Guinea
76-7, 78, 79, 220-1
South Africa *see also* activism - anti-
apartheid, politics
growing up 'coloured' 133
lifestyle 137
security police 137
Cummings, Barbara 1-2
currency 14, 112, 205
customs/immigration 37, 50, 184, 211,
237-8
bureaucracy of 45, 132
Cuthbert, Betty 13

Dare, Dan (*Eagle* comic-book character)
62, 67
daring *see* courage
Daughters of Charity 232
Daughters of Midas (King) 4-5
Davies, Martin 140-50 *passim*
death
of brother 140-1, 143, 146
of father 33, 49, 89-90, 141, 193-4
of grandfather 91
of grandmother 92, 203
of mother 20, 52, 133, 134
of parents 107, 116
of uncle 163
Deidrich, John 108
Democratic Labor Party (DLP) 14
demonstrations *see* activism/
demonstrations
Department of Urban and Regional
Development (DURD) 104
'developed' vs 'developing' countries
138, 238
Dickson, Susie 24
Different Lives (Scutt) 5
discrimination 197, 207, 210, 224,
225, 233, 243 *see also* Aborigines and
Torres Strait Islanders, racism, sexism
disappeared (Central/Latin America)
229, 236
distance/s *see* travel
Djaru people 8, 214-23 *passim*, 251
see also Aborigines and Torres Strait
Islanders; Aboriginal
Done, Ken 109
*Dr Wooreddy's Prescription for Enduring
the Ending of the World* (Mudrooroo)
189

economic rationalism 178, 197, 200,
240 *see also* John Major, Margaret
Thatcher, Thatcherism, Reagan
government, Ronald Reagan
education 3, 8, 14, 19, 20, 24, 34, 47,
54, 55, 64, 66, 67, 64, 73, 101, 118,
120, 122, 124, 127, 134, 159, 175-6,
181, 184, 190-1, 192, 193, 203, 212,
213, 216, 226, 232, 233, 235, 236,
242 *see also* Aborigines and Torres
Strait Islanders, Aboriginal, educational
institutions, travel - to study
Chamberlain Fellow in Legal Studies
131, 134

cross-cultural research 219-220
'11 Plus' 64
(il)literacy 226, 252
(non) recognition of qualifications 67,
    98, 213, 251-2, 261-2
of boys and girls 73
educational institutions
Australian Film and Television School
    (Aust.) 191, 193
Australian National University (ANU)
    (Aust.) 79
Birbeck College (UK) 19
Brisbane College of Advanced
    Education (CAE) 182, 191
British School of Brussels (Belgium) 51
Catholic Theological College (Aust.)
    145, 149
Charles Sturt University (Aust.) 195,
    198
Charles University (Czech.) 153
City University of New York
    (CUNY)(USA) 131-2
College of Technical and Further
    Education (TAFE) 159, 161, 233
Colleges of Further Education
    (FE Colleges, UK) 19
Columbia University (USA) 131, 132,
    134, 256
diocesan schools (Anglican)(HK) 120,
    258
Goroke Teachers College (PNG) 188
Griffith University (Aust.) 193
Harvard University (USA) 8, 141,
    214-23 passim, 251
    Graduate School of Education
        (HGSE) 214, 216, 217, 218, 222
    Kennedy School of Government
        219, 220, 222
Institute of Papua-New Guinea
    Studies 71, 78
Jesuit University (Central America) 39
Jews College (UK) 20
Koszalin Polytechnic (Poland) 202,
    203
La Trobe University (Aust.) 131, 132,
    234, 251
MacRobertson Girls High (Aust.) 101
Massachusetts Institute of Technology
    (MIT)(USA) 218
Military College of Science (UK) 47
Monash University (Aust.) 33, 35, 91,
    101

National Institute of Dramatic Art
    (NIDA)(Aust.) 23, 250
Oxford University (UK) 20, 21, 141,
    243, 252, 257
    Magdalene College 243
    St Anne's 20
    St Hugh's 20-1
Poznan University (Poland) 201
Queens College (UK) 20
Queensland Institute of Technology
    (Aust.) 176, 178, 191
Queensland University of Technology
    (Aust.) 175, 191, 193
Sacred Heart Girls College (NZ) 24
School of Aboriginal and Islander
    Administration (Aust.) 215
Shanghai University Engineering
    Science Textile Institute (China) 83
South Australian College of Advanced
    Education (CAE)(now University of
    South Australia)(Aust.) 216
South Australian Institute of
    Technology (SAIT)(Aust.) 215, 216
South Hampton University (UK) 180
Southern Methodist University 248
Stanford University (USA) 175, 187,
    193
Trent Park Training College (UK) 61
Tulane University (USA) 140
University of Adelaide (Aust.) 215, 251
University of British Columbia (Can.)
    102, 253
University of Cambridge (UK) 151-8
    passim, 249, 250
    Clare Hall 154
    Institute of Criminology 151, 249
University of Hong Kong (HK) 176
University of Melbourne (Aust.) 33,
    35, 213, 252, 260
University of Michigan (USA) 247
University of Natal (Africa) 131, 134
University of New Brunswick (Can.)
    107
University of New England (Aust.) 61
University of New South Wales
    (Aust.) 151
University of Queensland (Aust.) 23,
    183, 191, 193
University of South Australia (Aust.)
    216
University of South Pacific 188
University of Sydney (Aust.) 247

University of Toronto (Can.) 21
University of Victoria, British
  Columbia (Can.) 107
University of West Indies (UWI) 175,
  176, 179, 180
University of Western Australia
  (Aust.) 247, 251-2
Victorian University of Technology
  (inc. Western Institute) (Aust.) 159, 161
EEC/EC European Economic
  Community/European Community 51
eurocentracism 5-6, 7, 186
Evans, Hyacinth 180
Evans-Omerod, Beverley 179
expatriates 19, 21, 76, 77, 79, 120

Fareday, Lisa (Bin-Sallik) 215, 223
Fareday, Robert 223
Farrell, Janice 7, 43-54, 249-50, 259,
  260, 262, 263
Farrell, Roger 47, 49, 51, 250
fauna 7, 190, 211
  of Australia 7, 16-7, 22, 63, 69, 74,
    93, 108, 117, 124, 149, 241
    Blattodea cockroach 25-26
    blowflies/flies 25
    black swan 239
    crocodile 26, 190
    frilled-necked lizard 26
    kangaroo 108, 111, 128, 137, 176,
      190, 241
    koala 137
    kookaburra 17, 69
    mosquitoes 88
    wombat 32
  of Britain 69
  of Papua New Guinea/New Guinea 76
  of North America 117
    moose 96-7
Faust, Beatrice 14
Feel the Fear, and Do It Anyway 166
feminism/feminist 21, 22, 24, 27, 30,
  32, 35, 36, 116, 152, 163, 198, 212,
  224, 235 see also discrimination/
  Women's Movement, women's rights
  activism/international solidarity 13,
    27, 230, 234, 235, 236
  theory/challenges 13, 30
Figueroa, Carol 180
Figueroa, Peter (snr) 180
films/documentary/television series 65,
  68, 78-9, 185, 192, 194, 243, 244, 258

Australian film industry 14
Battle of Chile 35
Burke's Back Yard 124
Crocodile Dundee 98, 190, 258
Crocodile Dundee II 98, 258
E Street 199, 258
Flying Doctors, The 199, 241, 258
Home and Away 258
Neighbours 157, 199, 258
On the Beach 13
Partizans, The 239
Silver City 63
Skippy 241, 258
Stormboy 241
Tambo 76
Upstairs, Downstairs 48
Walkabout 241
Fingleton, Larry 195-200 passim, 248,
  249
Fingleton, Phillipa 197
Fingleton, Niall (Hennessy) 195-200
  passim
Fingleton, Sean (Hennessy) 195-200
  passim, 249
First National Women's Health
  Conference (Australia) 28
Flesh and Paper (Hanscombe and
  Namjoshi) 13, 16
flora 17, 18, 32, 178, 180, 190, 198,
  211, 242
  of Australia 7, 16-7, 22, 40, 68, 68,
    69, 74, 93, 155, 246
  of Britain 7, 18, 61, 66, 69
  of Greece 18
  of Papua New Guinean/New Guinean
    7, 75, 76, 77
  eucalypts/gum trees 16, 22, 40, 67, 69,
    77, 124, 128, 149, 155, 254, 263
  United States 96
food see culture/traditions
food parcels/ration card 54, 64, 129, 205
Forza e corraggio (With Strength and
  Courage)(National Italian-Australian
  Women's Association) 5
Frame, Janet 32
Franklin, Miles 6
Fraser, Dawn 13
freedom 57, 136, 137, 139, 165, 204,
  207, 223, 226, 242

games, children's 65
  in China 56-7

Gardener, Daisy (Williams) 240, 241
Gardener, Gisela 8, 239-46, 249, 257, 258, 259, 263, 264
Gardner, Ava 13
Glorious Age (Scutt) 1
Goethe, Wolfgang 166
Goldberg, Whoopie 29
Goldfields and Chrysanthemums (Bond) 5
Goods and Services Tax (GST) 31, 160, 167 *see also* Value Added Tax (VAT)
Gordon, Adam Lindsey 62
Gospel of Mark 150
Goss government 187
Great Mass (Mozart) 140
Greer, Germaine 244
gypsies 46-7

Hanscombe, Gillian 7, 13-22, 249, 257, 260, 262, 263
Hanscombe, Martin 13, 21, 22
Hawke, Robert J. (Bob) 14, 168
Hecate's Charms (Hanscombe) 13, 16-7
Hennessy, Ann 196, 198, 200, 249
Hennessy, Sylvia R. 8, 195-200, 248, 249, 250, 257, 261, 263
Henry, Alice 6
Henry, Kristin 8, 110-17, 254, 258, 260, 261
Hickling, Brian 175, 187, 190, 193
Hickling Hudson, Anne 8, 175-94, 250, 257-8, 259, 260, 261
Hickling Hudson, Alexis 178, 183, 186, 190, 193
Hickling Hudson, Dominic 173, 182, 183, 186, 190, 192, 193,
Higgs, Kerryn 15
Higman, Barry 176
Higman, Merle 176
Hillary, Edmund 65
home 8, 9, 31, 32, 37, 64, 86, 90, 103, 115, 128, 130, 131, 132, 133, 161, 162, 163, 179, 212, 237, 241-2, 251, 253 *see also* belonging, travel - returning home/'home'
'Back Home' 19
burial place 136, 193
homesickness 32, 40, 99, 113, 114, 146, 154, 155, 157, 162, 180, 227
loss of 'sense of belonging' 52
missing family/friends/home/places/ news 57, 88, 129, 135, 155, 170, 180, 196, 198

mother country/homeland 136, 243, 251
nostalgic memories of 45
'sent home' 91
to 'go home'/to retire to 64, 128, 130, 161, 210
housing 48, 49, 54, 55, 94, 123, 124, 178, 180, 197, 203, 204, 207, 225, 226, 240
army hut 48, 88
government hostel 105
isolated 93-4 *passim*, 262
migrant/refugee camp/hostel 63, 88, 211, 228, 232, 252
moving house 124, 146
Women's College, University of Sydney 101-2, 105
Hudson, Catherine 176
Hudson, Frederick 181
Hudson, Gillian 181
Hudson, Kathryn 181
humour 9, 129, 245, 263
Humphries, Barry/Edna Everage 63, 129, 134

identity *see* character/identity
immigration *see* customs/immigration
imperialism 14, 113, 227
industrial action/conditions 177
liquor strike (Can.) 106
pilots' strike (Aust.) 26
underground (UK) 166
wharfies (Aust.) 14, 62
initiative/enterprise 9, 124, 168
International Feminist Book Fair (first) 21
International Red Cross 231
'Irish jokes' 197, 249
Isaacs, Ian 187, 190
Isaacs, Isaac 34
Isaacs, Pat 179, 187, 190
IWDA (International Women's Development Agency) 224, 234, 252

Japanese occupation 58, 120
Jones, Ruth 27

Keating, Paul 168, 187
Kenyon, J.W. 139
Kerensky government 34
King, Norma 4-5
King, Martin Luther 133, 256

Kituai, Kathy 7, 71-9, 249, 253, 256, 258, 259, 263
Kituai, Robbie
Kiwi *see under* New Zealand/Aotearoa
Kolia, John 78
Koori/s *see* Aborigines and Torres Strait Islanders, Aboriginal
Ku Klux Klan 116, 136, 186

Labatut, A.J. 140-1, 143, 146
Labatut, Ann 142-3
Labatut, Elaine 143
Labatut, Fi 143
Labatut, Janet 8, 139-50, 253, 254, 263, 264
Labatut, Lois 143
Lacey, Rokiah (Bin-Sallik) 215, 223
Lacey, Rod 223
La Forest, Gerald 203
Laker, Richard 91-4 *passim*, 250, 258, 262
landscape 18, *see also* national, provincial or state landmarks/events
  Australian 7, 16, 25, 58, 65, 74, 85, 117, 155, 190, 199-200, 211, 240-1, 254
    beaches 7, 40, 64, 119, 240, 241, 245, 247
    tropical rain forests 70, 155, 211
  British 7, 45, 65, 154, 240, 245
    English countryside/Downs 61
  Canadian 103
  Caribbean 189
    beaches 180
  Chinese 7, 58, 85
  Dutch coast 240
  Eastern European 211
  Greece - beaches 201, 240
  Hong Kong - beaches 119
  Papua New Guinea/New Guinea 7, 75, 77
  North American 114, 117
Langbroek, Anne (Hudson) 176, 179
Langbroek, Jan, 176, 179
Langbroek, Jean Paul 176, 179
Langbroek, Kate 176, 179
Lange, David 24
Langer, Beryl 234
language 6, 31, 42, 64, 68-69, 75, 77, 85, 103, 119, 123, 128, 129, 161, 163, 182, 183, 185, 227, 233, 237, 254-6, 260-1
  accents 34, 46, 47, 111, 116, 128, 135, 140, 169-70, 245, 254, 260-1, 264
  American English/as language of imperialism/occupation 135, 227, 252
  Arrernte 55, 254
  Australian accent/Aust. English 21, 47, 98, 135, 156, 162, 169, 199, 250-1, 254
  Australian expressions/pronunciations 31, 63, 65, 85, 98, 109, 113, 119, 122, 123, 124, 156-7, 161-2, 169, 179, 183, 188, 189, 211-2, 258, 261
  Chinese accent/learning Chinese 55, 85, 252, 254
  compulsory French 51
  cost of English course 83
  English accent/expressions/pronunciations 48, 94, 199, 244, 261
  English cramming lessons 20
  English as a Second Language (ESL) 43, 232
  Irish accent 199, 249
  Jamaican English/accent/expressions 182, 183, 183-4, 250
  learning/speaking/teaching English 19-20, 39, 43, 55, 58, 118, 119, 206, 209, 212, 233, 241, 244, 245, 252, 261, 262
  learning/speaking Spanish 37, 41, 154, 228, 230, 234, 248, 259-60
  New Zealand accent/expressions 24, 31, 162
  non-English speaking 68, 232
  North American accent/expressions 47, 113, 114, 115, 129, 258, 261
  Pidgin English 77, 256
  problems 135, 260
  Scottish/Welsh accent 47, 169
  South African accent 135
  speaking/learning German 33, 254-5
  teaching Polish 209, 210, 254
  Viennese accent 34
lavatory *see* toilets/lavatories
Law Reform Commission, Australia 105-6
Law Reform Commission, Canada 103-6 *passim*
Lawson, Henry 66
Lee, Gloria 7, 53-60, 252, 254, 258, 263, 264
Lee, Olive 54, 55, 59-60, 252

INDEX

Lee, Peggy 60
Lee, Sarah 55
lesbian/lesbianism 13, 14, 15, 210, 235
  in exile 21
  love affairs 13, 18
  separatism 235
  writers 21
Levin, Bernard 170
literary criticism 13
Lopez, Ofelia 8, 224-38, 248, 252, 253, 255, 260, 261, 262

McCallum, Sandra K. 8, 100-9, 250, 256, 257, 258, 260, 263, 264
McKellar, Dorothea 65, 70
McPherson-Russell, Phyllis 180
Major, John 200
Malchevski, Dorota 8, 201-13, 248-9, 254, 260, 261, 263
Malchevski, Magdalena 201-13 passim, 254
Managua earthquake 38
Manley government 177
Manley, Michael 177
Mansfield, Katherine 20
Marche Militaire 24
marriage 47-51, 57-8, 59, 76-9 passim, 86, 87, 89, 92, 95, 115, 120, 128, 136, 142, 144-5, 147, 149, 155, 159, 160, 161, 204, 205, 208-9, 212, 225, 240, 241, 242, 248, 249, 253
  by proxy 5
  and forced/customary travel 3
  and status 77, 98, 233, 235
Matters, Muriel 6
meeting - at airport/wharf 37, 45, 85, 104, 122, 195, 228, 245, 262
Men, Sex, Power and Survival (Gardener and Williams) 239
Menzies, Robert 6, 14, 64
midwifery 44, 46, 196, 236, 250
migrant condition 132, 135, 136, 245, 251, 260
migrants 62, 66, 68, 133, 179, 260
  first generation 1, 34-5, 43-4, 123, 151, 249
  illegal 43, 250
  non-English speaking background (NESB) 245
  second generation 43, 123, 124, 249
migration schemes/policy 5, 6, 45, 59, 92, 94, 121 see also White Australia

Policy
  £10 pound scheme to Australia 87, 92, 121
Miller, Lena 4-5
Mills, John 244
Mills, Gladstone 180
Milton, John 64
miscarriages of justice - Birmingham 6, Guildford 4, Birmingham 6, Macguire 7, Winchester 3 197
Mock, Andrew 95-9 passim
Mock, Jan 8, 91-9, 250, 254, 258, 260, 261, 262, 264
Mock, Kevin 95-9 passim
Mock, Peta 95-9 passim
Modern Woman and Other Crimes, A (Chan and Terry) 139
motherhood 74, 76, 89, 225, 232, 235, 236, 261
Mozart, Wolfgang 74, 140
Murris see Aborigines and Torres Strait Islanders, Aboriginal
music 71-5 passim, 78, 79, 88, 176, 181, 208, 211
  bagpipe/didgeridoo 165, 262
  Carifolk singers 181
  country and western 254
  reggae 182, 250
My Country (McKellar) 65

NAACP (National Association for the Advancement of Coloured People) Legal Defence Fund 131
Namjoshi, Suniti 13, 16, 18, 21, 22
National Aboriginal Employment Development Committee 215
National Committee Against Discrimination in Employment and Occupation 215
National Health Service (UK) 197
national identity see character/identity
national, provincial or state landmarks/events
  Australia
    Adelaide Writers' Festival 18
    Anzac Day 15, 260
    Australia Day 76, 132, 251
    Bicentenary 222
    Botany Bay 2
    Brisbane River 178
    Centre, the 137

273

Collins Street 13
Commonwealth Avenue 67
Conniston Massacre 246
Daintree Rainforest 189
Eildon Weir 16
Flying Doctor Service 111
Free Store, The, Chappell Street 35
Goulburn Valley 16
Great Barrier Reef 137, 189
Great Ocean Road 16
ICI building - first 'skyscraper' 129
Kakadu National Park 26
Kerries 245
Kings Avenue 67
Kingsford Smith airport 195
Lake Burley Griffin 67
Lodge, The 168
Lone Pine Sanctuary 108
MCG (Melbourne Cricket Ground) 124, 258
Magnetic Island 24
Maralinga 245
Mataranka thermal springs 69
Moreton Bay 2
Myer Music Bowl 13, 108
New Theatre, The 129
Nurrungar 245
Pine Gap 245
Port Arthur 2
Port Fairy 16
Port Phillip/Port Phillip Bay 2, 16
Queen Street Mall 178, 182
Rocks, The 122
Roxeby Downs 245
Shrine, The 13
Snowy River Gorge 245
Southern Cross 122, 247
Stradbroke Island 189
Surfer's Paradise 189
Swan River 2, 145, 253
Sydney Harbour 87, 88
Sydney Harbour Bridge 122
Sydney to Hobart yacht race 35
Sydney Opera House 102, 108, 190
Tullamarine airport 15, 104, 245, 262
Western Tiers 29
Woolloomooloo dock 122, 256
Woolloongabba cricket ground 180, 258
Britain
  Ashfield Woods 61
  British Imperial War Museum 244
  Charing Cross Road 240, 241
  Chelsea 245
  Clapham Common 166
  Downs 61
  Edinburgh airport 164
  Edinburgh Fringe Festival 165
  Embankment Park 243
  Epsom Derby 61
  Greenham Common 240
  Harley Street 19, 20
  Heathrow airport 164, 165, 262
  Kentish Town Road 200
  King's Road 243, 245
  London Underground ('tube') 69, 166, 240, 244, 263
  May Balls/May Bumps 154, 254
  Oxford Street 200
  River Cam 69, 254
  River Mole 61
  Royal Court Theatre 245
  Royal Opera House 20
  Savoy Hotel 243, 264
  Sloane Square 245
  St Paul's Cathedral 243
  Thames/Thames Embankment 62, 243
  Yorkshire Moors 49
Caribbean
  Jamaican Folk Museum 180
  Sabina Park, Kingston 180
Central/Latin American
  Augusto Cesar Sandina Airport 38
  Coppelia Park, Central Havana 37
China
  Cultural Revolution 119
  Pearl River 55
  Shanghai airport 83
Empire Day 15
France
  Alps 50
  Mont Blanc 50
Germany/Poland
  Auschwitz, Bergen-Belsen, Dachau 243
  Rhein 241, 242
Greece
  Athens airport 210, 211
Guy Fawkes Night 32
Halloween 155, 222
Hong Kong
  Hong Kong Club 120
  minority clubs 120

Italy
  Alps 50
New Zealand
  Canterbury Plains 32
  Rangitata Gorge 26
  Southern Alps 32
North America
  Central Park/Station 128, 263
  French Quarter Festival 140
  Huston Women's Conference 248
  Mississippi River 140
  New York subway 128, 262-3
  St Charles Avenue 140, 253
  St Louis Cathedral 140
  Tiffany's 223
  Waldorf Astoria 223
  Wall Street 213
  White House 111
Remembrance Day 15
St Patrick's Day 63
nationality see citizenship/nationality
NATO (North Atlantic Treaty
  Organisation) 51
naturalisation/naturalisation ceremonies
  see citizenship/nationality
Nettlefold, Rex 178
New Australians 14, 123
new reproductive technologies (NRTs)
  30
New South Wales Child Protection
  Council 15
newspapers/comics/magazines 129,
  184-5, 205, 230, 243, 253
  Bikmaus 78
  Business Review Weekly 168
  Chronical of Higher Education 132, 251
  Digger 35
  Eagle 62, 63, 67
  Executive Women's Report, The 127
  Financial Times 20
  freelance reporting 39, 41
  Girl 63
  Guardian/Manchester Guardian
    63, 170
  Muse 71
  North American publications 129
  Observer 63
  Planner, The 176
  Times 170
  Women Australia 127
Niven, David 244
Norgay, Tenzing 65

Nunga see Aborigines and Torres Strait
  Islanders, Aboriginal
Nyunga see Aborigines and Torres Strait
  Islanders, Aboriginal

O'Brien, Margaret 4-5
Ockers 31
Ogier, Susan 8, 87-90, 260, 261, 262,
  263, 264
O'Gorman, Pam 176, 180
One Day She Catches Fire (Henry) 110
O'Reilly, Bernard 70
Our Tiem but not Our Plec (Our Time but
  not Our Place)(Kituai et al) 71
outsider 69, 75, 137, 157, 162, 264
  see also belonging, home
Owen, Liz 24

Pan African Congress 133
'Parents who Kill their Children' PhD
  thesis (Wilczynski, A.)
passion/passionate 40
  commitment 13
  images of 17
passport/visa 50, 83, 84, 88, 95, 102,
  103, 107, 118, 132, 136, 143, 201,
  206, 228, 250, 255
  bureaucracy in connection with 106,
    107, 136, 207
Paterson, Banjo 65
patriarchy see discrimination, feminism,
  Women's Movement
Peach, Blair 244
permanent resident 170
Pinochet, General 35
Pintubi 246 see also Aborigines and
  Torres Strait Islanders, Aboriginal,
  discrimination, racism
Pintubi Homelands Health Service 239,
  246
poetry 13, 16, 17, 71
political asylum 133, 205, 207
political prisoner 224, 229, 230, 231,
  252 see also activism/demonstrations,
  politics, violence against women
  delegations to/visits (El Salvador) 228,
    229, 230
  exchange of 230
  torture of 229, 230, 236
politics 15, 35, 39-40, 87, 133, 137,
  160, 162, 177, 196, 203, 205, 211,
  224, 226, 240, 252 see also

activism/demonstrations, Chilean
resistance, industrial action,
Sandinistas, Salvadoran peace
accords, Solidarity, Tian An Mien
Square
Anti-Nazi League (UK) 244
black/race and 21, 135, 138
Black and Tans 200
and change 41
communism 14, 119, 202, 204, 205,
225, 226, 240
of country 21, 32, 173-246
democracy 133, 136, 137, 213, 251
Easter Rising 200
11 November 1975 (Aust.) 104
and empowerment 25
environmental/green 24, 29, 30
fascism 243
'gender' 15
geo- 15
Grenada revolution (Carib.) 175
Left Connection/New Left Party
(Aust.) 195
Left Front (El Sal.) 230, 252
National Front (UK) 244
National Liberation Front (El Sal.)
230, 252
National Socialism 243
nuclear 24
nuns and 24
Peace Movement 245
radical youth vote/student 24, 162
right to vote 136, 251
sanctions 136
songs as 225, 226
Troops Out Movement (Ire.) 195
POW (prisoner of war)/camps 44, 62,
120, 124
pregnancy 20-1, 31, 36, 75, 121, 122,
196, 223, 230, 245, 257
President Sukarno 15
protests see activism/demonstrations,
Viet Nam war
public transport 88-9, 96, 97, 108,
237-8, 240, 249, 262, 263
Puentener, Anna 24
Puentener, Janine 23, 24, 31
Puentener, Marlies 7, 23-32, 250, 263,
264
Puentener, Rachel 24

racism/race relations 14, 51, 60, 66, 92,
111, 169, 176, 185, 120-1, 132, 196,
214, 223, 232, 239, 244, 246, 256,
263
Racial Discrimination Act 131
racial 'jokes' 31, 199
Ramirez, Lil Milagro 224
rape see violence against women
Rationalists 15
Reagan government 177
Reagan, Ronald 115, 260
refugees 36, 44, 124, 206-7, 208, 209,
211, 212, 232, 259 see also travel - as
refugee
special humanitarian program 207,
227, 248
work with 51
religion 13, 15, 23, 24, 27, 28, 34, 66,
68, 74-75, 103-5 passim, 116, 117,
120, 121, 140-1, 142, 147, 149, 159,
160, 167, 177, 194, 199, 210, 214,
218, 221, 224, 231, 235, 241, 243
Bible, Bible Belt 66, 116, 117, 226
Billy Graham Crusade 13
Buddhism 121
Latin 226
laying on of hands 149
liberation theology 224-5, 226
religious conversion 147-8
Rock 'N' Roll Review, The (comedy show)
129
Roots (play) 68
Rose, Lionel 122
rugby 31
All Blacks 31
Spring Bok rugby tour 24
Rushdie, Salman 132, 251

Salvadoran peace accords 42, 224
Samuda, Pauline 180
Sandinistas 35, 39
Saunders, Clara 4
SBS (Special Broadcasting Service) 168,
185, 260
Scutt, Jocelynne A. 1-9, 247-64
sexism 169 see also discrimination
Shakespeare, William 64
ships
MV Fairsky 67
SS Mon Tora 54
SS Ranchi 62
Skaubryn 67

SS Southern Cross 44
SS Strathnaver 92
SS Tjuluwah 121, 248
Simon, Jennifer 8, 164-71, 259, 260, 263
slavery 175, 176, 259
Slices of Wry (Henry) 110
Solidarity 202, 203, 205
Somare, Michael 221
songs
    Advance Australia Fair 124
    corroboree 57
    God of Our Fathers 15
    Land of Hope and Glory 15
    Mocking-bird Hill 63
    O Valiant Hearts 15
    political 225, 226
    Rule Brittania 15, 66
Spender, Dale 244
Spitzer, Hans 33
sport 13, 94, 120, 124, 180, 211 *see also* cricket, rugby
    learning to ski 103, 104, 257
Stanner, W.E.H. 246
State of Emergency (Poland) 204
Stead, Christina 1, 6
Students for a Democratic Society (SDS) 15
Sudden Infant Death Research Foundation 127
superstition 121, 123
Sybil The Glide of Her Tongue (Hanscombe) 13, 18
Sykes, Roberta 216

Take this Child (Cummings) 1-2
Talking Up a Storm (Henry and Derlet) 110
Taurua, Tui 8, 159-63, 249, 257, 258, 263, 264
television 14, 66, 77, 211, 230, 254 *see also* film/documentary/television series
£10 migration scheme *see* migrant schemes
Thatcher, Margaret 168, 196, 197, 200, 239, 240, 245
Thatcherism 22, 197, 240
Third Reich/Hitler/Goebbels 243, 257
Tian An Mien Square 84, 123, 184, 260
toilets/lavatories 88, 114, 232
To the Island (Frame) 32
tourist trips 19, 26

tradition *see* culture/tradition
transport *see* travel
travel
    and self-identity 98
    and single women 3, 85, 152, 209, 247, 248, 262
    around/within Asia 53, 56, 118, 199
    around/within Australia 1, 2, 4, 5, 7, 8, 16, 23-32 *passim*, 54, 55-6, 57, 58, 59, 74, 101, 105, 118, 139, 145, 146, 214, 159, 160-1, 212-3, 249, 253
    around/within Britain 13, 45, 46-9 *passim*, 50, 144, 153, 164, 166, 249, 259
    around/within Europe 33, 49-51, 153, 263
    around/within North America 8, 102, 133
    around the world 140, 142, 253
    as opportunity 99
    as refugee 119, 224, 227 *see also* refugees
    as single parent 224
    as tourist 208, 216
    backpacking 6, 8, 27, 152, 153, 158
    by air 20, 37, 38, 70, 83, 102, 105, 127, 144, 152, 159, 164, 178, 195, 207, 216, 223, 231-2, 236, 237, 241, 247, 248, 253, 262
    by bicycle/Vespa scooter 46, 92, 93
    by bus/coach/waggon 5, 67, 88, 89, 96-7, 248, 262
    by cable car 50
    by car/truck 16, 92, 97, 153, 190, 212-3, 249, 262
    by caravan 50-1, 62, 69
    by cattle train/rattlers 59
    by ferry/launch 19, 50
    by force/transportation/kidnapping 2-3, 4
    by four-wheel drive/Kombi 23, 25, 26, 250
    by sea 44, 45, 54, 62, 67, 87, 92, 111, 120-1, 260
    by train/Eurail pass 5, 16, 33, 88, 89, 153, 233, 249, 263
    cost of 1, 15, 25, 44, 89, 96, 104, 121, 130, 170, 178, 200, 227, 248
    distance/s 1, 9, 14, 29, 127, 128, 153, 165, 170, 178, 179, 189, 190, 196,

198, 211, 216, 225, 227, 231, 261, 262
for adventure 3, 36, 111, 165, 179, 242, 262
for art/writing 6, 22
for children's future 3, 92, 118, 196, 208, 237, 248
for education/knowledge/study 3, 4, 6, 54, 83
for fame/recognition/money 6, 84, 85, 151, 260, 262
for health 227, 229, 232, 236
for honeymoon/holiday 36, 121, 128, 132, 240
for independence 3, 151
for love, marriage 3, 5, 8, 67, 127, 127-8, 142-50 *passim*
for own future/security 3, 92, 110, 111, 118, 136, 151, 167, 196, 248
for political reasons 205, 227, 228, 248, 249
for prostitution 4
for work/business 3, 4, 92, 104, 205, 249, 259
from Africa 7, 131-8, 251, 256
from Australia 6, 7, 8, 13-23 *passim*, 33-42 *passim*, 43-52 *passim*, 53-60 *passim*, 67, 71-9 *passim*, 95-9 *passim*, 100-109 *passim*, 131-2, 151-8 *passim*, 214-23 *passim*, 248, 253, 260
from Britain 3, 7, 8, 51-2, 61-70 *passim*, 87-90 *passim*, 91-4 *passim*, 164-71 *passim*, 195-200, 239-46 *passim*, 249
from Caribbean 8, 175-94 *passim*
from Central/Latin America 8, 224-38 *passim*, 248
from China 8, 55, 57, 59, 60, 83-6 *passim*
from Eastern Europe 8, 201-13 *passim*
from Europe 5, 8, 24, 241-3
from Hong Kong 119-24 *passim*, 248
from New Zealand 7, 8, 23-32 *passim*, 159-63 *passim*, 249, 250
from New Guinea 254, 263
from North America 8, 11, 110-19 *passim*, 127-30 *passim*, 132-4, 135-6, 139-50 *passim*, 253, 260
from war 34
marriage impeding 57-8
on Concorde 167

on foot/in bush 1, 50, 59, 93-4, 262
on longservice leave 95
on International Teaching Fellowship 95
packing to 18, 50, 111, 143, 154, 241
parents'/family's reaction to 45, 52, 127, 142-3, 166, 167, 196, 201-2, 216, 228, 253, 259
reasons for 3, 5, 8, 36, 119, 121, 132, 159-60, 176-7, 248
visiting country of birth 18, 20, 31-2, 41-2, 67, 77-8, 86, 89-90, 95, 104-5, 107-9, 116-7, 130, 133, 138, 149, 157, 163, 181, 187, 193-4, 200, 201-2, 224, 227, 234-5, 237
to Africa 7
to Australia 3, 8, 23-32 *passim*, 51-2, 55, 59, 61-70 *passim*, 83-6 *passim*, 87-90 *passim*, 91-4 *passim*, 110-17, 118-24 passim, 127-30 *passim*, 131-8 *passim*, 139-50 *passim*, 159-63 *passim*, 164-71 *passim*, 175-94 *passim*, 195-200 *passim*, 200-13 *passim*, 224-38 *passim*, 239-46 *passim*, 248, 249, 253, 260
to Britain 6, 7, 8, 13-22 *passim*, 43-52 *passim*, 151-8 *passim*, 240-1, 243-4, 260
to buy goods 204
to Central/Latin America 7-8, 33-42, 260 *passim*
to China/Asia 6, 7, 8, 53-60 *passim*, 260
to escape husband/relationship 8, 160, 249
to escape suburban destiny 15, 249
to Europe 6, 7, 15, 16, 33, 34, 44, 49, 204, 205
to find roots/background 43, 69, 249
to goldfields 4, 5
to Hong Kong 54, 58
to India 91
to Malaysia 7
to the Middle East 26, 27
to North America 3, 8, 34, 96, 100-09 *passim*, 131, 214-23 *passim*, 251, 256, 262
to Papua New Guinea/New Guinea 7, 71-9 *passim*, 196
to search for birth mother 30
to see family 18, 20, 31-2, 41-2, 67, 77-8, 86, 89-90, 95, 104-5, 107, 116, 130, 138, 149, 157, 160, 163,

181, 187, 193-4, 200, 234, 237, 254
to see the world 59
to study 23, 34, 102-4, 151-8 *passim*, 214-24 *passim*, 247-8, 249, 256
via Central/Latin America 35
via Europe 16, 19, 128, 143-4, 201, 206-10, 253
via Far East 19, 54, 102, 122, 143
via North America 34, 35, 37, 128
via the Pacific 44, 102, 134, 216
with child/family 79, 87, 107-8, 110-11, 175-94 *passim*, 195-200 *passim*, 201-13 *passim*, 224, 232, 241
with partner/friend 3, 6, 18-20 *passim*, 21-2, 47-50 *passim*, 51, 76-9 *passim*, 119-24 *passim*, 143-9 *passim*, 152, 195-200 *passim*, 201, 205, 206-7, 210-12, 241, 247, 248
Tucker, Joan 180

UNIFEM (United Nations Development Fund for Women) 127
United Nations 133
uranium mining/nuclear threat 24, 239, 240
Uren, Tom 195

Value Added Tax (VAT) 167 *see also* Goods and Services Tax (GST)
Victorian School Reader 64
Viet Nam war 111, 113
and Australian troops 119
protests 14, 35, 87
R. and R. (rest and recreation) 119
and USA troops 119
violence against women 147, 204, 229, 230, 236, 252, 264
visa *see* passport

Wajda, Andrzej 68
Wayne, John 78, 258
Wendt, Jana 186
Wenig, Lynne 8, 127-30, 253, 261, 262, 263
White Australia Policy 14, 15, 119, 136, 256
white supremacy 7
Whitlam, Gough 94
Wilczynski, Ania 8, 151-8, 249, 254, 255, 256, 260, 263
Wilczynski, Janet 7, 61-70, 250, 253, 254, 259, 260, 261, 263, 264

Williams, Bill 239, 245
Williams, Lily (Gardener) 245
WINDS (Women's International Network for Democracy and Development in El Salvador) 224, 235
Women in Management 127
Women's Movement 191, 230, 234, 235, 236, 247 *see also* feminism
women's publishing 21
Artemis (press, Australia) 139
Jezebel (press, United Kingdom) 13
Khasmik (press, Australia) 13
Ragweek (press, Canada) 13
Spinifex (press, Australia) 13
Women's Press 241
women's rights to equality 27, 138, 218, 241
Woolf, Virginia 8, 241, 246
work 57, 139, 141, 242
and identity 112, 141-3
at rehabilitation (rehab.) hospital 145
teaching law 106-7, 108, 131-8 *passim*
to support husband 128
voluntary 51, 145
with aged 48, 233-4
with homeless people/youth 28, 51
with intellectually and physically impaired 27-8
with refugees 51
work permit 18, 97, 107, 206, 234
bureaucracy re 97
working holiday 18-20, 196 *passim*, 22, 23, 259, 263 *see also* travel
writing 16, 79, 139, 140, 146, 148, 192
becoming/being a writer 144, 146
of thesis 20, 21
short stories 146
Wright, Judith 16

X, Malcolm 133, 256

Yamagee people *see* Aborigines and Torres Strait Islanders, Aboriginal
Young Women's Christian Association (YWCA) 28

Zhu, Mickey 8, 83-6, 253, 255, 258, 260, 262, 263

ABOUT ARTEMIS PUBLISHING

Artemis Publishing is a feminist publishing house established to publish and promote women's writing. Artemis specialises in biography and autobiography, publishing the series 'Women's Voices, Women's Lives', series editor Jocelynne A. Scutt. Books in the series include *Breaking Through – Women, Work and Careers*, *As a Woman – Writing Women's Lives*, *Glorious Age – Growing Older Gloriously* and *No Fear of Flying – Women at Home and Abroad.*

Forthcoming books in the 'Women's Voices, Women's Lives' series include *Singular Women*, *Taking a Stand – Women in Politics and Society*, *Sisters*, *City Women, Country Women – Crossing the Boundaries*, *My Mother, My Daughter* and *Living Generously.*

Artemis also publishes feminist crime fiction, detection and mystery writing. Melissa Chan's *One Too Many* and Sue Neacy's *Murder in Northbridge* are to be joined by the Artemis crime anthologies, *A Modern Woman and Other Crimes* and *Calling Up the Devil and Other Misdemeanours*, edited by Melissa Chan and J. Terry.